GONE HOLLYWOOD

MG-2J130

GONE HOLLYWOOD

by Christopher Finch
and Linda Rosenkrantz

Weidenfeld and Nicolson
London

INTRODUCTION

Back near the dawn of the modern age, when time unwound at sixteen frames a second—back when the big pepper tree at Hollywood and Vine stood against a clear desert sky, and the fogs that rolled off Santa Monica Bay were pure as Mary Pickford's smile—an empire of fantasy came into existence on the shores of the Pacific Ocean. It was an empire conjured into being by the disenfranchised of the world—émigrés from Central Europe, chorus girls and vaudevillians tired of the boardinghouses of St. Paul and Missoula, ambitious mothers with talented offspring in tow, fleeing the constraints of provincial America, country boys raised on the mythology of Horatio Alger, working-class kids with nothing to lose— and it annexed the imaginations of people everywhere for more than three decades. In the United States alone, in the typical year 1930, an average of 90 million people a week went to the movies. This, then, was the prototype media revolution, and the most powerful of them all.

This book is about the era that came to an end more than thirty years ago, about the old Hollywood that vanished with the arrival of smog, antitrust suits, and television. It attempts to reconstruct the world of Pickford, Fairbanks, Chaplin, Valentino, Garbo, Gilbert, Dietrich, Shearer, Harlow, Cagney, Gable, Lombard, Bogart, and the Barrymores, recalling Tuesday nights at the Cocoanut Grove, fist fights at the Trocadero, gambling ships anchored just beyond the three-mile limit, and Sunday afternoon polo games out in the wilds of Brentwood. It is also about moguls and agents, about fabulous salaries and "moral turpitude" clauses, about extras and drugstore cowboys, about unions and strikes and all the consequences of the studio system. It recounts how gangsters became involved with the movies and how movie stars were drawn into politics. It describes how glamour was manufactured and how it was disseminated. This is the world, too, of Hedda and Louella, "Prince" Mike Romanoff and all the hundreds of peripheral characters—sob sisters, restaurateurs, domestics—who serviced the movie colony. In these pages we look at discoveries and screen tests and at marriage and divorce as practiced in the foothills of the Santa Monica mountains. This is, in short, a book about what it was like to live and work in Hollywood during its Golden Age.

It has been our intention to arrive at a broad overview of life in Hollywood from the time the movie industry first took root there until World

Introduction

War II. (Here, as elsewhere, the word "Hollywood" is used in its commonly understood sense of describing the entire Southern California movie industry and its attendant social life, irrespective of the geographic limits of the Hollywood postal district.) Many books have been written about this era. There have been histories, biographies, memoirs, exposés, profiles of studios, filmographies, studies of writers, directors, and cinematographers. Stars, critics, gossip columnists, and anthropologists have all made their contributions to the literature of Hollywood. As in no other field, the authors of these books run the full gamut from sheer trashmongers to academic mandarins. The most esoteric interests have been catered to, and yet, with one partial exception, there is no book that presents the kind of comprehensive picture we are essaying here. The historians have a primary concern for cause and effect and the sequence of events, the biographers are preoccupied with an individual and his immediate circle, the memoirists tend to take too much for granted, and so on. The partial exception is Leo Rosten's *Hollywood: the Movie Colony, the Movie Makers,* published in 1941 by Harcourt, Brace. This admirable treatise had the misfortune to appear at the time of Pearl Harbor and never found its audience. Rosten's book was an attempt to put Hollywood "under the microscopes of social science." The author's sense of irony makes for many entertaining passages, but his approach is essentially scholarly.

Our own intentions have been somewhat less scientific. Although we have not shied away from facts and figures where they seem pertinent, we have been more interested in telling the story in terms of personalities; less concerned with drawing conclusions than with finding the telling detail and presenting it for its own sake. Our approach diverges from Rosten's largely because we are writing at a different time. His book was compiled while the world he was describing was still in existence, its cast of characters constantly in the public eye, its legends still fresh in the minds of its readers. We are writing at a considerable remove from our subject, and our chief objective is to bring the period back to life.

Our aims correspond with Rosten's to the extent that we are attempting to present the whole panorama of Hollywood society—its work habits, its domestic idiosyncrasies, its leisure activities. The one area we have chosen to ignore is the actual art of the filmmaker, except insofar as it pertains to the shaping of Hollywood's social patterns. Since the projection of glamour, on screen and off, was critical to the image of Hollywood, we have included chapters on cinematographers, make-up artists, and costume designers. On the other hand, the reader will not find sections devoted to screenwriters or directors—though they make frequent appearances in a variety of contexts—because their skills seem to relate more to the art of the cinema than to the social life of the movie colony. (Many would argue that this was true of cinematographers, too, and we would not disagree, but certain top cameramen were celebrated for enhancing the appearance of stars, females in particular, and this draws them into our province.)

Since Hollywood was dominated by two intertwined systems—the star system and the studio system—it is the stars and leading studio executives who are our central characters. It is conventional to refer to these people—probably there were fewer than a hundred of them at any given time—as Hollywood "royalty," and this is not entirely inappropriate, since that is precisely how they were perceived both by the general public and by lesser members of the movie colony. Earlier artistocracies and plutocracies have been far wealthier and more extravagant than these motion picture people, but this was the first group in history to be awarded such a position of privilege by the common man, and to enjoy this privilege under conditions of daily public scrutiny. The stars were installed in the Hollywood pantheon to live out the fantasies of the theatergoers who had placed them there. Their values were, unlike those of any previous aristocracy, essentially those of the modern world. Everyone could identify with the satisfaction—however fleeting—of being driven to work in a customized Duesenberg as long as a streetcar.

There was far more to Hollywood, of course, than the stars and the studios, and it is a primary aim of this book to explore the backwaters of the movie business and the satellite industries that grew up around it. Talent scouts, casting directors, and coaches are all part of the story, as are business managers, lawyers, and publicists. To understand the life of the movie colony it is not enough to know about the public figures; one must also grasp the roles of the people working behind the scenes, for they too contributed to the impact of Hollywood on our culture.

It would be difficult to overestimate the force of that impact. The public was hypnotized by Hollywood. The extent of interest in the movie industry and its workers can be gauged by the fact that the Hollywood press corps, in its heyday, was the third largest in the country, after those assigned to New York and Washington. In 1940 there were 395 accredited permanent Hollywood correspondents, including 89 newspapermen, 77 U.S. magazine reporters, and 63 representatives of foreign periodicals. There were, in short, three or four journalists for every star of any consequence, including has-beens and singing cowboys. Studio publicity departments, obviously, did their utmost to see that this army of reporters did not go short of copy, as indicated by the fact that in 1939, 15,709 publicity stories were submitted to the Advertising Advisory Council and 109,083 stills. Seldom, if ever, have so many words and pictures been expended on so small a group of people, and yet the researcher still finds reliable information extremely difficult to come by. License with the truth was taken so freely that anything that originated in a studio publicity department—and this included the majority of newspaper and magazine stories—must automatically be regarded with suspicion. Happily, many veterans of the era are willing to share their recollections of it, but memories can be deceptive, and different eyewitnesses of a single event often supply widely differing accounts of it.

Even if it were possible, we would not banish the handiwork of the press agent entirely from these pages—no account of Hollywood would be complete without a few examples of his artistry—but for the most part we have attempted to untangle truth from legend. Certain stories, such as those about technical aspects of the industry, can be accepted at face value because there was no reason to distort the truth in the first place. Some we have chosen to believe because they were accompanied by convincing circumstantial detail, and others because the source has proven reliable in providing information verifiable elsewhere. In many instances, we have pieced stories together from a number of different sources, and to a large extent we have had to rely on intuition bolstered by several years immersion in the period while preparing this and earlier books. Although our aim has been to produce a true picture of the movie colony, we have not felt above giving the benefit of the doubt for the sake of a good anecdote. Such stories, even when not supported by strict documentary evidence, often serve to portray an accurate sense of the character of the time and place.

It is precisely that character which we hope to convey in these pages, along with the pleasure that we derived from unearthing the information they contain. We began the project by selecting a number of categories —agents, chutzpah, extras, gambling, nepotism, etc., about fifty in all— that could serve as a basis for our research. As we began to amass material, from archives, newspapers, trade papers, magazines, books, and personal interviews, we started a card index which eventually stretched to an enormous length. As it grew, some categories were abandoned and others added; some took on greater importance than we had anticipated, while others we had great hopes for proved to be uninteresting. The file took on an existence of its own and, since it was the determining factor in shaping the book, we have chosen to retain its alphabetical system for the organization of the final text.

We feel that this method of presenting the material has the advantage of allowing it to speak for itself. We are not normally diffident about offering opinions, but we wanted to avoid making this a didactic work—it was not our intention to force our material into some mold that conforms to currently held views about the old Hollywood. We simply wanted to re-enter that world as fully as possible and bring back our discoveries.

GONE HOLLYWOOD

ABOUT HOLLYWOOD.

Toward the end of 1907, the Selig Company of Chicago sent a troupe of players to Los Angeles to complete a film version of *The Count of Monte Cristo*. Interior sets were built in the rear of Sing Loo's Chinese laundry on Olive Street and exteriors were shot on the beach at Santa Monica. The Selig players then began work on another one-reeler, *The Heart of a Race Tout,* which is considered the first "story" film ever made entirely within the Los Angeles area.

The original nickelodeon had opened in Pittsburgh just two years earlier and already nickelodeons across the country were attracting 26 million patrons a week. As for Los Angeles, it was a rapidly expanding city—its population had doubled to 250,000 in barely half a dozen years. Parts of it still resembled a frontier town, but modern commercial buildings dominated the downtown area, and the oil boom, which hit at the turn of the century, had left its mark in many districts. Forests of oil derricks cut through residential neighborhoods, combining with frame houses, tele-graph poles, palms, and eucalyptus trees to create a bizarre suburban landscape. Henry Huntington's Big Red Cars connected Los Angeles (old-timers pronounced the name with a hard "G") to many outlying com-munities: Pasadena, Pomona, Long Beach, Monrovia, Covina, Glendale, Whittier, Newport Beach, San Pedro, Santa Ana, and others. Venice, with its canals and Italianate hotels, had opened to the public two years earlier, Santa Monica was a thriving resort town, and Ocean Park was the Coney Island of the Pacific. In 1907 construction began on the first house in the new community of Beverly Hills, and the area we now call the Sunset Strip was the site of the rural township of Sherman. Hollywood itself was a sleepy village surrounded by farms and citrus groves—the first lots there had gone on sale just twenty years earlier. Its one major landmark was the Hollywood Hotel, built in 1903 on a dirt road that was to become world-famous as Hollywood Boulevard. It was 1905 before the town could boast its first store, the Hollywood Cash Grocery at Sunset and Cahuenga.

Separating these various communities were vast tracts of undeveloped land. In some places, neatly planted rows of lima beans extended as far as the eye could see. Carnation fields flourished near Ocean Park and Redondo Beach, and everywhere in season, poppies bloomed on vacant

1

A GENERAL VIEW OF THE MACK SENNETT STUDIO, 1915.
CULVER PICTURES.

lots. Small towns were beginning to establish themselves on the fringes of
the San Fernando Valley, but most of the valley was still devoted to
agriculture, with the major portion of the land there belonging to a handful
of powerful ranchers.

In 1908 Selig built a new studio in the Edendale district, east of Hollywood, and the moviemakers' invasion of Southern California began in
earnest. The Majestic Film Company acquired a lot in Boyle Heights, and
the Lubin Company built a studio in Highland Park. Kalem and Vitagraph
both established units in Santa Monica, and a number of "outlaw" producers gravitated to the Greater Los Angeles area. Legend has it that it
was these "outlaws"—independents working outside the monopoly formed
by the Motion Picture Patents Company—who brought filmmaking to
Southern California. The strong-arm tactics of the Trust's goons did drive
some independents to Los Angeles—illegal film stock could be obtained
just across the border in Tijuana, which also offered safe refuge in case of
harassment—but most of the pioneer film companies in the Los Angeles
area were in fact affiliated with the Trust. What brought them West was
the climate, good locations, and cheap real estate.

In January of 1909, Biograph, the most powerful of all the Trust companies, sent a unit to Southern California. Headed by D. W. Griffith, it established itself in the Chutes Park neighborhood. Griffith took his troupe back East for the summer, but returned in the fall of 1910. By that time, ramshackle studios were springing up all over. On the East Coast, sets were already lit by klieg lights. In California everything—including interiors— was shot outdoors, since the slow film stock used in those days benefited greatly from natural illumination. Wall props—mirrors, framed photographs, fireplaces, and even windows—were often painted directly onto canvas flats, and muslin diffusers, strung on frames above the sets, were used to soften the harsh sunlight.

Filmmaking came to Hollywood proper in 1911, when David Horsley, an Englishman who had previously produced pictures in New Jersey, established a studio behind Blondeau's Tavern at Sunset and Gower. Horsley's Centaur Film Company, a very professional outfit, merged with Universal the following year. In 1915 Universal shifted to the giant spread it still occupies in the San Fernando Valley, and other studios looking for larger lots also relocated in what were then outlying districts. Thomas Ince, for example, established Inceville in Santa Ynez Canyon, at what is now the intersection of Sunset Boulevard and the Coast Highway. Hal Kern, later David Selznick's supervising editor, worked at Inceville in 1915 and recalls that, since the trolley car route terminated at the foot of Santa Monica Canyon, then the site of a Japanese fishing village, the studio would send out a stagecoach to pick up employees. Other studios, though, were taking root in Hollywood itself, mostly in the vicinity of Sunset and Gower, and the word Hollywood was beginning to be used colloquially to describe the entire Southern California movie industry.

By this time, Hollywood was being perceived as the epitome of glamour, although new arrivals in the movie capital were sometimes disappointed by the physical reality behind the glittering image. Colleen Moore, in her autobiography, *Silent Star,* describes her first impression of the Griffith Studio as she saw it in 1917. She was struck by the huge Babylonian set built for *Intolerance,* but not by the studio itself. "It was a large, three-story barnlike structure made of clapboard and painted dark green." Attached to it, "in a very makeshift manner," were a number of buildings. "It looked to me as if when they needed more room they just got together some old boards and added on another shack." It was in this period that Julius Stern, a producer of shoestring comedies, came up with a famous remark that has since been attributed to every poverty row producer in the business: "A rock is a rock, a tree is a tree—shoot it in Griffith Park."

The Los Angeles area did offer producers the advantage of varied and spectacular locations, many of them untouched by man—a big factor in the success of the Western genre that was to capture the imagination of the world. Soon the Santa Monica mountains and the Simi hills were dotted with Indian encampments, mining towns, ranch houses, and hurriedly erected facsimiles of Dodge City and Tombstone. Stars like Tom Mix, William S. Hart, and Hoot Gibson—some genuine cowboys, others barely able to mount a horse—became national heroes. Horse operas could be turned out cheaply and quickly, and dozens of producers capitalized on their success, but it was at Universal in particular that the Western was molded into its archetypal form.

If you lived in one of the new Hollywood apartment houses or bungalow courts in the late teens, a comfortable walk would bring you to Paramount, Fox, or any of a dozen other studios. If your work took you further afield, the trolley car system could generally be relied on. A Red Car went to Edendale, where the Mack Sennett Studio and several other lots were located; a Yellow Car would carry you to the Eastlake Park site of the Selig Zoo. Even Triangle, out among the virgin tracts of Culver City, could be reached by trolley, and eventually a line was built from Highland Avenue into the San Fernando Valley. Until this opened, however, reaching Universal City was a problem unless you owned a car. Extras would set off from Hollywood at dawn, hoping to hitch a ride through the Cahuenga Pass.

Paul Fix, who was to become one of the film industry's busiest character actors, arrived in Hollywood in April of 1922:

> There was nobody out here. Hollywood was a beautiful little sleepy town. Hollywood Boulevard was bordered with lovely homes. Where Warners Theater is now, there was a big lawn facing the Boulevard and a white gingerbread house that belonged to Paul de Longpré, one of the pioneers. There were a few shops and there was a restaurant at Cherokee called Armstrong & Carlton, and when you wanted to see movie stars, that's where you went. The studios didn't have commissaries then so at noon the actors converged on Armstrong & Carlton. At night there was nothing. It was very quiet.
>
> The Security Bank at Hollywood and Cahuenga, that was the skyscraper —it must have been all of four stories—and that intersection was the hub of activity, such as it was.

Two blocks east, at Hollywood and Vine, were the offices of *The Hollywood Filmograph*—a weekly trade paper aimed mostly at extras and bit players—and so this intersection became a meeting place for those in the lower echelons of the industry.

The twenties saw the population of Los Angeles expand at an incredible rate: close to three quarters of a million people moved there during the decade. Real estate boomed. Hucksters would shanghai people off the street, supplying them with box lunches and busing them out to the San Fernando Valley, where, in some areas, you could buy an acre for a nickel.

In those early days, the movie colony was a tight-knit group dominated by people in their twenties and thirties. In 1924 Betty Bronson was eighteen, Colleen Moore was twenty-one, Marion Davies and Gloria Swanson were twenty-seven, and Lillian Gish was twenty-eight. Harold Lloyd was thirty-one, Buster Keaton was twenty-nine—as was Rudolph Valentino— and Ramon Novarro and Irving Thalberg were both twenty-five. Bebe Daniels, who had been a star for almost a decade, celebrated her twenty-third birthday that year. (In the teens, producers had sought out fourteen- and fifteen-year-old girls because the camera, prior to the diffusion lens, was a pitiless instrument and women were often over the hill by the time they reached their early twenties.)

Few of the people in movies had had much formal education. Actors, directors, writers, cutters, cameramen, and lab technicians had acquired their skills on the job by a process of trial and error. For all its spectacular success, though, Hollywood was snubbed by most of the nabobs of the legitimate theater and by polite society. As late as 1931, when the City of Los Angeles celebrated its first 150 years, movie people were treated as pariahs. The industry raised thousands of dollars for the celebrations and staged a spectacular electrical parade, but the committee which organized the culminating Fiesta Ball decided to exclude all Hollywood personalities but Mary Pickford from its guest list. Under the circumstances, Pickford refused the invitation.

The highly publicized scandals of the early twenties had helped promote the picture of Hollywood as a debauched place devoted to orgies and riotous living. When Roscoe "Fatty" Arbuckle was made the scapegoat for the death of a young actress, he was crucified by the Hearst press. The still unsolved murder of director William Desmond Taylor provided the yellow press with another field day, especially since Mabel Normand was discovered in the dead man's house, burning love letters, while other evidence indicated that Taylor had been romantically involved with teen-age star Mary Miles Minter. Wallace Reid, one of the biggest idols of the period, died a drug addict, and Olive Thomas, Mary Pickford's sister-in-law, killed herself under circumstances that suggested a link to the narcotics trade. Thus, journalists were easily able to give the impression that life in Hollywood resembled the more lurid passages in the films of Von Stroheim and DeMille, and so the legend has come down to us. Indicative of the distortion involved is the fact that Wilson Mizner—adventurer, wit, and part owner of the Brown Derby—is often quoted as having said that living in Hollywood was "like a trip through a sewer in a glass-bottomed boat." What he did in fact say, in a 1927 *Photoplay* interview was, "The joint is as dead as a New York nightclub. I thought it was going to be like a delightful trip through a sewer in a glass-bottomed boat."

Just how shocking was Hollywood society in the twenties? There were people like Norman Kerry, Buster Keaton, John Gilbert, and Lew Cody who drank too much, and others, like Mabel Normand and Nazimova, who experimented with drugs. On the other hand, the colony had its full complement of teetotalers, and Conrad Nagel was apt to throw a fit if he heard anyone using off-color language. The Pickford-Fairbanks set was very self-conscious about maintaining the social proprieties and there were individuals like Lois Wilson and Sidney Franklin who were positively sanctimonious (Hollywood was dumbfounded, years later, when Franklin and Nelson Eddy exchanged wives). Long an influence in the theater, the Christian Science Church made many converts in the film community— Bessie Love and Conrad Nagel were early devotees. The Catholic contingent was powerful and, with many Jews prominent in the industry—

NORMA SHEARER AND HER BROTHER, DOUGLAS, HEAD OF THE M-G-M SOUND DEPARTMENT, POSE WITH SOME OF THE NEW TALKIE EQUIPMENT, C. 1928.

although few of them seem to have been especially religious—B'nai B'rith and other Jewish organizations came to play an important role in Hollywood's social life. Certainly there were devout partygoers and hell-raisers around town—money and fame giving their revelry a flamboyant edge—but most people were inhibited by wives, weak stomachs, and moral turpitude clauses in their contracts. Very evident too was the desperate striving for respectability that is the traditional neurosis of the newly rich. Also, and perhaps most important, movie people worked extremely hard. Although the fact that there were no lines to study in the silent era did permit more free time than in later years, and discipline on the set in the early, freewheeling days was sometimes lax, that soon changed. For the most part, Hollywood was an industrious and relatively sedate community.

The celebrities of the silent era were able to move about in society virtually unmolested. At Crystal Beach, in Santa Monica, major stars like Gloria Swanson could swim and sun-bathe without fear of being mobbed by their admirers. Fans might ask for an autograph, but they were in awe of their idols and seldom harrassed them.

Before the twenties were over, Hollywood had ceased to be the residential center of the movie colony. There had been a gradual drifting west to Beverly Hills, which was a much more exclusive place than Hollywood had ever been. Douglas Fairbanks once went as far as proposing the idea of building a wall around the entire city. A motion picture establishment was beginning to solidify, as F. Scott Fitzgerald noted in his 1928 story, "Magnetism," in which he describes a Hollywood party attended by members of the "old crowd"—people who had been in the early Griffith pictures:

> They had a dignity and straightforwardness about them from the fact they had worked in pictures before pictures were bathed in a golden haze of success. They were still rather humble about their amazing triumph, and thus, unlike the new generation, who took it all for granted, they were constantly in touch with reality. . . . With all this, they were still young enough to believe that they would go on forever.

The "old crowd" survived, but change was accelerated by the arrival of sound, which forced some members of the establishment into early retirement. Stars who had been brilliant mimes but lacked good speaking voices found themselves unwanted, and the hundreds of new people—both actors and technicians—who flocked to California destroyed the film settlement's village atmosphere forever. Paul Fix reports that the town was suddenly inundated with voice teachers:

> Every other storefront seemed to have been rented by one of them. And every actor you knew—if you saw them across the street, they were

all *projecting*. . . . They'd say, "HELLO, PAUL. HOW *ARE* YOU?" Enunciating clearly. "IT'S A BEAUTIFUL DAY, ISN'T IT?"

On the set, the mike man was the boss. The director might say, "Beautiful scene!", but the mike man would say, "You've got to take it again—can't hear the dialogue." Everything was on wax. The cameras were in big blimps that looked like iceboxes. The atmosphere was very tense. A red light would come on and the sound guy would holler, "Synchronize!" Then the director would yell, "Camera! Quiet! Nobody move!" After the scene was over, they'd play the disc back to see how it sounded.

Exterior shots now had to contend with extraneous noises such as passing traffic and low-flying aircraft. At Universal someone had the idea of sending a blimp up over the lot to keep airplanes away, but it had the reverse effect. Every pilot who spotted it would fly over to see what was going on. Consequently, all the studios had to build new soundproof stages. Fox was especially proud of its air-conditioned buildings, but these proved rather impractical because, when the hot lights were turned off, the actors and crew half froze to death. Within two or three years, the most serious of the technical problems had been solved. But by that time, Hollywood had changed forever.

Had you been a privileged visitor to Hollywood in 1931, you might have been escorted onto one of M-G-M's spanking new sound stages to see a rapidly rising star, Clark Gable, roughing up one of the studio's established queens, Norma Shearer, on the set of *A Free Soul*. Just across Washington Boulevard, on a vacant lot in the Palms district, you could have witnessed the other extreme of the movie industry, as Hal Roach's Little Rascals were dragooned through another of their brief adventures. The Little Rascal films were made in a freewheeling atmosphere that was reminiscent of the old Hollywood, plots being half planned, half improvised around a gag man's sketch, or an idea that had worked well in an earlier picture. Behind the stucco walls of the M-G-M lot, everything was slick, polished, and businesslike. Screenplays were written and rewritten by teams of highly paid specialists and each press release was part of a carefully thought-out strategy. Directors, cameramen, designers, musicians, and lab technicians were hand-picked for their ability to contribute to a master plan conceived with the intention of transforming mortals into demigods.

But the future of the movie industry did not look bright at that time. Hollywood had ridden out the first years of the Depression on the strength of the novelty of sound, but in 1931 box-office receipts began to slip badly. M-G-M and Paramount showed respectable profits at the end of the year, and Universal had a bumper season thanks to the success of *Frankenstein* and *Dracula,* but the industry as a whole went into a skid it did not pull out of till the mid-thirties. By the end of 1932, Paramount and RKO would

JOAN CRAWFORD STANDING WITH A TRUCKLOAD OF FAN MAIL, 1928.

JEAN HARLOW PAUSES, AT THE DOOR OF HER TRAILER, TO CHAT
WITH LEE TRACY DURING THE FILMING OF *Dinner at Eight*.

be on the verge of bankruptcy, and by the spring of 1933, Loew's, Inc.—parent company of M-G-M—was the only major film corporation that remained completely solvent.

These fiscal problems had the paradoxical effect of rejuvenating the industry. High-priced stars held over from the silent days were phased out and new players—some from the stage, some from the ranks of lower-paid contract artists, some practically picked up off the streets—were given their chance. Between 1931 and 1935, many of the faces which would dominate the movies for the next twenty years began to appear on screen. The one thing the new people had in common, for a while at least, was that they were drawing salaries which were a fraction of those the studios had been paying to displaced stars like John Gilbert, whose 1928 contract assured him of $250,000 per picture. Clark Gable, his heir at M-G-M, worked in 1931 for $350 a week—and appeared in no fewer than fourteen films during his first year under contract.

The Los Angeles area did not expand as rapidly in the thirties as it had in the twenties—the Depression was an effective damper—but it continued to change. The 1932 Olympic Games focused international attention on the city. Architectural landmarks, like the old Santa Fe depot and the County Jail, gave way to new public buildings, often in the *moderne* style. Wilshire Boulevard's Miracle Mile became one of the busiest commercial districts in the country, and new communities, such as Westwood Village, appeared amid the bean fields. As the trolley car system—the most extensive in the world—began to show signs of wear, the automobile became more and more important. Shopping areas were developed with the convenience of the car owner in mind, and drive-in restaurants—varying in idiom from colonial to streamline to proto-Pop—sprang up everywhere. The city's first drive-in movie theater opened at Pico and Westwood in 1934. By the end of the decade, the first freeway—the Arroyo Seco Parkway—was ready for the million-odd cars registered in Los Angeles County.

Throughout the Depression, Los Angeles remained relatively affluent. At the same time, though, migrant workers and "Okies" fleeing the Dust Bowl set up pathetic homesteads on the fringes of the city, while hobos roamed the jungles near the Santa Fe yards; a large shantytown thrived on Sepulveda Boulevard, and another near Universal City. Blacks, Chicanos, and poor whites crowded into old residential districts as the middle classes moved out toward the burgeoning suburban communities, and movie people began to seek out new areas in which to live. Some pushed west into Bel Air and Brentwood, while others crossed the hills and settled the more pleasant sections of the Valley. They no longer belonged to one tight little community, but could be found on either side of the Santa Monica mountains anywhere from Los Feliz to Malibu. The movie colony had become a loose cluster of intersecting circles—some centered upon studios, some upon geographical location, and some upon political belief. There was still a primary focal point, however, and that was now Beverly Hills.

An outlying community in the early twenties, Beverly Hills had become by 1930 one of the most prosperous and fashionable residential shopping areas in the country. Most roads south of Wilshire Boulevard were still unpaved then, but Wilshire itself, Beverly Drive, and Little Santa Monica were already lined with expensive stores and boutiques. Restaurants like the Wilshire Brown Derby, Armstrong-Schroeder, and Victor Hugo's catered to the movie crowd, and the Beverly Hills Hotel—after a brief closure—competed for the carriage trade with the newer Beverly-Wilshire. North of Sunset, irrigation had transformed arid canyons into subtropical gardens. Hillsides were cropped to accommodate spectacular homes which combined with the natural contours of the land and imported exotic vegetation to create the ultimate suburb, a lush hybrid of the Hanging Gardens of Babylon and the Alpes-Maritimes. Adjacent to these tamed acres, however, were wilderness areas where foxes and coyotes still roamed, occasionally descending into a well-tended yard to carry off a kitten or a lap dog.

As for Hollywood proper, show business had not abandoned it entirely. Movie people still frequented its clubs and restaurants. RKO, Paramount, and Columbia were in Hollywood, strung out along "Gower Gulch," and the Goldwyn and Chaplin studios were also located within the postal district. In addition, Hollywood had become the West Coast base of the broadcasting industry, and, during the thirties, both NBC and CBS built modernistic studios on Sunset Boulevard.

The Pantages, the Egyptian, the Chinese, and other big theaters on Hollywood Boulevard, and the Hollywood Hotel were still operating, but the street was already on its way to becoming just another tourist trap. By the thirties, Hollywood Boulevard had become the territory of innumerable eccentrics—flat-earthers, prophets, and religious extremists—the best known of whom was Peter the Hermit, who lived in a hut on the undeveloped slopes above Laurel Canyon. Reputed to have been a wealthy San Francisco businessman, Peter dressed in cotton pants and a thin cotton shirt all year long, wore a long white beard, and carried a wooden staff. He was on familiar terms with several movie celebrities and liked to discourse with them on a variety of subjects, from ethics to economics. Another character known to everyone in the industry was Memphis, a black newspaper vendor whose first pitch had been outside the Armstrong & Carlton Café. That famous group of characters, the drugstore cowboys, tended to congregate a few blocks away, at the corner of Sunset and Gower.

Joseph Cotten arrived in Hollywood in 1940 and recalls that the small-town feeling had not vanished entirely:

FANS PURSUE FRED MACMURRAY AS HE LEAVES THE PARAMOUNT LOT.

We drove down Sunset Boulevard and there were still residences on the street, where there are nothing but businesses now. There were photography studios there with still photographs out on the lawn—big, heroic blow-ups. Everything on Ventura Boulevard was shaped like a windmill or a hot dog. It looked like Disneyland.

There were two or three restaurants for the movie crowd and it was fashionable to put on a black tie and go to the Mocambo or Ciro's. We worked on Saturdays in those days, and then on Saturday night we all went out and had fun—just as you would in any other factory town.

Of course, Hollywood was not *quite* like any other factory town: Symbolically, Cotten's first home there was on Wonderland Avenue. As for the architectural oddities he noted along Ventura Boulevard, they were not confined to that one thoroughfare. The Big Red Piano Shop—constructed to resemble a big red piano—had been on Venice Boulevard since 1910. At Florence and Figueroa was a famous cocktail lounge, the "Zep," built in the shape of an airship. The Dark Room, a photography shop on Wilshire, had a storefront that was an oversize facsimile of an early Brownie camera, and there was an entire chain of restaurants each of which was built in the form of a giant chili bowl.

Prior to World War II, some of the subordinate workers were poorly paid, which led to labor unrest, but taxes and the cost of living were low, and you did not have to be a star to be comfortable. Bob Schiffer, a make-up man, remembers that his salary could be stretched to pay for a number of luxuries: "We made fifteen dollars a day—about the same as a cameraman—and on that salary I had an airplane, I had a racing car with a Miller motor in it, and I had a nice apartment."

The war changed conditions drastically. Although many people went into the service, the general population of Los Angeles began to expand rapidly again as people poured in to work at the aircraft factories and other defense plants. An acute housing shortage forced people to live in dormitories, converted garages, and even shacktowns reminiscent of the "Hoovervilles" of the Depression years. One unpleasant wartime arrival, not created by the war itself, was the smog, which first showed signs of becoming a serious problem in 1943. Parts of the city had always been foggy, and smudge-pot fires in citrus groves had long been a winter nuisance, but the smogs which began to hang over Los Angeles in the forties were altogether more sinister and had a strong psychological effect. For twenty-five years, Hollywood had been the primary image associated with Southern California. Gradually, smog was to become almost as powerful a symbol, representing the new megalopolis—"L.A."—which would eventually swamp the Hollywood of the Golden Age.

AGENTS.

The stereotyped image of the shifty-eyed, bloodsucking leech of a ten-percenter, the talent agent, dates from well before the birth of the American movie industry. Vaudevillians would joke about the performer who kicked his agent in the heart and broke his toe. Hollywood, however—for the first time in history putting entertainment on the level of big business—offered unparalleled opportunities for the men who sometimes liked to call themselves "artists' representatives." The money that could be made by a successful agent attracted some very strong personalities into the field. To deal with mogols, you had to be as ruthless as they were, and in their heyday, men like Charles Feldman, Myron Selznick, Leland Hayward, and Phil Berg had the kind of clout in the industry that only top studio executives could match. The beleagured executives never missed an opportunity to have agents lampooned on screen.

The most important early agency dealing with movies was headed by Edward Small, who started in New York in 1910, and is credited with being the first representative to handle actors for motion pictures. "In those days," Small has been quoted as saying, "agents were viewed as rats . . . they acted more like an employment agency, in addition to managing, giving legal advice, obtaining publicity and nursing the clients generally." Small was not famous for charm or subtlety, and would hit any key which he felt might produce the desired result. In 1920 he tried to interest Louis B. Mayer in the services of John Stahl, with the argument that the industry was lacking in Jewish directors. (Stahl got the job, but more for economic reasons than for being a *lanzman*.) A firm believer in self-promotion, Small published an illustrated yearbook, "The Link," which was mailed to the trade—something of an innovation in those days. At one time, the agency was the largest in the country, with Small instrumental in launching the movie careers of Clara Bow, Norma Shearer, Corinne Griffith, and many others. Increasingly involved in the picture business, Small moved the agency to Hollywood in 1924. The following year, he handed it over to his brother Morris (Maury) and became a producer, in which capacity he continued to enhance his reputation as the meanest man in show business. Under Maury Small, the agency was soon eclipsed by others, though as late as 1938 it still listed Rita Hayworth, Jack Oakie, and Lionel Barrymore among its clients.

Another early and sizable operation was inaugurated in 1920 by Ivan Kahn, who continued to run it until 1938, when he became chief talent scout for 20th Century-Fox. Among others, Kahn represented Lew Ayres, Joe E. Brown, Sally O'Neill, Olivia De Havilland, and Joan Fontaine. One of his favorite ploys was to be on hand at the train depot or airport when an important executive was about to leave for the East. In the course of exchanging greetings with the executive, Kahn would slip an envelope into his hand. Opening this envelope en route, the recipient would discover a succinct, laudatory description of one of Kahn's clients.

An agent with automatic access to the most powerful executive in Hollywood was Frank Orsatti, who entered the business largely because he was one of Louis B. Mayer's closest friends. This relationship began in the twenties when Orsatti became Mayer's bootlegger. Mayer used his political connections to keep members of the Orsatti family out of jail, and is said to have suggested that Frank himself might like to consider a line of work that was less likely to bring him into conflict with the law. In 1930 the company of Bren, Weber, and Orsatti was formed, with the partners being given to understand that the agency's clients would receive preferential treatment at Metro-Goldwyn-Mayer. A short time later, Orsatti bought out his partners, Milton Bren (an ex-USC athlete who went on to develop much of the real estate along the Sunset Strip) and Herman Weber. That done, Frank brought his brothers, Vic, Al, and Ernie (a former outfielder with the St. Louis Cardinals) into the business. Since it was common knowledge in the community that Frank Orsatti had a direct line to Mayer —he bought a house near Mayer's in Santa Monica and they saw each other daily—it was not difficult for the agency to develop a significant clientele, which leaned toward executives and producers, as well as such actors and directors—in and out of Metro—as Judy Garland, Edward G. Robinson, Frank Capra, Sonja Henie, Alice Faye, and Preston Sturges. The general attitude toward the Orsatti style is summed up in this story told by long-time M-G-M staff writer, John Lee Mahin: "I once saw Frank Orsatti carrying around a big volume of *Les Misérables*. I said, 'Did you read that, Frank?' He said, 'Christ, no—but I might be able to sell it to the old man.' "

Charles K. Feldman, whose agency—Famous Artists—became one of the bases of the current megacorporation, International Creative Management, began as a show business lawyer. While earning his law degree from UCLA, he spent summers working at various studios, at one point attaining the rank of second assistant cameraman on a John Ford film. By the time he opened his law offices at the corner of Hollywood and Vine in

1928, Feldman had some connections in the lower echelons of the industry and was becoming friendly with the Brown Derby crowd, including Eddie Small and Frank Orsatti, who began to use him as their attorney. One day, after working out a three-year, million-dollar contract for one of Orsatti's clients, Feldman realized that while his legal fee was $5,000, his commission as an agent would have been $100,000. It wasn't long before Charlie Feldman became an agent.

His first deal involved getting $5,000 a week for Gregory Ratoff—whose top salary until then had been $1,750—plus the absorption of his taxes and round-trip transportation to England, from Gaumont-British. These conditions were unheard-of in the industry at that time, and Feldman's reputation was established overnight. He went into partnership with Ad Schulberg, wife of B. P. Schulberg, general manager of West Coast production at Paramount. Her principal clients were Richard Bennett and his daughter, Joan. Through personal connections, they soon signed Charles Boyer and Claudette Colbert.

But Feldman got off to a shaky start. He made the mistake of wooing and winning an actress with whom Louis B. Mayer was infatuated—Jean Howard—which led to banishment from the M-G-M lot. In addition, Mayer supposedly had Feldman's house watched, and the names of all the agent's visitors reported back to him. (Feldman's eventual revenge came when Garbo insisted on Boyer as her leading man in *Conquest*. He persuaded Walter Wanger to let him negotiate with Mayer—and was able to extract a fee of $125,000 for Boyer. His return to professional and social acceptance was signaled when Mrs. Samuel Goldwyn sanctioned the Feldmans to throw a party in honor of her and her husband.) Feldman got into trouble at Warners as well, when client Ann Dvorak walked off the lot one day, enraged that a little known child actor was being paid twice her salary, and Feldman was accused by Darryl Zanuck—then head of production there—of encouraging the actress to break her contract. Feldman was denied entry to that studio, too, for a year, until he finally convinced Zanuck that he had not been responsible.

Mrs. Schulberg panicked and proposed a dissociation. Feldman hastily offered to buy her out, and when she unexpectedly accepted, he was forced to sell the contract of Sylvia Sidney, which he had just obtained with considerable difficulty, for $25,000, in order to fulfill his obligation. Borrowing on all his assets, he set up briefly in partnership with a former law associate, Ralph Blum, and then on his own as Famous Artists Corporation in 1932. (Ironically, in view of the brouhaha over Dvorak, Feldman became a close friend of Zanuck and Joe Schenck, gaining his clients a special entré at Twentieth.)

Feldman was among the first in his profession to realize the potential of the one-picture deal over the long-term studio contract for his star clients. Irene Dunne, for example, was under contract to RKO for $1,500 a week, which, for a forty-week year, brought her $60,000. When her contract expired, Feldman refused another term arrangement, demanding $150,000 per picture, which she got, beginning with *Magnificent Obsession* and *Show Boat*. A similar situation existed with Claudette Colbert, whose Paramount contract provided her with $2,500 per week. Feldman convinced her to accept a script which several other actresses had rejected, and demanded $150,000 for her services in the film, which was *It Happened One Night*. The agent next raised Charles Boyer's salary from $30,000 per picture to $125,000 for eight weeks' work—and it wasn't long before Marlene Dietrich, George Raft, and Tyrone Power were represented by Feldman.

Charlie Feldman was one of the pioneers of the package deal. Around 1935, he was hit with the idea of creating jobs for his clients rather than fighting for them, which he did by combining an available writer, actor, director, and producer client with a property that would fit all their talents. He would first buy a book or play, pay a writer to adapt it for the screen, and, if it turned out well, sell it with the proviso that one of his producers, directors, and/or actors had to go with it. He did this with *The Spoilers,* selling the story to Universal as a package which included his clients Dietrich and John Wayne.

Feldman was one of the first agents to enter independent production while still representing clients. In 1939 the Screen Actors Guild granted him a waiver to produce as well as continue with his agency. The office grew into one of the largest in the world dealing with film talent, grossing $12 million annually before Feldman sold out to Ashley Steiner in 1962.

An urbane, attractive, literate man, Feldman became an intimate of such moguls as Jack Warner and Sam Goldwyn, in addition to Schenck and Zanuck. One of the reasons frequently given for his popularity is that he was on record as never winning a game of gin rummy and never complaining when he lost. Much of his business was conducted over dinner at Romanoff's, where he was often seen conferring with clients and studio executives.

Myron Selznick would not have been caught dead socializing with a Warner or a Schenck. Myron was an embittered son of Lewis J. Selznick, who, in the early twenties, was one of the key figures in the motion picture business. In 1922 William Randolph Hearst offered several million dollars for a share in Lewis Selznick Enterprises, but Selznick wanted to retain autonomy. He was worth $23 million on paper at that time but, unfortunately, had overextended himself to the point where he was vulnerable to instant destruction—which was exactly what befell him. Myron, who was then twenty-three, and who idolized the father who had trained both him and his brother David in every facet of the business, from cutting to selling, felt that his father's rivals had banded together to ruin him, and Myron was out for bloody vengeance.

It took him a few years. After founding the abortive Selznick Pictures Corporation—not to be confused with his brother's later company, Selznick International—Myron settled in Hollywood and worked briefly as an assistant producer at United Artists. In 1927 he performed his first negotiation as an agent, doubling the salary of director Lewis Milestone (who happened to be his roommate). He then set up Myron Selznick and Company, declaring that he would represent only the foremost people in the industry. In a series of trade advertisements, he took aim at his father's old enemies at the major studios, proclaiming that he intended to procure for his clients a far greater percentage of the film companies' earnings than they had ever received before.

In a short time, the abrasive Selznick, with his more charming partners —first Frank Joyce, brother of silent star Alice Joyce, and later Leland Hayward—built Hollywood's most powerful agency, at one time controlling about 75 percent of the business and, by 1937, grossing $15 million a year. After convincing key directors and writers that they, too, required representation, the firm amassed a glittering list of three hundred of the most prominent creative talents, which included Carole Lombard, Kay Francis, Olivia De Havilland, Paulette Goddard, Katharine Hepburn, Vivien Leigh (whom Myron recommended to David for *Gone With the Wind*), Myrna Loy, Fredric March, Ginger Rogers, Ernst Lubitsch, Alfred Hitchcock, and George Cukor. According to Quentin Reynolds, in the May 28, 1935, *Collier's:*

> A word from him and any of his clients will walk out of any studio, including the one operated and headed by brother David Selznick. . . . Anything under $5,000 a week or less than $150,000 a picture is peanuts to Myron.

Before Myron, there had been a tacit understanding among the studios of nonproselytizing. If a performer's contract expired, or he was dissatisfied, he had to renegotiate with his own studio, because no one else would talk to him. This was the industry's internal control on salary levels, which Selznick and Hayward decided to smash. Among their clients were three of Paramount's top stars, Kay Francis, William Powell, and Ruth Chatterton, all of whose contracts were up for renewal. The agents were aware that Warner Brothers, who had been first with talkies, was eager to get new talent to expand its sound program, and in one fell swoop, they moved their three clients from Paramount to Warners, doubling their salaries in the process. This, and a similar move of Constance Bennett from Pathé to Warners, led to a changed climate, in which studio raids erupted for the first time. The new inter- and intra-studio competition led to higher and higher salaries. When Hayward got Sam Goldwyn to pay Ina Claire $50,000 per picture, the other stars at that studio insisted that their own contracts be revised accordingly. Myrna Loy, Fredric March, and Miriam Hopkins found that Hayward and Selznick could get them four or five times what they had been earning.

But it was Myron's manner, as much as his methods, which enraged the producers he dealt with. When he stormed into their executive offices, growling demands and abuse, they knew that the sniveling image of the Hollywood agent had been irrevocably reversed. In his autobiography, Pat O'Brien describes his first meeting with Myron, explaining how "a strange little figure wandered onto the set, a sort of tough Jewish leprechaun." Selznick asked O'Brien who his agent was and O'Brien said he didn't have one. Selznick said, "You have one now, sweetheart," adding that he wouldn't take a dime from the actor until he had improved on his current deal. O'Brien thought that that sounded fair enough, and only after having agreed to these terms did he think to ask his new agent's name. They became good friends and O'Brien was one of Myron's pallbearers when, in 1944, Selznick died at the age of forty-five.

The cause of death was portal thrombosis, which surprised nobody who had watched him burn himself out. For twenty-five years, his life had been a constant round of boozing, womanizing, and gambling—all of this spiced with the daily exercise of his vendetta against the studios. In the beginning, it was his anger which propelled him to success, but, by the late thirties, it was beginning to boomerang on him, and his heavy drinking did nothing to help. The moguls began to find ways to get back at him—Zanuck banned him from the 20th Century-Fox lot—and a number of his top clients, even the easygoing Carole Lombard, were antagonized into quitting the agency. Frank Joyce—an affable man but a formidable negotiator— died in 1936, and the following year Selznick split with his other partner, Leland Hayward, who promptly opened his own business.

After bouncing around for several years as a press agent and talent scout on both coasts, Hayward's career as an agent began one evening in 1926 at the Trocadero in New York. The proprietor was bemoaning his lack of customers, saying he'd pay three or four thousand a week for a major attraction like the Astaires, who could be counted upon to bring the patrons in. Hayward promptly called on Fred and Adele, who were appearing in *Lady, Be Good,* and signed them up for the Trocadero at four thousand a week. Their new agent collected four hundred weekly for the twelve weeks of their engagement, and concluded that this was a pretty good way to earn a living.

Even after his split with Myron, Hayward carried on the Selznick tradition of antagonism (albeit in a more playful manner) toward the studio bosses. Ben Hecht, in *Charlie,* wrote of Hayward's "disdain for movies and his larkish attitude towards the movie Pharaohs." Certainly, his methods were successful. With his new partner, Nat Deverich, Hayward went on to pull off such deals as obtaining $130,000 from RKO for *Stage Door,* $117,500 from Metro for an unsuccessful Broadway play called *Excursion,* and $250,000 for something named *Dark Eyes.* One notion of his which shocked studio brass came about when he sent identical telegrams to each company, announcing the fact that the almost published (production heads had seen galley proofs) *Saratoga Trunk* was not for sale, but could be *leased* for seven years for a mere $175,000. Although all the studios let out a collective howl, Warners agreed to the terms that afternoon.

Hayward, a man of considerable charm, was one of the first regular transcontinental commuters, maintaining headquarters in both New York and Hollywood, until, after a serious romance with one client, Kate Hepburn, he married another, Margaret Sullavan, and settled into Hollywood domesticity, which included a passionate interest in bread baking. (Film celebrities became used to having him interrupt their telephone negotiations with, "Excuse me while I take my bread out of the oven.") In her family memoir, *Haywire,* the agent's daughter, Brooke, described a typical Leland Hayward working day:

> On a quiet morning he might call the executives of five or six studios —Warner Brothers, Columbia, Paramount, MGM, RKO, for instance— to tell them, excitedly, that they should check the box office receipts and reviews of some play that had just opened in New York (having himself arranged to handle its motion picture sale an hour before). Then, having satisfactorily charged the atmosphere with the necessary delirium, he would leave the office before they could call back, have a relaxed lunch with a client at the Brown Derby and maybe do an hour or two of leisurely shopping. By the time he got back to the office, there would be twenty properly hysterical phone calls from the studios, all bidding against each other, and Father would calmly close the deal for the record price.

Although he had profitable relationships with Astaire, Rogers, Hepburn, Henry Fonda, Jimmy Stewart, Fredric March, Myrna Loy, Garbo, Miriam Hopkins, and many others, Hayward's interest began to drift away from the agency business. In 1940, with money raised from such aviation-minded clients as Stewart, Fonda, Cary Grant, and Hoagy Carmichael, he built Thunderbird Field, a small flying school near Phoenix for the training of army cadet pilots. In April of 1945 the Hayward-Deverich Agency merged with the Music Corporation of America, with Hayward getting a ten-year contract as an MCA vice-president, and MCA getting a stable which helped make it number one overnight.

Agents

In the natural course of things, clients jumped from agency to agency, looking for better deals, and nobody took greater advantage of this than Phil Berg and Bert Allenberg, who, in the late thirties and early forties—the period that separates the Myron Selznick era from the MCA era—headed the most powerful agency in town. Phil Berg came to Hollywood from New York in 1926, at the age of twenty-four, for love of actress Leila Hyams, whom he later married. Both their families disapproved of the romance and Berg's financial support was cut off. Faced with the need to acquire a good income to impress the Hyams family, he became an agent. Working against him was the fact that he looked extremely young, younger even than he was, and he was sure that he would not be taken seriously by leads, male or female. So he decided to concentrate instead on older male character actors, who, he reasoned, probably looked on everyone under the age of thirty-five as being young, and thus would not hold his extreme youth against him. The technique he employed was to approach an actor who he knew was getting $750 a week and say, "I hear you're only getting $900 a week. I think you're worth more than that and I can get it for you." After cornering the elderly character actor market, he managed to sign up some bigger names, like Wallace Beery and Edward Arnold, and gradually acquired younger talents, including Madeleine Carroll and Deanna Durbin. Far less flamboyant than Myron Selznick, Berg—who actually avoided publicity for himself, preferring to exert clout behind the scenes—was nonetheless a ruthless negotiator, and, by the time Allenberg (a former investment broker) became his partner in 1934, the agency was already a force to be reckoned with. Berg had no compunctions about poaching clients from other agencies. That, for him, was the nature of the business, and Myron Selznick's decline provided him with many opportunities to acquire major talents for his list. At its peak, around 1941, the Berg-Allenberg agency handled literally hundreds of motion picture talents—stars, featured players, producers, directors, writers—including many of the top names in the industry. It dealt extensively in literary and dramatic properties, representing major publishers like Doubleday and Scribner's, and received a percentage of all the important Hollywood movie series, such as the Andy Hardy pictures. Like the Selznick agency, it also offered its clients business management, and for years operated a 138-foot yacht, equipped with ship-to-shore lines in every stateroom, for its clients' convenience.

During World War II, Phil Berg went into the Navy and, soon after he returned, sold out to his partner Bert Allenberg, who, in turn, sold out to William Morris. William Morris, established in New York in 1898, had long had a Los Angeles office, but for years it handled mostly vaudeville players. Later a Hollywood branch was opened, with first Meury File, then Walter Myers in charge. Later still, Abe Lastvogel and Johnny Hyde helped the Morris agency to make steady inroads in Hollywood, but it still did not become a major force in the movie industry until it bought out the agency that Berg-Allenberg had built.

Nor did William Morris get all of Berg-Allenberg's clients. Many shifted to MCA, which was to dominate the scene for years. Dr. Jules Stein began his agency in Chicago, and by the early thirties it was by far the largest organization handling the big bands that were so popular in that day. In 1937 MCA opened a Hollywood branch, headed by Taft Schreiber, and a few years later, Stein moved to California himself. Before long, he and one of his top agents, Lew Wasserman, began to crack the movie market, acquiring stars like Bette Davis and Betty Grable, but it was not until after the war that MCA became a real power in the film industry.

Famous Artists, Selznick, Hayward, Berg-Allenberg, William Morris, and MCA—these were the giants, but a number of other important smaller agents operated in Hollywood in the thirties and forties. One of them, Michael C. Levee, started in films in 1917 as a prop boy at Fox. Three years later, he founded Brunton Studios, in partnership with Joe Schenck and Robert Brunton, which was later sold to Paramount. Executive positions with Paramount, United Artists, and First National preceded his becoming a talent agent in the thirties. A founder of the Motion Picture Academy and its first treasurer, and also the first president of the Artists' Managers Guild, Levee served as agent or manager for Mary Pickford, Joan Crawford, Bette Davis, Merle Oberon, Jeanette MacDonald, Greer Garson, Paul Muni, Leslie Howard, Dick Powell, Claude Rains, Franchot Tone, Cecil B. DeMille, Frank Borzage, Mervyn LeRoy, Douglas Fairbanks, Jr., Ben Hecht, and William Dieterle. In his biography of Paul Muni, *Actor,* Jerome Lawrence describes Levee as "an honest, direct, down-to-earth businessman who handled less than twenty top actors and directors and devoted all his time to them." Levee ran his organization from a large, comfortable Hollywood house, where he indulged his passion for gourmet cooking, often serving his clients delightful lunches on the patio while talking over upcoming contract negotiations.

Another highly civilized agent was Paul Kohner, who represented a great many Europeans, particularly, in the late thirties, anti-Nazi actors, directors, and writers who had fled Hitler's Germany. Brought over from Czechoslovakia by Carl Laemmle, Kohner started his movie career in the shipping department of Universal with William Wyler. He graduated to the position of producer at Universal, then at Metro and Columbia, being represented by Frank Orsatti. When he left Columbia, Orsatti invited him to join his agency, but Kohner decided to start his own instead. His client list gradually grew to include Pola Negri, Luise Rainer, Myrna Loy, Greta

Garbo, Dolores Del Rio, Rita Hayworth, Lana Turner, John and Walter Huston, Robert Taylor, Erich von Stroheim, and David Niven. Another client was screenwriter Salka Viertel, who, in her autobiography, *The Kindness of Strangers,* demonstrates how agents were still often in an uncomfortable position with studio executives. After seven years with M-G-M, Viertel brought Kohner in to negotiate a new contract. On the day that Kohner met with Eddie Mannix, a top Mayer aide, to discuss the terms of the new deal, Viertel received a call from the head of the story department, informing her that she was being removed from the payroll. Apparently Mannix was incensed to learn that the writer was daring to allow an agent to "barge in" on what he evidently thought of as a "family" relationship, especially since M-G-M had voluntarily increased her salary at regular intervals.

Minna Wallis and Ruth Collier, her partner for a short time, were among the few female agents of importance in Hollywood during the thirties. The sister of producer Hal Wallis, Minna was in Los Angeles for a visit when Erwin Loeb, attorney for her hosts, asked her if she'd like to fill in for his secretary for two weeks. She eagerly agreed and, during that period, another of Loeb's clients, Sam Warner, offered her a job at his studio. Preceding her brother there, Minna Wallis became casting director for Warners in the mid-twenties, also doubling as a one-woman wardrobe department in the days when the job consisted of going out and purchasing suitable garments in shops. When she decided to become an agent, she was staked by Myron Selznick and Leland Hayward to the sum of $10,000, which she paid back at the end of her first year, and before long she was representing Errol Flynn, George Brent, Eduardo Ciannelli, Clark Gable, and Myrna Loy. Being a socially prominent single female had its professional advantages. She would often ask one of her male clients to escort her to a party, thus making sure that he would be seen by the right people. This worked well when she was trying to interest M-G-M in Clark Gable. Wallis was one of the agents who formed personal attachments with their clients, in her case particularly Gable, who remained a close friend long after he switched to the Berg-Allenberg agency. When Wallis signed him, he was still working in the theater, at a salary of $350 a week. She took him out to Pathé, where they were doing a picture called *Painted Desert:*

> They liked him and I was able to get him $750 for his first picture. They said, "Of course you can ride." I said, "Of course he can." When we got outside, Clark looked at me and said, "Minna, you're crazy! I've never even been near a horse!" I said, "Well, you're going to be, starting right now." We went out to the Valley, where they had a riding school, and started him off. He went out there and practiced every day and when the picture was ready, he could ride as well as anybody.

Wallis describes the signing of another of her early clients:

I had my office on Sunset Boulevard, above La Rue, and one day the woman who worked opposite me was giving a cocktail party for her millinery shop. Lloyd Pantages came and he brought Errol Flynn, who had just arrived in America. I think he'd just done one scene—as a dead man—for Warner Brothers in England. As soon as I saw him, I said, "I've got to sign him, Lloyd!" He said, "He's yours." Errol came in that afternoon and signed a contract with me.

Like Minna Wallis, several other agents who made their marks in the thirties were related in some way to celebrities on the scene. There was the fourth Marx brother, Zeppo, with offices on Sunset Boulevard; Bing's brothers, Everett and Larry Crosby; Howard Hawks's brother, Bill; Sam Jaffe, brother of Ad Schulberg; and Edna Best's husband, Nat Wolf. Jack Sherrill, a former leading man, and Sue Carol, a former leading lady, both set up as agents. Sherrill persevered, but it wasn't long before Sue Carol was devoting all of her promotional energies to her husband, Alan Ladd.

Garbo's first agent-manager, Frank Edington—who had started his career as Sam Goldwyn's studio manager and comptroller and was later chief of production at RKO—has been credited with inadvertently creating his client's aloof image. In response to her complaints about being forced to pose in gym shorts with the USC track team (see PUBLICITY), he suggested she simply play hard to get. Edington also represented John Gilbert and was responsible for getting him the highest salary M-G-M had ever paid. In 1932 he entered into partnership with Frank Vincent—a white-haired, immaculately dressed man whom Rosalind Russell described as looking more like a senator than an agent—and they, together with a third partner, Frederick Brisson (Russell's husband), who joined them later, specialized in British actors and writers.

Other agents who moved in and out of the scene included Louis "Doc" Schurr, who had been one of Eddie Small's New York protégés; Charlie Morrison, who was briefly in partnership with Felix "Fefe" Ferry, then went on to open the Mocambo; Hal Cooley, Sam Lyons, Tom Fixdale, George Chasin, Wynn Roccamora, and Pat Di Cicco.

CAMERAMEN.

One of the shortest strikes in Hollywood history occurred in 1933 when M-G-M camera operators walked off the job. Management was not unduly concerned: Everyone assumed that the directors of photography—known, in those simpler days, as first cameramen—could climb up behind the big Mitchells in their soundproof "blimps" (sometimes called "bungalows") and carry on business as usual. John Lee Mahin recalls what happened:

> The rushes were unbelievable! There was a long scene in one of the big Garbo pictures—*Queen Christina*—in which she came down the palace steps, with a lot of action and dialogue going on. Bill Daniels was operating the camera and all you could see, the whole time, was Garbo's nose! Hal Rosson was on a picture and he forgot to rack over the whole day. Normally, you set up, you look through the viewfinder and you rack over. He forgot to rack over, and everything came out black. These fellows hadn't operated a camera in years. Louis B. Mayer took one look at what was going on and said, "Settle it! Settle it right away!"

The camera operators were given everything they wanted and returned to work.

This anecdote is not intended to belittle men like Daniels and Rosson —who were among the true artists of the Hollywood film—but is meant to illustrate the fact that the great cinematographers had little to do with the actual handling of the motion picture camera, a task they could safely delegate to an assistant. The director of photography had to be thoroughly familiar with the fundamentals of optics, the properties of various lenses and filters, the uses of different cranes, booms, and dollies, and a hundred other mechanical factors, but he would seldom place himself at the viewfinder except to adjust the pictorial composition. Composition was one major component in his artistry; another was light. The great cameramen were obsessed with light.

26

George Folsey—who received his first screen credit in 1919 and was for many years a mainstay at M-G-M—states, quite succinctly, "I have devoted my whole life to thinking about light." As a boy he had a job delivering groceries and remembers studying the way that gas lamps cast shadows in dim hallways. As a young cameraman in New York he took note of everything that might be of possible value:

> There were no schools then, so you learned as you went along. When I'd get on the subway, I'd look at the people and ask myself, "How are they lighted?" Wherever I was, indoors or out, I'd ask myself that question. . . .
>
> I'd go to museums and photographic galleries. I'd stop by at Perry MacDonald's salon. He photographed only men—he refused to photograph women—and he always had great character in those faces, and great skin texture. And nearby there was a man called Albin who had huge blowups of Dorothy and Lillian Gish. I'd study those and I'd look in the magazines and learn the names of the fashion photographers and watch what they did.
>
> If you absorb yourself in how a coffee cup is made, and you think about that to the exclusion of a helluva lot of other things, you can find out an awful lot about coffee cups and how they are manufactured. That's how I was about light.

Nothing could benefit a star more than this particular obsession. By orchestrating key lights and filters, reflectors and diffusors, the director of photography could make a beautiful woman seem more beautiful, or he could bring out the character in a man's face. The distribution of light and shadow can, of course, also be used to create drama and tension or frivolity, to give a film a look of stark realism or deliberately evoke an ambience of artifice. Given the Hollywood system, however, much of the cinematographer's energy was likely to be devoted to servicing the stars. As far back as 1919, Billy Bitzer was photographing the twenty-two-year-old Lillian Gish through a fine silk net, in order to make her appear younger—the first step toward the development of the rejuvenating diffusing lens.

Many stars had their favorite cameramen, with whom they worked on a regular basis. Mary Pickford started this trend, keeping Charles Rosher on salary the year round, permitting him to work on other films only when she didn't need him. Pickford, whose career depended upon looking youthful, appreciated Rosher's backlighting effects, which kept her darkening curls blond, and his skill with other lights kind to her complexion. It was Pickford herself who discovered the efficacy of using light from below

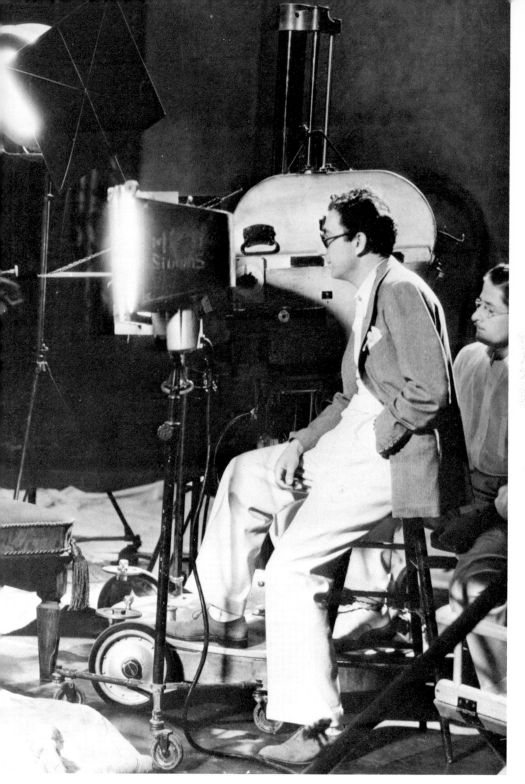

GRETA GARBO, C. AUBREY SMITH, ROUBEN MAMOULIAN,
AND CINEMATOGRAPHER BILL DANIELS (FAR RIGHT) ON THE SET
OF *Queen Christina*.

one morning when her mirror caught the sun's early rays and cast a particularly flattering light on her skin. This realization led to the use of "baby spots," which gradually became standard practice.

Pickford's husband, Doug Fairbanks, liked to work with Arthur Edison and Henry Sharp; Norma Talmadge had Tony Gaudio on most of her films; Harold Lloyd's favorite was Walter Lundin; and Chaplin placed great reliance on Rollie Totheroe. Even cowboy stars like William S. Hart and Tom Mix had their own cameramen, Hart working with Joe August and Mix with Dan Clark. Garbo and Shearer always demanded Bill Daniels, whose reputation may be gauged from the fact that John Barrymore's first words of advice to his sister, Ethel, when she arrived in Hollywood, were, "Get Bill Daniels. He'll make you look younger than the Mona Lisa." John himself, however, generally worked with Rosher, who had developed the Rosher Kino Portrait Lens, a soft-focus lens which was very kind to aging skin. It may be that Barrymore's advice to his sister was not entirely motivated by brotherly affection: possibly he was anxious to keep Rosher for himself. Certainly competition for gifted cinematographers was cutthroat. Constance Bennett refused to start work on *Outlaw Lady* unless she was lighted by Rosher, who had already been assigned to Helen Hayes, then busy on *What Every Woman Knows*. Bennett's temperament being legendary, Irving Thalberg acquiesced to her demand, pulling Rosher off the Hayes picture in the middle of production.

George Folsey was another cinematographer much in demand with M-G-M's female stars. For almost a decade, he lit all of Joan Crawford's pictures:

> Crawford was doing *Chained* with Clarence Brown, and he had been using Olly Marsh, who was an extremely capable cameraman—when he wanted to be. He'd been in the business a long time and had become, I think, a little jaded. He'd lost the drive and ambition he should have had. He'd find the easiest way to light a scene—everything came out kind of one tone—and Crawford needed *dynamic* lighting.
>
> So they brought me in to do the picture and there was a scene which called for her to sit at a table alone and drink a sherry flip. We were rehearsing this scene and all the stage lights were on, but ours went off—and *way* up on a catwalk was a little light that came down and hit Crawford absolutely beautifully. As you know, she used to wear those Adrian costumes with big white collars. The little light hit the collar and bounced up on her face. It was beautiful. . . .
>
> When I came to light the scene, I took a spotlight and ran it up in line with that other light—keeping it very soft. The spot hit the white collar and bounced up on her face, just the way I wanted it to. I put an optical

disc on the lens and she looked like she hadn't looked in years. . . . Well, she was so ecstatically happy with the results that from then on I could do no wrong.

Carole Lombard had an understanding that Ted Tetzlaff would shoot all her pictures, though later she did work happily with Harry Stradling. Bette Davis' favorite was Ernest Haller, and Greer Garson liked to work with Joe Ruttenberg. He had noted that she always photographed better when she held her chin up and devised a set of signals that would tip her off when it began to dip.

A cinematographer who worked with a star on a regular basis could help in a dozen different ways. Charles G. Clarke, who was assigned to Jeanette MacDonald during her brief stay at Fox, recalls that she was extremely cooperative—no youngster, she appreciated all that he could do for her—and so he was happy to oblige her with small favors: "She liked to go home at six, so she'd look at me and I'd say, 'I guess we'd better quit. She's getting rings under her eyes.' "

Since certain cameramen were considered to be specialists—though most cinematographers felt they could do anything, given the chance—they were often "cast" for a picture at a very early stage of preproduction, sometimes even before a director had been chosen. In other instances, the studio would arrange for several cameramen to shoot tests of a new prospect, generally female, and the one who seemed to have the most rapport with the subject would be assigned to work with her. This system was not much liked by cinematographers, who resented being pitted against one another.

A handful of stars themselves became lighting experts. Harry Stradling has been quoted as saying of Carole Lombard, "She knew as much about the tricks of the trade as I do." One of her problems was a scar on one cheek. Stradling wanted to eliminate it by bringing more light to bear, making it blend in with the surrounding skin tones. Lombard told him that a diffusing glass on his lens would do the job better, and he found that she was absolutely right. Preparing for one setup, she told him that there was a light missing on her right side and, sure enough, an inspection revealed that one of the sixty or seventy lights trained on her—a small key light—had burned out. She explained that a tiny patch of skin, above one cheekbone, felt too cool, so she knew something must be wrong. Loretta Young is said to have been another who could judge if a scene was correctly lit by the emission of heat from the lamps.

After working with Marlene Dietrich on *Stage Fright,* Alfred Hitchcock said, with a faint trace of malice, "Marlene Dietrich is a *professional*—a professional actress, a professional dress designer, a professional cameraman!" Edward G. Robinson has described how she would politely super-

31

intend camera placements and lighting, making suggestions so subtly and sexily that no one was offended. At one point in her career, she used to have a mirror mounted on the camera, alongside the lens, so she could check the lighting, but mostly she seems to have depended on heat rays to guide her. Many people have suggested that it was Josef Von Sternberg who taught Dietrich all she knew about lighting, but Lee Garmes, who shot most of her early Hollywood pictures, claims that Von Sternberg had very little to do with lighting her. In an interview published in Charles Higham's *Hollywood Cameramen,* Garmes said that after studying *The Blue Angel,* he lit Dietrich with a sidelight, so that one half of her face was bright and the other was in shadow. When the first day's rushes were screened, he realized that this was exactly the way that Bill Daniels was lighting Garbo and, not wanting to appear derivative, he changed—without telling Von Sternberg—to a "north light" effect which became the norm for all her future films and, to a large extent, helped define the Dietrich face. Garmes has nothing but respect for Dietrich's understanding of the cinematographer's art. "She had a great mechanical mind, and knew the camera. She would always stop in the exact position that was right for her."

Most actors, however, never developed this skill, as Charles Clarke remembers:

> Jeanette was a great girl to work with, and Tyrone Power was very helpful and considerate of the cinematographer's problems, but most of them couldn't care less about lighting. They'd expect to look good, but they wouldn't do anything to help you. They'd be so wrapped up in their performance that they felt they could land anywhere on the floor and somehow you'd take care of it. Their attitude was, "That's your problem, not mine."

In other instances, by Clarke's estimate, a star's interest in lighting did not always work to her advantage:

> There was a time when everyone wanted backlighting. A little bit was good, so a whole lot must be better—that was the theory. Stars wanted it, and some of them demanded it—and, if Betty Grable wants a lot of back-light, why you'd better give it to her. In some cases there was so much backlighting on people that they looked like they were on fire!

To achieve whatever effect was called for, the director of photography had an incredible arsenal of lamps at his disposal, ranging in size from "gimmicks"—tiny spotlights about the size of a beer can—to "sun arcs" (also known as "sixties"), five feet across and generating up to 3 million foot-candles. In between came lights with such felicitous names as "bon bons," "juniors," "crackerboxes," "rifles," "broads," "twins," "half-barrels," and "10-Ks." Conversation between the cinematographer and the "gaffer"—or head electrician (whose assistants were known as "juicers")—were conducted in an esoteric patois. Old-fashioned arc lights were called "ashcans"; the newer incandescent lights—which had the great advantage of being silent—in those days were referred to generically as "inkies."

"Silks" were frames over which had been stretched rectangles of raw silk. These were placed in front of various light sources to soften the illumination. "Barn doors" and "ears" were metal gates, attached to a lamp, which could be opened and closed to control the amount of light that was emitted. "Gobos," "flats," "flags," and "niggers" were black cloth shades used to block out unwanted light from the camera lens in order to avoid halation and other undesirable effects. Even when exteriors were being shot, many lights, silks, and reflectors were required. The cinematographer was paid to orchestrate these instruments, just as he was expected to choreograph camera movements.

CARS.

The star car was one of the most tangible and public manifestations of success in early Hollywood, and there are few chroniclers of the period who do not mention Tom Mix cruising the Boulevard in his motorized cow palace, its long hood decorated with a tooled saddle and steer horns, or Mae Murray, her costume aflutter with feathers, riding with chaffeur and footman to match her cream-and-black Rolls, her canary yellow Pierce-Arrow, or her more formal white Rolls. Clara Bow drove a flame-red Kissel convertible painted to match her hair, and was usually accompanied by two chows whose coats had been dyed the same shade. By 1919, Fatty Arbuckle had filled his multicar garage with a Rolls, a Stevens-Duryea, a white Cadillac, a Renault, and a $25,000 Pierce-Arrow outfitted with a cocktail bar and a toilet. In an effort to outdo Arbuckle, Sessue Hayakawa acquired a gold-plated Pierce Arrow. (Later, Clark Gable would insist that his Duesenberg be made one foot longer than Gary Cooper's pale green and canary custom model.)

AL JOLSON WITH HIS MERCEDES.

JOAN CRAWFORD IN HER CONVERTIBLE.

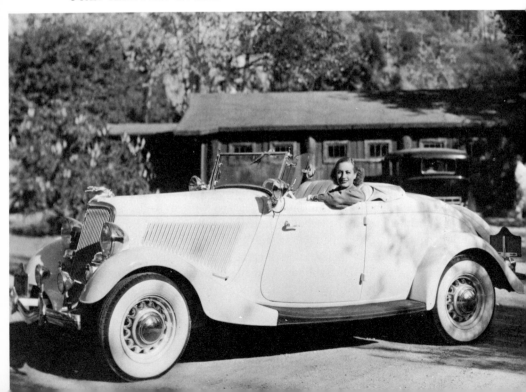

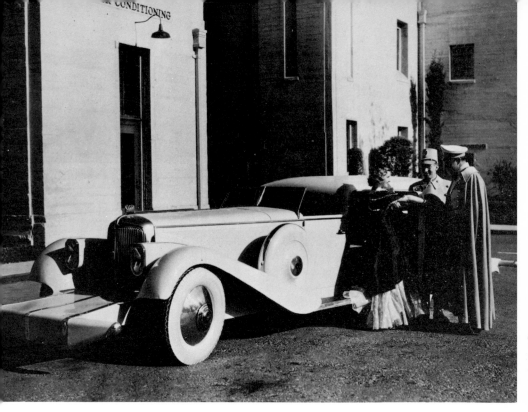

GRACE MOORE IN WHAT WAS REPUTED TO HAVE BEEN "THE
LONGEST CAR IN HOLLYWOOD."

RONALD REAGAN WITH HIS BUICK.

CARS

At a glance, the Hollywood limousine could be identified by color, mountings, and accouterments. Swanson's Lancia was upholstered in leopard skin. Francis X. Bushman drove a lavender Rolls in which, attended by servants in lavender uniforms, he smoked only lavender cigarettes. Valentino's cream-colored Mercedes and custom-built Voisin tourer had specially designed silver coiled cobras for radiator caps, and his Isotta Fraschini had silver mountings and panels of inlaid walnut and silver. Ralph Forbes's Cadillac featured a built-in dressing table, and the white MacFarland Jack Dempsey drove during his Hollywood years ran on monogrammed tires. To reduce the question of identification even further, Stepin Fetchit could often be seen in a pink Rolls, the trunk of which bore his name spelled out in neon. Buster Keaton, displaying more of a sense of humor, and usually wearing a cocked hat and an admiral's uniform borrowed from the Metro wardrobe department, drove a unique yachtlike thirty-foot land cruiser—complete with bunks for six, two drawing rooms, a gallery, and an observation deck—that had been specially built by the Fifth Avenue Bus Company.

CLARK GABLE WITH HIS CUSTOMIZED DUESENBERG.

During World War I, the Locomobile Company began construction of a special vehicle intended for the use of General Pershing. The war ended before it could be delivered to France, however, and Cecil B. DeMille—a car buff—bought the chassis for $12,500 and had coachwork fabricated for it in California. Later, he acquired a second Locomobile which he drove daily for fourteen years. He also owned a Cunningham touring model, a Lincoln limousine, a Cord roadster, and the first Model A Ford.

It was, of course, essential that the driver of the automobile be equal in elegance to his conveyance. Briggs, the driver of Marlene Dietrich's Cadillac, wore a mink-trimmed uniform and a pair of revolvers, while Jeanette MacDonald's chauffeur shared the front seat with the star's large sheep dog. And Constance Bennett's chauffeur sat outside her gleaming black Rolls, like a hack driver, while she rested comfortably within a velvet-lined compartment.

CHILDREN.

Under the Hollywood studio system, having a baby could be an expensive proposition for a female star. One contemporary report, published in 1933, estimated that the birth of Bebe Daniels' daughter Barbara had lost the actress $150,000 in salary, and suggested that it had also cost her her Warner Brothers contract. (It must be admitted that, although she had made the transition to sound, Daniels' popularity was slipping before childbirth became a factor.) Helen Twelvetrees gave up her $130,000 a year salary to have little Jack Woody, and lost *Bill of Divorcement* to Katharine Hepburn, and when she did return to work, her career never regained its momentum. Norma Shearer was operating from more of a power base, but even she suffered a setback when she became pregnant in 1930, losing the coveted lead in *Paid,* which husband Irving Thalberg had bought for her. (The part went to Joan Crawford, who made a big success of it.) Mae Marsh's decision to marry and have children, against the wishes of Sam Goldwyn, who owned her contract, destroyed her career, and it has been suggested that the time Gloria Swanson took off to have her second child, Michael Bridget, may have contributed to the waning of her popularity in the thirties.

WALLACE BEERY WATCHING "HOME MOVIES" WITH HIS WIFE AND
ADOPTED DAUGHTER, CAROL ANN.

At the very least, the months of work sacrificed to pregnancy and
childbirth cost an actress a good deal of money and often upset the studio.
When, in 1938, Dorothy Lamour was quoted as saying, "I want a baby of
my own and I want it before I'm twenty-five," alarmed Paramount officials
cautioned her that if she was serious, she should at least consider adopting.
(The threat they faced was an immediate one. Lamour was twenty-four at
the time of her statement.) Whether because of Paramount's advice or not,
she did eventually adopt—seven years later, after she had divorced and
remarried.

It is not surprising, then, that there was an exceptionally high percentage
of adopted children in the movie colony. Apart from the career and financial factors mentioned above, there was also the need for stars to preserve
their perfect bodies—although many of the adoptions were probably
motivated by infertility, altruism, and other normal considerations, and
it should be noted that a number of male celebrities also adopted children.
Among the large population of adoptive parents were Al Jolson and Ruby
Keeler, Fredric March and Florence Eldridge, the James Cagneys, the
Adolphe Menjous, the Wallace Beerys, Barbara Stanwyck and Frank Fay,

the Pat O'Briens, and Linda Darnell and Peverell Marley. Several couples had mixed families of natural and adopted children. These included the Harold Lloyds, the Joe E. Browns, Barbara Bennett and Morton Downey, the Harry Cohns, and Dick Powell and June Allyson.

A number of these children were placed by the Cradle Society of Evanston, Illinois, a rather elegantly appointed private agency, which also served as a refuge for "respectable" young pregnant women. The movie colony was able to establish connections to it through a few knowing West Coast lawyers. Miriam Hopkins, then single, adopted a five-day-old boy she called Michael from the society in 1932. George Burns and Gracie Allen found both their children at the same institution, with a great deal of accompanying public fanfare—*Photoplay* ran an article entitled "Her Adopted Children Remade Gracie Allen's Life" in April of 1937. There was a rather insensitive follow-up story several months later:

> When the Burns adopted their Sandra, Jack Benny was always around her. One day, he said to Mary, "What are we waiting for?" They presently started their baby shopping. Mary said, "I wanted a baby that really needed help, not a gorgeous darling that anyone would snap up at sight. We looked at a lot of babies . . . then I saw this one. Everything was wrong with her. She had a cast in one eye, she was undernourished, she had a skin rash and a cold on the chest. She wasn't a good-looking baby, but I liked her."

Other couples were not so amenable to the attendant publicity as the Burns and Benny families. Joe E. Brown warned the Warners publicity department to "cut out the word 'adopted' every time you mention my daughter." When Irene Dunne and her husband, Dr. Francis Griffin, adopted four-year-old Anna Mary Bush (called "Missy") from the New York Foundling Hospital, they decided to have the final papers processed in New York, in an effort to avoid the Los Angeles publicity. Despite their ploy, reporters and cameramen besieged their Manhattan hotel, with Miss Dunne denying the rumors that Missy was a foundling, stating that she had met the child's grandparents, "who are delightful and charming old people."

Miriam Hopkins (whose character witness was Dorothy Parker and who sent a friend out to Chicago to pick up little Michael) was not the only single female parent to adopt. Gloria Swanson adopted four-month-old Joseph, and Joan Crawford became the parent of Christina, Christopher, Cathy, and Cynthia, between marriages. In 1937 Loretta Young, following a year's sabbatical from the Hollywood scene, was said to have adopted two little girls from a local Catholic orphanage. The elder was then supposedly reclaimed by relatives, while Miss Young kept baby Judy—who for years has been rumored to have been her own child, fathered by Clark Gable.

Cecil B. DeMille, notoriously callous on the set, could be quite the opposite in private life. In 1920 nine-year-old Katherine Lester, the Canadian-born daughter of a British father killed in the battle of Verdun and a Swiss mother who died of tuberculosis, was placed in a Los Angeles orphanage. DeMille's wife, Constance, a director of the institution, would frequently bring the shy, serious girl home with her, and it wasn't long before Katherine was a legal member of the family. In 1922 a frail baby boy with rickets was found in a parked car outside the DeMille estate. The child, who was named Richard, was gradually restored to health, and formally adopted in 1940.

Several other film personalities wanted to take responsibility for children who struck their fancy. In addition to Mae Murray's interest in the six-year-old Loretta Young (see DISCOVERIES), director Herbert Brenon

JACK BENNY GREETS WIFE MARY LIVINGSTON AND DAUGHTER JOAN.

and his wife became so fond of little Anne Shirley that they tried to adopt her. Marion Davies made an eight-year-old boy who peddled newspapers on Washington Boulevard, outside the M-G-M gate, her private ward, and George Raft once offered to adopt a boy who had legal and behavioral problems, but at the last moment, the child's parents declined.

Raising a child in Hollywood was a formidable task. Everyone in the movie industry worked long hours, six days a week, had scripts to study at home and complex social responsibilities, so the children's welfare often had to be entrusted to a series of nurses and nannies. (Few communities at that time boasted as many women breadwinners as the movie colony did.) There was great competition for the better nurses available, and new parents were often pestered with phone calls from quack "mother's helpers," claiming to represent some current educational or hygienic cult. The spotlight of publicity, too, made for a difficult parent-child relationship. (In the early days, when stars were supposed to be single, children were sometimes trained to deny their parentage.) Again, many stars came to the wealth and glamour of the movie world directly from difficult childhoods and broken homes, never having experienced normal family life and having no model to emulate, so it is not surprising that in some cases their notions of the correct way to rear children were rather bizarre.

An extreme instance of this has been made public in the revelations printed about Joan Crawford since her death. Crawford had a dramatically harsh early life and achieved her position as a *grande dame* of the movies by sheer will power and discipline. (It is said that when she first went to M-G-M, she was so lax in her personal hygiene that wardrobe women were in the habit of picking up her discarded clothes with sticks.) No one in Hollywood transformed herself more completely to attain stardom, and Crawford felt that the qualities that had enabled her to make this transformation could somehow be transmitted to her adopted children. Above all, they must learn self-control. The three girls were obliged to dress in stiff organdy frocks and frilly party dresses, Christopher in velvet Fauntleroy suits, and when guests were present, they were required to bow and curtsy like overdressed windup toys. According to Crawford's biographer, Bob Thomas, when visitors were taken to the children's quarters one evening—to inspect their wardrobes—they were surprised to find Christopher tied to the four corners of his bed. "Oh, he likes to kick off the covers and suck his thumb," was the hostess's explanation. Thomas also reports that Crawford would punish the boy by locking him in closets, and was known to pull down his pants and spank him in public. She also cut off Christina's long blond curls because she thought they were making her vain.

The two younger girls—Crawford insisted on referring to them as "the twins," although they were born a month apart to different women—were not treated quite so harshly, but they were still subjected to the rages that their mother flew into if she found a closet untidy. All four children were sent to a series of private boarding schools, and sometimes were left there through the school vacations. Christopher tried to run away several times and, as a teen-ager, was put into a correctional institution after a shooting spree with a BB gun. But every so often, particularly if photographers were to be present, Crawford enjoyed planning expensive surprises for her family. One Easter, for example, employees of Stanley Medeiro, a floral designer who catered to the movie crowd, rose at dawn and placed on the Crawford lawn five-foot-tall bunnies, dressed to match the children's Easter outfits, carrying baskets of candy and flowers. The following year, Joan's new husband, Alfred Steele, sporting an Easter bunny costume, hopped around the garden for the children's amusement. Unfortunately, Christina reports in her own book, many of the toys and other gifts were taken away by Mommie Dearest as soon as the press left.

The Crawford pattern of child rearing was military discipline interspersed with occasional acts of indulgence. More often, in the movie colony, the reverse was true. Hollywood children tended—as many of them have since admitted in sorrow or anger—to have had too much of everything, and special occasions like birthdays were apt to be treated as an excuse for a Busby Berkeley production number, with young children already participants in the status race, competing to have the best corps of circus entertainers on hand or the most elaborately architected birthday cake. (They were aware almost from toddlerhood how much money each of their playmates' fathers earned.) In 1939 the Edward G. Robinsons threw a spectacular party to celebrate the sixth birthday of their son, Eddie, Jr. (always called Manny). Manny practically grew up on the Warners lot—Harry Warner was his godfather—and at an early age was known in Beverly Hills for his ability to impersonate his father's famous tough-guy delivery. By his own account, Manny was crazy about jails—he had been on so many prison sets—and so a child-size jail was built for him, complete with bars, locks, and other appropriate accessories. His parents had found a police chief's uniform for him in Chicago, and it was a natural to plan his birthday celebration around a penal theme. Instead of receiving invitations, his guests were subpoenaed (on regulation State of California forms), and a Black Maria was borrowed from the studio to convey them to the festivities—the Beverly Hills police provided an escort. Once everyone was there, Manny had a wonderful time locking up his peers—the Crosby boys, the young Selznicks, John Barrymore, Jr., Peter Gahagan Douglas—and his father, then eating the Alcatraz-shaped birthday cake. A swarm of photographers dutifully recorded all this and the party was such a success that it was featured on the front page of the Los Angeles *Times* the following day.

JOAN CRAWFORD AND HER FOUR ADOPTED CHILDREN SAY GRACE IN
THE WARNERS COMMISSARY.

Manny's life was a privileged one—kidding between takes with Bogart,
Cagney, and Raft—and his father was obviously aware of the dangers
of overindulgence. He considered sending his son to a public school,
but in the end gave into pressure from friends and sent Manny to a military school, hoping the discipline would benefit him. Manny became increasingly disturbed, feeling that his father worked so hard that they had
no time together. The only thing that seemed to unite the family was
crises, and so Manny, in his early teens, began to manufacture them.
There were joy rides in stolen cars, traffic violations and crashes, and
before long, Manny's old friends in the Beverly Hills police department
were getting to know him in a new way.

Growing up in the movie colony was, then, far from a charmed existence. In *Los Angeles* magazine several years ago, Budd Schulberg recalled the horror of being driven to Los Angeles High School—a tough,
inner-city public school—in a Lincoln town car customized to resemble
an eighteenth-century royal coach, complete with gold *petit point* and
gold-tipped coach lights, driven by a chauffeur whose maroon livery
matched the car's upholstery. Schulberg and his sister were so embarrassed
that they would hide on the floor and slip out of the grotesque vehicle a
couple of blocks from school so they could arrive on foot.

On Monday mornings in the early thirties, many children could be seen

43

CHILDREN

EDWARD G. ROBINSON, JR. (MANNY), ON THE WARNERS LOT.
CULVER PICTURES.

descending from other chauffeur-driven vehicles near the intersection of
Melrose and Wilcox, the site of the Black Foxe Military Academy.
Founded by Earle Foxe, a leading man of the silent era, and Captain
Black, an ex-army officer, this was a weekly boarding school that was
much patronized by the movie colony. The common sentiment was that it
was chic to have a son in military uniform. (Many of the daughters of
Hollywood society, such as the Mayer and DeMille girls, attended the
Hollywood School for Girls; several of the next generation of less formal
parents—the Henry Fondas, Gary Coopers, and Laurence Oliviers—
favored the Brentwood School.) Soon after Charles Lindbergh's son was
kidnapped, however, in 1932, the limousines outside the academy gave
way to anonymous-looking sedans. Kidnap fever had gripped wealthy
parents from Los Feliz to Santa Monica. The two eldest Chaplin boys
were students at Black Foxe. They spent their weekends at their mother's
home on Rossmore Avenue, and on hot nights, they tossed and turned in
bed because burglar alarms had been installed on every window, meaning

that none of them could be opened after dark when the system was turned on. Ann Harding, after receiving a couple of notes threatening her daughter Janie, bought a trained police dog and hired a bodyguard. Harold Lloyd took similar precautions on his estate after receiving phone calls from a self-proclaimed kidnapper; Irving Thalberg, Jr., who lived at the ocean, was never allowed on the beach without an adult; and Bebe Daniels and Ben Lyon were given a terrible fright when their little daughter disappeared with her nurse—both later found, unharmed. Everyone in the public eye suddenly felt themselves vulnerable. For the nation's most precious child, J. Edgar Hoover himself came to California to oversee the setting-up of elaborate electronic protection systems at the home of Shirley Temple.

COACHES.

Movie executives and producers prided themselves on their ability to spot diamonds in the rough—young men and women who had that charismatic flash of personality or beauty that would come across on screen—but rough gems need to be cut and polished. As a consequence of this, coaches of all kinds flourished in Hollywood. If you needed to learn to walk, enunciate, ride, fence, or make love, someone could be called upon with the appropriate expertise.

One of the earliest advisers to the stars was Elinor Glyn, self-proclaimed arbiter of glamour, creator of "It." She generously shared her repertoire of tricks with certain chosen people, showing them how to project themselves romantically. It was she, for example, who claimed credit for advising Valentino to kiss the open palm of his leading lady's hand in *Beyond the Rocks*—a sensation in its day. A later arbiter of glamour was the designer, Adrian, who took some time from his fashion sketching to coach the nubile Lana Turner in stance and poise, teaching her to walk regally (which at the same time allowed the shy girl to avoid looking people in the eye). At Paramount, Zee Silvonia, an ex-Follies girl, was in charge of training the younger contract players in carriage and grace, and David Selznick hired Anita Colby as a "personality consultant"—

which in modern terms might be called "image maker." To take one instance, Colby advised that the public imprint of Joan Fontaine should be "smart, feminine, and refined."

The coming of sound created a desperate need for vocal coaches to eradicate accents, denasalize tones, sharpen diction, lower registers, etc. Metro imported from Italy Dr. Mario Marafioti, who had been Caruso's throat specialist and later became the mentor of Grace Moore. His arrival was considered sufficiently important to justify Louis B. Mayer himself heading the party that greeted him at the Santa Fe depot. According to Frances Marion, Marafioti "listened to all the young chorus girls to see if he could find any latent talent." Another arrival at the beginning of the sound era was Laura Hope Crews, a well-known stage actress with impeccable diction. It is said that Gloria Swanson, at the suggestion of Sam Goldwyn, brought Crews to California, at a salary of one thousand a week, so that the Broadway star could help the Hollywood goddess prepare for her first talkie. Others report, however, that it was Norma Talmadge— the possessor of a ripe Brooklyn accent—who, at the advent of sound, slipped off quietly to New York, returning in the company of Crews. (If this version is true, it did not succeed in helping Talmadge make the transition to talkies.) Colleen Moore and Mary Pickford were coached by another distinguished Broadway actress, Constance Collier, for one hundred dollars an hour. When news of these fees reached the Great White Way, scores of Shakespearean actors packed their bags and headed for the Coast. Norma Shearer's diction was improved by two of the most noted actresses of the day, Mrs. Patrick Campbell and Mrs. Leslie Carter. Humphrey Bogart, early in his career, spent six weeks helping Charles Farrell to modulate his speech.

Katharine Hepburn and Bette Davis notwithstanding, it was colloquial speech that came to dominate as the sound era progressed. Still, daily sessions with the studio dramatic and diction coaches were on the schedules of every rising contract player. At 20th Century-Fox, in the late thirties, there was a well-organized drama school, supervised by Florence Enright, where newcomers were coached before they even took their screen tests. (See DISCOVERIES and SCREEN TESTS) At Metro, Oliver Hinsdell ran the "School for Stars," which began with a course in imitating classical statues. Candidates for fame would study photographs of "The Winged Victory of Samothrace" or Cellini's "Perseus" to learn the arts of standing and walking. Among other coaches performing similar tasks were Alice Kelly and, later, Helena Sorrell at Fox; Lillian Burns and Grace Fogeler at Metro; Phyliss Laughton and Charlotte Clary at Paramount; Malvina Dunn and Sophie Rosenstein at Warners; and Benno Schneider at RKO and, later, Columbia.

Early on, when Columbia was dickering with Rita Hayworth's agents, Morris Small and George Chasin, about whether or not to exercise her next option—which would have meant raising her salary from $250 to $300 a week—the agents suggested applying the $50 in question toward drama lessons with Grace Fogeler, which proved to be a satisfactory compromise. Lillian Burns became a key figure on the M-G-M lot, not only teaching the stars to emote and enunciate, but going over their scripts and even rewriting dialogue to make it more comfortable for them. Harry Cohn was quoted as saying of her, "She is the only woman I know who could run a major studio." (Not everyone was so enthusiastic about a drama coach who got involved with script decisions. When Mayer received the phone call announcing her resignation, a leading director who was with him is said to have remarked, "That's the best thing that's happened to the studio in thirty years.")

Another well-known early dramatic coach was Josephine Dillon, first wife of Clark Gable. Before either of them reached Hollywood, she had transformed the awkward, fairly high-voiced Billy Gable into the matinee idol whose rich husky tones and lopsided, seductive grin were, in some part at least, her inspiration. Sitting with him at a piano, she gradually lowered the register of his voice, tone by tone. Other pupils of hers included Valentino, Gary Cooper, Nelson Eddy, and Lupe Velez, but not all were so illustrious. The May 10, 1934, *Hollywood Reporter* recounted, "Valerie de Lorenzo, Brown Derby waitress, has been signed for the MGM stock company. She was discovered by an MGM writer, and after being coached by Josephine Dillon, passed her tests successfully." In the film *The Lady and the Monster,* Dillon was offered a minor role, so that she could be on the set to instill confidence in its leading lady, Vera Hruba Ralston. Ginger Rogers' omnipresent mother, Lela (see MOTHERS AND OTHERS), was employed by RKO to develop embryonic talent for the studio's stock company, receiving in return a fat salary and a 250-seat theater on the lot.

Paul Fix, who ran little theater groups, as well as appearing in films from the early silent days, became John Wayne's unofficial coach:

> Loretta Young had told me that he wanted to meet me. He said that he had a chance in the business, but goddam it, he couldn't act and he knew it. He wanted me to put him in a play or something, to get some experience. Well, I couldn't do that because what he didn't know was so basic. For instance, I had to tell him that when he was standing, and wanted to turn to the left, to automatically put his weight on his right foot, so he could turn. He was so tense and wooden that he would just stand, and if he wanted to turn around, he'd lose his balance. I told him he had to be like a prizefighter and be on his toes all the time. He'd come to my house at night before he had a scene the next day and we'd go over things for him to do, natural things, but he insisted that he couldn't recall what I said, and so then he wanted me to come on the set with him.

COACHES

It wasn't long before Paul Fix was appearing in almost every John Wayne film. But because no self-respecting director would have put up with overt coaching on the set, Fix devised a set of signals:

> Duke had a wonderful natural expression where he'd furrow his brow. It was very effective on the screen, but then he'd work it to death, so I had one signal that meant "knock it off." Or if he was too lackadaisical, I'd do something else which meant "get up on your heels, bring it to life!" Another sign I used meant "get the words out so they don't drag."
>
> Once, when we were doing a picture called *Pittsburgh,* Randy Scott got wise to it. He said to Duke, "Goddam it, you've got Paul over there, why can't he help me too?" So Randy would watch me too. And the topper was that before the picture was finished, Marlene Dietrich would come over and she'd say, "Paulie, how am I doing?"

Subtle signals were also worked out by Paul Muni and his wife, Bella, who was always coaching from the sidelines. Muni's biographer, Jerome Lawrence, said she had "a Yiddish way of shrugging her face" when a scene displeased her. On those occasions, the scene was usually reshot.

Erasing foreign accents was an obvious problem with imported stars. It is said that Garbo was so timid when she first came over that she insisted on learning English from her black maid. Fox employed Zacharias Yaconelli, an Italian, to improve Carmen Miranda's American speech (which may explain a great deal). Ingrid Bergman was coached by Ruth Roberts to help diminish her Swedish accent. Some years later, Roberts was called upon to assist Loretta Young in acquiring one for *The Farmer's Daughter,* working with her eight hours a day for six weeks.

Other accents, too, had to be created and destroyed; the making of *Gone with the Wind* involved many such problems. Even before casting was completed, dialogue coach Will Price spent weeks working on Joan Bennett, Paulette Goddard, and Jeffrey Lynn's pre-test accents. Clark Gable flatly refused to even attempt southern speech. Butterfly McQueen had lost any trace of dialect during her years in New York and had to be coached by Hattie McDaniel. In addition to Will Price, Selznick engaged Susan Myrick, a Georgia newspaper columnist friend of Margaret Mitchell, known as "The Emily Post of the South," to advise on both speech and manners. After almost every take, Victor Fleming would turn to her for approval, asking, "Okay for Dixie?"

The task of wringing North Carolina out of young Ava Gardner's speech was assigned to her coaches at Metro-Goldwyn-Mayer. For the role of the cockney trollop in *Man Hunt,* Joan Bennett spent weeks working with English character actress Queenie Leonard, who also tried to train Alan Ladd to impersonate a British flier in *Joan of Paris* ("It wasn't easy," admits Miss Leonard). She also assisted Hume Cronyn with his cockney accent in *Lifeboat,* while Tallulah Bankhead was drilled in phonetic German for that film by Paula Miller. For *Romeo and Juliet,* John Barrymore was tutored by his old Shakespearean mentor, Margaret Carrington (sister of Walter Huston), and Norma Shearer studied for months under Constance Collier—who was also engaged to help Luise Rainer with her English before she made her screen debut and to coach Paulette Goddard after Selznick put her under contract.

Although dubbing could always be resorted to, the numbers of musical coaches were legion. Roger Edens, who had been Ethel Merman's accompanist, was a key member of the M-G-M music department—later he became a producer—writing special material and arrangements for many artists and exerting a tremendous general influence on the character of the musicals produced by the Freed unit. One of his most important contributions was as Judy Garland's vocal coach. Thirteen-year-old Judy was placed in his charge as soon as she signed with Metro, and he was largely responsible for developing her mature style. Under her mother's guidance, Judy had been imitating torch singers like Helen Morgan, working in idioms that were entirely inappropriate to her tender age. Edens guided her toward a more natural style, and wrote new material— such as "Dear Mr. Gable," a gloss on "You Made Me Love You"— tailored to her personality. Edens was the single most significant influence on Judy's early screen career. When she was asked to do vaudeville impersonations for *Babes on Broadway,* however, Elsie Janis, an old vaudeville hand, was called in to coach her. Fanny Brice helped Claudette Colbert when the latter played the title role in *Zaza.* According to George Cukor, the former Follies star advised Colbert, "Kid, when you sing a ballad, you'll find it a comfort to touch your own flesh." To make her point, Brice showed Colbert how to place her hand at the base of her throat while she was singing.

Among the influential dancing teachers—some of whom were also dance directors—were Ernest Belcher, LeRoy Prinz, Ernst Matray, Maurice Kusell, Albertina Rasch, and Rita Hayworth's father, Eduardo Cansino, who specialized in Spanish dancing. Belcher, whose daughter became Marge Champion, taught the fundamentals of ballet to everyone from Vilma Banky to Betty Grable; Loretta Young started when she was only six years old. The Fanchon & Marco Dance School, whose students included Ann Miller, Shirley Temple, and Jane Withers, was later directed by Ethel Meglin, after which the children (Judy Garland was one) were called "Meglin Kiddies." Ernst Matray had been trained by Max Reinhardt to choreograph crowd scenes (as LeRoy Prinz did for DeMille) and often coached dramatic actresses with little formal dance training, such as Vivien Leigh for her *Swan Lake* ballet in *Waterloo Bridge,* Joan Crawford for the

EDUARDO CANSINO, DANCING COACH, WITH HIS DAUGHTER,
RITA HAYWORTH.

Swedish folk dance in *A Woman's Face,* and Greer Garson for her vaude-ville act in *Random Harvest.* More esoteric still was Albertina Rasch, one of whose chores was instructing Norma Shearer in the intricate court dances of the Bourbons in preparation for *Marie Antoinette.* For *Swing High, Swing Low!,* Carole Lombard hired Al Siegel to coach her vocally and LeRoy Prinz to improve her dancing. Dance director Prinz would often help such stars as Marlene Dietrich and Claudette Colbert privately (at $250 an hour), working out bits of business for them. And when Clark Gable was required to perform his now famous soft shoe for *Idiot's Delight,* M-G-M called in Mickey Rooney's father, Joe Yule, to teach him the elementary tricks of the trade.

There were a number of independent dance studios in Hollywood, such as the Rainbow School, the Falcon—where Alexis Smith was the star pupil—and Perry's. The latter, on Highland Avenue, was a place where people like Jeanne Cagney, Doris Duke Cromwell, and Sally Rand came to study or practice ballet, tap, acrobatic, Spanish, Gypsy, and Oriental dancing, with a staff which included, at one time, the young Agnes de Mille. Drama schools for all ages abounded off the lot too. The Lawler Professional School—generally known as "Ma Lawler's"—had a full academic curriculum, but placed primary emphasis on acting, dance, and vocal lessons. Sometime students included Mickey Rooney, Judy Garland, Jane Withers, Anne Shirley, Anita Louise, Mitzi Green, and Virginia Weidler. For adult performers, Maria Ouspenskaya set up a private studio of dramatic arts based on her Moscow Art Theater training.

Other specialists, from acrobats to archers, were also called in when needed. Yakima Canutt taught horsemanship to Gene Autry and John Wayne—neither of whom was crazy about horses. Howard Hill was hired to inculcate the basics of archery to twenty-two stock actors and the six principals of the 1938 *Robin Hood.* But despite his coaching, in the big tournament scene, Errol Flynn did only the long shots, while Hill himself would shoot the actual arrow that hit dead center, as the camera moved in to show only the target. Jack Dempsey gave some boxing lessons to Valentino for *Cobra,* and Jimmy Cagney, although he had done some amateur fighting when he was young, in preparation for *City for Conquest* spent three intensive weeks of boxing training in Palm Springs with former professional Harvey Perry.

Two men were almost solely responsible for forming the swashbuckling image of romantic swordplay presented to several generations of movie-goers. Henry J. Uyttenhove, the Belgian fencing master at the Los Angeles Athletic Club, trained Douglas Fairbanks for *The Mark of Zorro,* his first film in that genre. But it was his countryman, Fred Cavens, who at eighteen graduated from the Belgian Military Academy as the youngest fencing master of his day, who was primary in setting the style and technique of

51

the Hollywood duel. When Fairbanks saw Cavens' work in a film of Max Lindner's, he said, I must meet this man!" and immediately put him under contract. At the age of eleven, Cavens' son Albert began working for Fairbanks as well, demonstrating his father's routines:

> I started fencing when I was about nine years old. My dad gave me lessons and then he would teach me the choreography of what he was going to do. He had learned foil, sabre and epée in the Army, but as far as period weapons were concerned, you could take them out of historical books, but the method of their use was what my father created.

Father and son trained and doubled such cinema heroes as John Barrymore, Montague Love, Basil Rathbone ("He took a fencing lesson every day and became absolutely proficient at it—his attitude and his style were absolute perfection"), Errol Flynn ("He worked very, very hard at the beginning, but later it was difficult to get him to come to the rehearsal hall"), Tyrone Power ("We used to go out to his home to rehearse. I often doubled him. When he had a permanent wave, I got a permanent wave"), Maureen O'Hara ("stupendous"), and Joan Fontaine ("She fenced like a man"). After Uyttenhove, the Cavens' only serious competition came from a former pupil of Frank's named Ralph Faulkner, who had been a 1928 and 1932 Olympic champion. Faulkner opened a school of his own and worked on such films as *The Prisoner of Zenda*, choreographing routines for Ronald Colman and Doug Fairbanks, Jr.

COAST TO COAST.

In this age of jet transportation, it is perhaps difficult for us to grasp just how isolated Hollywood once was from the rest of the country, and especially from the East Coast. When Griffith produced *The Birth of a Nation* and Chaplin was making his Keystone comedies, there was not even a telephone link between California and New York.

Broadway wits warned show business friends who were headed for Hollywood, "Don't buy anything there you can't put on the *Chief*," and for years the Santa Fe's *Chief*—one of the great trains of the twenties and thirties—was Hollywood's lifeline to the world east of the Mississippi.

CHARLES LAUGHTON AND ELSA LANCHESTER DESCENDING FROM A
FOKKER TRIMOTOR.

JUDY GARLAND AT THE END OF A COAST-TO-COAST TRAIN JOURNEY.

You boarded the *Chief* in Pasadena (never in L.A. if you had any pretense to elegance), and, until 1936, the journey to Chicago took about two and a half days. There you had a few hours before changing to the New York Central's *Twentieth Century Limited* for the overnight ride into Manhattan. (This Chicago stopover provided M-G-M's local publicists with an opportunity to service their stars: A studio representative would always be on hand to meet the Chief, shelter the star from his fans, and keep him entertained—Clark Gable liked to be taken to the Chicago Zoo.)

In the earliest days, the *Chief* had no dining car. Instead, the train stopped at various Santa Fe depots where there were Harvey House restaurants. One meal, for example, was served in Albuquerque, another (fresh trout in season) in eastern Colorado, a third in Kansas City. In the early twenties, a breakfast car was added to the train, and, soon after, full dining service, in the grand manner, was provided on board. One of the first dining cars was captained by an imposing man called Pete Schroeder, who later became a well-known Hollywood figure, first as *maître d'* of the original Brown Derby and then as co-owner of Armstrong-Schroeder's in Beverly Hills (see RESTAURANTS).

In 1929 the Santa Fe Railroad, in conjunction with the Pennsylvania Railroad and the Transcontinental Air Transportation Corporation, offered a combined rail and air coast-to-coast service which cut the Los Angeles to New York journey to a mere two days. You boarded your plane at the Grand Central Air Terminal in Glendale at 8:45 in the morning and flew across the desert all day, with three refueling stops, arriving at an airfield outside Clovis, New Mexico, at 6:45 in the evening. In Clovis, you transferred to a Santa Fe train which carried you overnight to Waynoka, Oklahoma. Leaving your sleeping car there, you boarded another trimotor plane and flew to Columbus, Ohio, with stops at Wichita, Kansas City, St. Louis, and Indianapolis. Arriving at Columbus at 7:15, you climbed aboard a Pennsylvania Railroad train, the *American,* which deposited you in New York at 9:50 the following morning.

The service was inaugurated with a great flurry of publicity. The first plane to leave Los Angeles, on July 8, 1929, was christened by Mary Pickford and piloted by Charles Lindbergh. Given the primitive state of civil aviation in those days, however, schedules were not always adhered to. The least squall could disrupt a flight, and during the winter it was often impossible to fly at all. Because of this, and the fact that planes could carry very few passengers, the *Chief* remained the main lifeline to the East.

In May of 1936 the Santa Fe Railroad updated its L.A. to Chicago service, naming its new train the *Super Chief*. Hauled first of all by two snub-nosed diesel engines nicknamed "Amos 'n' Andy" (later streamline diesels were used), the *Super Chief* cut the time for the trip to Chicago by over fifteen hours. (The *Super Chief* operated once a week; the old *Chief* continued to provide its regular service on other days.) All new stainless-steel coaches were built for this train with luxurious interiors featuring motifs and colors borrowed from the art of the Pueblo Indians. The fabrics imitated Navajo blankets—the looms that wove them being deliberately programmed to drop an occasional stitch—though light fixtures and other modern devices were essentially art deco in feel. Coaches were named for various Pueblos. The lounge car, for example, was the Acoma, and the diner was the Cochiti. The Cochiti offered an elaborate meal service—everything from caviar to Cheshire cheese with guava jelly was available—at very reasonable prices. Salmon poached in white wine, for instance, cost seventy cents. (On the westbound trip, people who wanted trout the second day out placed their orders on the first evening. The chef then wired ahead to Las Vegas, New Mexico, where fresh-caught brook trout were put aboard.) The *Super Chief* could sleep 104 passengers in a variety of private compartments and convertible section cars. The train was air-conditioned, unlike the sometimes desperately hot *Chief;* there was a barbershop, and radio and recorded music were available in every room. A star would travel in his or her own suite of rooms, which included a shower, the females often traveling with hairdresser and manicurist.

By the end of the thirties, larger, safer, all-metal, all-weather aircraft, like the Douglas DC-3, were making cross-continental flight much more attractive for the average passenger. Now you could reach New York from L.A. overnight, though it still involved many refueling stops. American Airlines "Flagship" service made a dozen stopovers between the two cities as it followed the southern route with touchdowns at, among other places, Phoenix, El Paso, Dallas, Memphis, Nashville, and Washington, D.C.

Sleeping berths were available on many overnight flights, and the airlines did all they could to provide the same comforts that could be found aboard trains. It would be more than a decade, however, before flying became the norm for most· people. The *Super Chief* remained an important Hollywood institution until well after World War II. The executives who traveled to New York on business, the stars and writers who hurried back to Manhattan when they had a long enough vacation, had grown used to the luxury of the Santa Fe service. The ride on the *Super Chief* was a social event in itself. You were almost certain to find friends aboard, and the trip to Chicago often turned into a two-day poker game, or an extended drinking session. For touted newcomers arriving in California for the first time, it was virtually *de rigueur* to arrive aboard the *Super Chief,* since it was traditional for the press corps, aided by studio publicists, to provide a suitable media welcome at the Pasadena station.

COMMISSARIES.

With his commissary as with everything else, Louis B. Mayer wanted to be best, no matter what the cost. And since he considered his wife, Margaret, the finest cook in the world, he had M-G-M's head chef spend several weeks at his home, observing in particular just how her famous chicken soup was made—by taking fat kosher hens, stewing them in a large pot overnight, then separating the broth from the chicken. It would be served by spooning the rich, clear liquid over chunks of chicken and delicate matzoh balls. Good enough (at thirty-five cents a bowl), Mayer hoped, to keep an errant scriptwriter from wandering into a Culver City bar and risking an afternoon's work.

The M-G-M commissary, designed by Cedric Gibbons and decorated in green and chromium, had a seating capacity of 225 and served lunch each day to 1,200 people. The various production companies on the lot were given staggered lunch hours, so that a room full of extras in formal dress might be replaced by an army of grizzled ranch hands. Seating was controlled by an efficient hostess named Frances Edwards. Shop talk, intramural gossip, and practical gags abounded as professional co-workers segregated themselves into a Publicity table, a Wardrobe table, a Legal Department table, and so on, with a long star table in the center of the room—at which few stars ever sat. The Music Department table attracted some of the talented younger people—Mickey Rooney, Judy Garland, and Elizabeth Taylor, usually with her pet chepmunk, Nibbles, on her shoulder.

The liveliest group was to be found at the so-called Directors' table, which was located on a screened-in wooden porch off the main room. Among the regulars—with veteran writer Joe Farnham at the head—were Spencer Tracy, Clark Gable, Bob Taylor, Eddie Mannix, Billy Grady, Frank Whitbeck, Howard Strickling, Otto Winkler, Victor Fleming, Woody Van Dyke, Tay Garnett, Harry Ruskin, gagman Dick Noonan, Sam Zimbalist, "Pop" Leonard, Clarence Brown, King Vidor, Mervyn LeRoy, and Norman Taurog. There had to be a certain amount of consistency among the cast of characters because every day, when lunch was

THE SILVER ROOM OF THE CAFÉ DE PARIS AT 20TH CENTURY-FOX,
LOOKING THROUGH TO THE MAIN DINING ROOM.

finished, waiter Billy Fies, who took care of the table for seven years,
would pass around a metal bird cage with three dice. Each person would
spin the cage in turn, with the low man paying the entire group's bill—
including Billy's regular $5.50 tip—but he had the consolation of eating
free for the rest of that week. Leon Ames recalls how flattered he was to
join the big table on his first day at the studio—until he was stuck with
the check for eighteen people's lunch. He never sat there again.

When Lupe Velez was working at Metro, she sat near the veranda, but
would pop into the kitchen to inspect what was on the fire, rather than
ordering from the menu. Irving Thalberg dined regularly with his ten
associate producers in the "executive bungalow," while Mr. Mayer, a
prodigious eater, would lunch in a small private room in the commissary
building, often spending half an hour table-hopping on his way. Garbo
supposedly only appeared in the studio lunchroom four times in her
sixteen years at Metro, preferring to remain in her velvet-draped dressing
room, where she would munch on raw vegetable salads and Swedish rye
crisp, apple pie, cheese, and milk, or her favorite imported caviar, mixed
with chopped onions and chives.

BETTE DAVIS IN THE WARNER BROTHERS COMMISSARY.

COMMISSARIES

M-G-M was happy to cater to the culinary idiosyncracies of its luminaries. Lionel Barrymore kept a special brand of bacon reserved for his exclusive use in the storeroom, and his fried eggs had to be timed to the precise second. He also had a relish made by a retired colonel in Connecticut, from his own vegetable garden, shipped to the commissary each week. His brother, John, would phone for his particular brand of coffee ($1.10 per cup) to be sent over five or six times a day. Hygiene fanatic Joan Crawford insisted on her dishes being scalded before she used them —although, being a perpetual dieter, she rarely had much more than black coffee and soda crackers (spread with mustard) for lunch. Greer Garson kept her weight in check by lunching on hot sauerkraut juice. (Fans were fed a steady diet of information about the stars' favorite dishes, learning, for example, that Alan Ladd loved Spanish omelets, that Robert Montgomery ordered double servings of green apple pie, that Lon Chaney doted on steak tartare, and John Barrymore on Philadelphia scrapple and lamb curry.)

The Warner Brothers commissary, run by Katharine Higgins, consisted of three sections: an enormous restaurant with hundreds of tables and a large counter, for all studio crew and extras (food prices in the room were on a sliding scale, varying for those seated at tables with tablecloths, those at tables without cloths, and those at the counter); a greenroom for stars, featured players, writers, directors, and publicists; and an executive dining room for the Warner brothers, their executives, and one star—Al Jolson. The head chef, a man named Rader, was Swiss, and was assisted by a Chinese, an Italian, a Mexican, a Dutch, and a French cook —as well as twenty-four Americans. Every day at five, Miss Higgins would confer with the assistant directors of each current production, to ascertain how many crew members would be working the following day, so she could place her orders. In addition, she was responsible for providing the 120,000 box lunches needed yearly for the 20 percent of all pictures filmed on location.

Studio dining facilities could become factors in executive power struggles. At Columbia, Harry Cohn instituted a private dining room for himself and his minions after he was denied entrance to the Brown Derby for being in shirt sleeves. He would sit in stony silence, at the head of a long table, and listen to his invited underlings discuss the affairs of the day, waiting for an opportunity to pounce and strike. In 1938 Cary Grant, after making two successful features for Columbia, was asked to dine regularly with the executives. Grant spent a few days listening to the shop talk, scoldings, and football scores, then requested to be permanently excused. One of the more grotesque attractions of Cohn's dining room was an electrically charged chair, operated by a button near the studio head's foot, and usually reserved for humiliating timid newcomers. When a tired

ELIZABETH TAYLOR, SEATED BETWEEN HER MOTHER AND DARRYL
HICKMAN, IN THE M-G-M COMMISSARY, 1944.

Frank Capra was the victim of its shock one day, the director smashed
the chair to the floor, reducing it to splinters. Cohn soon replaced it with
another.

On the Paramount lot, Cecil B. DeMilles' seven-foot-long table was
called "The Throne." It sat on a platform above all the other tables in the
room, affording DeMille and his companions a lofty view of luncheon
activity. After several years of this, a memo came down from the front
office, suggesting the elimination of the platform. Since DeMille was attracting all the attention of the visiting press, other Paramount stars were
losing valuable column space. Paramount's commissary, managed for
over twenty years by Pauline Kessinger, was M-G-M's closest rival in the
area of the homey touch. The little squares of fresh corn bread on all the
lunch tables were the specialty of studio head Y. Frank Freeman.

In the mid-thirties, organized labor on the RKO lot boycotted the
commissary when its employees with union affiliations were dismissed.
The Fox commissary, called the Café de Paris and attractively decorated
with brightly colored paintings of the studio's stars, was the setting of
Shirley Temple's birthday parties (which consistently made her a year
younger than her true age). Its headwaiter, Nick, was the former headwaiter at the Vine Street Brown Derby. Here there was a traveling cart,
from which roasts were carved to order, and what many people considered
to be the best food in town.

CONTRACTS AND BILLING.

After their agents had engineered satisfactory financial deals with the studios, many of the stars would demand any number of special clauses in their contracts to protect their individual idosyncracies, vanities, and phobias. Most common were specifications concerning working hours, billing, travel arrangements and script, cameraman and cast approval. As early as 1916, when Mary Pickford re-signed with Adolph Zukor, her contract stipulated that her weekly salary of $10,000 be drawable on Mondays, as an advance against royalties from the Mary Pickford Motion Picture Corporation, of which her mother was treasurer; that she receive star billing, and a "first-class individual studio" in New York for her exclusive use. Some demands in the old days were more basic. Maurice Costello signed with Vitagraph on condition that he would never have to wear a hammer in his belt (to avoid being called upon to help out the carpenters).

W. C. Fields, when he joined Mack Sennett, had definite ideas about when he wanted to be paid: a clause stated that of his weekly $5,000, he had to get $2,500 on Monday morning and the other $2,500 on Wednesday. Ben Hecht once demanded $5,000 in cash at the end of each week, and made the further provision that if Sam Goldwyn spoke one word to him, the deal on *The Unholy Garden* would become void. After Hecht hadn't handed anything in for two weeks, Goldwyn finally called him, saying, "Ben, this is purely a social call." "That cancels the deal," said Hecht, who then collected his $10,000 and left.

Contract provisos concerning the presence or behavior of other people were not unusual. Mae West made it part of her agreement for *My Little Chickadee* that W. C. Fields had to abstain from drinking on the set. Dorothy Arzner insisted on a special clause stipulating that she would not be required to attend conferences aboard Harry Cohn's yacht, and producer Sam Bischoff went even further, getting a written guarantee that he wouldn't ever have to speak to Cohn. In 1934 George S. Kaufman won a contract clause assuring him that he would not have to discuss the story of *Roman Scandals* with Eddie Cantor. The terms of William Powell's deal with Paramount asserted that he would never have to appear in a Von

Sternberg film, and Columbia negotiated Paul Muni's wife, Bella, off the set of *A Song to Remember*. On the other hand, Carole Lombard's pact with Paramount provided for her whole crew to be employed with her, assuring job security for cameraman Ted Tetzlaff, electrician Pat Drew, favorite grips, prop men, etc. Lombard also had written approval of story, director, and casting, while Muni's contract allowed that if he refused three scripts, and then Warners rejected the three he provided as alternatives, he would be placed on half salary until a mutually acceptable project could be found.

Other clauses in fine print (known in the trade as "boiler plate") provided for comfort and convenience. Joan Crawford was guaranteed that the temperature on her set be maintained at 68°. Irene Dunne was legally assured that after completion of each of her films, she could return to her husband in New York, and that she be given ten days' notice before the start of her next assignment. Clark Gable, as soon as he was in a position to demand the privilege, worked a strictly enforced nine-to-five schedule (this at a time when it was commonplace for actors to be required to work till midnight and later.) Gable also had a flight clause appended to his Metro contract, specifying that he would only fly in planes with more than two engines, flown by licensed pilots, and that he had to be informed in advance of the make of the plane. In Thomas Mitchell's contract with David Selznick, there was a guarantee that, because of his fear, the actor would not be required to ride a horse (although he was later tricked onto one by Victor Fleming). Gene Tierney's Fox contract specified that she would not be required to change the color or length of her hair, and that her slightly crooked teeth would not be altered. Susan Hayward's contract with the same studio also prohibited the cutting of her hair. Grace Moore's contract stipulated that she could not exceed a 135-pound weight limit and, on her mother's insistence, Shirley Temple's contract barred her from the Fox commissary—except on her birthday—a precaution that was intended to protect her from being "petted and pampered."

From the earliest days, studios often insisted on clauses that were intended to safeguard the image they wished to project of a given star. Matinee idol Francis X. Bushman was forbidden to reveal that he was married and the father of five children. (Eventually, the truth came out and the subsequent scandalous divorce was responsible for the rapid collapse of his career.) When Cecil B. DeMille made *King of Kings*, in 1926, both H. B. Warner, who played Christ, and Dorothy Cummings, who played the Virgin Mary, were required to sign documents stipulating that they would not accept any role for five years which might reflect on their parts in the religious epic. Although it wasn't part of the deal, DeMille also urged them to avoid night clubs and—during production—not to be seen swimming, playing cards, riding in convertibles, or attending ball games. With the rise to power of the Hays office, it became common practice for studios to include morals clauses in their standard contracts, giving them the right to release a player in the event of a scandal. Such clauses could give the production company very specific powers over a star's private life. The "moral turpitude" rider that David Selznick inserted into Vivien Leigh's *Gone With the Wind* contract had the intended effect of forcing Laurence Olivier to move out of their shared residence. (He moved in with Leslie Howard.) When Selznick began to groom Jennifer Jones, he made her sign a contract which—echoing the earlier Bushman pact—forbade her to be photographed with her husband or sons. When, soon after, Robert Walker began to establish himself as a rising star at Metro, this edict was promptly disregarded.

Not all contract negotiations were successful, of course, as can be illustrated by two examples involving Irving Thalberg. Edward G. Robinson has described in his autobiography how, in 1930, Thalberg offered him $1 million for three years, promising a major star build-up. Robinson and his agent expressed interest in such a deal provided the actor was only required to make one to one and a half pictures a year, and was given plenty of time off to continue his Broadway career. Thalberg demurred, observing that—while he appreciated Robinson's devotion to the stage—the actor should keep in mind that live theater was probably on its last legs and about to be replaced by talking pictures. No compromise was forthcoming, and Robinson, upon leaving Thalberg's office, promptly threw up. Harry Carey had a similar experience with Thalberg, who had offered him a long-term star contract at a fabulous salary. The one stipulation was that he must live in Hollywood, so as to be available for publicity. Carey declined, saying, "I don't want anyone telling me where to live."

But some people just didn't take the whole thing that seriously. Wallace Beery was presented by Louis B. Mayer each year with a long legal document, and each year Beery would tear it up in Mayer's presence, then dash off a simple agreement in longhand. It always ended with the words, "Quitting time is 5:30 P.M. punctually."

Most actors who signed with a major studio, including many who became stars, had to make do with the standard contract—a document that was loaded heavily in favor of the employer. This generally called for the actor to be bound to the studio for a seven-year period, with the studio—but not the performer—able to exercise an option to discontiuue the agreement at six-month intervals. If the studio did pick up the option, the performer's salary was usually increased. The standard contract also contained provisions that enabled the employer to assign the employee to any role in any picture, no matter how inappropriate or mediocre, and to loan the employee to any other production company. Refusal to play a

UNDER THE WATCHFUL EYE OF LOUIS B. MAYER, SEVEN-YEAR-OLD JACKIE COOPER SIGNS A LONG-TERM CONTRACT WITH M-G-M IN 1932.   CULVER PICTURES.

role, or to be loaned out, would result in suspension without pay, and this led to some of the most celebrated confrontations in movie history.

In 1936 Warner Brothers refused Bette Davis the role she had sought in *Anthony Adverse* and assigned her instead to a picture called *God's Country and the Woman*. Davis would have none of this and was immediately suspended and taken off the payroll. When Ludovic Toeplitz, a British-based entrepreneur, offered her a deal to make two pictures in Europe, she promptly set sail for England. Warners issued an injunction to prevent her working for Toeplitz, and she responded by filing suit against the studio, charging restraint of trade. A British court decided in Warners' favor and Davis was forced to return to California, yet her battle can still be counted as a partial victory for the performer. Warners not only overlooked the damages that had been awarded against the actress, but also made genuine efforts to find her better scripts. It was in 1936, too, that James Cagney entered into a court duel with Warners. He had attempted to break his contract on the grounds that he had been cast in five pictures in the previous twelve-month period (his agreement stipulated four), and because—here is an instance of lawyers picking up on a technicality—his friend Pat O'Brien was billed above him in the fifth of these films, *Devil Dogs of the Air*. While waiting for the case to be settled, Cagney made two pictures for First National, a poverty row company. Again, the courts decided in Warner Brothers favor, and Cagney returned to the studio. Like Davis, however, he found that his efforts were rewarded with more respect and worthwhile assignments. In the thirties, studios automatically added suspension time onto the length of a player's contract. This practice faced a court challenge, in 1943, from Olivia de Havilland. Once again, the studio involved was Warner Brothers, which claimed that the actress owed twenty-five weeks' work to make up for time spent on suspension during the previous seven years. In this instance, the actress, strongly supported by the Screen Actors Guild, won the case, and seven years was officially endorsed as the upper limit of any contract between a performer and a production company.

Contracts would often specify that the star's name would have to be first in all advertisements, in letters larger and of greater prominence than any other name. (The phrase "greater prominence" came into use when it was discovered that smaller lettering could be made to overpower larger lettering by the skillful manipulation of design, type face, and color.) This effectively meant that some major stars could not be cast together because both had the same "top billing" clause in their contracts.

The question of billing was not simply a matter of ego gratification. It could play an important role in salary negotiations, often with ugly consequences, give publicists nightmares, and it could lead to bad feelings, tantrums, and lawsuits. Even close personal friendships could not be allowed to interfere with the strict etiquette of billing. Given their well-known romantic involvement, it is interesting to discover that Spencer Tracy insisted on being billed above Katharine Hepburn in the advertising for *Adam's Rib*. Both Tracy and Humphrey Bogart were eager to do *The Desperate Hours* together, but neither would accept second billing.

Ben Lyon recalls a billing dispute in which he was involved during the making of *Hell's Angels*.

> I was loaned to Howard Hughes from Warner Brothers. My contract with Warners stated first billing, but after Jean Harlow had been working on the picture for three or four months, I learned through the grapevine that Howard was going to star her over me. I was furious! I used to have a hell of a temper! So one day there was a meeting between me and Howard and his lawyer, Neil McCarthy, in Howard's office, and we were shouting at each other over this billing. I said, "My contract calls for first billing and I've worked for it all my life and I'm gonna have it!" Finally, McCarthy jumped up and he said, "All right, goddam it, Ben Lyon, if you want first billing, we're gonna give it to you. We'll put your name in six-foot letters across the top of every poster that's up in the United States. But goddam it, we'll put it up in watercolor, and the first rain will wash it off." Well, I thought that was hysterical. I said, "Neil, anybody who could think of an argument like that deserves to win. Bill me any way you want." The picture came out and I was billed first.

Things did not always work out so amicably. Irving Thalberg wanted to borrow Grace Moore from Columbia, to star her with Maurice Chevalier. But Harry Cohn would only agree to the loan if she received top billing, and Chevalier protested that he had been a star for twenty-five years and refused to change his position now. The deal was never made and Chevalier left Hollywood shortly after.

In *Life with Father,* Irene Dunne and William Powell were to have equal billing. But there was still the puzzle of how to avoid placing one name before the other, and an ingenious solution was reached. While the credits rolled on screen, flashing lights alternated the two names in the top spot. In magazine and newspaper ads, Dunne's name would appear first one day, Powell's the next.

A few stars elected to be flexible about billing or to stay out of the competition altogether. On *Juarez,* Paul Muni requested a waiver of the provision in his contract that stipulated he get sole star billing above the title, feeling that Bette Davis deserved an equal share. And Bing Crosby always insisted that someone be co-starred with him, saying that he didn't want to have to carry the blame if the picture failed.

Costume.

In many cases, clothes were important in the definition of a star's image, and a handful of designers—Adrian, Howard Greer, Travis Banton, Irene, Orry-Kelly—achieved considerable celebrity in their own right. (Surprisingly enough, most of the other designers were often downgraded in the thirties and early forties, frequently not receiving screen credit for their work.) Although Paramount, Fox, and Metro had fairly extensive wardrobe departments by the early twenties, most studios had a rather casual attitude towards clothing their performers, at least until the arrival of the sound era. Walter Plunkett, who costumed the actors for *Gone With the Wind* and is considered by many to be Hollywood's greatest exponent of period dress, became head of the FBO costume department in 1926:

> It was part of the drapery department. The men in charge of drapery went out and bought or rented clothes, or gave yardage to the maids who pinned it on. . . . The first day I went to work there, they told me that a girl who was playing a mysterious queen in a Tarzan picture was having trouble with her costume and they asked me if I would get to her dressing room and see what I could do. When I got there, I found her maid—a clumsy black girl—trying to pin three or four yards of beaded chiffon. She had no idea what she was doing, so I pinned it onto the actress's bra and draped it around her and that was the costume for the day. It was the customary way of doing things.
>
> Generally, they shot so darned fast in silent films that the costume wasn't needed again. If it was, you'd mark where the pins had been and try to reproduce it the next day. If it didn't quite match, I don't think people really cared that much. Mostly, though, I was in charge of buying and renting.

Western Costume was already the main source for rentals, though another company called United was in competition with them for a while. Oriental clothes were rented from a man in Chinatown. Plunkett was dissatisfied with what he could get from these outlets, however, and per-

THIS PHOTOGRAPH, TAKEN IN THE TWENTIES, SHOWS HOWARD
GREER IN HIS WARDROBE DEPARTMENT AT PARAMOUNT.

suaded the front office that money could be saved by buying a couple of
sewing machines and hiring dressmakers. At first, these were housed in a
single room at the back of the property department, but when RKO took
over the studio in 1929, conditions improved rapidly and a real costume
department was created with offices for the designers, fitting rooms, work-
rooms, and ample space to store stock costumes.

Physically, one costume department was much like another, but the
atmosphere of each was greatly influenced by the temperamental and
sometimes arrogant characters who ran them. The top costume designers
tended to be men and women with strong ideas, whose willfulness occasionally verged on hysteria. At Warner Brothers, for example, Orry-Kelly's
rages were legendary. On one occasion, when an actress refused to emerge
from her mobile dressing room for a scheduled fitting, Kelly is said to
have shaken the trailer until she abandoned it in terror. Travis Banton
eventually fell apart under the pressure, taking to drink and mysterious
disappearances, but during his reign at Paramount he was sufficiently

powerful to have a clause in his contract stipulating that he would not be subject to interference from the stars he dressed. Adrian—once cruelly described by *Fortune* as a "tall, twittering hunchback"—ruled the M-G-M wardrobe department like some Valentinoesque sheik.

In fairness, the designers were often given ample reason to unleash displays of temper. While, for the most part, stars would leave cinematographers to their own devices and seldom seemed to have fought with their make-up men, many had strong views about the kind of clothes they should wear—particularly in films with contemporary settings. After 1936, except for the occasional picture of an actress he considered a personal friend, Walter Plunkett gave up doing modern dress films because he had become so exasperated with the problems they provoked:

> Everyone wants to stick his nose into the modern things—the directors' wives, secretaries, actresses with rather bad taste. It's far easier when you can tell them, "I love your idea, but it's just wrong for the period." That gets them the hell off the set and out of your hair.

On one occasion, needing a single modern costume for a picture that was otherwise in period dress, Plunkett decided to buy an outfit from Adrian's Beverly Hills shop:

> I called up and said we'd like to make an appointment. The actress and I went over there and Adrian received us charmingly. Then he told me I could sit in the waiting room while he dressed her. I said, "But Adrian, it's my film and I'm buying the outfit and I know the requirements of the set, and I have to see what I'm getting. "Well," he said, "I can't have another designer work with my things! I'm sorry." It was so bitchy.

Some actresses were easy to dress and some were not. As David Chierichetti points out in *Hollywood Costume Design,* Travis Banton was especially fortunate in that most of Paramount's top female stars—such as Carole Lombard, Kay Francis, Miriam Hopkins, and Claudette Colbert —had figures that were perfectly in tune with the taste and line of the period, so that Banton was able to concentrate on creating elegant clothes without having to bother about disguising serious defects. Mae West, it's true, did not have a figure that approximated in any way the high-fashion ideals of the thirties, but Mae West was Mae West and it was not difficult to design costumes which suited and enhanced her camp personality, especially since most of her films were period pieces. Banton's greatest success, however, was with Marlene Dietrich, who had the panache to carry off his most daring and innovative conceptions.

ADRIAN WITH GRETA GARBO.

COSTUME

At Metro, Adrian had far more obstacles to overcome. Jean Harlow had a perfect body, but her aversion to underwear caused certain problems with the Hays Office. Beneath one costume, she was persuaded to try various brassieres, but still her nipples showed through, until a special bra was devised, one which had tips of fur-lined tin. Less well endowed M-G-M stars were provided with false breasts, perfect in every detail, each neatly labeled and stored on a shelf in the wardrobe department.

Joan Crawford, during her early years at Metro, managed to work off the muscle she had developed as a young hoofer, but there was nothing she could do about her broad shoulders and hips. Adrian dealt with this brilliantly by turning the flaw into an asset, emphasizing the shoulders with pads and huge flaring white collars which drew attention away from her hips (see TRENDSETTING). Garbo, too, had broad shoulders, but, in her case, they were combined with narrow, boyish hips, so Adrian worked at minimizing the shoulders. His penchant for clean lines and geometric pattern came into play in most of Garbo's modern dress pictures, in which he tended to use her torso as an armature on which to hang art deco-like optical illusions.

Norma Shearer had indifferent legs, but, since she tended to play the *grande dame,* Adrian was generally able to conceal them between long skirts and slinky, flowing gowns. As for Jeanette MacDonald, when she came to the studio she was quite heavy and special foundation garments had to be designed for her, but she soon lost weight and achieved an almost perfect figure. In the process, however, her face became emaciated and Adrian had to compensate for this with hats and collars that made it appear broader.

Men, for the most part, supplied their own clothes—except for period pictures—and were reimbursed by the studio. Only at M-G-M, according to Plunkett, was it at all common for men's sports coats, for example, to be made up on the lot. Plunkett remembers a great rack of suits and jackets made for Walter Pidgeon and reports that Metro employed "the most beautiful tailors in the world."

> There wasn't anyone who could beat them. There was one big shop at the studio that was strictly men's tailoring. When I arrived, there was a man who had been a tailor in New York and another who had come from Germany. They were both very good, but I preferred the German. He could drape a silk Roman toga or make a tweed suit or a coat of armor—anything.
>
> After they died, we got a Mexican family. One man made exquisite coats, a brother made pants that were perfection and other brothers followed through. They run the tailor's shop at Universal now.

CRIME.

When John Dillinger, eulogized throughout the land as Public Enemy Number One, was shot down outside the Biograph Theater in Chicago, it was just after watching Clark Gable portray a suave mobster, Blackie Gallagher, in M-G-M's *Manhattan Melodrama.*

"Die the way you live," says Blackie at the end of the picture, headed for the electric chair.

The ironies of this conjunction have been duly noted: the star as gangster, the gangster as star.

A few months earlier, Dillinger had devised an ingenious plan to rob a savings bank in Greencastle, Indiana. Members of his gang would pose as a crew from Paramount Pictures in town to film a bank holdup for an upcoming production. While they set up outside the bank, Dillinger and a cohort were to enter the bank, wearing theatrical make-up and carrying machine guns. Once the robbery had been carried out, the "crew" would film the getaway, then make its own escape before onlookers realized that this was not the world of make-believe.

Criminals had been fascinated by movies and the movie industry from the very beginning, when motion pictures started to pay huge returns on small investments and producers and theater owners were sometimes backed by prominent underworld figures. Arnold "The Brain" Rothstein —the man behind the Liberty Bond fraud of 1918 and the Black Sox scandal of 1919—was a major investor in Loew's, Inc., M-G-M's parent company. A little later, mobsters like Longie Zwillman—one of the rumrunners Rothstein bankrolled—were attracted to the glamour of Hollywood society and fascinated by the sexual magnetism of stars like Jean Harlow, who were viewed as extremely prestigious conquests. At about the same time, Hollywood discovered that crime could be made to pay on screen. Criminals, from Al Capone down to the punks who rolled winos on Skid Row, were flattered by the attention. Stars like Jimmy Cagney and Edward G. Robinson gave hoodlums a style to imitate, and the staff writers at Warners kept them in hard-boiled dialogue.

The cultural exchange program between the studios and the underworld proved mutually advantageous and soon Hollywood became a mecca for criminals. They flourished at all levels—from the neurotic gunmen, crooked club owners, and slick-haired blackmailers who inhabit Raymond Chandler's stories, up to the big-time mobsters like George Raft's pal, Benjamin "Bugsy" Siegel.

Los Angeles provided an ideal climate for them, having long been run by men who treated the law as though it were made of India rubber. Through most of the twenties and thirties, the city was controlled by a group of men known locally as the Combination, who paid off law-enforcement agencies and provided protection for a variety of illegal activities, from gambling to prostitution, in return for fiscal tributes said to amount to $50 million a year. The lords of this feudal system enjoyed the support of a large segment of the Los Angeles press, with corruption reaching its peak under the administration of Mayor Frank L. Shaw. It is claimed that his underlings collected a dime for each towel used in every brothel throughout the city. Shaw's regime crumbled when a real estate man named Ralph Gray sued a former police commissioner, claiming he had not been paid for services rendered to Shaw during the 1933 mayoralty campaign. This precipitated a recall election in which Shaw was defeated by Fletcher Bowron, who broke up the Combination's political machine and forced many early retirements in the Police Department and the D.A.'s office.

The executives who ran the motion picture industry were pragmatists who had no real difficulty getting along with politicians like Frank Shaw. The producers understood the exigencies of *real politik*. Filmmaking was a high-risk industry and people got things done any way they could, even if this meant handing out money and favors to people close to the Combination. When D. A. Buron Fitts ran for re-election in 1940, he was heavily supported by the studio bosses—especially Louis B. Mayer—who poured thousands of dollars into his campaign fund. This was quite legitimate, of course, but insiders saw this support as payment for numerous services rendered, such as the golden silence in which Fitts had wrapped the mysterious death of Paul Bern, Harlow's husband.

It was an everyday matter for studios to enrich the funds of police benevolent societies when stars were careless enough to get caught in situations which might attract unfavorable publicity. Occasionally, an especially obliging officer might be rewarded with a sinecure post. According to one source, Blayney Matthews got his job as head of security at Warner Brothers in this way, having—while employed as an investigator for the D.A.'s office—given evidence that absolved an important studio employee in a hit-and-run accident.

Al Capone's visit to Los Angeles in 1927 aroused terror in those true to the Combination. Could it be that the Chicago mob had designs on their land of milk and honey? The detectives who were assigned to visit Capone were greeted warmly. He told them he had heard so much about California that he had to see it for himself, and, after offering the detectives a drink, assured them he was returning to his own bailiwick the following day. As soon as the train carrying Capone was safely on its way, the detectives' visit was leaked to an acquiescent press, which obliged with such headlines as CAPONE TOLD TO BLOW: GANG CHIEF ROUTED.

When Capone paid a return visit a few years later, Howard Hawks invited him to see rushes of *Scarface*. Capone reciprocated when Hawks was next in Chicago, throwing a party in his honor and presenting him with a miniature machine gun.

The big-time gangster who spent most time in Hollywood in the early thirties was Longie Zwillman, one of the nation's top bootleggers. He had business interests in L.A., but the great attraction for him was Jean Harlow. Zwillman made many visits to Hollywood, generally renting a bungalow at the Garden of Allah. Harlow was not the nymphomaniacal bombshell of popular legend, but it does seem certain that she had an early affair with Zwillman. He was obsessed with her and for years she wore a platinum bracelet he gave her, which was hung with tiny objects, including a pig (to represent her eating habits) and a miniature man of the world (to represent himself). This was much admired by Harlow's friends and seems to have started the charm-bracelet craze.

Even aside from her relationship with Zwillman, Harlow was not unfamiliar with the world of crime. Her unscrupulous stepfather—who swindled her out of much of her money, claiming to invest it in such fictitious enterprises as a Mexican gold mine—was an ex-barber and ex-small-time hood named Marino Bello, who claimed acquaintance with mobsters like Capone and Johnny Torrio.

Ironically, it was the move toward unionization in the film industry that gave organized crime its first toehold at the studios. Long before Hollywood artists and craftsmen decided to form guilds, projectionists all over the country had belonged to the International Alliance of Theatrical Stage Employees and Moving Picture Operators—IATSE—the union which was to provide leverage within the film industry. The inspiration for this came from a pair of tin-horn Chicago operators named Willie Bioff and George Browne. Browne, already an officer in the union, was the front man and Bioff appears to have been the brains.

Their first target was Balaban and Katz, the biggest theater owners in the Chicago area. The chain's employees had been forced to accept a 20 percent pay cut and Bioff informed the company's front office that this cut would have to be rescinded or there would be a strike—unless Balaban and Katz preferred to make a lump sum payment to Browne and himself on behalf of the union's welfare fund. After some haggling, the theater owners agreed to pay them $20,000, the bulk of which—laundered by an obliging attorney—went into the conspirators' pockets.

The new-found affluence of Bioff and Browne came to the attention of Frank Nitti, a Capone lieutenant, who saw the potential of the scheme and called in Louis Lepke, a major East Coast crime figure, to discuss what could be done on a national scale. Lepke said that he could arrange for Browne to be elected to the presidency of the union—a feat accomplished at the next national convention—and it was agreed that Bioff, having displayed a gift for extortion, should continue as the power behind Browne's throne.

When Bioff arrived in California in 1934, IATSE membership was at a low ebb, but the threat of mob strong-arm tactics helped swell the ranks, and by the spring of 1935, he felt that he was ready to make his move. He was given the go-ahead in December and suddenly the industry was threatened with a nationwide projectionists' strike. This first show of power actually benefited union members in that it won them a closed-shop agreement with theater owners and production companies. Apparently, the industry bosses did not even suspect an underworld plot and blamed the whole thing on FDR and creeping socialism.

That this was an error became evident when Bioff suggested that, if suitable annual payments could be made, such problems might be avoided in the future. After the specter of socialism, his demands must have come as a ray of sunshine. Bioff talked a language the bosses understood: He was offering sweetheart contracts and all he wanted in return was money.

The amounts involved were relatively modest, ranging from $100,000 per annum for the larger companies down to $25,000 for producers along Poverty Row. At first, payments were made directly to Bioff at the Garden of Allah. Later, things were done more surreptitiously: 20th Century-Fox emissaries were instructed, in one instance, to hand the company's tithe, wrapped in brown paper, to a bellboy at the Warwick Hotel in Manhattan.

Presumably, Bioff would have upped the ante in due course, but his scheme was staved off thanks to the efforts of legitimate union organizers, supported by an anti-Bioff campaign in *Daily Variety* and a series of syndicated articles by Westbrook Pegler. Robert Montgomery persuaded the Screen Actors Guild, of which he was president, to back an investigation of Bioff which quickly came up with a number of unsavory facts, including the information that he was a convicted pimp, still wanted for jumping bail in Illinois several years earlier. When Bioff and Browne were brought to trial, they squealed on their Chicago bosses. Frank Nitti killed himself rather than serve another term in jail.

Curiously, in light of this contravention of the mobster's code, Bioff and Browne survived their prison terms. Bioff, using the name William Nelson, later showed up in Arizona and somehow became a good friend of Senator Barry Goldwater (who has repeatedly denied that he knew about the man's past). That friendship came to an end in Phoenix one day in 1955, when Willie Bioff climbed into his pickup, turned the key in the ignition, and was blown to smithereens.

The threat of strike action was not the only form of intimidation considered by Bioff at the time of the shakedown. He is said to have told George Raft that, because Warner Brothers was holding out on him, he had planned to have a lamp dropped on Jimmy Cagney's head during the shooting of *Each Dawn I Die*. Supposedly, the plan was called off because Raft was Cagney's costar and had friends who did not want to take the risk of hurting him or his career.

Fox executive Joseph Schenck was not so lucky. Bioff had needed "clean" money to buy a ranch and Schenck had been foolish enough to accept $100,000 in cash from the IATSE kitty, in exchange for a personal check. The IRS became interested in this transaction and brought tax evasion charges against Schenck. Faced with this, he agreed to co-operate with the government in establishing the case against Bioff and Browne. The income tax charges were dropped and he was permitted to plead guilty to a single charge of perjury, for which he was sentenced to a year in jail. He was paroled after four months and later received a pardon which restored his full civil rights.

The biggest underworld name to operate in Hollywood in the thirties and forties was Benjamin Siegel—generally called "Bugsy," though not to his face. A handsome man with a taste for flashy clothes, he was Meyer Lansky's partner; between them, they controlled a gigantic gambling empire in Florida. Lansky's business acumen had made him one of the two or three most influential figures in organized crime. Siegel was not in Lansky's intellectual league, but he was a sharp operator with a sure instinct for the quick buck, and, since he was also gregarious and charming, he was a logical choice to become the syndicate's ambassador to Hollywood.

Like his friend Longie Zwillman, Siegel seems to have visited the Coast several times in the mid-thirties, making the move permanent at the end of 1937. Although it has been suggested that he was sent out to supervise the activities of Bioff and Browne, it seems more likely that his presence in L.A. was encouraged by his New York associates as a counterweight to Bioff and Browne, whose primary allegiance was to the Chicago mob. In any case, Siegel devised his own shakedown scheme by grabbing control of the extras guild. An extras strike could be almost as devastating as a strike by projectionists, and studio bosses were happy to make Siegel "loans" in return for his co-operation in ensuring that Hollywood productions continued to feature casts of thousands.

CRIME

It was conventional, during Siegel's earliest period in Hollywood, for columnists to describe him as "a New York playboy," and, with his constant companion, the Countess Di Frasso—an East Coast heiress who had married into the Italian aristocracy before carving a niche for herself in Hollywood society—he did his best sustain this image. The countess, who met Siegel on the rebound from an affair with Gary Cooper, knew everyone who was anyone in the movie capital.

Given the climate of gossip in Hollywood, it seems naïve to believe that Siegel's real business was not known from the outset. Certainly William Randolph Hearst, who had no desire for organized crime to move into Hollywood, was under no illusion and it was not long before his Los Angeles *Examiner* began to hint at Siegel's connections with the mob. If anyone was still in doubt, they were given a strong hint when, in 1940, Siegel was booked for the murder of a minor hood named Harry Greenberg. Why Siegel participated in this killing is something of a mystery. There was a contract out on Greenberg, but it has been assigned to a competent hit man named Allie Tannenbaum, so there was no need for Siegel to soil his hands. Perhaps he had some personal score to settle with the victim.

Siegel was arrested and jailed without bail, but, luckily for him, a new D.A.—John Dockweiler—had just been elected, reputedly with the aid of a large financial contribution from Siegel. The mob had supported Dockweiler with an eye to getting rid of Buron Fitts—the choice, it will be remembered, of the studios—who had been conducting a noisy campaign against the fleet of gambling ships which operated outside the three-mile limit (SEE GAMBLING). Siegel was soon back at his house in Holmby Hills, but a few months later he was arrested again for the same crime. A new witness had come forward, but when this witness died in a mysterious fall from a hotel window, the charges were dropped once more and Siegel resumed his career.

His main concern was to organize gambling and prostitution on the Coast, to which the wartime economy added the almost limitless possibilities of the black market. The movie colony was vital to his image, however, and he continued to hobnob with stars and producers. The Countess Di Frasso having been ditched, he dated starlets like Wendy Barrie and Marie McDonald. Show business did a great deal for him, and he reciprocated by providing show business with a spectacular new showcase—Las Vegas.

Until 1947, Vegas was a dusty little desert town which had enjoyed a brief boom during the building of Boulder Dam. There were a few small gambling spots there, but business was light. Vegas still looked like a frontier town and the city fathers were inclined to think they should play up the Wild West angle in the hope of attracting more tourists. Siegel had other ideas. Realizing that fast highways and planes could make the city highly accessible, he hit on the scheme of building a huge casino-resort there. He raised $6 million—mostly from his underworld friends—and within a matter of months, the Flamingo was open to the public, with Jimmy Durante, George Jessel, and Xavier Cugat headlining.

It was an immediate hit. Its flashy decor and atmosphere of crude hedonism caught the imagination of people living through the drab period of emotional letdown and material shortage that followed World War II. Soon there would be half a dozen huge casino-resorts along the Las Vegas Strip, most of them controlled by the Syndicate, a fact that gave mobsters an enormous influence over the performers who entertained there. When gangsters had operated speakeasies during Prohibition, they had been in a position to make or break the careers of singers, comedians, and band-leaders. (Mob-owned jukeboxes had also been an important consideration for aspiring vocalists.) Now the pattern was repeated in the Nevada desert.

Benny Siegel did not live to see all this. No one knows for sure what he did to upset the criminal fraternity—probably he became too greedy —but, in any case, his former friends decided to do away with him. On June 20, 1947—just a few months after the Flamingo was opened—Siegel was in L.A. He had a haircut at the Beverly Hills Club, then went to the home of his current girl friend, Virginia Hill. She was away in Europe, but an old New York buddy, Allen Smiley, joined him there.

They were chatting about old times when a series of shots was fired through a window. One bullet hit Siegel smack in the eye.

DISCOVERIES.

Featured prominently in the mythology of every schoolgirl in the forties was the tale of Lana Turner being discovered while sipping a soda at the counter of Schwab's drugstore on Sunset Boulevard. Her biographers have told us that she was in fact enjoying a malt at Currie's Ice Cream Parlor, across the street from Hollywood High, where the then-redheaded sixteen-year-old was supposed to be attending classes. (*Daily Variety* of November 1, 1937, however, states that she had been discovered a year earlier at a place called Tops on Sunset.) Reputedly, she was spotted by Billy Wilkerson, publisher of the *Hollywood Reporter,* who brought her to the attention of the Zeppo Marx Agency. Henry Willson, the agency's young vice-president, began taking the girl around to various studios, but, publicity releases to the contrary, there was no great rush to sign—or even test—her. The casting director at 20th Century-Fox actually called Willson to reprimand him for wasting his time on a girl with so little talent. It wasn't until Mervyn LeRoy hired her for *They Won't Forget,* at Warners, that her career was launched. LeRoy took her across to Metro when he moved there, and she was gradually groomed for stardom.

The myths were self-perpetuating, simply because people *wanted* to believe that they could be noticed walking down Dream Street and become a star overnight. Occasionally something like that did happen. Maureen O'Sullivan caught the eye of director Frank Borzage at a Dublin International Horse Show dinner-dance in 1930. Ellen Drew was working at Brown's Confectionary on Hollywood Boulevard when she attracted the attention of an agent who set up a studio test. Bruce Cabot was the host-manager of the Embassy Roof Club when he became friendly with Dolores Del Rio, who introduced him to David Selznick and executives at Paramount. During the search for Scarlett O'Hara, hat model Edythe Marrener, later Susan Hayward, was spotted by Selznick's wife, Irene, and was soon on her way to Hollywood. Jean Parker was seen by a scout as she was taking part in a school pageant in Glendale. Fred MacMurray was playing saxophone in the pit orchestra of the Broadway musical *Roberta* when Paramount scout Oscar Serlin noticed him clowning around and offered him a few months of free dramatic training and a screen test. Rin-Tin-Tin was discovered among a litter of pups in a trench during World War I.

In the early days, everyone connected with the business considered himself a talent scout. A cameraman would bring his pretty niece in, a carpenter his wife's cousin. In the early thirties, however, talent scouting emerged as a profession, and one by one the studios began to employ people whose sole function was looking for potential stars. By 1935 these scouts were headquartered in New York, and in that year one of them listed his main sources in the November *Ladies' Home Journal:*

1. Broadway shows
2. Touring companies
3. Stock and repertory companies
4. Radio
5. Vaudeville and picture-house stage shows
6. Night clubs
7. Opera
8. Models
9. College drama societies
10. Dramatic schools

11. Other amateur performances
12. Dance recitals
13. Song recitals
14. Photographic studios
15. Periodicals
16. Sports
17. Old screen tests
18. Hotel shows—morning musicales
19. Beauty pageants
20. Lectures
21. Kiddie shows
22. People who just walk in off the street

In 1936 Oscar Serlin, in New York on behalf of Paramount, investigated 1,500 possibilities a week, and interviewed 200 of them. Of these, about 100 a year were given some training and about 25 would be sent to Hollywood. Rufus LeMaire, who worked at several studios, brought 167 people to Hollywood in his first eighteen months on the job. Billy Grady, who had known Louis B. Mayer in the nickelodeon days when he booked acts for Mayer's theater in Haverhill, Massachusetts, had a checkered career as actor and agent (representing W. C. Fields for fourteen years) before he became a talent scout and M-G-M's casting director. For three years, he saw every show on Broadway, sending a succinct daily report to Metro. He moved to the Coast in 1937 and immediately proved himself by finding two Chinese water buffalo for *The Good Earth*. According to Ezra Goodman's *Fifty-Year Decline and Fall of Hollywood,* approximately 5,000 people a year were auditioned for M-G-M. Fewer than 1 percent were ever given screen tests and only a couple of those tested were likely to be signed. Billy Grady estimated that Metro invested $150,000 in any potential star before any return could be shown. Against that investment, he guessed that a star was worth at least $2.5 million to the studio.

By the end of the decade, *Daily Variety* was reporting that reason was beginning to prevail in the studio scouting departments:

> No longer do the Coast scouts head eastward in April, making a swing of every university campus and every little theater, then crashing the strawhatters for the balance of summer. No longer are production and other execs permitted to charge pleasurable European travel against talent-finding funds. . . .
>
> With general tightening up on aimless scouting, film companies have shuttered their New York and Chicago testing quarters. . . . Scouts are now equipped with 16 mm. cameras, which they operate themselves in running off a few hundred feet of film for submission to studio biggies.

DISCOVERIES

The greatest percentage of stars who eventually endured in Hollywood
—Bette Davis, Humphrey Bogart, Spencer Tracy, Paul Muni, Kay Francis,
Miriam Hopkins, Edward G. Robinson, Katharine Hepburn, Pat O'Brien,
James Cagney, Joan Blondell, Robert Montgomery, Fredric March,
Claudette Colbert, Sylvia Sidney, Fred Astaire—were first noticed on the
Broadway stage. Los Angeles and its immediate environs, however, also
had a healthy theater community, and scouts and agents kept a close watch
on talent appearing locally. The most famous of southern California
theaters was the Pasadena Playhouse, at which Robert Young, Eleanor
Parker, Dana Andrews, Victor Jory, Robert Preston, Randolph Scott,
and Victor Mature were all seen before moving on to screen careers.
Goldwyn scout Marty Martyn found Laraine Day at the Long Beach
Playhouse, and Susan Peters attracted the attention of a Warners scout
while appearing in a Los Angeles showcase production of *Holiday*. In
December of 1932, M-G-M's Ben Piazza attended a performance of
Journey's End at Pomona College and was favorably impressed with the
leading man, Arlington Brugh. At Piazza's invitation, Brugh visited the
studio. He said that he wanted to finish his last year of college and—after
the young man had given a weak reading from Noël Coward's *Private
Lives*—Piazza agreed that he should. Brugh returned in June and, following more than a year of coaching sessions with Oliver Hinsdell (see
COACHES), was tested, signed at thirty-five dollars a week, and given the
name Robert Taylor.

Agent Minna Wallis was instrumental in the development of several
careers. In 1925 she was at Warners, serving as a one-woman casting and
wardrobe department, when:

> Henry Waxman, who did beautiful photographs, came over one day
> with these fantastic pictures of a girl. He said, "Minna, you've got to sign
> this girl!" It was Myrna Loy. I said, "Well, we're doing a picture with
> Lowell Sherman, and instead of making a test, I'll have her sit next to him
> while they're photographing him. We'll be able to see better than in a test
> because it will be more natural." And the next day, when we were looking
> at rushes, Jack Warner said, "Who is that girl next to Lowell Sherman?
> That's a girl I want to get!" And we signed her up for $75 a week.

One purpose of Louis B. Mayer's annual European jaunts was to add
new stars to the Metro heavens. Greta Garbo, Hedy Lamarr, and Greer
Garson were his personal imports (though, as is well known, Garbo came
as an appendage to Mauritz Stiller, thrown into the deal like a minor league
pitcher). Producer Harry Rapf picked Joan Crawford out of a chorus of
forty-five dancers appearing in a show called *Innocent Eyes,* in which she
was a "beaded bag" in a "Living Curtain" number and "Labor Day" in a

holiday routine. Allan Dwan spotted Carole Lombard playing baseball on the street when she was twelve years old, and John Huston discovered Sydney Greenstreet on the stage when he was sixty-one.

Veteran director Henry King was responsible for the emergence of several major stars. When he was casting *The White Sister,* he and his wife were in the audience of a Broadway play in which Ronald Colman made a brief appearance. King's wife said, "Now, there's the man you want to play Giovanni," and King arranged for an interview, during which Colman told him that he would love to be in pictures, but all the reports on him in England said that he didn't photograph well. King, however, persisted. He decided to test him anyway and deliberately asked Colman a number of embarrassing questions to distract him from the camera. Once the actor recovered from his surprise, he found that he was able to relax. Next, King asked him if he would object to a change of hair style:

> He had a pompadour way up high and it made his face look this long. So I slicked it right down with pomade and ran another 400 feet, asking him a different line of questions. By now he had forgotten the camera and he was a human being. I said, "Would you mind if I took a few more liberties with you?" He said no, so I took a retouching pencil and drew a small moustache. He said, "I had an injury during the war. A piece of shrapnel hit me in the lip and I can't grow a moustache." I said, "Well, we can make moustaches that look pretty real." When I had finished, I said, "Mr. Colman—would it surprise you if I said you were 90% on your way to Italy to play Giovanni?"

Gary Cooper had been a Hollywood extra and featured player in two-reelers for a while when King recognized his star potential and gave him his first important role in *The Winning of Barbara Worth.* Cooper had been hired as a rider on the picture, but King found himself using the young man as a stand-in for one of the main supporting players who had been signed for the part, but was still off working on a Lubitsch picture. King, having completed whatever he could without the missing actor, tried Cooper out in one minor scene, just to see what he could do and to keep the crew occupied. Cooper played it so well that King decided to go one step further. There was a particularly difficult scene, in which the character has just ridden across the desert, knocks on a door, and drops down, exhausted, and King determined that if Cooper could handle it, then he would give him the part, instead of waiting for the absent actor.

> I met the boy at the studio at eight in the morning and I wet his face and patted it with Fuller's earth, and I let it dry, and we walked and talked and walked and talked for about three hours, until he was good

and tired. I said, "Now look, if I asked you to knock at that door, then just turn loose and fall, could you do that?" He assured me that he could.

Just as the crew was ready to go, the property man informed King that Sam Goldwyn wanted to see him. Goldwyn asked what the hell he thought he was doing with "that damn cowboy." King explained the situation and Goldwyn walked off, grumbling, "Sometimes I think you just do what you can to make me mad." King returned to the set and had the prop man signal for Cooper to come up and knock at the door:

> Ronnie Colman opened the door and there stood the most pathetic figure you ever saw in your life. It startled Ronnie Colman so that the fellow was just a few inches from the ground before Colman got hold of him and just turned his face to keep his nose from hitting the floor. I said to my cameraman, George Barnes, "If you want to make a close-up of this, make it quick! We're never going to get it again!"

Goldwyn sent for King again and said, "Why didn't you tell me that this was a great actor? . . . He's the greatest actor I have ever seen!" King asked how he knew that. "I was peeking through that hole in the black flat," said Goldwyn.

King had worked with Tyrone Power, Sr., in the early days and so was pleasantly surprised when Ty Power, Jr., stopped by his office one day to introduce himself. King was casting *Lloyds of London*. He had already tested Don Ameche, but decided that he would like to test Power, too. Darryl Zanuck gave his permission for this without telling King that Power had just been taken off a picture the day before because the director said he couldn't do anything with him. King repeated the test sequence he had done with Ameche, which called for the character to age from sixteen to sixty-five:

> When the test with Ty was run, Zanuck saw something in it but he said nothing. He asked, "Which one do you people like?" and everyone said "Don Ameche, Don Ameche." Zanuck said, "Henry, who do you like?" I said, "This boy, Power. He's a little more versatile, he's a better looking boy, and furthermore, we need new talent. Two or three years from now, I think this boy will be the top leading man in motion pictures." Zanuck said, "Put him in the picture before I change my mind."
>
> I'd been working about ten days when Zanuck said, "Henry, I've been watching the rushes every day and this boy is great. I don't want anybody to hurry you and I don't want you to let anything go. If we'd used Fredric March or somebody like that, it'd cost us $250,000. We're paying this boy peanuts. I want you to spend the extra money on his performance."

Occasionally, people were discovered right on the lot. Ann Dvorak was an assistant dance director at Metro. Virginia Bruce was a teen-ager taking a studio tour at Fox when she was spotted by director William Beaudine and signed for twenty-five dollars a week. Richard Arlen was making a delivery, by motorcycle, at Paramount when he collided with a truck and broke his leg. The studio doctor apparently thought it might be diplomatic if Arlen were offered extra work and passed the word on to the casting director.

Established performers were often able to give newcomers a boost. When Gretchen Young was a six-year-old extra, she was noticed by silent star Mae Murray, who was so taken by the child that she tried to adopt her. The girl's mother, struggling to raise several children by herself, refused the offer, but she did allow the little girl to live with the star for a year, during which time she was tutored by a German governess and given dancing lessons with Ernest Belcher. Several years later, in 1927, Gretchen drew the attention of Colleen Moore, who went to Al Rockett, head of talent at First National, and persuaded him to place the girl under contract. It was then that she was rechristened Loretta, after Colleen Moore's favorite doll.

Lillian Gish arranged for Mary Astor to test for D. W. Griffith. When John Barrymore saw photographs of her, he requested that she be considered for his leading lady in *Beau Brummel* (whispering to her during the test, "You are so goddamn beautiful, you make me feel faint"). Barrymore was responsible for giving William Powell his start and was repaid, years later, when Powell refused to replace him in *Romeo and Juliet*. Al Jolson recommended James Cagney and Joan Blondell to Warner Brothers after seeing them on Broadway in *Penny Arcade,* and Leslie Howard threatened to walk out on *The Petrified Forest* unless Humphrey Bogart was given the role of Duke Mantee.

It took Howard Hughes two years to shoot the silent version of *Hell's Angels,* with Ben Lyon and Norwegian-accented Greta Nissen, but when sound came in he decided to scrap most of it and find a new female lead. Lyon recalls:

> Howard tested every girl in Hollywood—Jane Peters before she became Carole Lombard, June Collier, Ann Harding—but none suited him. One day, after two or three months of this, Jimmy Hall and I were wandering around a Christie Comedy set, watching them film a ballroom scene, and I saw a girl—I've never seen anything like it in my life. It wasn't known as platinum hair then—just silver. And a black satin dress—you knew she had nothing on underneath—that showed every curve of her body. I said, "My God, Jimmy, look at that! There's the girl for *Hell's Angels!*"
> When they finished the scene, I walked over and introduced myself.

I said, "How would you like to play the lead in *Hell's Angels?*" She said, "I'll bite. What do I have to do?" I said, "Just meet me here at 12:30 and I'll take you to see Mr. Hughes." When she broke for lunch, I took her up and said, "You wait in the outer office." I went in and said, "Howard, I've found the girl for *Hell's Angels.*" When I brought her in, he said, "If you think she can do it, hold the crew and shoot a test tonight when she finishes work."

At 7:30, we gave her two pages of dialogue, which she learned in about five minutes, they got her an evening gown out of wardrobe, and we made the test together. Next day, Howard saw it, went mad about it, and signed her for $125 a week. When I found Jean Harlow, she was getting $5 a day.

D OMESTICS.

Once a movie personality had purchased or built a suitable residence—unless, of course, he was pursuing the simple life on a walnut ranch—it was essential to acquire a suitable household staff. He might have his business manager arrange for this, or he could call Mrs. Patten's agency on North Beverly Drive, or he might first check the personal ads in the Hollywood trade papers, where servants sometimes announced their availability, as in this 1938 example from *The Hollywood Filmograph:*

Gustavo Leah Ibn Singh
ARABIAN
DESIRES WORK—WITH LADY OR GENTLEMAN—bachelor or family. Very efficient in the work specified: Butler, Cook, Valet, House-Boy, Riding Instructor in Mounting and Alighting from Horse. 29 years in the service of British Nobleman in London, England

There were probably more domestics employed by the film colony than in any other community of comparable size, but there was no tradition of service, so that relationships between master and servant were sometimes bizarre. Louis B. Mayer, for example, never became completely accustomed to dealing with domestics, and even when he was the highest paid executive in the nation, he still found it necessary to try to impress his hirelings, as John Lee Mahin recalls:

Mayer had a Swedish butler. Sonny Whitney was at the house once and I was sitting there when Whitney left and the butler came into the room. "Now George," says Mayer, "that man is one of the richest men in the country." He always had to tell the butler about everything. He told him that Whitney was worth so many millions and the butler asked him what he did with it. Mayer said, "What do you mean, what does he do with it? He's going to put it in pictures."

Sometimes domestics found it difficult to take their employers seriously. Clara Bow, despite her flamboyance when she first became a star, felt herself to be so inept socially that, rather than risk going to parties and restaurants, she would stay at home and play cards with her servants. When Judy Garland was married to David Rose, the people running her house couldn't stop thinking of her as little Dorothy in *The Wizard of Oz,* which did not make for a smoothly run ménage. Anyone entering service in Hollywood had to be prepared for just about anything. The Japanese valet of Douglas Fairbanks (who later returned to Japan to become a movie producer) was a former acrobat who allowed his master to throw him about for the sake of a practical joke. W. C. Fields did not subscribe to conventional ways of summoning his staff. Instead, he carried a Halloween horn, on which he'd sound a blast when he needed something—more often than not a shaker of martinis.

Domestics were not entirely a luxury in Hollywood. Movie people worked long hours and much was expected of them socially. It would have been almost impossible for them to run their households without help. The considerable staff at Pickfair, which usually numbered about fifteen, had separate quarters comprising a gabled cottage for the head man and a dormitory for the maids, butlers, gardeners, grooms, etc. The entire staff would be invited to join the guests at the main house when home movies were being screened.

New arrivals in town were often in particular need of help. When the Charles Laughtons first came to Hollywood, Paramount found them a run-down stucco house on La Brea Terrace in the Hollywood Hills. Unfamiliar with the California life style, they relied heavily on Rogers, their chauffeur-houseman, who drove Charles to work and did all the cleaning, shopping, and cooking.

Many lasting relationships developed between employer and employee. Bette Davis retained one maid, Dell Pfeiffer, for twenty years. Mamie Cox was Marie Dressler's maid and housekeeper for nineteen. Tall, handsome, and well-dressed (he could wear Gable's clothes) Rufus Martin was Clark Gable's major-domo for two decades, maintaining an impersonal relationship with his master, but able to duplicate his voice on the telephone. Gary Cooper's dresser, Cracker, was devoted to him, and Tommy Turner, secretary, chauffeur, and valet to Ronald Colman, empathized with his employer to the extent of whispering hoarsely when Colman developed laryngitis.

The dean of the aristocracy of movie star maids and valets was unquestionably George Arliss' veritable Jeeves of a manservant named George Jenner. A large, humorless Briton, Jenner, who had already been with Arliss for twenty-seven years in 1933, would appear on the set every day, precisely at 4:30, wearing a derby and carrying a cane, and—whether a take was in progress or not—would remove Arliss' hat or outer garment. This was the signal that the day's shooting was at an end.

There were also studio employees who in effect doubled as domestics. Harold Garrison, better known as Slickem, ran the shoeshine parlor at M-G-M, and was known for his skill at accompanying his work with little song-and-dance routines. At the same time, he would serve as chauffeur to Thalberg and other executives—it was he who gave the police an account of Paul Bern's movements on the night he died—and he had the reputation of being the confidant of stars, executives, and workers alike.

DRESSING ROOMS.

From the silent period on, an important symbol of status on the lot was the dressing room—although the term is something of a misnomer, since it was used to include everything from a rambling villa to a luxury apartment on wheels. As with so many other things in Hollywood, Mary Pickford set the tradition of the glorified bungalow when she built her five-room stucco Norman cottage on the United Artists lot, furnishing it with antiques brought from the chateau of Baroness Burdett-Coutts. A butler and cook were always on duty. In the mid-twenties, Colleen Moore knew she had arrived when First National built a special bungalow for her at the studio. Hispanic in style, it was constructed around a patio containing a fountain and a live oak. There was a living room with a high beamed ceiling and a fireplace, a large bedroom, a kitchen, a wardrobe room, and a bathroom with a sunken tub. To accommodate idle moments, the bungalow came equipped with a grand piano and a shady back porch.

The first portable dressing room was Norma Talmadge's circus wagon-type affair, which was pulled around the lot by prop boys. (The inside walls were covered with shirred chiffon—said to resemble nothing so much as a baby's bassinet.) Gasoline-propelled dressing rooms were introduced in the form of a birthday gift from Irving Thalberg to his wife, Norma Shearer.

At M-G-M, caste standing was expressed without ambiguity. For a dozen years or so, all of the dressing rooms were located in an old frame building built up against the studio walls, with rooms assigned in order of star power, from Garbo and Shearer and Crawford on down. Men were housed at street level and the women were on the second floor, where the rooms gave onto a long wooden balcony which was reached by a flight of steps. (A sign posted at the foot of the stairs read NO MEN ALLOWED TO GO UPSTAIRS.) A porch ran around the building, and Lionel Barrymore has described how everyone would sit out there, "Tilting our chairs back, as drummers used to sprawl on hotel piazzas on summer nights." Later, in the thirties, new dressing rooms were built nearby—white stone cubes like something designed by Tony Garnier for one of his model cities.

Standing apart from these was Marion Davies' fourteen-room bungalow, which was in fact a Mediterranean-style villa, built for her in 1926 because, according to Davies herself, she got tired of running up the steps to the women's quarters in the old building. The Davies bungalow, which Chaplin dubbed "The Trianon," cost $75,000, was filled with Hearst antiques, and run by a full staff of servants. It allowed her privacy—there was a large lawn where she could, in her own words, "roll on the grass and kick and groan and scream and roar and holler"—but it also served as a social center in which Hearst and Metro executives could entertain distinguished visitors. However, when Hearst and M-G-M had a falling out over certain roles which were going to Norma Shearer rather than Marion, the bungalow, which had been constructed in breakaway sections, was carted across town to the Warner Brothers lot on a fleet of ten flat-bed trucks. (It was finally moved to Benedict Canyon and sold as a private home. Louis B. Mayer lived in it for a time.)

Constance Bennett moved to M-G-M at the height of her popularity, in 1931, and for a while her elegantly furnished rooms became second only to Davies' in prestige. Norma Shearer was fond of entertaining in her suite. While she was making *The Barretts of Wimpole Street,* for example, the cast would stop work every afternoon and congregate there to enjoy the eggnogs she liked to prepare. In 1932, after Robert Montgomery lost a heated argument with Mayer over a salary raise, he was presented the consolation prize of a barber's chair in his dressing room.

At RKO, Ginger Rogers' quarters were enlarged and embellished each year, until she had her own self-contained complex, which included a kitchen, bedroom, sitting room, hairdressing and make-up rooms, wardrobe and fitting rooms, etc. At 20th, Shirley Temple inherited Lilian Harvey's ten-room bungalow, which was redecorated to suit the less sophisticated tastes of its new mistress.

The readers of fan magazines and women's periodicals were, apparently,

PAUL MUNI OUTSIDE HIS PORTABLE BUNGALOW DURING THE
FILMING OF *Juarez*.

avid for news of the rooms in which their favorites dressed and undressed, and the studios gladly provided them with frequently updated information pertaining to expansions and refurbishments. In March of 1931, for instance, *Modern Screen* characterized Garbo's three-room bungalow as suffering from a "masculine severity," the living room papered in a "strange green tapestry." And when Clara Bow took over the Pola Negri suite at Paramount, the fans were informed, the living room walls were done over in gold leaf (and then covered with autographed photos of other stars), on the floor were rugs of old gold, and her dressing table was ebony with golden curtains and lights.

The *Woman's Home Companion* of August 1940 also devoted considerable space to the decor and color schemes preferred by screen notables. Rosalind Russell, for example, favored royal blue and chartreuse, with light woodwork, while Myrna Loy opted for lime green, tan, and Chinese red, with light birch and rough-textured fabrics. Jeanette Mac-Donald's sitting room featured "treasure tables" and hanging shelves for her Dresden statuette collection. Joan Crawford, at that time, had selected Victorian furniture against a background of powder blue, red, and white. Norma Shearer's "cool and restful" muskmelon green and peachy orange room had built-in corner seats for comfort. Bette Davis (who was one of the few people to actually live in her suite at times during production) had requested a New England motif appropriate to her origins, and was given green, brown, and cream-colored chintz, a comfy green davenport, and a mahogany four-poster bed. Robert Taylor and Clark Gable had, not unexpectedly, rooms of knotty pine with leather-upholstered furniture and hunting prints on the wall. Other sources tell us that Gable's suite consisted of dressing room, sitting room, and bathroom. Along with the sporting prints, there were many photographs and a devastating caricature of the star drawn by an artist at the Disney studio. During his romance with and marriage to Carole Lombard, a bud vase stood in front of her photograph. When he was working, it always contained a single red rose which she had sent to him each morning.

Quite naturally, the players' hobbies and special interests were reflected in their quarters. Lionel Barrymore converted his into a combination office-art studio, equipped with a piano and the copper plates and etching tools he used for printmaking. Buster Keaton's deluxe trailer on the M-G-M lot, which contained a fully equipped kitchen and a well-stocked bar, became the center of studio dissent and a focus of heavy drinking after his marriage to Natalie Talmadge broke up and he took to living there. Ken Maynard had a secret compartment and exit built into his, to allow himself and his tightrope-walker girl friend to make unobserved getaways. One room of Tom Mix's suite at Universal was outfitted as a gym, complete with a regulation boxing ring, punching bags, and parallel bars. W. C. Fields insisted on a front porch being added to his dressing room so that he could sit and rock himself into oblivion on pleasant days.

But there were some people who really didn't care. Carole Lombard required only a chair and a small table, at which she put on her own make-up. Garbo refused, for some time, to move into Metro's fancy new building, preferring her old dressing room. And when George Sanders was told he could have his quarters redecorated only if he promised to stop making rude remarks about the head of the studio, he decided that that was altogether too high a price to pay.

EXTRAS AND STAND-INS.

At the opposite end of the scale from the star who was battling for a nine-to-five clause in his contract, in order to work one hour less a day, was the army of extras struggling to put in as many extra hours as they could, their livelihoods at the mercy of Central Casting.

Before the Central Casting Corporation was set up by the Hays Office in 1926, the bit player situation had been one of total chaos. In the early twenties, thousands of people—the majority of them young women—poured into Hollywood looking for extra work, certain that it would lead to instant stardom. There were dozens of applicants for every job and work was often assigned on the basis of favoritism, bribery, and sexual services rendered. It seems probable that many female extras worked as prostitutes on the side—each of them posing a threat of scandal to the industry—and this became one of the factors that led to Will Hays establishing the Central Casting reorganization. In 1925 a group of film executives had consulted a New York research firm, the Russell Sage Foundation, which sent a special investigator to Hollywood. His findings led to the State Labor Commission recommending that the Motion Picture Producers and Distributors of America (which represented 95 percent of the industry), set up a free, centralized bureau to provide a reliable pool of talent, and to protect extras from the ordeals of making rounds. This would also enable casting directors to place bulk orders, such as forty-five policemen or two thousand Chinese. By 1937 the office was assigning about six hundred players a day and there were some fifteen thousand names on file. From time to time the bureau was forced to place a moratorium on

GARY COOPER, FAR LEFT, AS AN EXTRA IN A QUICKIE WESTERN
CALLED *Three Pals.*

adding new names to the list. In the thirties, in fact, rumblings from Washington prompted the setting up of a committee of people from outside the industry who requested studio casting directors to send lists of recommended extras so that Central Casting's pool could be reduced.

All of this did little to alleviate the plight of the extra. Those who did manage to work from time to time often spent much of their earnings on clothing and maintaining their appearance. In 1934 *Photoplay* described extra girls living five and six to a room, sharing clothes and expenses. Others at that time were in a shantytown—one of the Depression's

WITH HIS STAND-IN AND CECIL B. DEMILLE, FREDRIC MARCH
VIEWS A SCENE FROM *The Buccaneer* ON A MOVIEOLA, 1938.

"Hoovervilles"—out near Universal City. *Photoplay* even found one pair of girls residing in a tent.

Robert Parrish, in his *Growing Up in Hollywood,* has given a description of what happened when you called Central Casting's office in the Taft building at Hollywood and Vine:

> When the casting switchboard answered, "Central," you gave your name. The operator would repeat it to the casting directors and then give you instructions for the next day's work. "Report to RKO studio at 7:30 A.M. Summer school clothes. Panchromatic make-up. $5 and overtime. Director Seitz." More often, there was no job for you and the operator said, "Try later," usually in a nasal voice. For a long time, they just said "nothing," but the extras complained that it was too discouraging, so it was changed.
>
> You always kept phoning until you got a job or Central Casting closed the switchboard. The phone was the lifeline. The words "try later" became a joke password with Hollywood's extras. If you asked to borrow money, you were likely to be told "try later." Some years afterward, Frankie Darro opened a bar called the "Try Later," where extras met to discuss their hopes and fears, exchange wardrobes, call Central Casting, and even drink.

In 1936 only 58 out of 5,500 men and 20 out of 6,500 women averaged three or more days work a week; the 1,500 children registered only four days work a *year*. Extras were earning $3.25 to $35 a day, depending on their wardrobes and special talents, appendages and fearlessness. There would be additional fees for a natural beard, for getting doused by rain (which would bring you a "wet check") or falling off a horse (which would produce a stunt check). Most of the types needed for dramatic films fell into about forty groups, including dress men and women ("society" types who wore clothes well—and supplied their own), juveniles, bellhops, bald men, butlers, beards (or "beavers"), riders, dwarfs, dope fiends (in appearance only), Negroes, Orientals, Latin types, German types, pretty girls, homely girls, dowagers, healthy children, peaked children, etc. On a particular card might be a notation like, "Beard grows very fast—can develop a swell, tough stubble overnight" or "Character, comic, crook, bumps." ("Bumps" meant that the extra was not averse to being handled roughly). An enterprising young Los Angeles intern kept a casting index of freak medical cases. He could supply on demand men or women lacking one or both legs, a man with the shakes or a woman with a harelip. A list of such "atmosphere" players needed for the next day would be filed at three o'clock on the preceding afternoon.

THE FAMILIAR FACES AT THIS BANQUET ALL BELONG
TO THE DOUBLES OF FAMOUS STARS.

EXTRAS AND STAND-INS

Despite the fact that the average extra's yearly income in the mid-thirties was $161.36 a year, the movie-struck players kept calling, as reflected in this verse by extra Ruth Roozef, printed in the January 26, 1935, *Hollywood Filmograph:*

> Hello Central, give me Heaven—
>   Heaven, give me a call!
> Send me to MGM at seven
>   In old street clothes for fall—
> Always dialing 3–7–11
>   As evening shadows fall—
> Anxious hours! "Try later" even
>   Can't keep hope in thrall.
> Hello, studios, don't you want me?
>
> What? No requests at all?
> Rains and cancellations haunt me—
>   And beans begin to pall.
> Muddy nightwork—nothing heeding,
>   I'm glad to take it all.
> Central Angels! Hear my pleading—
>   Heed my need of a call.

By 1940 the situation had degenerated once more. Mobster Bugsy Siegel had taken over the extras' union and was manipulating it to his own advantage. (See CRIME.) Some extras, seeking special attention, were leaving cash bribes inside preselected volumes in a Hollywood Boulevard bookstore, where they were picked up by a studio casting director. Exasperated producers called in Howard Philbrick, former FBI agent and head of the California Motor Vehicles Bureau, to set up stricter standards of employment.

Some directors continued to take matters into their own hands. Woody Van Dyke had a "panic list," a roster of once successful movie people—including D. W. Griffith—who had been forgotten by the public and badly needed work. Whenever Van Dyke started a picture, he would send this "panic list" to casting director Billy Grady, who would hire some of the old-timers. John Ford had a similar arrangement at RKO. Grady himself organized an annual Casting Directors Ball, to raise money for sick and needy extras.

One step removed from the extra was the stand-in, who differed in that he rarely had any ambition to progress further up the ladder. Once in a while an extra would become a stand-in, such as Priscilla Lane's double, Alta Mae Smith; and Paulette Goddard's, June Kilgour, was one of the few to occasionally earn separate billing in small speaking roles. The work was more regular than that of an extra, but the salary was roughly the same as a dress extra's, $16.50 a day—although a few of the top stars personally paid handsome bonuses. Some became close friends with the person they were doubling—Sally Sage with Bette Davis, "Red" Breen with Jimmy Cagney, Don Turner with George Brent. "Dutch" Pettit—who later stood in for Paul Muni and Humphrey Bogart—was with Richard Barthelmess for so long that he took on many of the star's speech and acting mannerisms. Bob Hope's long-time double, Jack Robbins, was adept at aping Hope's comic delivery. On the other hand, there were stand-ins who never exchanged words with the stars they represented, such as Lillian Kilgannon and Marlene Dietrich.

It didn't happen often, but a few stand-ins did go on to substantial success themselves. Joel McCrea stood in for Wallace Reid, Valentino, and, most often, Arnold Grey. When their fortunes reversed, Grey doubled for McCrea. Gilbert Roland was Ramon Novarro's stand-in for *The Midshipmen* and Ann Dvorak stood in for Joan Crawford, who had doubled for Norma Shearer in *Lady of the Night* in 1925 (a possible cause of their later antagonism). Often, the person chosen for the job would be a relative or an old friend. "Slim" Talbot came from Montana with Gary Cooper, and Mary Lou Islieb was a neighbor of Shirley Temple's, the daughter of a banker who worked with Shirley's father. Deanna Durbin's stand-in for her first two films was Dorothy Sherrill, the daughter of her agent, but the girls began to grow at different rates and Dorothy had to be replaced.

At least three different stars have been credited with inadvertently originating the stand-in system: Mary Pickford, Pola Negri, and Marion Davies. Pickford's cameraman, Charles Rosher, used a be-curled mannequin on a wooden frame (nicknamed Maria), so that his star could relax between takes. Another story has it that Pola Negri couldn't stand still long enough for the technicians to spot their lights or the cameraman to focus, so one of her directors began to use a store dummy for the preliminary work, an idea which immediately caught on and spread. But still the dummy was usable only for stationary setups, and production would often be halted waiting for a star to appear and action walk-throughs to begin. On *Zander the Great,* director George Hill, weary of waiting for Marion Davies, hired a young woman named Vera Bennett to stand in for her, and before long nearly all stars—particularly the females—had stand-ins. By 1938 only the Ritz Brothers were still using wooden dummies.

Extravagance.

During the economic boom years of the teens and twenties, the extravagant Hollywood life style, as presented to the public, became the ultimate symbol of the American dream. It might be thought, then, that when the market crashed and the Depression set in, people would have turned against Hollywood's values, and, indeed, there were isolated manifestations of resentment: on a few occasions, for example, stars were booed and jeered at movie premieres. For the most part, though, the motion picture elite became more admired than ever. In the slumping economy, the escapism provided by the movies took on a new significance and the rich life style acted out by its stars also served, for many people, as a kind of tacit promise that everything would turn out okay in the end. The stars, after all, had not inherited their immunity to the consequences of the Depression; they had won it by means of talent, hard work, and sheer chutzpah. The movie celebrity was presented as an example of what the ordinary guy could attain if he wanted success badly enough.

In his 1941 book, *Hollywood: The Movie Colony,* Leo Rosten downplayed the extravagance of life in Hollywood, pointing out that one need only look to East Coast establishment society of the recent past to find examples of profligacy and vulgar taste that easily eclipsed anything essayed in Beverly Hills. The industrial barons of Fifth Avenue, Newport, and Long Island did in fact build larger and more ostentaious mansions, stage bigger and more pretentious parties, and generally behave in a way that would have cowed the big spenders of Hollywood, but the key difference is that the extravagance of the East Coast plutocracy was not much in the eye of the general public—the establishment shunned publicity—while the extravagance of Hollywood became, virtually, a pageant staged for the masses. Everyone knew about Pickfair. Everyone watched, on the newsreels, as Rolls-Royces, Duesenbergs, Packards, and Hispano-Suizas deposited their human cargo, adorned with silk hats and ermine capes, at the portals of Grauman's Chinese. Hollywood extravagance of behavior and display was as much a part of show business as the movies themselves.

100

MARLENE DIETRICH DEMONSTRATES THE MANNER IN WHICH
A STAR WAS EXPECTED TO TRAVEL.

Extravagance

In 1941 two thirds of all American families earned between $1,000 and $3,000 annually. A further 27 percent had incomes—often derived from relief handouts—of between $500 and $1,000. A middle-ranking movie star earned as much in a week as a middle-class family did in twelve months. And major stars, top executives, some producers and directors —even a few writers—earned far more than that. Given this contrast, it was natural for the general public to perceive the Hollywood life style as the apotheosis of splendor. Despite the fact that many movie people were thrifty and concerned with husbanding their incomes, or with investing any surplus in outside ventures (see INVESTMENTS), there was always plenty of money in circulation in Hollywood, and the way in which it was spent was often highly visible. The flaks had no difficulty in projecting a picture of Hollywood as a community of prodigal sons and daughters, a picture of which the public never tired.

Back in the early twenties, Universal erected a large electric sign in Times Square advertising Erich von Stroheim's forthcoming picture *Foolish Wives*. It was billed as the first million-dollar movie, and a dollar sign was substituted for the "S" in Stroheim's name. Stories about Stroheim's extravagance as a filmmaker are well known. He is said to have delayed shooting on *Foolish Wives* for a full day because the gold rims on a thousand champagne glasses were a quarter of an inch too narrow, and in *The Merry Widow* he insisted that all the soldiers wear silk underwear. Stroheim was, of course, making a fetish of such expensive details as a way of inspiring his cast and crew to levels of realism that were then unheard-of in Hollywood. Others followed his example. William Randolph Hearst demanded that an ancient warship be gilded, rather than painted, for a Marion Davies picture, at an increased cost of several thousand dollars. Director Herbert Brenon once held up a scene while a prop man scoured Hollywood for a British fifty-pound note. When it was found, he sealed it in an envelope and handed it to an actor who was supposed to be carrying an envelope containing a fifty-pound note. This tradition was beginning to die out when *Gone With the Wind* was being made, but David Selznick insisted that petticoats be trimmed with authentic Alençon lace and that shoes be hand-stitched by an Italian bootmaker, explaining to Ann Rutherford, "You are a rich plantation owner's daughter. The wardrobe will make you stand taller, prouder."

Such attitudes on set helped foster extravagance off the lot, and extravagance often degenerated into ostentation—the press agent's best friend. One actor installed a $60,000 cut-glass bathtub in his home, another had all his personal possessions monogrammed in diamonds, while a third, Tom Mix, had his monogram emblazoned in lights above both gates of his mansion. Barbara La Marr returned from a European shopping spree with twenty-two trunks which contained, among other trifles, six ermine coats. Valentino carried his silk sheets with him wherever he traveled. Lilyan Tashman never wore the same dress twice and, according to Colleen Moore, once went so far as to repaint her dining room dark blue for an Easter Sunday brunch because she thought it would set off her golden hair to the best possible advantage. Paulette Goddard, with possibly the slightest bit of help from a publicity man, trimmed her Christmas tree with bits of ermine one year and, on another occasion, appeared at a party in a sarong decorated with ten-dollar bills. It is said that Jennifer Jones always tried on at least a dozen pairs of new hose before selecting one, then tossed the others to her maid to be disposed of. Jean Arthur refused to wear any pair of stockings more than once, but she did have a pragmatic reason to offer for her behavior. When wardrobe mistress Emily Sundby pointed out to her that the stockings would fit better after they had been washed, the actress retorted that she was doing it merely to spite Harry Cohn. Cohn himself would wear his monogrammed silk shirts only once before giving them to his children's nanny, who sent them off to her father in Scotland. Clark Gable—not known as the most generous of men with his money— always carried two or three thousand dollars in cash.

Such tidbits do not define a life style, but they are the stuff that press releases were made of, as well as being symptomatic of the competitiveness that was a very real fact of life in Hollywood.

FALSE STARTS.

Tales of Clark Gable's early adventures in the oil fields and of Spencer Tracy's frustrated medical ambitions were among the favorites of studio publicists and Hollywood journalists. They made good copy because they seemed to tell us something about the stars—they fit their characters so perfectly. In fact, Gable left the oil fields as soon as he could, after only a brief apprenticeship, and Tracy had promised to study medicine in order to placate his parents. (Gable, on the other hand, *had* dreamed of becoming a doctor before he was smitten with the acting bug.)

Biographical research has since clarified many such legends, but the publicist's hand is not easily eradicated. The following is a list of pre-movie careers and studies that have been ascribed, at one time or another, to various stars and featured players.

Ameche, Don	Studied law at the University of Wisconsin
Autry, Gene	Railroad telegrapher
Ayres, Lew	Studied medicine at the University of Arizona; worked as musician
Barrymore, Ethel	Trained to become a concert pianist
Barrymore, John	Attended Slade School of Art in London; employed by the New York *Evening Journal* to illustrate Arthur Brisbane's column for eighteen months
Barrymore, Lionel	Artist. Attended Art Students League in New York for over a year
Baxter, Warner	Was head of Travelers Insurance Company's Philadelphia office
Beavers, Louise	Leatrice Joy's personal maid
Bendix, William	Played minor league baseball
Bickford, Charles	Studied engineering at MIT
Bow, Clara	Typist; doctor's receptionist
Brown, Joe E.	Played semi-pro baseball
Carroll, Madeleine	Taught French
Colbert, Claudette	Studied commercial art
Cooper, Gary	Majored in art at Grinnell College; came to Hollywood with hopes of becoming an animator
Costello, Lou	Prize fighter
Cromwell, Richard	Artist. Became known for the masks he did of Garbo, Crawford, etc.; did murals for Colleen Moore's home.
Cummings, Robert	Entered Carnegie Tech for engineering
Dietrich, Marlene	Studied the violin at the Berlin State Academy of Music until she suffered muscle damage

Dix, Richard — Studied medicine at the University of Minnesota

Dvorak, Ann — Assistant to choreographer Sammy Lee

Francis, Kay — Real estate broker, public relations woman

Garson, Greer — Head of market research and information department of Lever Brothers in London

Greenstreet, Sydney — Spent two years as tea planter in Ceylon

Hamilton, Margaret — Kindergarten teacher

Hussey, Ruth — Advertising copywriter

Huston, Walter — Engineer

Karloff, Boris — Expected to be placed in the British Consular Service in China, like two of his brothers

Kerr, Deborah — Ballet dancer. Made her debut with Sadler's Wells Ballet

Landi, Elissa — Published two novels before appearing in American films

Laughton, Charles — Sent to London to train for the hotel business at Claridge's

Luke, Keye — Studied architecture and design at the University of Washington; was an RKO advertising artist

MacMurray, Fred — Saxophonist

March, Fredric — Studied economics; was a trainee at the National City Bank, New York

Menjou, Adolphe — Attended Cornell for a course in engineering

Montgomery, Robert — Writer

Patrick, Gail — Studied law

Price, Vincent — Studied art history at the Courtauld Institute in London

Raft, George — Boxer, baseball player, dancer, gigolo

Rathbone, Basil — Insurance agent

Reid, Wallace	Property man
Robeson, Paul	Admitted to the bar
Ryan, Robert	Journalist
Sanders, George	Majored in textiles at the Manchester Technical College
Scott, Randolph	Degree in engineering from the University of North Carolina
Stewart, James	Studied civil engineering, then architecture
Stroheim, Erich von	Austrian Army officer, then newspaperman
Taylor, Robert	Concert cellist
Tone, Franchot	After being graduated from Cornell, planned to teach languages
Valentino, Rudolph	Trained in agriculture, worked as gardener
Welles, Orson	Studied painting at the Chicago Art Institute

Fan Magazines.

Newsstands in the thirties and forties displayed a dizzying array of fan magazines—*Photoplay, Motion Picture, Movieland, Modern Screen, Silver Screen, Screenland,* plus dozens of ephemeral competitors—all purporting to bring the secrets of Hollywood to filmgoers in Brooklyn and Baton Rouge, Columbus and Kalispell. The millions of predominantly female readers who bought them each month could turn the pages and find photographs of the latest fashions modeled by their favorite stars, advice to the lovelorn, and beauty hints. They learned about Errol Flynn's adventures in the South Seas and Clark Gable's bout with amnesia. They were told how Kay Francis kept her figure and were made privy to symposiums at which stars were asked their opinions on everything from the moral consequences of women wearing slacks to the factors contributing to an ideal marriage. They could learn what Adolphe Menjou liked and disliked in the opposite sex and why Bette Davis was unhappy with her

Warners contract. They could read how the Fredric Marches were bringing up their children and discover who had aspirations to be an opera star and who still dreamed of becoming a famous surgeon. In the dense pages of these periodicals, Hollywood's faithful were given "candid" glimpses of their favorites at work and play—the grit and the glamour—and could indulge their own fantasies of upward mobility through short stories in which girls from the Midwest, on vacation in California, were swept into the arms of handsome actors or used their native smarts to finagle screen tests. Everything the fan could reasonably hope for was crammed into these publications, from polls and questionnaires and horoscopes of the stars to decorating hints for Mother and leg art for Dad.

Most of these magazines reviewed current films—sometimes quite pithily—and developed columns and features that recurred in each issue. *Photoplay,* for example, had Cal York's "Monthly Broadcast" of gossip and trade news (Cal York was simply an abbreviation of California–New York) and regular articles on physical and mental fitness written by Madame Sylvia, who was forever exhorting her readers to "keep lean, babies, keep lean"—advice which she backed up with exercise suggestions such as, "Stimulate the thymus gland, in the center of the chest, with massage, at the same time digging into the shoulder muscles." A typical example of Sylvia's prose occurred in the June 1935 edition under the heading "How to Get Rid of the Depression Blues":

> So you've been through the Depression. And you tell me that the worry and the mental stress and the heartache of these last few years have left their mark upon you. Your letters say that you're nervous, run down, pepless, melancholic. And I'll add something to that. Your circulation is probably terrible too. And you blame it all on the Depression. When the only person to blame is yourself!
>
> Listen to me! The Depression was darn good for you. Before the crash, when money was rolling in, you were soft—physically and mentally. . . .

Whenever possible, Sylvia made her point with the help of movie personalities. Thus, in another 1935 piece titled "Happiness for Every Girl," she advised her readers that they should not allow their flaws to get them down:

> Now look at Claudette Colbert. She has handicaps too, but she overcomes them by the sheer force of her personality, her alertness, her vitality. . . .

Every fan magazine had its equivalent of Cal York's column, but *Motion Picture* went one step further, keeping its readers on their toes with a

107

regular feature called "The Gossip Test," which included such challenges as:

> Who is the movie actress who was recently accused of beating a less known film player?

The answer to this particular question, buried toward the back of the magazine, was:

> Lilyan Tashman was charged with beating Alona Marlowe when Lil found her in her husband's [Edmund Lowe's] dressing room.

Another staple of the fan magazines was the Miss Lonelyhearts column, usually with a star, such as Bette Davis, nominally providing the advice. Although the fan magazines were quick to inform their readers that stars employed stand-ins and stunt men to double for them on screen, there was never a hint—needless to say—that ghost writers were generally employed to compose the features that appeared under the stars' by-lines. There was no suggestion, either, that much of the material that appeared between the table of contents and the ads for Ex-Lax and Max Factor was actually provided by studio publicists. When a star was photographed with an interviewer at the Vendome or the Brown Derby, the photographer took care not to show the table setting laid for the third person present at the luncheon—the studio representative who was always on hand to guide the conversation away from potential reefs and shoals.

Actually, there were brief periods when the magazines showed some independence. In 1933 and 1934, for example, when the Hays Office was tightening its grip on the industry, several of the more prominent movie periodicals showed signs of revolt and for a while became relatively bold in their choice of material. *Photoplay* ran articles like "Undraped Hollywood"—a sort of paean to nudity—"Lupe and Johnny were Lovers," and "I Had to Leave John Gilbert"—all with suggestions of spice which anticipated the editorial approach favored by fan magazines in more recent decades. *Motion Picture* ran some fairly sexy pictorial spreads—one celebrating Goldwyn's *Roman Scandals* revealed an unusual amount of flesh for the time—and even launched an attack on Will Hays, blaming the puerile values of the Production Code for blunting the talents of people like Mae West.

This mini-rebellion did not last long, however. Without the cooperation of the studios—and the advertising revenues they provided—the fan magazines could not have survived and the industry brought them back into line by forcing the editors to sign a pledge to "cleave to a policy of clean, constructive and honest material," and to divest themselves of "false and otherwise salacious material." The Hays Office compiled a list of "acceptable" writers and issued them cards without which they were forbidden access to any Hollywood lot.

The fan magazine business had its beginning in 1909 when Eugene V. Brewster launched *Motion Picture Stories,* a monthly which offered brief novelizations of current Vitagraph movies, illustrated with still photographs, provided by the producers to publicize their films. Deluged with mail, Brewster instituted a question-and-answer feature supplying readers with information about their favorites. It was in *Motion Picture Stories,* which was then distributed at movie box offices, that Mary Pickford was first identified by name—like other players, she did not receive screen credit in those early days. By the time the magazine had been in existence for a year or so, it became clear that the readers wanted to know much more about the real people behind the characters they saw on screen, and Brewster began to publish photographs of popular performers accompanied by a few paragraphs of biographical material. In 1911 the name of the publication was changed to *Motion Picture Magazine,* and the editorial content gradually took on the general appearance of the modern fan magazine.

A typical early issue of *Motion Picture* ran to almost two hundred pages in a smallish format—about the size of *National Geographic*—and contained several stories based on movies, along with such features as "Art Gallery of Popular Players," printed on glossy paper, word portraits of current stars, "The Photoplay Philosopher," "How I Became a Photoplayer," and "Funny Stories That Are True: by the Players Themselves." Articles aimed at aspiring screenwriters were a staple. In "Where to Get Photoplay Plots," for example, Henry Arthur Phillips informed his eager readers: "Plot material is the telltale dust of Deeds that lies heavy behind the curtain of Commonplace Events. . . ."

Readers' letters continued to be used, since they boosted circulation and offered a feeling of participation and influence. Many of them were addressed to favorite stars and offered advice on warding off the evil eye, as well as efficacious remedies for anemia and constipation. Cartoons were distributed throughout the magazine, as were poems, of which the following is a representative example:

> "We should worry" about the weather.
> We're off to the picture show together.
> We'll brave the wind and ice and snow,
> For we can't miss a moving picture show.

Motion Picture was, at the outset, backed by the all-powerful Motion Picture Patents Trust Company and it prospered mightily. Eugene Brewster employed his new-found wealth to promote a redheaded young actress named Corliss Palmer, setting up his own production company and using the magazine to showcase her charms. Although she was an attractive enough woman, her histrionic gifts evidently did not impress the film-going public, and the project ended in disaster. *Motion Picture* passed into other hands and Brewster died penniless.

The initial success of *Motion Picture* inspired dozens of competitors, one of which was *Photoplay,* first published in Chicago, then a thriving center of the film industry, in 1911. It was, for the first three years of its existence, a marginal operation, and in 1914, deeply in debt, it fell into the hands of the W. F. Hall Printing Company, which called in a young man named James R. Quirk, in the hope that he might be able to reverse the fortunes of the ailing publication. Quirk had been a top editorial aide of John F. Fitzgerald—grandfather of John Fitzgerald Kennedy—on a short-lived Boston newspaper, but his chief qualification for the *Photoplay* job was that he had been enormously successful in turning *Popular Mechanics,* which had been facing bankruptcy, into a highly profitable venture. Quirk was to dominate the fan magazine field for the next eighteen years.

Quirk's name first appeared on the *Photoplay* masthead in January of 1915. At that time the magazine was almost identical, in format and editorial content, with *Motion Picture.* Under Quirk's guidance, it became livelier almost immediately. He cut down on the number of mini-novelizations and—sensing the authentic interests of his readers—began to publish articles such as "Who's Married to Who in the Movies?" Within the limitations of the format, he started to jazz up the layout, breaking away from the almost Victorian solemnity still favored by the other publications, and he commissioned cover art that managed to convey some of the freshness of the movies themselves.

In October of 1917 he startled his competitors by switching to a larger format—the size of the modern fan magazine—which allowed his layout artists to vary the visual texture still more. *Motion Picture* followed suit six months later. At about the same time, Quirk began to look around for fresh writing talent to further enliven his magazine. In 1918 the name Louella Parsons made its first appearance in *Photoplay* and that same year he approached Adela Rogers St. Johns, then a young Hearst journalist, asking her to supply him with regular features under her own name and a variety of pseudonyms, offering her thirty-five dollars a story. In the same year, he instigated the Cal York column, the first of the real movie gossip columns, to which Mrs. St. Johns contributed many tidbits. Having grown up in Hollywood, the daughter of the noted attorney Earl Rogers, she was on familiar terms with many of the stars, and so was ideally equipped for this kind of work. Before long, she was being featured on the masthead as West Coast editor.

Quirk was not without his rivals. William Fawcett, a native of Minneapolis, returned from World War I with his bags crammed full of copies of

La Vie Parisienne. He reproduced the French drawings, along with suitably saucy captions, and issued them in a magazine which he called *So This Is Paris!* As the French material began to wear thin, he supplemented it with pictures of movie sirens in mildly provocative poses, retitling his publication *So This Is Paris—and Hollywood!* This soon became *So This Is Hollywood!* and, when studio gossip began to accompany the pictures, *Hollywood Secrets. Hollywood Secrets* then became *Screen Secrets,* and finally *Screen Book.* Meanwhile, Fawcett launched a new publication called, quite simply, *Hollywood,* and completed his stable by acquiring the venerable *Motion Picture Magazine.*

Quirk, however, remained the czar of the fan magazines, and his *Photoplay* set the style and tone which the others strove to imitate. In the early days, he sometimes served as amateur talent scout, publishing photographs of unknown aspirants who were later signed by studios. His editorial column—called first "Speaking of Pictures," then "Close-ups and Long Shots"—was hard-hitting by the standards of a subculture given to flattery as a way of life. He was not afraid to attack men like Zukor, Laemmle, and Mayer and often risked reader disapproval by knocking some of their favorite stars. He took digs at Garbo—"Perhaps she has nothing to say!" —accused Pickford of being aloof, and, a decade before Hedda Hopper took up the cause, chastised Chaplin for not applying for U.S. citizenship.

It was Quirk who commissioned Terry Ramsaye's *A Million and One Nights*—a classic history of the American cinema—and ran it in thirty-six installments under the title "The Romantic History of the Motion Picture." Among other occasional contributors to *Photoplay* were H. L. Mencken, George Jean Nathan, F. Scott Fitzgerald, Theodore Dreiser, and Sherwood Anderson; staff writers included Robert Sherwood, Willard Huntington Wright ("S. S. Van Dine"), and Sally Benson.

In 1930 a magazine called *New Movies* made its appearance. What distinguished it had nothing to do with either format or content: it looked like all the others, but it was distributed through dime stores and sold for ten cents, as opposed to *Photoplay*'s twenty-five cents. Most magazines were quick to respond to the challenge, setting off a fierce price-cutting war, which Quirk refused to join, insisting that he could provide better value for money by maintaining his standards and continuing to sell his magazine for a quarter. At the height of this battle, in August of 1932, he died of a heart attack at the age of forty-seven.

Quirk's assistant since 1914, Kathryn Dougherty, managed to maintain his standards for a couple of years until, in 1934, *Photoplay* was taken over by Macfadden Publications. It then seemed destined to become just another fan magazine, although, in 1937, under the editorship of a self-promoting magazine writer named Ruth Waterbury, a final effort to break the mold was made. In imitation of picture magazines like *Life* and *Look,* the *Photo-*

play format was enlarged and a much greater emphasis placed on slick photographic material, so that the periodical became a kind of glossy chronicle of café society, Hollywood style. Unfortunately, editorial standards seldom matched its visual merits, and in 1940 the magazine returned to its conventional format, losing its distinctive personality once and for all, though it retained one of the largest circulations in the field. What had in fact happened was that Quirk and his staffers had evolved a successful formula for the fan magazines that others were able to reproduce without difficulty, and big publishers and syndicates like Dell, Macfadden, and Fawcett simply took it over, producing a dull sameness throughout the business.

A couple of hundred free-lancers filed occasional stories with the "fannies"—as they were called—but it is generally acknowledged that the great majority of features was written by a small group of specialists numbering perhaps thirty or thirty-five. A few top writers—such as Grover Jones, Gilbert Seldes, Kyle Crichton, and Quentin Reynolds—were men, but for them the fan magazines were generally a secondary source of income. Jones was a successful screenwriter, Seldes was the author of books like *The Movies Come from America,* and Crichton and Reynolds were both staff editors of *Collier's.* Most of the writers, however, were women—often referred to disparagingly as either "sob sisters" or "chatter-chippies."

Adela Rogers St. Johns was the prototype for this group and an authentic "personality" herself. She had an energy and stylistic flair which placed her high above the rest. She soon graduated to national publications like *Cosmopolitan* and, by the early thirties, had largely abandoned the fan magazine field to her imitators.

With Adela gone, Gladys Hall—active from 1925—became the de facto leader of the sob sorority. She produced an average of half a dozen stories a month for the fan magazines, though she was eclipsed in terms of sheer logorrhea by the phenomenally prolific Sonia Lee, who spoke her stream of prose into a dictating machine and displayed a canny ability to make each story read exactly like the last—a talent that probably endeared her to editors and studios alike. One of the most popular of the feature writers was Liza Wilson, who was reputed to have been the best interviewer of the group. Sara Hamilton specialized in syrupy love stories, while others like Kay Proctor, Ida Zeitlin, Marian Rhea, and Katherine Hartley were reliable work horses. Among the men, Howard Sharpe was another writer specializing in heavy "love interest," while Kirtley Baskette—author of the celebrated *Photoplay* story "Hollywood's Unmarried Husbands and Wives" —anticipated the kind of journalism that later became the staple of *Confidential.* Their long deadlines also worked to the disadvantage of the magazine writer. For example, Joan Crawford gave the exclusive news (she hadn't told her husband yet) of her impending separation from Douglas

Fairbanks, Jr., to her good friend Katherine Albert at *Modern Screen*. But the thirty days until the magazine would appear was just too long for Crawford to keep her secret, and she finally blurted it out to Louella Parsons, losing Albert her scoop.

None of these people became wealthy writing for the fan magazines. In the mid-thirties, the top publications occasionally paid as much as $125 for an article, but the average fee was closer to $50, or $75 for a "name" writer. Even the most prolific, like Sonia Lee, were hard pressed to make $10,000 a year. It was rumored at the time that some of the regular contributors supplemented their incomes by taking handouts from studios which were prepared to pay well for the suppression of material unflattering to their valuable employees, although it's doubtful that many of these writers were in any position to have much information worth suppressing. Most of them gladly accepted the fantasy of Hollywood glamour dished out by the studios.

Although every journalist in Hollywood was reliant to some extent on the good will of the studios, most of those employed by newspapers, wire services, and major magazines managed to retain a degree of independence and self-respect. The sob sisters, on the other hand, were—after the 1934 crackdown—"kept women." Not only were they unable to conduct interviews without the presence of a studio publicist, often they were also required to submit questions in writing beforehand and the text of the finished story had to get a studio okay—which was not granted routinely. Writing in *Coast* magazine in 1939, Carl Cotter quoted an example of a story submitted to M-G-M which mentioned the fact that Virginia Bruce enjoyed dancing until the wee hours. When the piece was returned by the studio, "until the wee hours" had been struck out and penciled above was the correction: "Virginia likes to get all her dancing over with by twelve o'clock." Given the limited literary skill of most fan magazine writers, these conditions tended to produce a flatness of both style and content—especially since the "angle" from which a story was written was often thought up by a studio publicist, rather than the writer, and offered to several different writers at the same time.

The history of Hollywood, as presented by the fan magazines, is for the most part ludicrously unreal—but the magazines are fascinating documents because they did accurately chronicle the folklore of the American film industry as it emerged. They gave the studios a direct line to the hard-core fans and served the important function of giving the stars an existence—however fantasized—separate from the roles they played on screen. More than any other organ, the fan magazine was responsible for perpetrating the dualistic mythology of Hollywood—that in addition to the idealized lives projected on the screen, there was the actual/dream existence of Screenland.

FIGHTS.

In October of 1944 Herman Hover, then the proprietor of Ciro's, half-facetiously announced his intention of setting up a prize-fight ring at his club, to accommodate the brawlers who were slugging it out so regularly on the dance floor. Perhaps because the pressures of the home front were beginning to make themselves felt, 1944 was indeed a vintage year for Hollywood scraps. On one night alone that season, Mike Romanoff was tangling with racing driver Barney Oldfield, Charles Bickford was pummeling a couple of strangers for what he considered to be unpatriotic remarks at the Somerset House restaurant, and there was a headline-making melee at Tommy Dorsey's Sunset Plaza home. This latter involved Dorsey and his wife along with Jon Hall, Ann Sheridan's ex-husband Eddie Norris, Winston Churchill's third cousin Jane, a Panamanian actor named Antonio Icaza, a butcher knife, broken beer bottles, the D.A. and the FBI. It all started when Mr. Hall gave Mrs. Dorsey a supposedly friendly pat on the back.

From the beginning, the rages of the movie colony were expressed in fisticuffs—in the clubs, on the set, at parties, and at home—it wasn't for nothing that Bogart's nickname for his wife, Mayo, was "Sluggy" while Errol Flynn called his mate "Tiger Lil." Louis B. Mayer was a celebrated one-punch artist, always more than willing to fight for what he believed in, particularly the sanctity of womanhood, and especially motherhood. Once, while shooting his silent version of *The Merry Widow,* Erich von Stroheim told Mayer that the film's heroine was a whore. L. B. said, "I don't make pictures about whores." To which the director replied, "All women are whores." Mayer promptly knocked Stroheim to the floor, threw him out of the office, and barred him from the lot. A similar incident occurred when John Gilbert was making *The Widow in the Bye Street,* adapted from John Masefield's poem about a woman forced by circumstances to turn to prostitution. On this occasion, Gilbert said that his own mother was a whore, causing Mayer to fly at him screaming, "I ought to cut your balls off!" In the lobby of the Alexandria Hotel (the scene also of an epic confrontation between John Barrymore and Myron Selznick,

114

which resulted in black eyes for both) Mayer accused Charles Chaplin of besmirching the name of his ex-wife, Mildred Harris Chaplin (who happened to be under contract to Mayer), and kayoed the comedian with one wallop. Mayer was never fond of Sam Goldwyn and, becoming enraged with him in the showers of the Hillcrest Country Club, knocked him into the towel cabinet. Goldwyn threatened to sue for a million dollars, but Mayer convinced him that such an action would cast a dim light on the entire industry.

A famous battle, which went down in Hollywood history as "The War of the Red Noses," took place at the Cocoanut Grove when a party of drunks directed some unkind wisecracks at Al Jolson, who was notoriously easy to rile. At the start of the fracas, Abe Lyman and his band rushed from the men's room and struck up a frenzied fox trot, but they were too late to prevent a general free-for-all. Women could also get into the act. Lupe Velez and Lilyan Tashman came to blows in the powder room of the Montmartre Café in 1932.

In December of 1935 Spencer Tracy squared off with William Wellman because of a remark the director made about Loretta Young at the Trocadero; at another night spot, Harry James and George Raft had a big confrontation over Betty Grable. In 1937 Arline Judge was the subject of a fight between millionaire Dan Topping and agent Pat di Cicco (according to James Robert Parrish, witness Woody Van Dyke claimed that the contestants missed each other so often that it got to be a bore). At Ciro's one night, a patron was needling Johnny Weismuller, who was doing his best to avoid physical combat. But his wife, Lupe Velez, jumped right in and began to punch the man, screaming, "You beeg ape! You leave my man alone!" Even at the sedate Enchanted Lilac Society Ball, Oleg Cassini thrashed someone he thought was cutting in on his wife, Gene Tierney.

One of Hollywood's most publicized skirmishes took place at the Mocambo, when Errol Flynn flattened Jimmy Fidler, who had touched a sore spot in his column:

> Errol Flynn, whose love for his dog, Arno, has been much heralded, didn't even bother to go get his body when it was washed ashore. That's how much he cared for him.

Fidler's wife grabbed a fork and stabbed Flynn in the ear. The columnist later charged the star with assault, but the case was settled out of court. A later account offered another motivational factor:

> Fidler, when interviewed, did say that previously he'd refused $2,500 which had been offered him to give a favorable review to The Prisoner of Zenda.

FIGHTS

In addition to the night spots on the strip, private parties were another frequent fighting arena. In the early days, Norman Kerry and Mickey Neilan began to argue at a party at Gloria Swanson's mansion. When they started to go outside to slug it out, their hostess said no, that would draw too much public attention, so she locked them in a coat closet and they pounded each other for twenty minutes in the dark.

Writer John Monk Saunders knocked out Herbert Marshall at a dinner party given by Ernst Lubitsch for Max Reinhardt, and at a party at Ann Rutherford's Beverly Hills home, restaurateur Stephen Crane slugged it out with Turhan Bey in the garden over Crane's future wife, Lana Turner. Before friends could separate them, Crane had a black eye and Bey's face was a network of scratches.

On-set differences sometimes erupted into violence, too. Character actor Charles Lane remembers Jimmy Cagney flattening a director who had persisted in interrupting him and making him repeat a simple line. Cagney then phoned Jack Warner and said, "You can come and pick up your boy. I just laid him out." During the filming of *Manpower,* tensions developed between Edward G. Robinson and George Raft, possibly because Raft was interested in Marlene Dietrich at the time and thought Robinson might be, too, but also because of Raft's gnawing insecurity. Raft's biographer, Lewis Yablonsky, has said that the actor resented Robinson's persistent advice about how to handle lines and business, interpreting this as a put-down. During one take, blows were exchanged—photographs of which made the front pages—until the pair was finally separated by Alan Hale and Ward Bond. A couple of years later, in 1943, Raft had trouble with Peter Lorre when the two were working on *Background to Danger.* In a scene which called for Raft to be tied up by Lorre and Sydney Greenstreet, Lorre began to improvise by blowing smoke into Raft's face, laughing sadistically. The minute he was untied, Raft dashed into Lorre's dressing room and clouted him.

GAMBLING.

In a 1937 letter to Maxwell Perkins, F. Scott Fitzgerald wrote from Hollywood that Ernest Hemingway was in town to raise money for the Spanish War Relief, and that Miriam Hopkins, in support of the effort, had been seen handing Hemingway thousand-doller bills as she won them at the gaming tables. Gambling, inevitably, was a passion with the movie colony and flourished in a variety of forms, legitimate and otherwise. Prior to 1935, the track and casino at Agua Caliente were much frequented by the movie crowd. Joe Schenck had more than $400,000 invested in these enterprises, most of which he lost when, in 1935, the Mexican Government outlawed gambling. By that time, however, Southern California had its own race tracks.

If Louis B. Mayer was pre-eminent as a breeder of thoroughbreds (see also RACING), Harry Cohn was Hollywood's most fanatical bettor. (Mayer seldom placed a wager of more than twenty dollars.) Cohn and his brother Jack had been bowling sharks in their youth, but the race track was Harry's real love. His annual vacation consisted of a month at Saratoga, and it was possible to determine who was in favor at Columbia simply by observing Cohn's boxes at Santa Anita and Hollywood Park. A firm believer in inside information, Cohn is said to have paid a man called Buzzy Appleton up to $25,000 a year for tips, while bookies roamed freely in the Columbia administration building. Curiously, however, Cohn disapproved of any but his executive employees gambling, except in his company. When he caught a group of writers shooting craps on Christmas, he sent for the police and had them arrested. Another Christmas, he found some laborers playing cards and fired them on the spot. Farley Granger has said that he was once summoned to Harry Cohn's office, where he was informed that he had been won from Sam Goldwyn the previous evening, in a gin game.

Cohn's gambling reached its peak in the forties when he is believed to have averaged between $5,000 and $10,000 a day on bets. This continued until he experienced a disastrous thirty-day losing streak at Saratoga, dropping about $400,000. At this point he received an ultimatum from his brother, who controlled the company's finances in New York, warning that unless he stayed away from the track, he would be removed by the Board. In all probability, this came as a relief. Harry did conceive a new passion for football, but managed to keep it under reasonable control, confining himself to fifty-dollar bets on college games.

Prior to a major clamp-down in 1938, there were any number of well-protected gambling joints in and around Hollywood. In *The Big Sleep,* Raymond Chandler presented a fictionalized portrait of one of the ritzier spots, calling it the Cypress Club, which bore a distinct family relationship to real life gaming houses like the Clover Club and the Colony. The Clover Club was above the Sunset Strip, just west of the Château Marmont. It was operated by Nola Hahn and Eddie Ness, and its *maître d',* Marcel Lamaze, went on to become a popular restaurateur himself. The Colony Club, discreetly situated behind a screen of shrubbery on a side street south of Sunset and run by Lew Wertheimer, who was alleged to have had ties with the Detroit Purple Gang, featured entertainment by major show business acts like the Ritz Brothers. When the Colony was forced to close, Wertheimer was placed on the 20th Century-Fox payroll. Apparently Joe Schenck had lost so much money at the club that he owed Wertheimer a substantial favor.

Dorothy Parker once referred to Hollywood money as "congealed snow," and the movie colony's big gamblers seem to have shared her sense of its unreality, losing money almost more quickly than they could earn it. B. P. Schulberg, a compulsive gambler, dropped $100,000 at the Clover one evening and returned a short while later to lose another $40,000. (Executive IOUs were considered about as solid as government bonds.) Poker was a popular activity in private homes during the thirties and forties, and all-night, no-limit games were commonplace. Regular high-stakes players included Sam Goldwyn, Carl Laemmle, Eddie Mannix, Joe Schenck, Sid Grauman, Ben Hecht, Norman Krasna, Harpo Marx, and David Selznick (swallowing Benzedrine to stay awake). Both David and Myron Selznick had inherited their passion for gambling from their parents—Lewis was estimated to have lost about a million dollars a year for several consecutive years, and it was not unusual for his wife to join in the games. Only one other woman, Constance Bennett—considered among the best players in town—was habitually welcomed at these sessions, where it was not unusual for participants to lose $40,000 or $50,000 an evening.

Another favorite gambling spot was the Beverly Hills Club—a health spa on Roxbury Drive—which was opened in 1924 by Elmer Perry, a gambler who used its facilities and his friendship with movie people as a front for high-priced card games. In the thirties, while Errol Flynn, Howard Hughes, Edward G. Robinson, Tyrone Power, and other luminaries were working out in the gymnasium there, Perry was also catering to a different kind of clientele—for when the Beverly Hills police found twelve men playing poker in the back room there quite early one morning, they learned that eleven of them had criminal records, two being reputed associates of the Purple Gang. Perry was prosecuted, found guilty, and fined, but not before dozens of civic leaders had dashed to his defense. One prominent rabbi praised the club for its "air of refinement."

Not discouraged by this blot on his reputation, Perry linked up with a one-time rumrunner, Antonio Stralla—better known in the underworld as Tony Cornero—who operated a gambling ship, the *Rex* (in Chandler's *Farewell, My Lovely,* it appears as the *Royal Crown*), which was moored off Santa Monica, in full view of the shore. At night, ablaze with lights, it became an inescapable presence for strollers in Palisades Park and for movie stars and moguls in their beach-front mansions. Elmer Perry helped set up expeditions to the *Rex*—three barges and a fleet of water taxis being available to ferry passengers out to the ship.

Tony Cornero was the most colorful of the individuals who sought to side-step the law by setting up floating casinos outside the three-mile limit. His earliest venture of this sort was the *Tango,* which began to operate off Venice Beach in 1929 and was still stationed there ten years later, though Cornero no longer had an interest in it. It was commonly assumed that both the *Tango* and the *Rex,* as well as other vessels anchored off Southern California, enjoyed the backing of East Coast gamblers affiliated with the Syndicate, but Cornero always claimed that he had managed to stay independent, a claim that was publicly substantiated by his mortal enemy, Los Angeles District Attorney Buron Fitts. Fitts was just one of many lawmen to conduct campaigns of harassment against the gambling ships, an effort that started in 1929 when a gang of hoodlums who had shot and killed a policeman in Long Beach took refuge aboard one of the floating casinos.

The *Rex* was by far the most ambitious of these ventures. Originally a steel-hulled British barkentine, built in 1887, it had had a varied career before Cornero had it converted at a cost of $300,000. It sported a 250-foot glass-covered gaming deck which offered faro, roulette, and craps. A lower deck featured dancing and entertainment, a café, and more plebian forms of gambling, such as bingo. Bob Gans—known as the slot-machine king of L.A.—had provided 120 one-armed bandits.

The *Rex* operated twenty-four hours a day and on busy nights would hold close to 2,000 pleasure seekers. (Disliking the word "suckers," Cornero called them "squirrels.") There was a payroll of 325, with pit bosses earning $25 a shift and croupiers $15. The pretty girls used as shills were paid $5 for eight hours' work. The daily gross profit, as Cornero cheerfully admitted, averaged in excess of $10,000. Security was tight. Business was conducted behind steel doors, and armed bouncers frisked arrivals for guns and cameras. Mindful of the fact that another gambling ship, the *Monte Carlo,* had been boarded one foggy dawn and robbed of $40,000, Cornero had batteries of machine guns installed fore and aft.

Although it faced constant court battles—fought by Cornero's mouthpiece, Joe Fainer—the *Rex* operated quite openly. Cornero hired skywriters and took out full-page advertisements in local papers. He courted editorial attention, always emphasizing the quality of the food and entertainment offered. In fact, the food is said to have been good and inexpensive, and at least one future movie star, Rita Hayworth—then still one of the Five Cansinos—performed on board.

The Hollywood crowd was much in evidence. Uncle Carl Laemmle, boss of Universal, was often seen at the faro table, and William Fox's partner, Winfield Sheehan, was another regular. Faro, which was not featured on the other gambling boats since it does not give the house much of an edge, was the big attraction for these high rollers. Cornero realized that it was the movie crowd who generated publicity and that he could break even on the faro tables and still get rich from the nickel-and-dime trade attracted by the ship's glamorous reputation.

All this came to an end in July 1939. The previous year, pressure from the D.A.'s office had forced Cornero to move the *Rex* first to Redondo Beach and then to the Santa Catalina Channel. This latter station was twelve miles off shore and Cornero found that few "squirrels" were prepared to make that long a boat journey in order to lose their shirts, and so, in 1939, he moved the *Rex* back to its old anchorage off Santa Monica. This made him vulnerable to the D.A.'s harassment once more, but business was soon back to normal.

In the end, however, it was not D.A. Fitts who closed down Cornero's racket. Earl Warren had become attorney general of California, and, perhaps heeding the political mileage Thomas Dewey had obtained from crime busting, he launched an all-out campaign against the gambling fleet. Among his legal pretexts was the notion that the owners had been operating water taxis without registering them as public vehicles. Boarding parties were sent out and the *Tango* and *Showboat* were surrendered without opposition, but Cornero was not so easily dislodged. There was a nine-day siege, during which he turned fire hoses on Warren's men and threatened to hoist the Japanese flag. Eventually, a deal was made. Cornero was given his freedom, in return for which he paid a modest fine, and the authorities got the opportunity to smash roulette wheels and slot machines for the benefit of eager newsmen.

In 1946 Cornero and Elmer Perry decided to give the floating casino idea one more whirl, this time using a refurbished mine layer called the *Lux.* Almost immediately, it was seized by the Coast Guard. Urged on by Earl Warren—now governor of California—it declared that the vessel was a hazard to navigation. Not long after, Perry was gunned down in the street near the La Brea tar pits. The Beverly Hills Club was taken over by restaurateur Tiny Naylor, who operated it as an eminently respectable establishment.

There would never again be anything like the gambling ships because Las Vegas, just a few hours' drive from L.A., would soon provide gambling on a scale undreamed of in the thirties. Tony Cornero survived just long enough to become part of the Vegas legend. It was he who built the Stardust—one of the earliest showplaces on the Strip—but, before it was quite finished, he dropped dead while shooting craps at the Desert Inn. He was $10,000 behind at the time.

GIFTS.

Bountiful gift-giving—being secure enough to share your riches—was a logical extension of the accumulation of personal possessions. Female guests at George Raft's flashy home would sometimes unfold their dinner napkins to discover a hundred-dollar bill or a piece of fine jewelry. At "Paradise," Cecil B. DeMille's ranch, women found bottles of perfume confected from blossoms grown on the ranch alongside their place settings. At cocktail time in "Paradise," a valet would bring in a basket full of baubles —costume jewelry, French perfume, gold compacts—which the female guests could examine before dinner. Gathering at the billiard table, they would roll balls to determine the order in which they could choose these gifts. After dining, they had the chance to inspect them again, then make their selections. Often DeMille would throw in a costly uncut gem and derive considerable pleasure from the fact that it was not chosen over the less valuable trifles.

Fans were particularly intrigued by the romantic tokens exchanged by star couples. If one is to believe the February 1931 issue of *Photoplay*, Douglas Fairbanks, Jr., gave Joan Crawford a portable dressing room for Christmas, which stepmother-in-law Mary Pickford was going to furnish for her. Among Pickford's gifts to Doug, Sr., were an oyster-shaped swimming pool, a bar shipped from a Nevada saloon, and a .45 pistol supposed to have killed twenty German soldiers in World War I. As a wedding present for his bride, Lupe Velez, in 1933, Johnny Weismuller purchased a thirty-four-foot schooner he christened the *Santa Guadalupe.* By the following Christmas, Lupe was giving Johnny a pair of boxing gloves with a card reading, "Darling. So you can punch me if I leave you again." Barbara Stanwyck gave Bob Taylor the horse he rode in *Billy the Kid,* and George Raft gave race horses to two of his girl friends, Virginia Pine and Betty Grable. Carole Lombard sent Gable a Ford ambulance painted red as a Valentine's gift. (The public wouldn't read about the hand-knitted penis warmer she reputedly gave him until thirty-five years later.) Lombard was legendery for her generosity, but often her acts of kindness had a prankish twist. An ex-Sennett bathing beauty, she sent Sennett's assistant director, Eddie Cline, a dozen custard pies every Christmas, and director Norman Taurog was the recipient of a two-hundred-pound bear. The ailing W. C. Fields once received a live piglet and a bicycle from Carole, commemorating a long and slovenly story Fields had once told her. The gift perked the comedian up sufficiently for him to be evicted from the hospital for riding down the corridors with the pig on a leash.

Studios would throw in the bonus gift of a new car or yacht or plane at the signing of a mutually beneficial contract with a major star or—like the $10,000 ermine coat Universal gave Deanna Durbin following *Three Smart Girls*—at the successful completion of a film. In 1922 Jesse Lasky presented Valentino with a set of gold-plated golf clubs. At Christmas and on other suitable occasions, barrelsful of presents were heaped upon the powerful gossip columnists. Louella Parsons acquired a mirrored bathroom in this way, courtesy of Carole Lombard, and Hedda Hopper's gray French poodle, Beau Beau, was a gift from Ann Sheridan.

When a production was completed, it was traditional for the crew to give the director a gift and for the star to dispense mass largess upon the crew and fellow cast members. After one of Mae West's films, she presented vanloads of expensive luggage to everyone, adding a diamond-and-sapphire-studded watch for the director and a gold and chromium desk set for the producer. Marion Davies' postproduction gifts were proverbially lavish. Pat O'Brien recalls receiving a wrist watch from her, after they made *Page Miss Glory* together, every numeral of which was a baguette diamond. Norma Shearer, a perfume fanatic, gave bottles of $30-an-ounce scent to all the female principals of one of her pictures. To commemorate the first anniversary of Joan Fontaine's contract with his studio, David Selznick presented her with a complete set of bone china, as well as a $30,000 bonus check. By their second anniversary, however, the relationship had degenerated to the point where his gift was a potted plant with a $5 price tag attached.

In a class by itself was the gift John Barrymore's pals sent him for his fifty-fifth birthday: a nude girl wrapped in cellophane and tied with a big silver bow.

GOOD GUYS.

Every veteran grip or gaffer in Hollywood has his repertoire of stories about both temperamental prima donnas and unflappable pros. It is almost impossible, for example, to find anyone with a bad word to say about Jean Harlow or Carole Lombard. They are examples of stars who did not take their position in life too seriously, arrived at the lot on time, worked hard, knew their lines, understood the camera, took direction well, got along with their costars, and generally helped create a relaxed atmosphere on set. Understandably, such actresses were adored by crews, and by almost everyone they came into contact with. Another of these was Barbara Stanwyck. Even the ultra-critical Cecil B. DeMille was lost in admiration for her, stating in his autobiography that he had never worked with an actress more co-operative or less temperamental. Dolores Del Rio, Joan Blondell, Rosalind Russell, Rita Hayworth, and the young Lana Turner were other favorites with crews. Marlene Dietrich is said always to have been ready to take the time to commiserate with and reassure her co-workers, and was almost as famous for her soothing chicken soup as was the M-G-M commissary. Make-up man Bob Schiffer reports that when he worked with her, she would often present him with strudel and pies she had just taken out of the oven.

Many top performers came from working-class and lower-middle-class backgrounds and, despite their acquired wealth and burgeoning aspirations, felt very much at home with the working stiffs on the set. Clark Gable's dressing room door was usually open and he liked nothing better than to take a prop man aside for a discussion of his newest hunting rifle or fishing rod, or to straddle a sawhorse and play a few hands of a cardgame called "gedunk" while waiting for the next setup. One trick Gable indulged in, along with a few other performers—Marion Davies and George Raft, for instance—infuriated the front office, but endeared him to his co-workers down on the sound stages. Sometimes, toward the end of the day, he would deliberately fluff his lines so that the extras could either collect overtime or —since Gable had a five o'clock quitting hour written into his contract— get another day of work. Raft would also persuade casting directors to pack

ONE OF THE MOST POPULAR STARS ON THE M-G-M LOT WAS
JEAN HARLOW, HERE SHOWN EMERGING FROM A MOBILE
BATHROOM.

as many extras as possible into crowd scenes, many of them his old buddies
from New York.

Some top players were well known for their acts of generosity, while
others preferred to bestow their kindness less publicly. Marion Davies was
the guardian angel of first Metro then Warners, coming to the aid of anyone
in need, from the crippled mother of an electrician to an office boy requiring an eye operation. At Christmas, dressed in her red and white clown
costume from *Polly of the Circus,* Marion would bring in dozens of her
hardly worn dresses and ask each extra to choose one, then she would
hand out hundreds of baskets containing the makings of complete turkey
dinners. Joan Crawford quietly turned over a percentage of her income to
pay for medical aid for the underprivileged, and for twelve years supported
a four-bed ward, for the use of her co-workers, at Santa Monica Hospital.

Aside from such gestures of generosity toward the studio "family,"
Hollywood personalities became involved with organized philanthropies of
all kinds. There was hardly anyone who did not participate, at some time
or another, in charity concerts at places like the Shrine Auditorium or
benefit radio broadcasts. Many others made more direct contributions to a
wide range of charities. Norma Shearer donated all her radio earnings to

ROSALIND RUSSELL, SEEN HERE AT A CAST PARTY WITH FRED MACMURRAY AND CREW MEMBERS, WAS A FAVORITE OF HER CO-WORKERS.

the National Foundation for Infantile Paralysis, Loretta Young was president of the St. Anne's Foundation, an adoption service for unwed mothers, and Bette Davis headed the Tailwaggers, an organization that—as well as caring for abandoned dogs—trained Seeing Eye dogs for the blind. Probably, though, no one in Hollywood gave more to charity than Marion Davies, and it is said that, by the late twenties, her philanthropies accounted for a greater proportion of her spendings than her grandiose homes and lavish entertainments. In 1926 she acquired several acres in Los Angeles as the future site of the Marion Davies Children's Clinic, which opened in 1932, largely financed by her own $2.1 million donation. In the fifties she gave another $1.5 million toward the building of a children's wing at the UCLA Medical Center.

There are few areas of philanthropy that have not benefited from the Hollywood movie colony, but always they have been particularly concerned with looking after their own, and the most remarkable example of this has been the success of the Motion Picture Relief Fund. This had its roots in the World War I Motion Picture War Service Association, which was founded in 1918 to provide for the wives and dependents of studio workers who had gone into the service. In 1921 a Hollywood branch of the Actors'

125

JOAN BENNETT OFFERS SANDWICHES FOR A GOOD CAUSE.

Fund of America was formed and began to perform charitable work within the community. (One of the first beneficiaries of this program was a widow living in a tent with her four children. The Lasky studio provided materials and labor to improve their living quarters, and extra work was found for the woman.)

In 1923 the Motion Picture Relief Fund—the present body—was incorporated, with Joseph Schenck as its first president and Mary Pickford as vice-president. The Board of Trustees included Harold Lloyd, Douglas Fairbanks, Mae Murray, William S. Hart, Cecil B. DeMille, Jesse Lasky, Donald Crisp, Hal Roach, and Irving Thalberg. Rev. Neal Dodd—an Episcopalian clergyman who portrayed ministers in many Hollywood movies—was the chief administrator of the Fund, which began by giving modest handouts. In 1932 a payroll deduction plan was instituted which made the possibility of the Fund becoming a kind of social security system for the motion picture industry seem quite feasible. Soon after Jean Hersholt was elected president of the Fund and George Bagnall treasurer in 1938, this became a reality. In 1942 the Motion Picture Country House —a retirement home for ex-studio employees—was opened on a forty-eight-acre site in Woodland Hills. Six years later, a hospital was added to the complex. Today that hospital has 180 beds and is equipped to the highest standards. (Outpatient care is provided both there and at the Fund's headquarters on La Brea Boulevard.)

Money for the Fund's programs has come from a variety of sources other than payroll deductions. "The Screen Guild Show"—a once popular radio show—provided over $5 million, and many prominent movie world personalities have made substantial personal donations or bequests.

GOSSIPS.

In the heyday of the hollywood gossip column, it was estimated that Hedda Hopper and Louella Parsons enjoyed a combined daily readership of about 75 million. Many other columnists added to the weight of information, trivia, and innuendo that rolled from the presses, but these two women— former friends who became archrivals—wielded a kind of power that in retrospect seems almost incomprehensible. This power derived from their own ambition and ruthlessness, from their position of journalistic privilege

Gossips

—their flagship papers were the two most influential in Los Angeles, hence those read by the Hollywood community—and from the fact that each arrived on the scene at precisely the right moment.

Gossip can be titillating, even years after the fact, but gossip in the present tense can be explosive. Daily journalism gave Hedda and Louella the opportunity to break a story at breakfast tables from coast to coast before it had even filtered down to the fashionable watering holes of the movie colony; they were so far ahead of the game that often a star's secret was common knowledge while he was still deciding whether or not to confide it to his best friend. The monthly fan magazines could not compete with this immediacy, and only the daily trades, with their extremely limited circulations, were substantial rivals.

Apart from their instinctive grasp of how to manipulate people and information, the two women could hardly have been more different. Louella, for all her vagueness—real and cultivated—and despite her prosaic appearance, seems to have been a woman of passion, never happy unless she was in love. The movies and love (seen through the filter of movies) were her life. Hedda, by contrast—although a great beauty in her day—apparently eschewed romantic attachments in the long years after the dissolution of her marriage to stage star De Wolf Hopper. She was as incisive as Louella was hazy, and, while she too was a defender of Hollywood, she saw it from the position of one who had long known it from the inside. She had strong political views and once—before becoming a columnist—was announced as a candidate for local office. (Louella, conversely, was capable of writing, in April of 1939, immediately following the fascist invasion of Albania: "The deadly dullness of the last week was lifted today when Darryl Zanuck admitted he had bought all rights to Maurice Maeterlinck's *The Bluebird.*") Hedda found her calling after years of struggle and failure in other fields. Louella recognized her vocation at a relatively early age, and her career followed an ascending curve of success until finally she lapsed into self-parody.

Louella Parsons was born Louella Oettinger in 1880 in Freeport, Illinois. Her parents were of Jewish descent, but were practicing Episcopalians (Louella was later to become an ardent Catholic); her father and brother operated a small clothing store. She was in her twenties when the movies became a national phenomenon and she was entranced from the beginning. She was married briefly to a man named John Parsons, by whom she had her only child, Harriet, then—after working for a spell in the syndication department of the Chicago *Tribune*—she landed a job as story editor at the Essanay Studio in the same city, contributing occasional scenarios of her own. Laid off by Essanay, she compiled a book called *How to Write for the Movies,* published in 1915, then began to do film reviews and movie columns for the Chicago *Record-Herald*. In one feature,

128

LOUELLA PARSONS WITH HEDY LAMARR.

"Seen on Screen," she included news of the stars and snippets of interview material, and it was from this that her gossip column evolved.

Meanwhile, she appears to have become the wife of Jack McCaffrey—a riverboat captain—though later she refused to speak of this marriage, and the records of it have been lost. In 1918 Louella moved to New York, where she became motion picture editor of the *Morning Telegraph*. Captain Jack accompanied her, but now she met another Irish charmer, Peter Brady—a union leader and a banker with extensive political connections—and Louella dumped the captain in his favor.

After becoming acquainted with Marion Davies in New York around 1919, Louella ran against the tide by praising Davies' films. In 1922, after her sterling defense of Marion's performance in *When Knighthood Was in Flower,* William Randolph Hearst invited Louella to join the staff of the New York *American,* where she was promoted to motion picture editor in 1924. She did not visit Hollywood until she went there as Marion Davies' guest in 1925. Later that year, Louella returned to California to recuperate from a bout with tuberculosis, and the following year she moved permanently to Hollywood, living in an apartment at the Villa Carlotta and supplying her copy to Hearst's *Examiner.*

It has often been suggested that Hearst was in Louella's power because she was aboard his yacht at the time of the mysterious death of Thomas Ince. There are those who believe that Hearst killed Ince and that Louella witnessed the crime, but there is, in fact, little hard evidence to support the murder theory. In any case, Louella can hardly have been present, since Ince died several months before she first set foot in California. The truth seems to be that Hearst employed Louella because she helped sell newspapers.

During her New York period, Louella had begun to develop a definite format for her column, perhaps inspired by the chatty local news sections in the small-town papers she had grown up with. She also started to cultivate her celebrated journalistic mannerisms—writing of "madcap Mabel Normand" and exclaiming "Tempus sure does fugit!"—but as yet her tone was generally benign. Only after she was well established in the Hollywood community did she begin to show her teeth.

One of her first campaigns—it seems harmless enough now, but made considerable waves at the time—was for candor about the marital status of stars. At that time, studios were in the habit of concealing the information that many of their players were married, but Louella succeeded in changing this policy, which had far-reaching consequences for the future of the gossip column as a genre. If the public did not know that a star was married, what mileage could a columnist get out of the fact that the person in question was seen out with someone other than his wife? Or that a divorce was in the offing?

Over lunch at the Vendome, or during a party at Pickfair, Louella would often seem detached and distracted, drifting from table to table and group to group like some vagrant blimp buffeted by random breezes. George Eells, author of *Hedda and Louella,* suggests that Louella carefully cultivated her eccentric social manner as a kind of camouflage that enabled her to float from conversation to conversation without running the risk of appearing deliberately rude. Her progress might seem absurd, and might provoke chuckles behind her back, but it got her to where the gossip was juiciest. In her office, across the street from the *Examiner,* she was anything but vague, banging out her daily columns plus reviews and a full page for the Sunday paper. By phone, she checked with her intelligence network, which included switchboard girls, telegraph operators, beauty parlor employees, doctors' receptionists, and so forth. Her power was such that she could reach Hollywood's elite simply by picking up a phone, but it was her anonymous sources who supplied her with many of her biggest breaks. A star could not send roses to his girl friend without considering the possibility that the florist might dial Louella the moment he left the shop.

Louella's one regret about moving to Hollywood had been the fact that she had to leave Peter Brady behind in New York. On a trip East to visit her beau, she met Dr. Harry Martin—better known as "Doc" or "Docky" —who was also traveling on the *Chief.* As a medical student, Docky had been looked on as having a brilliant future, but he was rather unambitious and spent much of his time drinking and brawling. A urologist, he had come to specialize in the treatment of venereal disease and was, at the time of his first auspicious encounter with Louella, house doctor to the establishment of Lee Frances, the madame of Hollywood's choicest bordello. Louella was so enchanted by this unlikely suitor that she soon forgot Peter Brady. After her marriage to Docky, Louella's network of medical informants became staggeringly efficient. Through him she established hot lines to the laboratories where rabbit tests were performed, so that she was often able to print with confidence that a certain celebrity was pregnant before the mother-to-be had heard the news from her own doctor.

As Louella's husband, Docky was awarded with a $30,000-a-year post as studio physician at 20th Century-Fox. Such sinecures were not unusual in Hollywood, so this might not have attracted much comment had not so many people doubted his professional competence. Primarily, these doubters were disturbed by Docky's apparent drinking problem, though Louella herself seems to have accepted the situation with equanimity. According to one famous anecdote, when informed that her husband had passed out at a party, Louella replied, "Don't disturb him. He has to operate tomorrow."

As Louella became more entrenched, her column became more and more catty. She had counted many of the stars of the silent period as her personal friends—she and Bebe Daniels were virtually inseparable—and she treated them accordingly in print. Newcomers were not always so fortunate. She wrote, for instance, of "the buxom, blonde Mae West, fat, fair and I don't know how near forty." Mae West arrived in Hollywood as an established Broadway star, and this, it seems, made her a natural target for Louella's bile. She could, on the other hand, be extremely kind to the neophyte working his or her way up from the ranks. Such aspirants presented no threat to established values, and their gratitude might be useful, in time. If Louella was not especially political, she was very much for the establishment and so was apt to apply the thumbscrews once in a while to the likes of Melvyn Douglas, who showed mildly leftist leanings. But if she had a pet hate, it was intellectualism. Her column exalted the taste of the *pompier,* and anyone who threatened to contaminate Hollywood with high culture was given short shrift.

Fearing Louella's claws, stars courted her. Carole Lombard made a point of calling her once a week, and would drop by her house with little gifts she felt Louella just had to have. Later, Lombard went through much the same routine with Hedda. Both columnists were showered with floral tributes the year round—their homes must have looked like greenhouses —and at Christmas they were inundated with expensive gifts (see GIFTS). But, more significantly, celebrities did their best to stay in favor by channeling information that might help flesh out a column.

By the mid-thirties, more and more people were beginning to resent Louella's power. Rival publications printed attacks on her, and there were rumblings in the executive suites of the major studios. One bone of contention was the fact that she had become very sloppy, relying on her memory for "facts" rather than bothering to check things out in the files. (It had been estimated that upwards of 50 percent of her items were fallacious.) Louella shrugged these errors off by printing bland apologies and retractions. More serious, from the studios' point of view, was that they had recklessly granted her a forty-eight-hour exclusive on key stories —which did little to endear studio publicists to other reporters. The industry, acting in unison, tried to rescind this deal, but Louella demonstrated her powerful position by breaking stories about contracts—quoting specific terms and salaries—before they were even signed. Apparently, she was getting this information from agents—notably Myron Selznick's partner, Frank Joyce—presumably in return for favorable attention to be shown toward their clients. The studios protested and Louella agreed to stop the practice, so long as her forty-eight-hour exclusive was restored.

It was in this climate that Hedda Hopper made her debut as a columnist, at a time when there were many people in Hollywood willing to lend a hand to anyone who showed promise of giving Louella some serious competition. According to Hedda's own account, Howard Denby of the Esquire Features Syndicate approached her to write a column for him, on the advice of Andy Hervey of the M-G-M publicity department. Hervey told Denby that Hedda was the person he went to when he needed inside information. Her first columns appeared in the Los Angeles *Times* and a dozen other papers in 1938.

Hedda Hopper was born Elda Furry in Holidaysburg, Pennsylvania, on May 2, 1885. Her family were Quakers and her father was in the meat business. At the age of twenty-two, Hedda made tracks for Broadway, where she quickly rose from chorine to playing leads in musical comedies, despite a rather mediocre singing voice. In New York she became the fifth wife of De Wolf Hopper, a prominent stage star of the time—a man older than her father. They had one child, De Wolf, Jr. (called Bill), but the marriage was not a success and ended in divorce.

Hedda had been to Hollywood with her husband in 1915, at the time of his abortive film career, and in 1923 she decided to try her luck there herself. Although a striking woman, she was then close to forty, and no one was prepared to groom her for stardom, but she managed to eke out a living playing a variety of small parts in big pictures and bigger parts in programmers. One of her greatest supporters was Louella, who gave her dozens of plugs and at one point dubbed her "Queen of the Quickies."

Despite her stage background, the arrival of sound did not advance her career, and in the early years of the Depression—although under contract to M-G-M—she was living in a gloomy basement apartment, saving every penny she could to send her son to the fashionable and expensive Catalina Island School, spending whatever was left on her showy wardrobe (of which Louella kept her readers abreast, especially the famous hats), and on trips to Europe, generally in the company of screenwriter Frances Marion, Hedda's closest friend.

At the same time, her sharp wit and gracious bearing kept her very much in the social swim. She had known Marion Davies since 1921 and was a frequent guest at San Simeon, which was enough to put the seal on her acceptability. Hearst enjoyed her company and would often ask her to show new guests around the estate, claiming that she knew it as well as he did. At M-G-M also, she was frequently called upon to escort visiting VIPs, but none of this did anything to further her acting career. As the thirties progressed, her roles became slimmer and slimmer, and she had to find new ways to supplement her income. For some time she had made a little money on small real estate deals, and this continued, but she also began to accept modeling jobs, always fighting to provide for her son in a manner befitting a young gentleman.

In October 1935—probably through the good offices of Marion Davies —Hedda began her journalistic career, writing weekly Hollywood fashion articles for the Washington *Post*. Louella blessed this enterprise in print. In 1937 Dema Harshbarger of the NBC casting office in Hollywood— later Hedda's business manager—succeeded in placing her on a number of radio programs to chat about a variety of show business topics. Shortly after came her big break with the Esquire Syndicate.

At first, it seems, Hedda had considerable doubts about her ability to write a daily column, but she agreed to give it a try. Her initial efforts were bland in the extreme and gave Louella little cause for concern. After a couple of months, however, Ida Koverman, Louis B. Mayer's executive assistant, decided to give Hedda some advice. Mayer himself may have been behind this move, as he strongly felt Louella needed some competition, but Mrs. Koverman was a powerful figure and could have been acting on her own initiative. She was a close friend of Hedda's and considered her a political ally. (Koverman, formerly secretary to Herbert Hoover, was a major force in the California Republican party.) In any case, Mrs. Koverman threw a hen party for Hedda—inviting Norma Shearer, Jeanette MacDonald, Claudette Colbert, Joan Crawford, Sophie Tucker, some press

HEDDA HOPPER EXCHANGING SOME GOSSIP WITH JUDY GARLAND, AS DAVID ROSE LOOKS ON, 1941.

people, and others—using the occasion to warn the guest of honor that her column would get nowhere if she tried to be everybody's best friend. It was time, Hedda was told, to stop pulling her punches.

Hedda heeded this advice and the column began to catch on. By the middle of 1939, Louella must have realized that she had a real fight on her hands. The battle would continue unabated for more than two decades, as the pair connived to outwit each other in their pursuit of the scoop. Now it was impossible to give your story, whatever it was, to one woman without incurring the public wrath of the other. A few people—like Ginger Rogers, who had been excommunicated by Louella for refusing to appear on her radio show—were delighted by Hedda's ascendancy. Most, though, wishing to offend neither columnist, found the new situation decidedly disquieting.

Hedda, given her background, had a ready-made set of informants— producers, performers, directors, crew—and she was ruthless in pursuit of a story. When Lana Turner married Bob Topping, Hedda is said to have telephoned the press agent of the Beverly Hills Hotel, where the couple was holed up, and demanded the number of their bungalow. Her plan was to enter, disguised as a maid, in the hope of catching the newlyweds in bed together. When not engaged in such subterfuge, she worked out of a cluttered office, half a block from Hollywood and Vine, which her onetime leg man, Jaik Rothenstien, has described as being crammed with hat boxes, battered furniture, and scrapbooks. Paste and scissors were always ready on her ancient desk and the walls were covered with framed pictures, ranging from an Adrian fashion sketch to a Bugs Bunny cartoon. Of the dozens of eight-by-ten glossies on display, only two—portraits of Marie Dressler and Grace Moore—were of women.

The attitude of the industry toward Hedda and Louella was decidedly ambiguous. The nervousness they provoked was virtually universal, but there were few people who were prepared to risk translating their secret resentment into open hostility, though occasionally people did revolt. Joan Bennett sent Hedda a skunk as a Valentine gift, accompanying it with a card that read:

> Here's a little Valentine
> That very plainly tells
> The reason it reminded me so much of you—(*over*)
> It smells!

More often, the tone of communications with Hedda was essentially fawning, as can be judged from her collected papers—letters, telegrams, transcripts of interviews—which are now in the archives of the Academy of Motion Picture Arts and Sciences. The following wire, for example, is dated November 15, 1940:

> HEDDA YOU OLD HOPTOAD. FIRST YOU WENT TO
> TEXAS. NOW YOU'RE IN ARIZONA. THAT'S COW
> COUNTRY AND THAT MEANS COWBOYS. AND COW-
> BOYS MEAN LOTS OF FUN FOR ALL AMERICA.
> SO HAVE A GOOD TIME. BUT FOR GOSH SAKES
> DON'T FORGET TO COME BACK TO US. REGARDS
> AND SUCCESS TO THE "ARIZONA" GANG.

This was signed by Gary Cooper, Bill Boyd, John Wayne, Harry Carey, and Roy Rogers. In June of the following year, Hedda received this telegram:

> DEAREST HEDDA: I OWE YOU THE BIGGEST
> APOLOGY OF MY LIFE AND HERE IT COMES.
> DRAKE SAID QUOTE THE MAGAZINE PEOPLE LOOK
> AND LIFE HAVE TO MEET THEIR DEADLINE SO WE
> MUST SHOW THEM THE PICTURE NO MATTER
> HOW BAD OR INCOMPLETE VERY SOON UNQUOTE.
> I SAID MUST WE. HE SAID WE MUST. FADE OUT.
> FADE IN. INSERT TRADE PAPER. QUOTE WELLES

SHOWS HIS PICTURE TONIGHT UNQUOTE. CLOSEUP.
MY FACE REGISTERS HORROR AND OTHER MIXED
EMOTIONS. AMOUNTS TO THIS. I DIDN'T KNOW
WHAT TIME IT WAS. FULLY REALIZE I HAVE
BROKEN A SOLEMN PROMISE THAT YOU'D BE THE
FIRST TO SEE KANE. PLEASE UNDERSTAND AND
FORGIVE. COME TONIGHT IF YOU MUST BUT IT
STILL STINKS. MANY KEY SHOTS ARE MISSING OR
ONLY THE TESTS ARE CUT IN AND WE NEED
MUSIC LIKE BRITAIN NEEDS PLANES. LOVE.
ORSON

Some of the biggest stars in the business, including a few who are generally considered fearless rebels against the system, showered her with bouquets—both literal and metaphorical—and notes of endearment. It should be remembered, however—and for this reason it would be unfair to quote some of the more extreme examples—that Hedda had long been a colleague and friend of some of these people, so it is not always easy to know where friendship leaves off and fear begins.

The publicists, press agents, and such who dealt with Hedda and Louella on a daily basis found that the two had different vices and virtues. Hedda is generally accused of a greater tendency toward catty malevolence. According to one story, Merle Oberon, the target of a great deal of flak in the column, asked to have a meeting with Hedda. Lunch at the Vine Street Derby was arranged, and Oberon asked what she had done to arouse Hedda's ire. Hedda is said to have replied, "Nothing, dear. It's bitchery, sheer bitchery." Not everyone took this kind of thing without retaliating. Joseph Cotten (after having been accused of romancing Deanna Durbin) kicked Hedda in the behind and Ann Sheridan once dumped a dish of mashed potatoes in her lap.

Still, Hedda is reputed to have been more trustworthy than Louella in some ways. If you gave her a story "off the record," she would generally —unless given good cause not to—respect the confidence. Usually, too, she declined to take advantage of her position arbitrarily, whereas Louella —especially in her later years—was apt to do so just for the hell of it. Tom Jones, who was for a while in charge of press relations at the Cocoanut Grove, recalls that when Louella was invited to an opening, she would invariably say that she was sorry but she had invited a dozen guests to dinner that night. It was understood, of course, that the Grove management would then suggest that she bring her guests along at the room's expense. Louella would accept and then encourage her companions to order the most expensive items on the menu—this was such an established routine that the management included it as an item in opening-night budgets. Hedda, on the other hand, never asked for special favors.

In retrospect, the keys to the success of these women seems to have been their timing, their drive, their energy, and their flamboyance. But even more, it was that they recognized Hollywood as the ultimate American small town and they treated it as such—satisfying their readers' nostalgia for the fast-vanishing world of the close community, with its gossip of everyday happenings and occasional scandals to which everyone is privy.

There was, of course, one columnist in America more powerful than either Parsons or Hopper. Walter Winchell, whose Sunday evening radio broadcasts made his voice familiar to millions who never saw his column, appeared in a few movies and visited Los Angeles every year—staying at the Ambassador and working out of the 20th Century-Fox publicity department—but he never felt at home in California. He printed plenty of Hollywood stories, but, since he was not part of the film colony, he did not exert the same day-to-day influence there that was enjoyed by the two women.

Sidney Skolsky, while scarcely enjoying the same kind of reputation as Hedda, Louella, or Winchell, was considered an unusually accurate reporter and built up a respectable following. Born in New York City, he began his career there as a press agent for Earl Carroll, then took over Mark Hellinger's gossip spot on the New York *Daily News* before moving to L.A. to join Louella at the *Examiner*. (Hellinger, meanwhile, became a producer—first at Warners, then at Universal—and served as one of Hedda's key informants.) In his first column for the Hearst press, Skolsky printed the impeccably correct information that Greta Garbo would not marry Leopold Stokowski. Unfortunately, Louella had a front-page story that same day announcing that the famous couple *had* made wedding plans. Louella never forgave Skolsky for this and seems to have put pressure on her boss to get rid of her new rival. Skolsky found that some of his best stories were being cut from his column without explanation. Piqued by this, he submitted his resignation. He had no doubt who had been behind the deletions, and, encountering Louella in a restaurant a few weeks later, he vented his feelings—and the vehemence behind this gesture can be judged by the fact that he was a chronic hypochondriac—by biting her arm.

Other syndicates were ready to welcome Skolsky. With no staff, and using Schwab's drugstore as an office, he worked on the run—hitching rides from studio to restaurant to party, since he did not drive. He was notoriously persistent, even managing to sneak onto a closed Garbo set. (He was caught and thrown off, but not until he had his story.) On another occasion he had the satisfaction of spanking Shirley Temple. A friend of Clifford Odets', he was the most liberal of the columnists—at the opposite pole from Hedda—and probably the most literate.

Gossips

Sheilah Graham—later famous as F. Scott Fitzgerald's mistress—arrived in Hollywood in the mid-thirties after working as a C. B. Cochrane showgirl in London and writing fiction for the Bell Syndicate in New York. As a gossip columnist for the North American Newspaper Alliance, she established a reputation for independence, resisting studio pressure on a number of occasions. (At one point she refused an M-G-M demand that she submit her column to the studio for censorship.) Her power was always relatively limited, however, and never posed much of a challenge to the front-runners.

Among lesser lights, Frederick Othman and Robin Coons represented UPI and AP respectively. Erskine Johnson and Jimmy Starr were second-stringers for the Hearst papers. (When Louella was on vacation, her daughter Harriet—billed as Parsons, Jr.—or Jerry Hoffman, her top leg man, pinch hit for her.) Lloyd Pantages, of the theater family, also had a shot with the Hearst chain, and George McCall, an ex-*Variety* reporter, had his brief moment of glory, catching Stokowski at a jam session and nicknaming him "Stoky."

A more prominent figure was Jimmy Fidler, whose column was carried in 187 papers by 1939. Fidler had been a bit player, Sid Grauman's assistant, and a press agent. In the latter occupation, he started out with Famous Players-Lasky, then went independent, building up a clientele that included Valentino, Wallace Reid, Edmund Lowe, Janet Gaynor, Clara Bow, and Gloria Swanson. His business prospered until he made the mistake of suing Constance Bennett for services rendered, scaring off a number of other clients. At about this time, however, in 1933, Dorothy Jordan asked him to help her prepare for a radio interview. He conducted the interview himself and more followed: In 1934, he was given his own radio gossip show. The following year, he began a newspaper column for the McNaught syndicate.

After Parsons and Hopper, Fidler had the best network of informants in Hollywood. He was so secretive about his sources that he had his spies identify themselves on the phone by code numbers rather than by name. A pugnacious little man, he made himself unpopular in Hollywood with his critical "open letters" and his frank discussions of the private lives of various celebrities. After enjoying the none-too-rare distinction of being punched out by Errol Flynn (see FIGHTS), he always traveled with a bodyguard.

For all the success of his column, he was perhaps most famous for his radio show, "Jimmy Fidler in Hollywood," sponsored by Drene shampoo, in which—despite a high-pitched voice—he managed a fair imitation of Winchell's staccato delivery, ending each show with, "Good night to you and you and especially to you!"

Radio, in the late thirties and forties, provided an important extension to the gossip column, but it was not an easy medium to master. Sidney Skolsky, despite his cleverness with words, never came across well over the air waves, but Hedda, the trained actress, did. Louella failed in attempts at radio "columns" in 1928 and 1931 before scoring a considerable success with "Hollywood Hotel," a show that combined musical numbers, interviews, and sketches, interspersed with gossip and the background chatter of "fans" ("Isn't that Ida Lupino over there?"). While Louella received $1,500 a show, her celebrity guests each got a case of Campbell's soup. When the Screen Actors Guild ruled that members could no longer work below scale on radio, except for charity, Louella's show quickly died.

Homes.

Few aspects of Hollywood have supplied its critics with more occasions for sarcasm and irony than its domestic architecture. Evelyn Waugh, given to drooling over mildewed examples of the Gothic Revival—as long as they had the good fortune to be crumbling into his native landscape—failed to recognize that the comic opera chateaux and overblown cottages of Southern California drew their inspirations from sources not far removed from those that produced the English "folly." Writers born east of the Great Divide thought it permissible to re-create a Tudor manor house on the Palisades of the Hudson, or in some garden suburb of London, but found it wholly inappropriate to indulge the same nostalgic impulse in the foothills of the Santa Monica mountains. Many were disturbed by the failure of fashionable Hollywood architects to observe a strict unity of idiom. The practice of, for example, grafting a chimney copied from Hampton Court onto a building that was otherwise an approximation of a Spanish-American ranch house was generally frowned upon by those raised in more conservative architectural circles.

All the criticisms could be reduced to one basic objection: "Hollywood has no tradition of its own." The charming wooden "California" bungalows, still to be found in the older sections of Los Angeles, along with more ambitious buildings, such as the ones designed by architects like Greene and Greene, had provided the beginnings of a native style, but it

139

did not lend itself to the kind of grandeur that movie celebrities envisioned for themselves. Nor did the more radical modernists, like Richard Neutra and Rudolph Schindler, find many clients in the movie colony. Most stars and executives were seeking the traditional comforts and the conventional symbols of success that they had missed in childhood, and there were any number of architectural firms quite willing to indulge their clients' fantasies, however naïve, with little regard for either historical precedent or the teachings of the Bauhaus. Movie people welcomed the license to live in homes that were part movie set, part playground. Charlie Chaplin's was actually built by studio carpenters, who, however skilled, were not geared toward building for posterity. Sections of the house fell off from time to time (friends secretly nicknamed it "Breakaway House"), and neighbors half expected a strong breeze to topple it into Benedict Canyon.

In the early days, before the drift to Beverly Hills, there were many fine homes on Sunset Boulevard, west of La Brea. Beyond Highland, on Sunset, was a British colony. Other clusters of fashionable houses were situated east of Hollywood, in Los Feliz, and in the hills overlooking Cahuenga Pass. At that time, quite a few successful people still lived in apartment buildings, such as the La Ronda and the Andalusia, many of which were built around courtyards with fountains and Spanish tile. The most exclusive of these buildings was the Garden Court, which, for a number of years, refused to take tenants from the movie industry, making an exception only for the British and very proper J. Stuart Blackton. Other modish apartment buildings were situated on Franklin Avenue, where there was another British colony, just east of Gower.

From the beginning, though, people who made it big wanted their own suitable baronial manses. When Mary Pickford married Douglas Fairbanks in 1920, his gift to her was a hunting lodge built on a ridge between Benedict and Coldwater canyons. A reporter dubbed the lodge "Pickfair," and, after extensive remodeling and expansion, the large, L-shaped Tudor-style dwelling became the first of the showcase homes to catch the public imagination. (When, in 1932, Mary had Pickfair redecorated by Elsie de Wolfe as a gift for her husband, it was national news.) It was the proto-typical movie star residence, complete with imposing gates, stables, a tennis court, miniature golf course, and Beverly Hills' first swimming pool —with its own sandy beach. (As a matter of record, the movie colony's first swimming pool seems to have been installed a couple of years earlier at Francis X. Bushman's home on Grace Avenue in the Hollywood Hills.)

Others soon followed Fairbanks' example. Harold Lloyd acquired a sixteen-acre estate and built a huge villa in the Italian Renaissance style. Called "Greenacres," the building was set in meticulously landscaped grounds that featured a waterfall and a golf course. John Barrymore bought "Bella Vista," a modest hacienda that had been erected for King

Vidor, and expanded it into a rambling estate that eventually consisted of sixteen separate buildings containing forty-five rooms. Situated on a knoll above Sunset, overlooking the Los Angeles littoral and the ocean, were the two main buildings, joined by what one visitor described as "a sort of Turkish Pergola." Below these structures were two swimming pools, a well-stocked trout pond, a bowling green, a skeet-shooting range, an aviary filled with exotic birds, garden sheds, and quarters for a dozen servants. In the main buildings were a library—containing a notable collection of first editions—a gun room, and a trophy room which housed, among other things, a crocodile shot by Barrymore's wife, Dolores Costello, the mounted remains of a 560-pound marlin, a stuffed giant turtle, and a dinosaur egg (at that time, the only one in private hands). Guests could be entertained in an English tavern or in a frontier bar that Barrymore had had shipped down from Alaska. Supposedly, however, he preferred a quiet patio beside one of the pools, where he ate many of his meals at a rickety card table. When Bella Vista fell into disrepair, its owner took to referring to it as "that Chinese tenement."

Barrymore's good friend and drinking companion, W. C. Fields, also aspired to the life style of some eccentric squire transplanted from the pages of Fielding or Smollett. One of his homes, on DeMille Drive (a name Fields deeply resented) in Los Feliz, was an opulent complex of broad stairways and paneled rooms which he did his best to furnish like a pool hall. Outside was a lily pond, on which bobbed a toy sailboat presented to him by his secretary. In 1941 Christopher Quinn—the three-year-old son of Anthony Quinn and his wife, Katherine DeMille—fell into this pond and drowned, causing the distraught Fields to quickly sell the house.

Greta Garbo apparently had little time for Hollywood decorators, and only bothered to furnish two rooms of her Beverly Hills home—the bedroom and the drawing room—leaving the rest quite bare. Another European star, Emil Jannings, lived in a huge pseudocolonial mansion on Hollywood Boulevard, which he had rented from Joseph Schenck. It had a large garden, with the obligatory swimming pool and tennis court, and a gigantic living room filled with a forest of lamps of all shapes and sizes. The Jannings residence was full of animals—yapping chows, squawking parrots, and chattering monkeys—and at the foot of the garden was a chicken coop where the actor kept hens and roosters named for Garbo, Valentino, Pola Negri, Jack Gilbert, Conrad Veidt, and other notables who had earned this distinction, according to Josef Von Sternberg, by bringing a tribute of sausage meat.

Although the eccentric mode always flourished in Hollywood among those whose backgrounds permitted them to relish the absurdity of their situation, most Hollywood personalities were far more conventional. By

Overleaf, JOHN BARRYMORE IN HIS "CHINESE TENAMENT," 1931.

thinking of their homes as expressions of status, and being concerned with aggregations of symbols intended to signify "success," "good taste," and "respectability," they differed little from the *nouveaux riches* of any other sector of society. In her book *A Cast of Thousands,* Jill Schary Robinson described the lower rungs of Hollywood status seeking in the mid-thirties, when her father, Dore Schary, was an up-and-coming screenwriter. People rising in that world sought out large Mediterranean-style houses—"anything stucco with arches somewhere in the construction and embellishments of spikey black iron." These homes, it seems, tended to be furnished in a style she described as "vaguely Chinese," and each had to have a room decorated "like a lanai with tropical leaves printed on cushions. No-one was exactly sure what a lanai was, but the consensus was that it looked like a banana tree inside the house and all you had to do to achieve the desired effect was call up Ritt Brothers Tropical Furniture Co. I *guess* the lanai made everyone feel carefree and chattery, like monkeys having a cocktail party in Guam."

Those in the higher reaches of status seeking, of course, were more apt to have their homes built to order, and would seek the services of an architect with a reputation for manipulating the appropriate symbols. There were a number of firms that could work comfortably in a variety of idioms, ranging from the Monterey style through American Colonial and

MARLENE DIETRICH'S LIVING ROOM.

CLAUDETTE COLBERT POSES BEFORE HER HOME.

Rustic English to French Provincial. Other architects, like George Vernon Russell, were fond of blending stylized Regency with a soupcon of Streamline Moderne or a dash of Old Connecticut, as is well exemplified in the homes he designed for Sam Goldwyn and Billy Wilkerson, publisher of the *Hollywood Reporter*. Eclecticism was the norm. When John W. Myers and Edla Muir were called upon to design a home for the parents of Shirley Temple, they produced a fairy tale synthesis of rustic, Queen Anne, and Arthurian elements worthy of a painting by Burne-Jones or Rossetti. A few celebrities, favoring native western imagery, opted for the "ranch home" style developed in the late thirties by Cliff May and his followers.

The imagery of the house might be drawn from any source, but its floor plan seldom had anything to do with the floor plan of its ostensible model. Details might be essentially correct, but proportions were generally changed. These buildings were, with few exceptions, low and horizontal, functional and comfortable. Given the mild climate, an abundance of French doors was usually provided to allow for an easy flow between inner and outer space. Gardens, terraces, and patios served as ancillary rooms. However "antique" their exteriors, these houses were basically modern, from their all-electric kitchens to their four-car garages.

HOMES

William Powell's house, built adjacent to the Beverly Hills estate of automobile tycoon E. L. Cord, was designed by J. E. Dolena. It was a neoclassical pavilion built on a wooded lot that featured twin tennis courts with galleries for spectators. Jean Harlow helped decorate it, and, despite its rigorously traditional appearance, it was wired for all kinds of electric gadgetry. Alarm bells warned of the arrival of visitors, all doors could be operated by foot switches, and all major rooms were equipped with bars, one of which could be transformed into a grill at the touch of a button, a spit rising from the floor and charcoal burners emerging from a closet. Living there seems to have had all the charm of living inside a pinball machine, as Powell explained to the readers of *Picturegoer:*

> I built a house of dreams that turned out to be a house of devilish gadgets. The secret panels and disappearing doors never worked right. I'd push one button to go into the parlor and I'd find myself in the kitchen or garden. There were thirty-two rooms in that house and in every one something unexpected was happening. I've been haunted by weird nightmare memories ever since.

It was not surprising that studio-trained set designers were often called in to give interiors the right Hollywood panache. Ginger Rogers' hilltop home, off Coldwater Canyon, was largely the work of Van Nest Polgase and the RKO art department. Harold Grieve began his career as an art director at the Marshall Neilan studio and soon went into business on his own, eventually designing many interiors for celebrities like Miriam Hopkins and Paulette Goddard, who lived in a gingerbread rustic right out of a Silly Symphony. Grieve was capable of being as imperious as his clients. In *Silent Star* Colleen Moore describes how she was introduced to him just as he was launching his own business:

> I looked at this tall, thin young man . . . and feeling like a movie star, I suppose . . . I said, "How nice. I'd like to have you do my bathroom for me."
>
> He gave me an amused look. "Either I do your whole house, Miss Moore, or nothing."

According to the same source, Grieve used to claim that he covered his office rent each year just redoing John Gilbert's guest bedroom and bath:

> Hoping to marry Garbo, Jack had the bedroom done in European style with painted Venetian furniture, the bathroom in black marble with gold fixtures. When he married Ina Claire instead, the bath was torn out and redone in pink marble, the bedroom in peach color with French furniture.

MR. AND MRS. PETER LORRE AT HOME.

THE PROJECTION ROOM AT CECIL B. DEMILLE'S LAUGHLIN
PARK HOME, C. 1937.

After Jack married Virginia Bruce, the pink marble was replaced with
white, the bedroom done in pale blue and white with Early American
furniture.

A screening room was, of course, essential to the well-appointed Hollywood home, since everyone wanted to be able to entertain his guests with
the latest features and newsreels. For some reason, though, it was considered *de rigueur* in most circles to disguise the function of the room
when it was not in use, thus—when showtime arrived—bookcases slid
back to reveal screens and Renoirs were taken down to uncover projection
ports.

In the three-story colonial that William Randolph Hearst built for
Marion Davies on the beach at Santa Monica, it was the library that
transformed into a screening room, the screen itself rising from the floor
at the touch of a button. This house, where Hearst spent much of his time,
was scarcely less opulent than his "ranch" at San Simeon (see SAN
SIMEON). Discounting the servants' quarters—all that remains today—
there were in excess of one hundred rooms, half of them with their own

148

bathrooms. As with San Simeon, walls, ceilings, and whole chambers of this house were brought piecemeal from Europe. One room was finished entirely in gold leaf, and outside there was an enormous marble pool that could be crossed by a marble Venetian bridge. More than two thousand lockers were provided for guests who chose to swim in this pool or dip in the nearby Pacific.

The Santa Monica beach front—sometimes called "Millionaire's Row" —was fashionable years before Malibu was. Ben Lyon, who, with his wife, Bebe Daniels, owned four of the houses there, explains that when they first moved to the beach it was just a summer resort:

> Then people realized that winter is the best time at the beach. It's warmer in Santa Monica in winter than in town, and cooler in the summer. There was a wonderful colony along there. As you rode down the ramp from Ocean Avenue, Marion Davies was off to the right, and Harold Lloyd, Norma Shearer, Louis B. Mayer and Jesse Lasky had houses off in that direction. We were to the left of the ramp and down our way were George Bancroft and Leo McCarey. Fay Bainter was next to us, and Norma Talmadge built a lovely house—a little isolated, out on its own— probably the best built house on the beach.

MARION DAVIES' SANTA MONICA BEACH HOUSE, 1937.

HOMES

Constance Talmadge also had a house there—a rambling affair with a gymnasium—which was shared for some time by Cary Grant and Randolph Scott. Laura La Plante had a Tudor cottage at the beach, and Pickford and Fairbanks owned a Santa Monica house, but it was seldom used until after their divorce, when Fairbanks lived there for a while with his new bride, Lady Sylvia Ashley. One of the last homes to be built along that stretch of beach front was Darryl Zanuck's.

From the Coast Highway, these Santa Monica homes—most of which are still standing—appear quite modest. Looking down on them from the heights of Palisades Park, however, one can gain some idea of just how palatial they are—wings thrusting out to enclose swimming pools, tennis courts, and courtyards dense with tropical vegetation. Some are variants on the Monterey style, while others evoke echoes of Newport and Cape Cod.

Among the less pretentious homes at the beach was one of those belonging to the Lyons, but it launched the career of a man who, along with Harold Grieve, is one of the most famous interior designers to have come out of Hollywood. Billy Haines was once a leading man in silent films, and Ben Lyon recalls that this small beach house was Haines's first commission as a designer:

> Later, it got to the point where he wouldn't touch a job under a quarter of a million, but we had this little broken-down cottage on thirty feet of frontage and we said, "Bill, we want to make this attractive so we can rent it." He enclosed the porch and made it part of the living room and made it all nautical, and he decorated everything in red, white and blue. The bill for the whole thing, including some of the furniture, was twenty-five hundred dollars. Today, if he were alive, he wouldn't get you a chair for that.

Haines went on to establish an international reputation, but much of his work was done in Hollywood, and, like Harold Grieve, he knew how to make a star feel like a star. For Carole Lombard, he designed a drawing room hung with six shades of blue velvet and filled with Empire furniture. In her bedroom he placed an oversize bed, covered in plum-colored satin, on either side of which were mirrored screens. Later, when she married Clark Gable, Lombard learned to live in more homey surroundings.

Each personality had his own particular requirements. At Edward G. Robinson's home on Rexford Drive, a badminton court was torn down to make way for an art gallery. Josef von Sternberg's Neutra house near Chatsworth was built to withstand earthquakes and was partially surrounded by a moat. Among W. R. Hearst's most ardent disciples was Winfield Sheehan, who rose to power as William Fox's right-hand man.

RANDOLPH SCOTT AND CARY GRANT ENJOY THEIR POOL.

For his opera star wife, Maria Jeritza, Sheehan built a miniature castle on forty acres in Hidden Valley, an hour's drive north of L.A., and furnished it with a variety of costly *ameublements* plundered from all over the world. On the grounds he had a tree from every state in the Union planted, each in a bed of its native soil. Jack Warner was another who liked to surround himself with the treasures of Europe—one unkind visitor nicknamed his home San Simeonette.

It should be noted that in Beverly Hills many nonmovie millionaires—like Carrie Guggenheim, George Lewis, Francis Betiller, and Edward Doheny—vied with the Hollywood crowd in both ostentation and architectural capriciousness. E. L. Cord built an eighty-seven-room mansion with white marble floors, a ballroom, a shooting gallery, an organ chamber, and an eighteen-car garage. Cord's hobby was raising chickens, and on the grounds was a chicken coop with mahogany walls, satin drapes, and gold feeding vessels.

But it was the stars' homes that the public was interested in, and the double-decker buses of Tanner Motor Tours conducted pilgrimages through the flatlands and the hills—though frequently there was nothing to be seen behind the high walls but an Italianate chimney stack or an undulating roof designed to simulate thatchwork.

HOTELS.

When the motion picture industry first settled in Hollywood, the Hollywood Hotel was by far the most prominent structure in the sleepy little village. Originally a winter haven for wealthy visitors to California ("No Dogs or Actors Allowed"), it was not long before many stars took up residence there. Tourists, clanging down Hollywood Boulevard on one of the Big Red Cars, would crane their necks as they traveled between Highland and Orchard, hoping for a glimpse of Mae Busch or Wallace Reid on the porch of this sprawling, vaguely Hispanic building. There was a dance every Thursday evening, at which it was commonplace to see Valentino and Rambova, Thalberg and Shearer, John Gilbert and the other stars of the day making their entrances down the long circular staircase. M-G-M set designer Cedric Gibbons once enlivened the proceedings by driving his car up the steps of the hotel and into the ballroom. Because of the hotel's prime location, rooms were at a premium there. Suites were unheard-of, so Elinor Glyn would rent two adjoining rooms and convert one into a sitting room by throwing brightly colored cushions onto the bed to make it seem like a sofa. Charlie Chaplin, in his autobiography, described the place as "a fifth rate, rambling, barnlike establishment" and preferred to stay at the other famous hotel of those early days, the Alexandria.

Located downtown, at Fifth and Main, not far from the Santa Fe depot, the Alexandria served as a meeting place for stars, producers, directors, and money men, and it was here, in the pre-trade paper era, that gossip was exchanged over breakfast, lunch, dinner, or a midnight snack. The male-only bar was patronized by the likes of Chaplin, Griffith, Mayer, and Fairbanks, while Pickford, Swanson, Mabel Normand, and the other ladies gathered in the lounge reserved for them. In the mornings the main lobby, with its marble columns and crystal chandeliers, looked like a stock exchange. The huge oriental carpet covering the floor was dubbed the "million-dollar rug" because so many deals were consummated on it. The "million-dollar rug" was once "stolen" by Sid Grauman as a practical joke. Grauman sent to the hotel a crew of men who announced themselves as cleaners, produced false credentials, rolled up the famous carpet, and drove off with it in a truck. When it was realized that no cleaning had been authorized, the police were notified and the "theft" of the rug became front-page news in the local papers. After several days, there were still no clues and the manager of the Alexandria—a good friend of Grauman's—found himself a prime suspect in the conspiracy. Grauman invited him to a major premiere at his Egyptian theater, and as the curtain rose on the live show, the hotel manager was shocked but relieved to see the chorus girls performing on his precious rug.

Mrs. Margaret Anderson, the first manager of the Hollywood Hotel, moved in 1912 to the brand-new Beverly Hills Hotel, which the Rodeo Land and Water Company had constructed amid the beanfields about a mile north of the Beverly Trolley depot, from which a narrow-gauge line was built to serve the hotel. With Mrs. Anderson came many of her famous guests, and, for a decade and a half, the Beverly Hills was to be the most successful hostelry in the area, its atmosphere a dash exotic, with caged monkeys and tropical birds displayed in the lobby. The opening of the Beverly Wilshire in 1928 and the stock market crash of the following year forced the temporary closure of the Beverly Hills Hotel. For three years it remained shuttered, until 1933 when it reopened as the half-Hispanic, half-Deco landmark we know today, complete with pool, ritzy bungalows, banana leaf wallpaper, and, of course, the Polo Lounge (converted from what had formerly been a children's nursery).

Another early favorite was the gracefully colonnaded St. Mark Hotel in Venice, opened in 1905. This, along with the nearby Waldorf, was the place to spend a weekend at the beach. Later, the Grand Hotel in Santa Monica became a popular spot for breakfast overlooking the Pacific. In downtown Los Angeles was the Continental Hotel, much frequented by vaudevillians, and among the most popular of the residential hotels was the Chateau Marmont, opened in 1927—a neo-Gothic fantasy planted on the hillside above Sunset Boulevard. Its understated gentility made it a favorite with New Yorkers and Europeans. Garbo found its atmosphere very much to her taste and often stayed there for extended periods. (Die-hards still claim she owns the place, though there is little evidence to support this rumor.) When Jean Harlow married Hal Rosson, they lived at the Marmont for a year in an all-white suite that looked not unlike a set for one of her movies.

Almost opposite the Chateau Marmont, on the south side of Sunset, was the Garden of Allah, which consisted of a couple of dozen Mediterranean bungalows clustered around an oversize, kidney-shaped swimming pool. Built by silent star Alla Nazimova, in 1927, and opened with an eighteen-hour party, it soon became the temporary home of many Hollywood writers and some of the less inhibited stars. According to legend, life at the Garden of Allah was one long, drunken party, punctuated by Dorothy Parker aphorisms and the frequent splashes of John Barrymore falling into the pool (which was the largest in Hollywood). The acknowledged genius in residence was Robert Benchley, and other writers who stayed there, at one time or another, included Ernest Hemingway, Scott Fitzgerald, Marc Connelly, Thomas Wolfe, Donald Ogden Stewart, George S. Kaufman, John O'Hara, and Lucius Beebe. It was the Algonquin Round Table gone Hollywood, with a dash of Broadway and *Vanity Fair*. Among the actors, Charlie Butterworth was Benchley's alter ego, and other sometime guests included Garbo, Errol Flynn, Bea Lillie, Buster Keaton, Louis Calhern, Ruth Chatterton, Fanny Brice, Orson Welles, Marlene Dietrich, Joe E. Lewis, Humphrey Bogart, and Lauren Bacall. William Powell and his wife, Carole Lombard, lived at the nearby Colonial House, but swam in the Allah pool. The Garden of Allah was also a favorite with musicians, from Paul Whiteman to Artie Shaw and Woody Herman, and nonresidents like W. C. Fields could often be found there, drinking in the piano bar, drinking around the pool, or partying in one of the bungalows.

If the Garden of Allah was a somewhat unstable state of mind, the Biltmore Hotel, erected in 1923, was an altogether more proper institution. It was here that the Mayfair Society, a social club dominated by the big names of the twenties—Mary Pickford, Tom Mix, Billie Dove, Norman Kerry, Jack Warner, and others—first held its snobbish, self-conscious, white-tie dinner dances. Later these were also staged at the Ambassador, the Beverly Wilshire, and other *venues*. For many years, however, the Biltmore continued to be a popular dancing place, as well as the place to be after a football game. The Roosevelt Hotel, on Hollywood Boulevard, was built by a syndicate headed by Joe Schenck, and, for a while, its "Blossom Room" was the Wednesday night meeting place of the colony. But far more important was the Ambassador Hotel, on Wilshire, the epitome of ostentatious opulence, from Harold Wilson's monumental *moderne* sculpture at its entrance to the grandiose swimming pool which came complete with a white sand beach and an Egyptian colonnade. What made the Ambassador famous to movie fans throughout the world, however, was the fact that it was the home of the Cocoanut Grove (see NIGHT-CLUBS).

INVESTMENTS.

While many of the stars were frittering away their weekly fortunes on hundred-foot schooners, garden fetes, golden goblets, and silk undershorts, a number of more cautious types were looking ahead to a future of sagging profiles, and began diverting funds into more solid assets. Bing Crosby is said to have camped for days in the outer office of a Los Angeles investment broker, who had previously refused to deal with show business people, until the man finally agreed to help him handle his money. Other stars were equally determined to use their film earnings to purchase security.

The following list represents both investments made by various movie personalities at the time of their initial success, and—in instances such as Crosby and Gene Autry—the extent of the financial empires that they eventually built up.

Abbott and *Costello* each owned a restaurant.

Richard Arlen subdivided sixty acres and built houses on it.

Edward Arnold owned and supervised a large orange grove.

Gene Autry, one of the most successful of Hollywood businessmen, owns 50.1 percent of Golden West Broadcasters (which controls five television stations and the California Angels baseball team), a Palm Springs hotel, a 175,000-acre Arizona ranch, other ranches in Texas and Oklahoma, four music publishing companies, oil wells, controlling stock in the Madison Square Garden rodeo, in addition to which he has substantial interests in two newspapers.

155

Investments

Lucille Ball and *Judy Garland* both invested in flower shops. Later, of course, Lucille Ball became one of the owners of Desilu Studios.

Binnie Barnes owned four London dress shops and a Beverly Hills apartment house.

Richard Barthelmess, Jackie Coogan, and *Mary Pickford* all built and operated miniature golf courses.

Wallace Beery, himself a licensed pilot, invested heavily in a major transcontinental airline, and was a silent partner in his brother Noah's trout farm. Like Donald Crisp, Douglas Fairbanks, C. B. DeMille, Jean Hersholt, and other Hollywood personalities, Beery also served as a bank director.

Ralph Bellamy and *Charles Farrell* built and owned the Racquet Club in Palm Springs. Bellamy sold out early, but Farrell did not relinquish his ownership till 1959, at which time he accepted one million dollars and an invitation to remain as the club's manager.

Constance Bennett owned a company manufacturing cosmetics and also endorsed the products of Fashion Frocks, Ltd., which sold clothes bearing the label "Designed by Constance Bennett." With Claudette Colbert, William Goetz, Al Jolson, Eddie Mannix, Joseph Schenck, and Darryl Zanuck, she was on the Board of Directors of the Arrowhead Springs resort. Bennett was one of many Hollywood personalities (others included Clarence Brown, Charles Chaplin, Claudette Colbert, C. B. DeMille, Richard Dix, Corinne Griffith, Rochelle Hudson, Allan Jones, Fred MacMurray, L. B. Mayer, Mary Pickford, May Robson, Lupe Velez, Mae West, Bert Wheeler, and Anna May Wong) who owned bungalow courts, apartment houses, office buildings, and warehouses.

Jack Benny had investments in real estate, cattle, and Texas oil and was a partner—along with Walt Disney and Spike Jones—in a Denver bowling alley. With Claudette Colbert, Bing Crosby, Phil Harris, Danny Kaye, Humphrey Bogart, José Ferrer, and Barbara Stanwyck, Benny was among the principal stockholders of a twenty-one-acre Palm Springs trailer park called "Blue Skies Village."

Edgar Bergen owned a block on Sunset Boulevard.

Charles Bickford owned a gold mine in San Bernardino County, a string of gas stations, a parking garage, and a controlling interest in two whalers operating off the Mexican coast. With New York fashion designer Joan Storm, he started the House of Bickstorm.

Walter Brennan owned a 12,000-acre cattle ranch, a movie theater, and a motel, all in Oregon.

George Brent operated several service stations and a supermarket.

Billie Burke financed a salad dressing company.

Eddie Cantor ran the antique and gift shop next to the Brown Derby.

Harry Carey operated a highly regarded horse ranch, conducted rodeos, and marketed cattle and alfalfa.

Lon Chaney, Jr., raised turkeys and owned a men's clothing store.

Gary Cooper had a string of dude ranches in Idaho and Montana.

Donald Crisp was an early investor in parcels of land that now constitute a good part of downtown Los Angeles.

Bing Crosby was a major stockholder in the Del Mar race track, Texas oil property, and a frozen fruit juice firm. He also owned a 25,000-acre cattle ranch, started an ice-cream business, and was a partner in Decca Records. His sporting investments included owning 15 percent of the Pittsburgh Pirates and 5½ percent of the Detroit Tigers, and at one time he purchased a half-interest in a promising welterweight fighter called Freddie Steele. With Harold Lloyd and Paul Whiteman he was a major stockholder in radio station KMPC and—along with Errol Flynn, Bob Hope, Fred MacMurray, Tony Martin, Ken Murray, Rudy Vallee, and Johnny Weissmuller—he was once a partner in the Pirates' Den night club.

Bebe Daniels was the proprietor of a dress shop and also owned real estate in Santa Monica.

Cecil B. DeMille owned a large fruit ranch, a cotton plantation, and a 1,700-acre pheasant ranch, which shipped over 200,000 birds a year. In 1919 he founded the Mercury Aviation Company and established an airfield at what is now the corner of Wilshire and Fairfax. In 1923 he became a major stockholder of the Biltmore Hotel and a few years later was elected to the Board of Directors of the Brown Derby restaurants. He was also president of a real estate syndicate which played a significant role in developing the San Fernando Valley.

Reginald Denny was in the airplane rental business and headed the largest model airplane factory in the United States.

Richard Dix raised dogs.

Brian Donlevy invested in tungsten mines in the Mohave desert.

Irene Dunne owned half a block of real estate in Beverly Hills' most exclusive business section, an interest in the Beverly Hills Hotel, and a sizable chunk of the Ojai Valley Inn. She also made investments in oil and, with her husband, Dr. Francis Griffin, helped finance a Las Vegas theater and housing project.

Stuart Erwin owned a vineyard.

Glenda Farrell subdivided land and built houses.

Clark Gable, Al Jolson, Victor McLaglen, Myrna Loy, Robert Taylor, Spencer Tracy, Hal Wallis, and *Jack Warner* all had investments in citrus groves, ranches, and livestock.

Greta Garbo invested in real estate in the Beverly Hills business district.

Cary Grant bought 1,200 acres in the Brazilian jungle.

Bonita Granville financed a beauty parlor.

Alan Hale invented a fire extinguisher and movable theater seats.

Jack Haley started buying business and residential lots in North Hollywood, a section of the San Fernando Valley, in 1927.

Sonja Henie owned a block of large apartment houses in Chicago, an import-export business in New York, and held sizable amounts of stock in Madison Square Garden and in ice palaces in Chicago, Detroit, St. Louis, Indianapolis, and Los Angeles.

Bob Hope invested in real estate on the grand scale, as well as in oil and a dairy in Columbus, Ohio. He also became part owner of the Los Angeles Rams and the Cleveland Indians.

James Wong Howe once owned two Chinese restaurants.

Allan Jones and *Robert Young* owned a riding academy and stable in Bel Air.

Alan Ladd owned a chicken ranch and a hardware store.

Mitchell Leisen owned a men's clothing store, for which he occasionally purchased tweeds while traveling abroad.

Edmund Lowe owned a hothouse.

Joel McCrea bought a working ranch in 1931 for a mere $19,500. A few years later, Union Oil of California was negotiating to lease a small section of the property for in excess of a million dollars.

George Macready and *Vincent Price* were partners in the Price-Macready Gallery, which existed for two years in the early forties.

Fred MacMurray, like Bob Hope, built up vast real estate holdings. With John Wayne, he purchased a hotel in Acapulco.

Zeppo Marx and *Barbara Stanwyck* were partners in Marwyck Stables, where many successful race horses were bred.

Victor Mature invested in a furniture and appliance store, a TV store, and a concession manufacturing meatballs.

Louis B. Mayer invested in oil and real estate. Becoming interested in thoroughbred horses in the late thirties, he acquired a ranch at Perris and in half a dozen years became the most important breeder of race horses on the West Coast. (In 1945 the New York Turf Writers Association named him breeder of the year.) On a less exalted level, he also owned a pool hall and bowling alley.

George Murphy marketed a rubbing liniment developed by his father.

Conrad Nagel built a large block of stores in Beverly Hills, and owned and operated a popular market there.

Merle Oberon has built up an emerald collection which some experts have estimated as being second only to Queen Elizabeth's in value.

Pat O'Brien was one of the original investors in the Del Mar race track, and financed a dress and hat shop run by his wife.

Gail Patrick personally managed the children's clothing store she owned in Beverly Hills.

Walter Pigeon invested in oil.

ZaSu Pitts raised prize tomatoes and lettuce on her small ranch.

Tyrone Power owned the Tyrone Apartments in Los Angeles.

Ginger Rogers purchased and operated a 1,000-acre dairy ranch in Oregon.

Charles Ruggles owned dog kennels.

Ann Sothern was a silent partner in a chili parlor.

James Stewart was a partner in a charter airline service.

Preston Sturges, having invented kissproof lipstick at the age of sixteen, built a factory manufacturing diesel engines and at one time owned two Hollywood restaurants.

Loretta Young financed a charm school and made substantial real estate investments.

KEEPING FIT.

Since failure to stay in shape could cut a Hollywood performer's career short, most studios employed health experts to ensure that their contract players stayed in peak condition. One of the most famous experts was Sylvia Ulbeck—commonly known as Madame Sylvia—who started by running the fitness program at the old Pathé studio, where she operated out of a little stucco bungalow which was dubbed the "Torture Chamber." Madame Sylvia specialized in such excrutiatingly painful massages that it is said that her radio was equipped with a special amplification system in order to drown out the moans of her victims. Later, she became a *Photoplay* columnist and a private health consultant to many stars, including Norma Shearer, Elsie Janis, Ramon Novarro, Ronald Colman, Douglas Fairbanks, Jr., ZaSu Pitts, Marion Davies, and Ruth Chatterton (see also FAN MAGAZINES and MAKE-OVERS). Joseph Kennedy, during his brief spell at FBO, attempted to contract for Sylvia's service on an exclusive basis for Gloria Swanson.

Swanson was an early fitness fanatic, as was Douglas Fairbanks. Although a superb natural athlete, Fairbanks worked strenuously at staying in top physical shape, exercising regularly in his fully equipped gymnasium-dressing room with his personal trainer, Chuck Lewis (also his closest friend and traveling companion, who collaborated on devising the stunts for Fairbanks' movies.) In the late thirties, Spencer Tracy, in addition to lifting weights, etc., became obsessed with massages, requiring at least one a day. W. C. Fields worked out with his trainer, Bob Howard, in Fields's exercise room, occasionally boxing, but more often using the rowing machines (as he bellowed sea chanteys), riding a stationary bicycle (drinking martinis at the same time), or using the Indian clubs or steam bath. Joan Crawford was a jogger years before the word was invented. It was her habit, on the way to work in the morning, to stop her limousine, step out, and run for a mile or so with her chauffeur following at a discreet distance. Sam Goldwyn and his wife, Frances, always had their driver drop them a couple of miles short of the studio and would complete the journey on foot.

At M-G-M new male contract players would be assigned to Don Loomis for an assessment of their physiques. In the case of Robert Taylor, for example, Loomis' verdict was that the shoulders were too narrow and the

CHARLIE CHAPLIN SPARS WITH DOUGLAS FAIRBANKS, 1918.
CULVER PICTURES.

neck too thin, and that the subject would have to be resculpted through the use of bar-bell exercises. Before long, Taylor's weight increased from 148 to 168 pounds, his chest gained 5 inches, and his neck went from 14½ inches to 16. Another beneficiary of the Loomis workshop was Jimmy Stewart. In four months he gained twenty pounds, his chest expanded by 4 inches and his neck by 2—mainly through Loomis' "heavy resistance exercises."

Off the lot, gymnasiums and health clubs, such as the Los Angeles Athletic Club, the Beverly Hills Club (see also GAMBLING), and Terry Hunt's on La Cienaga Boulevard, saw as many stars as the Cocoanut Grove. The L.A. Athletic Club dated back to the early silent period and became the main headquarters for the businessmen and bachelors of Hollywood. Charlie Chaplin joined under the auspices of Mack Sennett, and the twelve dollars he paid weekly for his room entitled him to the use of the elaborate gymnastic facilities and swimming pools of the club. Terry Hunt had run the gym at Paramount, under the sponsorship of Ernst Lubitsch, and later held a similar position at United Artists. His club attracted such female clients as Marlene Dietrich, Rita Hayworth, Olivia De Havilland, Joan Bennett, Ida Lupino, Paulette Goddard, Betty Grable, and Ingrid Bergman. The sexes were strictly segregated, the women's rooms lit, by request, with a dim green light, the men's brightly illuminated. The men's facilities at Hunt's were used by Clark Gable, Cesar Romero, Johnny Weissmuller, John Payne, and many others. Payne was so muscular at the beginning of his career that he looked ridiculous in suits, so Hunt devised a program to trim him down. When Robert Taylor was assigned the role of a prize fighter, he worked out at the club every evening. Several actors liked to don boxing gloves and spar with Hunt for the fun of it. Gary Cooper did so on a regular basis until Hunt accidentally blacked his eye, costing him several days' work.

LOVE, MARRIAGE, AND DIVORCE.

It would be impossible to exaggerate the impact that Hollywood has had upon American attitudes toward romance and the art of making love. The films produced there provided millions with models of courtship behavior, and the off-screen liaisons of the stars—the greatest ongoing soap opera of the day—enthralled the vast audience that paid daily tribute to the gossip columnists. It may well be that, on average, the Hollywood crowd was no more promiscuous, no more adulterous, than many other segments of society, but never before had one small group of people been subjected to such intense scrutiny. Every flirtation, every marital tiff—real, imagined, or contrived—was subject to the attentions of the eager press corps. Studio publicists knew that romance was a sure way of keeping a name in the public eye, and they promoted it for all it was worth.

Trying to penetrate the surface of the love life of the Hollywood colony in its heyday is a little like attempting to psychoanalyze the population of Pasadena from a helicopter. What, for instance, does it mean that, at various times, Loretta Young's name was linked with those of (in alphabetical order) George Brent, Ricardo Cortez, Clark Gable, newspaperman John McClain, Joseph Mankiewicz, Wayne Morris, David Niven, tennis star Fred Perry, Gregory Ratoff, screenwriter Robert Riskin, Gilbert Roland, Cesar Romero, restaurateur Herbert Somborn, James Stewart, director Eddie Sutherland, Spencer Tracy, and Jock Whitney? Or that Cesar Romero was portrayed as the dashing escort of almost every lovely lady in Hollywood—especially those under contract to his own studio, 20th Century-Fox, which apparently encouraged a convenient round-robin system of dating? Co-starring with someone important at the Trocadero could be almost as useful as co-starring with a hot actor in a film, as far as building a newcomer's image was concerned. East Coast socialites and international playboys also made suitable escorts for the rising starlet.

So much of this was stage-managed that it is almost meaningless, except insofar as it helps us understand the way the system worked. Homosexual stars, for example, could be provided with acceptable dates from the studio's pool of contract players, so that their sexual preference was effectively disguised. This is not to suggest that Hollywood was devoid of real romance, however—indeed, there is every reason to suggest that the opposite was true. The movie industry provided a climate in which every kind of liaison—from the mildest infatuation to the wildest affair—could thrive, and it was populated by people who were reminded daily of their sexual attractiveness, whose stock in trade was seduction. The fact that you were in the same business did not necessarily make you impervious to another star's public charms, or unflattered by his interest in you. In some cases, at least, actors and actresses had an urgent need to prove their virility or appeal in the bedrooms of the real world. It was not easy to play the great lover on cue if you had doubts about your ability off screen. Then again, the entire ethos of Hollywood was predicated on glamour and romance. It would have been almost churlish of the privileged not to have taken advantage of their situation.

Publicists were fond of inventing love affairs between co-stars, for the benefit of the box office, but we should not be too cynical about reported on-set romances because many did occur, love scenes played for the camera evolving into real-life passion in full view of grips, gaffers, prop men, and

163

script girls. Instances of this include Clara Bow and Gary Cooper on the set of *Children of Divorce,* Loretta Young and Grant Withers in *Too Young to Marry,* John Gilbert and Greta Garbo in *Flesh and the Devil,* John Gilbert and Virginia Bruce in *Downstairs,* Mary Pickford and Leslie Howard in *Secrets,* Ann Dvorak and Leslie Fenton in *The Strange Case of Molly Louvain,* Clark Gable and Joan Crawford in *Dance, Fools, Dance,* Clark Gable and Elizabeth Allan in *Men in White,* Clark Gable and Loretta Young in *Call of the Wild* (in this case the romance is reported to have affected the shooting schedule and the supporting cast to the extent that one actor, Walter Connolly, said he felt like an intruder on the set), Loretta Young and Spencer Tracy in *A Man's Castle,* Spencer Tracy and Joan Crawford in *Mannequin,* Spencer Tracy and Katharine Hepburn in *Woman of the Year,* and Bette Davis and George Brent in *Dark Victory* —to name a few.

There were several stars, such as John Barrymore and Marion Davies, who had the reputation of making a play for almost all of their costars. Marion Davies was, of course, involved in the strangest of Hollywood love affairs, her liaison with William Randolph Hearst—a marriage in all but name—which lasted more than thirty years, until his death in 1951. Hearst, her patron as well as her lover, was Davies' senior by thirty-five years and was understandably prone to jealousy. (Some of the people who chose to believe that he shot and killed Thomas Ince aboard the Hearst yacht also suggest that he mistook the director, in the dark, for Charlie Chaplin, whom he suspected of having an affair with his mistress.)

Barrymore's notoriety preceded him to Hollywood. According to most accounts, he began his sexual career at the age of fourteen with his father's second wife. Among his subsequent East Coast conquests were the celebrated Elsie Janis and Evelyn Nesbitt. In Hollywood his attention focused upon, among others, the seventeen-year-old Mary Astor. When they were preparing for *Beau Brummel*—Barrymore was then forty-two—he would send his car for Mary and her mother every Sunday, and when they arrived at his hotel suite, he would charm the older woman into remaining on the veranda so the lovers could have the interiors to themselves to "rehearse."

Errol Flynn was the archetypal example of a star with a seemingly insatiable libido—and a custom-built Darrin Packard with seats that reclined at the touch of a button. His sometime boss Jack Warner has related that Flynn once estimated he'd had sex some 12,000 to 14,000 nights of his life. Given that Flynn died at fifty and that this estimate was apparently made some time before his death, the mathematics of this lead to startling conclusions. Unfortunately, however, Flynn's Don Juanism did not lead him to Nirvana—he himself said that he had never "found his own soul" and in his autobiography bemoaned the fact that he was "nothing but a phallic symbol."

Seemingly shy Gary Cooper was attracted to flamboyant types like Clara Bow and Lupe Velez. (His romance with the latter was squashed by Cooper's mother, who took an instant dislike to the Mexican star and did her best to promote something between her son and Evelyn Brent, by way of distraction.) Later, Cooper had a long affair with Dorothy Di Frasso, the New York-born countess by marriage, who trained him in the social graces before she moved on to mobster Bugsy Segal (see CRIME), and Cooper married a wealthy socialite. Other unlikely ladies' men were Burgess Meredith and James Stewart. Columnist Jimmy Fidler, given to greater precision than Errol Flynn, has reported that Stewart dated 263 "glamour girls" before he left Hollywood for the Air Force. Frank Sinatra, during his early years at M-G-M, is said to have kept a master list of his star conquests behind his dressing room door. As for George Raft, he told his biographer, Lewis Yablonsky, that the phone would start ringing every evening around midnight, no matter where he was. "I was in the little black book of every high-class hooker in Hollywood." Raft's confidant, Mack Grey, estimated that the star averaged two women a day, for years.

GRETA GARBO AND JOHN GILBERT ON THE SET OF *Love*. CULVER PICTURES.

COUNTESS DOROTHY DI FRASSO AND GARY COOPER AT A
COSTUME PARTY, 1933.

All this has more to do with lust than romance, and before we move on, it would be appropriate to look at the casting-couch syndrome. This was certainly a reality of Hollywood life, though it's difficult to judge just how prevalent it was, since, generally speaking, both parties had an interest in keeping such things quiet. Most of the European-born, first-generation moguls appear to have been as romantically conventional as the movies they produced. Louis B. Mayer, for example, made awkward attempts at lechery—among those he pursued around his desk were Jeanette MacDonald and Hedda Hopper—but he seems to have derived most of his pleasure from the chase itself; when Hopper threatened to surrender, he panicked. He did fall in love with Jean Howard, and, although they had never had physical contact, when she rejected him in favor of Charlie Feldman (see AGENTS), Feldman was barred from doing business on the M-G-M lot. Later love interests of Mayer included Ann Miller and Ginny Simms. When his forty-year marriage began to disintegrate in the early forties, the boundlessly energetic Mayer perfected his rhumba technique and embarked on a nightly routine of escorting a succession of starlets to the fashionable clubs and cafés, until he married Lorena Danker, the widow of an advertising executive, in 1948.

Mayer's top musical producer, Arthur Freed, was one executive who did have the reputation of propositioning girls who came to him seeking work, and there were, no doubt, many others throughout the industry, at all levels, who took advantage of their positions from time to time. David Selznick, when his marriage to Irene Mayer was coming apart, and before his romance with Jennifer Jones, seems to have been another. The king of the casting couch, however, was Harry Cohn, who felt that any female employed by Columbia was his by *droit de seigneur*. Nor was he particularly subtle in his courting techniques, being fond of calling starlets on the set and whispering obscenities into the phone. When he mistakenly became convinced that John Wayne was after one of the contract players he himself had designs on, Cohn had Wayne dropped from the studio payroll and attempted to keep him from working elsewhere by starting a smear campaign which suggested that Wayne was quarrelsome and drank on set.

Howard Hughes, in his role as Hollywood mogul, was not above using his power to boost his love life. When he was told that a young woman in whom he had expressed an interest was involved with an actor, he had a part written for her boyfriend in a picture that was just going into production, offered him a handsome contract, and sent him off to an out-of-state location, where he would be kept busy for several weeks.

It was quite understandable that women whose profession was glamour should be drawn to men whose stock in trade was the enhancement of beauty. Linda Darnell married Peverell Marley, the cinematographer who shot her screen test and her first three features at Fox; Joan Blondell and Merle Oberon married cameramen George Barnes and Lucien Ballard; and Jean Harlow was for a while married to another important director of photography, Hal Rosson. Janet Gaynor married M-G-M costumer Adrian, and Gene Tierney wed designer Oleg Cassini. Ann Sheridan and Betty Hutton had flings with make-up artist Perc Westmore, and Martha Raye and Rosemary Lane both married his brother Bud, while Donna Reed made her vows to another make-up expert, Bill Tuttle.

Actresses seem to have been very attracted to literary figures, both in and out of the industry. Paulette Goddard, following her secret marriage to Charlie Chaplin, met H. G. Wells—then in his late seventies—at the premiere of *The Great Dictator,* and became so infatuated with him that she pursued him to every stop of his American lecture tour. Later she married novelist Erich Maria Remarque, who was also her senior by several years. Joan Bennett was for a while involved with George Jean Nathan, Binnie Barnes with Moss Hart, and Miriam Hopkins had relationships with John Gunther and Bennett Cerf (whom Sylvia Sidney married). Luise Rainer wed Clifford Odets, and Carole Lombard had romances with publisher Horace Liveright and writer Robert Riskin, who later married Fay Wray. Among the most publicized of such romances was Mary Astor's affair with playwright George S. Kaufman, which became the focus of a scandalous divorce case. According to Sam Marx, in *Mayer and Thalberg,* Jean Harlow was introduced to Thomas Wolfe at M-G-M and told that he was an important novelist. Obviously attracted to him, she offered him a ride home and everyone took due note of the fact that they arrived at the studio together the next morning, dressed just as they had been when they left.

With reference to Paulette Goddard's interest in older men, it should be noted that the older woman syndrome was also prevalent in Hollywood. Before he married Lauren Bacall, Humphrey Bogart had three wives, each significantly older than himself. Clark Gable's first two wives, Josephine Dillon and Ria Langham, were, respectively, sixteen and seventeen years his senior. Gable may have been drawn to maternal women because he had never known his own mother, who died when he was seven months old. In any case, his first two wives—like Bogart's first three—helped him considerably with his career. Josephine Dillon was instrumental in developing the Gable mystique (see COACHES), and Ria Langham effectively refined it—even sending him to her dentist to have his teeth fixed.

If Hollywood offered its audience lessons in love-making and romance, it had an equally profound effect on attitudes toward marriage and divorce. The fact that breaking up came to be as newsworthy as getting together

THE WEDDING OF JEAN HARLOW AND PAUL BERN, 1932.

THE WEDDING OF LANA TURNER AND STEPHEN CRANE; LINDA
DARNELL AT RIGHT.

tended to generate a cycle of impermanent relationships that ran counter to the American puritan tradition. The successful and enduring marriages (like those of the James Cagneys, Fredric Marches, Ray Millands, George Murphys, Walter Pigeons, Joel McCreas, etc.) received scant notice as the divorce rate in the movie colony soared way above the national average. The image of movie personalities drifting from romance to romance and from marriage to marriage with apparent impunity had a decided effect on attitudes all over the world—despite the fact that many of the pressures on these marriages were unique to show business and that much of the information broadcast to the public was false.

Everything about the film star liaison was invested, by press agents and journalists, with special significance. Back in the silent era, Hollywood weddings were staged like movie premieres. When Rod La Rocque wed Vilma Banky in 1927, thousands lined the streets and the police had to use force to keep the crowds under control. Nor were the fans alone in their hysteria: the invited guests were so carried away by the solemnity of the occasion that they fought over the seating arrangements. The entire event was staged by the Goldwyn publicity department, which also footed the bill.

There were occasional echoes of this tradition in the thirties, such as the Jeanette MacDonald–Gene Raymond wedding in 1937, where fifteen thousand fans congregated near the Wilshire Methodist–Episcopal Church and 150 policemen were called in to maintain order. The bride was attended by Ginger Rogers, Fay Wray, Helen Ferguson, and Mrs. Johnny Mack Brown, while Nelson Eddy sang "I Love You Truly" and "Perfect Love." By this time, however, such lavish weddings were the exceptions to the rule. The Depression, along with an increasing demand for privacy by the stars, had reversed the tide of extravagance, and it now became the job of publicity departments to keep the wraps on marriage plans and facilitate elopements to Santa Ana, Santa Barbara, San Diego, Las Vegas, and Yuma. Stunt flyer Paul Mantz, known to the press as "The Honeymoon Pilot," made a light plane available to celebrities like Lana Turner and Artie Shaw, who wanted to hop over to Reno or Vegas to tie the knot. Lupe Velez and Johnny Weissmuller, Constance Bennett and Gilbert Roland, Laurence Olivier and Vivien Leigh, Joan Bennett and Walter Wanger, Judy Garland and David Rose, and Barbara Stanwyck and Robert Taylor (after one unsuccessful attempt) were among the couples who managed to sneak away quietly. Loew's president, Nicholas Schenck, assisted Joan Crawford and Franchot Tone in their arrangements by having his good friend, the mayor of Englewood Cliffs, New Jersey, contrive for the clerk to bring the license to his home, where the couple was wed. Similarly, when Ronald Colman was marrying Benita Hume at his San Ysidro ranch, the county clerk brought the license application to them

THE WEDDING OF NORMA SHEARER AND IRVING THALBERG, 1927.

MR. AND MRS. CLARK GABLE (RIA LANGHAM) WITH NORMA SHEARER
AT THE *Grand Hotel* PREMIERE.

for completion and then, instead of placing it in the stack of the day's transactions, which would have exposed it to the scrutiny of the press, hid it under the counter.

The Gable-Lombard nuptials became an instance of high-level, high-priority M-G-M intrigue. Publicist Otto Winkler (who was later killed with Lombard in a plane crash) was assigned the task of finding a location that was accessible in one day, yet not likely to be under press surveillance. He chose the First Methodist–Episcopal Church in Kingman, Arizona—a small town three hundred miles southeast of Los Angeles. Gable, on a two-day furlough from *Gone With the Wind,* had to hide in the rumble seat when they stopped for gas, while Lombard, in pigtails and jeans, had no difficulty in passing for an ordinary traveler.

Even with the restrictions placed on it by the Hays Office, Hollywood continued to produce pictures that displayed a rather cavalier attitude toward the marriage vows. In many classic Hollywood comedies, life is portrayed as a confused but entertaining prelude to the act of becoming betrothed, but some—*The Gay Divorcee,* for example—are actually constructed around the machinery of annulment. A number of melodramas, the so-called women's pictures of the thirties, present marriage as a condition of unmitigated misery and treat divorce as an essential tool of emancipation. The fact that the denouements of such pictures tended to be engineered with chicken wire and wishful thinking did not diminish their impact.

In real life it was tough to stay married in Hollywood. A star's merest flirtation was likely to be broadcast from coast to coast, a fact which could place a considerable strain on a relationship. (It must have been trying, to say the least, to learn of your husband's alleged transgressions from the morning paper.) The Hollywood environment was full of what later came to be known as groupies, both male and female, and there were the additional problems of sudden wealth, career rivalries, possessive mothers, and a dozen other factors. It was not unheard-of, for example, for a studio to disapprove of a match involving one of its stars, making the other partner very uncomfortable.

Public pressure could work in many ways. In the mid-thirties *Photoplay* published an article on Hollywood's happiest unmarried couples, among them Gable and Lombard and Charlie Chaplin and Paulette Goddard. The piece caused an uproar—from the same fans who had avidly followed these romances from the sound stages to the Trocadero—and it wasn't long before almost all the couples mentioned found themselves at the altar.

The most famous marriage in Hollywood's history, that of Mary Pickford and Douglas Fairbanks, was bracketed by divorces. When Fairbanks' first wife, Beth, announced to the world in 1918 that their marriage was at an end, the press was at first afraid to print the fact that Mary Pickford was involved, despite the knowledge that this was an open secret in Hollywood and was made crystal clear by Beth Fairbanks in press conferences. A little over a year later, when Pickford severed her ties to Owen Moore, the whole business was conducted with extreme secrecy, and the validity of the Nevada divorce itself was questioned. The celebrated couple hesitated before taking the marriage vows, fearing that their careers might be destroyed by the public's traditional prejudice against divorce and immediate remarriage. It was not until they were greeted by wildly enthusiastic crowds on their European honeymoon that they were really convinced that their popularity could survive the scandal. The Pickford-Fairbanks marriage did more to promote the acceptability of divorce in America than any other single event.

In 1933 Pickford received a cable from Fairbanks, who was in England, admitting that he was in love with Lady Sylvia Ashley and would not return to Pickfair. Pickford had lunch at the Vendôme with Frances Marion and Louella Parsons. Marion, who had already seen the cable, urged Pickford to show it to Louella, who promised not to publish the story. Parsons kept her word for six weeks, but when she heard that the Los Angeles *Times* was about to scoop her, she released the news to the world in banner headlines.

In February of the same year, *Variety* published a synopsis of Hollywood divorce statistics for 1932. Of the 102 examples given, it was noted that 84 were attributable to "that Hollywood influence." A few of the cases mentioned were as follows:

PLAINTIFF	DEFENDANT	REASON
Loretta Young	Grant Withers	Nonsupport
Esther Muir	Busby Berkeley	Tore her dress off at a dance
Agnes Miller	Tim McCoy	Gone Hollywood
Dorothy Perry	Stepin Fetchit	Wife beating
Mary Poulson	Bull Montana	Made faces at her
Lowell Sherman	Helene Costello	Called him a ham actor
Helene Costello	Lowell Sherman	Feared for her life
Monte Banks	Gladys Frazier	Her chronic disappearances
Bobbe Arnst	Johnny Weissmuller	His brother lived with them
Vivian Duncan	Nils Asther	He spoke to his mother in Swedish

MR. AND MRS. CLARK GABLE (CAROLE LOMBARD) AT A PREMIERE.

HUMPHREY BOGART AND WIFE, MAYO METHOT.

Twenty-six years later, *McCall's* printed an article by Leonard Slater, titled "The Disgrace of Hollywood," which went into some further instances of the movie crowd's divorce syndrome. In 1934, when Joan Crawford divorced Douglas Fairbanks, Jr., she reported that he would sulk for days at a time and refuse to talk to her, and when Gloria Swanson cut her ties to Michael Farmer, that same year, she said, "He was offered a small part in one of my pictures and it hurt his pride." The year 1935 produced a good crop of newsworthy divorces. Helen Morgan complained that Maurice Maschke squirted sparkling burgundy all over the apartment, and Dorothy Gish explained that life with James Rennie was intolerable because he would come home at three in the morning, drunk, and awaken her in order to "talk incessantly on all sorts of subjects." Dr. Franklin Thorpe said that he did not like the fact that Mary Astor earned more than he did, and Virginia Cherrill characterized Cary Grant as sullen and quarrelsome. Barbara Stanwyck sought a divorce from Frank Fay on the grounds that he was morose, and Elizabeth Mae Keaton pleaded that she did not think that her husband, Buster, was funny. It was a bad year for cinematographers. Joan Blondell brought suit against George Barnes, saying, "He preferred a book and a highball to talking to me," and Jean Harlow similarly complained that Hal Rosson read in bed. The following year, Harmon Nelson, Jr., also grumbled that Bette Davis read in bed. In 1939 Betty Grable divorced Jackie Coogan on multiple grounds, citing his failure to come home at night, his auctioning off most of their wedding gifts, and his hampering of her career. The following year, Greer Garson parted company with Edward Snelson, finding it unacceptable that he insisted on her accompanying him to India; Lana Turner said Artie Shaw was jeopardizing her well-being, and Hedy Lamarr complained of Gene Markey, "He never told me about himself. He wouldn't talk but sent me notes."

While some of these complaints have the ring of truth, it should be remembered that the plaintiff was often a skilled performer and that Hollywood divorce lawyers—men like Jerry Geisler—were probably the most able and practiced in the world. Often the issues at stake were far more complex than is suggested by the *McCall's* piece. To take a couple of examples from the vintage year of 1935, for Barbara Stanwyck to have described Frank Fay as "morose" was more than kind. He was a hopeless alcoholic—it is said that *A Star Is Born* was partially based on their marriage—and had inflicted considerable psychic pain on her. When she financed a Broadway show, attempting to help him make a comeback, he simply failed to put in an appearance at the theater after the first night. Hoping to show him of unsound mind, Stanwyck testified that when he drove past a church he would remove his hands from the steering wheel and pray, and on one occasion, she said, he had fallen into their child's crib in a drunken stupor and kept the boy awake with his snoring. Similarly, Dr. Thorpe had more on his mind than salary inequities. He had found his wife's diary with its graphic accounts of her affairs with George S. Kaufman and others, and his lawyers leaked excerpts to the press. She countered with evidence that he had enjoyed liaisons with several Busby Berkeley dancers.

Year after year, details of marital splits hit the front pages. When Tom Mix's wife, Vicky, divorced him in 1930, she told the court that he frequently frightened her by twirling a loaded .38 on his finger. Dick Foran's wife testified that he tried to poison her. Martha Raye, whose marriage to Bud Westmore lasted only three months, admitted it was tough to choose between her mother, "who made me what I am today," and Bud, "who can make me up better than anyone else." Kay Francis claimed that Kenneth McKenna nagged and harassed her, ridiculed her choice of friends and style of dress, and cast aspersions on her acting ability. Ruth Chatterton, too, attested that George Brent was unsociable toward her friends. She also complained that he refused to talk to her for weeks at a time and was critical when he did address her. (Brent, in response, hinted that he was growing weary of the perpetual presence of his wife's former husband, Ralph Forbes—even at the breakfast table.) Sylvia Sidney charged that Carleton Alsop "engaged in a studied plan to destroy their marriage, berating her in the presence of others." Her earlier husband, Bennett Cerf, took the matter more lightly, declaring, "One should never legalize a hot romance." Cerf was an outsider, of course. He failed to take note of the fact that one could not get the full publicity value out of a hot romance unless you were prepared to take it to the accepted conclusion.

As divorce became commonplace in Hollywood, so did spectacular settlements. Some people have suggested that Mary Pickford "bought" her divorce from Owen Moore for as much as a million dollars, although recent biographers have estimated that the figure was actually more like $100,000 or $150,000. Douglas Fairbanks, however, settled $500,000 on Beth before marrying Mary. Lita Grey's complaint against Charlie Chaplin ran to forty-two pages. He protested that it was a plot to destroy his reputation, but finally agreed to give the girl (she was still in her teens) $625,000 in cash, and to set up a $200,000 trust fund for their two sons. Along with interest on deferred payments and lawyers' fees, it was estimated that the divorce cost him over $950,000. When Constance Bennett cut herself free from playboy Phil Plant, she accepted what was reported to have been a cool million.

The figures in other divorce settlements were less breath-taking, but they were often crippling to some of the well-known personalities who, although phenomenally well paid by the standards of the day, did not have the good fortune—enjoyed by Pickford, Fairbanks, and Chaplin—

MARY PICKFORD LEAVING THE WITNESS STAND DURING COURT
PROCEEDINGS OF HER DIVORCE FROM DOUGLAS FAIRBANKS.
CULVER PICTURES.

to be partners in one of America's largest production companies. Court costs and legal fees alone could be staggering and, around 1930, movie people began to turn to the newly available possibility of the Mexican divorce. In those days, Mexican divorces could actually be obtained by mail. Attorneys like S. S. "Sammy" Hahn, who had many motion picture clients, established ties with Mexican lawyers and supplied them with Spanish translations of the appropriate documents. When the Mexican lawyer received them, he filed a notice of intent to divorce by placing an advertisement in a local newspaper. A month later, the divorce would be granted and become final. This cost about $1,000 plus perhaps $10,000 for lawyers' fees, and it offered great advantages to actors or directors who could not afford to take time off from work. Nancy Carroll was one of the first to obtain a Mexican divorce, as was Grant Withers, when he was anxious to marry Loretta Young.

After the divorce headlines became yesterday's news, it was an accepted phenomenon in Hollywood for ex-spouses to become pals—in such an insular working community, this was practically a necessity. Carole Lombard, in her divorce action against William Powell, called him "cruel and cross." To friends, she is said to have complained that "the son-of-a-bitch is acting even when he takes his pajamas off." A short time later, however, she was "delighted" to be co-starring in a film with him. The movie colony's casual attitude toward divorce disturbed E. B. White sufficiently for him to write a piece for *Harper's,* published in July of 1939, titled "One Man's Meat." In it, he warned that "the Hollywood tradition of post-marital affection is having its effect everywhere on the culture of our land," adding, "marriage is becoming a stepping-stone to the idyllic life which lies ahead for graduates of the course."

MAKE-OVERS.

When the Hollywood make-up man went to work, usually at around six in the morning, he had to try to envision how the face that confronted him would appear—magnified a hundred times—to patrons in the front rows of Grauman's Chinese Theater and Radio City Music Hall. The top studio make-up artists were imaginative, resourceful, earthly individuals who bore no resemblance to the effete prima donnas perpetrated for laughs in such movies as the Selznick production of *A Star Is Born.* (Some were temperamental, many were hard drinking and hard living. Bob Schiffer, a top man in the field who has been active in Hollywood since the early thirties, remarks that there is something a little crazy about make-up artists as a group. "A lot of them die in bed, smoking, things like that. I guess it comes from looking at women too early in the morning.") Simply staying abreast of the times was a constant challenge. Each new technical innovation—whether it was panchromatic film (black-and-white stock sensitive to the full range of visible colors), incandescent lights, or Technicolor—required them to overhaul their skills, often in the most radical of ways. In effect, they were asked to reinvent their art over and over again.

Dominating the field was the extraordinary Westmore clan. George Westmore—a British barber from the Isle of Wight, who perfected his skills in Cleveland by preparing prostitutes for their customers—set up the first Hollywood make-up department at the Selig studio in 1917. He preferred to free-lance, however, often calling at the stars' homes before they left for the lot so that they could arrive in full make-up. Everybody sought George's services. Mary Pickford had been famous for her blond curls before George arrived on the scene, but it was he who augmented her baby-fine tresses with hair pieces that used locks shorn from hookers at Big Suzy's French Whorehouse, in Beverly Hills, where he was continuing his nocturnal studies and experiments. (All the Westmores were famous for their wigmaking skills.) George sired twenty children, and all six sons who survived childhood became top make-up artists. Between them, they headed the make-up departments at every major studio except M-G-M— and even there they were welcome on a free-lance basis.

The four older sons were born in England and had accompanied their father on his peregrinations around Canada and the United States. Mont, the eldest, worked for Cecil B. DeMille and free-lanced successfully before heading the make-up department for Selznick International. Perc and Ern were twins and bitter rivals. Perc was top man at First National and Warner Brothers for a quarter of a century (heading a staff of twenty to thirty sculptors, hairdressers, wigmakers, plastic workers, etc.), and Ern— thought by some, despite his drinking problems, to be the most gifted of all—held the same position at RKO. Wally, the fourth son, ran Paramount's make-up department, and Bud was in charge at Universal for twenty-three years. Frank, much the youngest—he represents virtually a third generation—has thrived as a free agent in the age of the independent producer, and, with Muriel Davidson, has recorded the entire saga in *The Westmores of Hollywood.* Despite their frequent and eloquently expressed differences—this was a family of egocentrics and Perc in particular was almost intolerably arrogant—they managed to combine their studio

DOROTHY LAMOUR WITH WALLY WESTMORE, HEAD OF THE
PARAMOUNT MAKE-UP DEPARTMENT, 1940.

duties with a highly profitable outside business, the House of Westmore, which catered to both stars and the wealthy matrons of Southern California.

The Westmores did have a few peers. Jack Dawn, overlord of the M-G-M make-up department, was every bit as imperious as any of the Westmores. The staff he assembled in Culver City included the likes of Bill Tuttle—a master technician, still active today—and was a match for that at any other studio.

The creation of glamour was not a very glamorous business. The hours were terrible and you were asked to look at the idols of the Western world in terms of their flaws and shortcomings. When you were starting out, things were even worse. Bob Schiffer remembers his beginnings at RKO:

> I was assigned to work on *The Last Days of Pompeii* and there were these big crowd scenes with hundreds of extras. In those days we had a gallon jug of "Bole Armenia"—ground up earth colors in a water and alcohol base—and all these nude men would line up every morning and you'd have to spread this crap all over them. They were supposed to be slaves. I told myself, "I'm getting out of this business!"
>
> On *Blonde Venus,* which starred Dietrich, we did the same thing, but with women—which made it a little more interesting. In those days we didn't have body makeup girls. Now we're just allowed to work down to the collar bone.

In her autobiography, *A Life on Film,* Mary Astor recalls that the make-up booths were—at six-thirty in the morning—at least relatively quiet after the din of the hairdressing department, where everyone was shouting to be heard above the roar of the driers. She writes, too, of the early days when her face would be coated with grease paint—Stein's #2 —until every pore was filled, then dusted with powder until it became a mask. The lipstick used then was dark red, but it had to be carefully applied because reds tended to read as black on the crude black-and-white film stock used in those days. If the lipstick was applied too lightly, however, it would come out white on screen. Astor also recalled brown eye shadow and black mascara, used along with "something that was called 'cosmetique,' a black cake of guck that was melted over a spirit lamp." This "guck" was applied to the eyelashes, with a match or a toothpick, to create a "beading" effect, serving much the same purpose that false eyelashes do today.

A little later—still in the twenties—Astor and Perc Westmore experimented by blending Stein's Pink with a touch of eye shadow. The results, she reports, were miraculous: "Bones began to show, skin looked natural. . . . It was the beginning of panchromatic makeup." Perc and his brothers,

185

along with Jack Dawn and others, were always attempting to improve the palette that was available to them. The Max Factor company, originally established in a small store at Third and Hill streets in downtown Los Angeles, was the main supplier of cosmetics to the movie industry, and it diligently kept in touch with these developments at the studios. It was at Factor's first shop that cameraman Charles Rosher created a special make-up for Mary Pickford's complexion, coded 7-R, which is still in use today. Major advances in make-up developed at Factor were outlined in an ad in the *Hollywood Reporter* of May 10, 1934, under the headline:

A PARADE OF HITS

1920—The first make-up to give natural tones to the skin

1923—The first perspiration-proof liquid body make-up

1926—The "under-water" make-up

1928—The perfection of Panchromatic make-up

1929—The first sunburn, water-proof make-up

1934—Satin Smooth—a make-up of delicate tones that photographs beautifully

By 1940 make-up was such an organized discipline that M-G-M's department could handle twelve hundred actors an hour.

More than make-up, however, was sometimes required. Cosmetic surgery was relatively common in Hollywood as early as the twenties—Rudolph Valentino had his bat ears operated on—and in 1932 it was reported in *Modern Screen* that one plastic surgeon alone, Dr. Josif Ginsberg, had performed over a thousand operations on Hollywood personalities in the previous two-year period. Bebe Daniels, Carmel Myers, and Vivienne Segal all had their noses remodeled, and a spectacular transformation was achieved when a sizable lump was removed from Johnny Weissmuller's nose, prior to his debut as Tarzan. Nor was Valentino the only one to have his ears fixed: George Raft's were made over early in his film career.

According to an article which appeared in *Collier's* in 1932, bat ears could be held flat with the aid of a fine (virtually invisible) fishskin net. This same net could be used to produce the effect of a face-lift, a method that was employed to make John Barrymore appear ten years younger for his role in *Eternal Love,* an early talkie. Douglas Fairbanks' double chin was eradicated by the application of heavy shadow—though cameramen had to be careful to avoid catching him in profile against a light background. *Collier's* readers were told that a girl could achieve "the tender-sweet look" of Hollywood stars by painting her eyesockets with Vaseline, that discolored teeth could be given a coat of collodion enamel paint which would last the day, and that more serious dental problems could be rectified by "shells" which slipped over the teeth like thimbles.

Corrective measures were sometimes so drastic as to create new problems. The make-up people on Lana Turner's second film, *The Adventures of Marco Polo,* shaved off her eyebrows and they never grew back. Another major female star developed a bad complexion at the height of her career. She traveled to Europe to have the top layer of facial tissue literally scraped away, then returned to Hollywood with wonderfully smooth skin —so smooth that make-up just slid off it.

Often, though, only minor cosmetic adjustments were needed to create an effective screen image. When Perc Westmore was confronted with Joan Crawford, early in her career, he did just three simple things. First he brushed her hair off her forehead, then he used lipstick to change the contour of her mouth, and finally he wiped the mascara off her lower lashes. When Merle Oberon arrived in Hollywood in 1934, she was given rosebud lips and finely penciled eyebrows, then her eyes were made to appear exotically slanted.

Margaret Sullavan was acknowledged to have been a glowing presence —one of the most attractive and captivating women ever to achieve Hollywood stardom—yet she required a relatively radical make-over. One difficulty was that her face was more than normally asymmetrical. To rectify this, her eyebrows were shaved so that the line of the right brow could be raised. Since the right side of her jaw was lower than the left, and her mouth slanted down in that direction, the corners of her mouth were raised with lipstick, and lipstick was also used to reduce the distance between her lips and her nose. In addition, a mole was removed, a shell was put on one tooth, and her brown hair was dyed blond.

On stage, Ruth Chatterton, too, had been considered something of a beauty, but the camera was not kind to her. She had particular difficulties with her nose, which appeared rather bulbous on screen. Writing in *Photoplay* in 1937, Madame Sylvia described how she worked on the Chatterton nose every day for weeks until she had massaged away the excess flesh, so that it could be photographed without casting "weird and unattractive shadows." Chatterton was very proud of her complexion and received daily facials from a woman named Ada Mae, who, according to Mary Astor, administered pats, strokes, and pinches to the star's features, at her Beverly Hills home, while she entertained a retinue of admirers— "mostly young men."

When Alice Faye first came to Hollywood, crevices between her teeth were filled with cement, but as soon as it became evident that she was in pictures to stay, she was sent to a dental surgeon and in a few months had a beautiful smile. In her early films, Faye was usually presented as a rather tough, brassy type, but when Fox merged with 20th Century, Darryl

MAKE-OVERS

Zanuck ordained a softer image for her. The hard pencil-line brows were thickened, her curls were unkinked, and the heavy bleach job that had been her trademark was abandoned in favor of a more natural hair color.

Change of hair color is one of the more obvious ways in which an image can be altered. When Joan Bennett was under contract to Walter Wanger (but before they were married), he starred Hedy Lamarr in his production of *Algiers*. Insiders were amused at the fact that the two women were virtual look-alikes, except for the fact that Lamarr was brunette and Bennett a blonde. When Tay Garnett was set to direct Joan in *Trade Winds* the following year, he remarked on the resemblance and suggested that it might be fun to make Joan a brunette for the picture. This was meant as a one-time gag, but everyone liked her so much with dark hair that she decided to keep it. In fact, the transformation was so successful, she found herself being offered much better parts.

In Rita Hayworth's case, hairline and color were both changed. As Margarita Cansino, she had played a number of small parts as a natural brunette, but when she was being groomed for stardom, Helen Hunt, Columbia's top stylist, suggested that Rita's tresses be lightened to auburn, and that her hairline—which was low on her forehead—be altered by means of electrolysis. Rita agreed willingly to the former and reluctantly to the latter, knowing it would be a long, painful process.

Bob Schiffer was Hayworth's regular make-up man for years and considers her to have been a great natural beauty, but explains that—as was the case with most glamorous women—there were always a few minor adjustments to be made before the star could be submitted to the scrutiny of the camera:

> One eye was a little smaller than the other, so I used to take a false eyelash and place it at an angle, then glue her own eyelash to it, just to even her eyes out.

Always, of course, the make-up artist and the lighting cameraman would be working in close collaboration, as Schiffer indicates:

> Rita was always lit, in those early pictures, for one particular close-up. What the cameraman would do is take a baby spot and he would look for little rings under the eyes—which Rita had a habit of getting—and he'd bring that spot up until he had eliminated them, then he'd take a huge key light and bring that up till it shadowed the baby spot. That's one reason she looked so beautiful in those days—they'd throw four or five of these long, static close-ups into every picture.
>
> Once the cameraman had done all that, I'd come in and work around the eyes. I had a little palette with different colors, and they'd wait till I was satisfied.

188

GENERAL VIEW OF A STUDIO MAKE-UP ROOM.

FILTER Nº 1
ANITA LOUISE
JOSEPHINE HUTCHINSON

FILTER Nº 2
JEAN MUIR
PATRICIA ELLIS
MARIE WILSON
JEANNE MADDEN

FILTER Nº 3
GLENDA FARRELL
WINIFRED SHAW

FILTER Nº 4
BETTE DAVIS
JOAN BLONDELL
OLIVIA DI HAVILLAND
CAROL HUGHES

FILTER Nº 5
MARGARET LINDSAY
JUNE TRAVIS

FILTER Nº 6
RUBY KEELER
KAY FRANCIS

STARLETS POSE WITH PERC WESTMORE FOR A DEMONSTRATION
OF FILTERS USED FOR VARIOUS SKIN TYPES.

Some of the biggest stars had very strong ideas about what the make-up
man should or should not do. Norma Shearer, apart from demanding her
own cinematographer, Bill Daniels, also insisted on a very pale and ghostly
make-up called Silver Stone. This was not just a casual whim. It meant
that Daniels would have to light every scene with special care, keying on
Shearer's face, often to the disadvantage of her co-stars. Garbo was another
who worked with Daniels and who wore very pale make-up, presenting
the same problem. Stars were often reluctant to step out of their image,
even where the part clearly called for it. In *The Good Earth,* for instance,
Luise Rainer had a scene where she was supposed to be digging for
jewels with her bare hands. But when Bob Schiffer tried to put dirt under
her fingernails, she promptly reported him to the front office, furious at
this assault upon her manicure.

Some people were far less temperamental. Carole Lombard, who was
very matter-of-fact about the business of glamour, liked nothing more than
sharing its secrets. One of those to benefit from Lombard's generosity was
Martha Scott, soon after her arrival in Hollywood:

She called me over to her dressing room—she was shooting *Made for Each Other* with Jimmy Stewart—and she drew the shape of my face. She said, "Now, I've done this for myself—I have a very strange face—my makeup chart looks like a map of war-torn Europe—and you have some of the same problems I do, one of which is a square jaw." And she gave me some tips which I think about to this day.

In the panchromatic era, men had little need for special cosmetic care, though most male stars had a favorite make-up man who worked with them regularly. Clark Gable, for example, was generally made up by Stan Campbell. Aside from major dental problems and the like, men were not expected to be as flawless as their female counterparts. Had Robert Taylor been a woman, it's very probable that something would have been done about his nose, the tip of which pointed slightly to the left. It was straightened on just one occasion—for his role in *Camille*—with the aid of cosmetic putty.

Make-up problems for men did arise when they were playing character roles. During the filming of *The General Died at Dawn,* for example, Wally Westmore's staff had great difficulty in making Akim Tamiroff look

VIRGINIA BRUCE, WITH DIRECTOR EDWIN L. MARIN, BEING PREPARED FOR A SCENE, 1936.

sufficiently Chinese. Jack Dawn was called in to consult, but he was unable to come up with a satisfactory solution. Lewis Milestone, the director, suggested that they try to build Oriental eyelids on the actor's own with the kind of liquid rubber used at that time by dental technicians. When that didn't work, Milestone had Wally make casts from the eyelids of a Chinese actor, then apply these to Tamiroff's eyes.

Lon Chaney is the classic example of an actor who built his roles around physical transformations that were achieved with the aid of make-up devices he invented himself. In *The Horror People,* John Brosnan has described the torture that Chaney endured for the sake of convincing characterizations. For the three months it took to make *The Hunchback of Notre Dame,* he wore a rubber hump weighing seventy pounds, which was secured to a harness and pads that were designed to prevent him from standing erect. Over this he wore a tight-fitting rubber suit—unbearably hot—covered with animal hair, and his facial make-up included a contraption that made it impossible for him to close his mouth.

For *The Phantom of the Opera,* in order to achieve the effect of skull-like features, Chaney's make-up was partially created by celluloid disks placed inside the cheeks to make them seem hollow, a device inserted into his nose to spread the nostrils (also used at times to make black character actors appear more Negroid) and raise the tip, and protruding false teeth to which were attached prongs to stretch back his lips. So often did he play cripples of one kind or another that he actually became one himself. Harnesses such as that worn for *The Hunchback of Notre Dame* damaged his spine, and the crude contact lenses he once wore to simulate blindness affected his eyesight.

Another master of character make-up was Jack Pierce, who was the real creator of Frankenstein's monster and the other sinister denizens of Universal's horror pictures. During the filming of *Frankenstein,* it took three and a half hours a day to build the monster's features on Karloff's face. Cotton wool pads were covered with artificial skin to change the contours, layer upon layer of grease paint was applied to Karloff's eyelids, and plugs were glued to his neck. To create a feeling of bulk, Pierce designed a costume which weighed close to seventy pounds—the built-up boots alone weighed twenty-one pounds apiece. For *The Mummy,* produced the following year, Pierce made Karloff's skin look like flaking ashes by applying a thick paste to the normal make-up base, then baking it dry with heat lamps.

Character make-up was a full of tricks as glamour make-up. To simulate scars, for example, collodion—a nitrocellulose solution that dries to a tough, shiny, elastic membrane—was applied to the skin. Occasionally, fishskin was also used to approximate scar tissue, though it tended to produce painful attacks of dermititis.

CHARLES LAUGHTON BEING MADE UP FOR *Mutiny on the Bounty.*

It might be thought that Hollywood would have been anxious to keep these secrets from the fans, fearful that such knowledge would detract from the illusion on screen, but the reverse was true. Just as stars' real names were regularly printed in the pages of fan magazines, so details of their physical flaws and step-by-step descriptions of the mysteries of make-up—using top personalities as examples—provided the bases for dozens of feature articles. Readers were told that Ern Westmore eliminated a bump on Claudette Colbert's nose by drawing a fine white line down the middle of the offending feature. They were informed that Johnny Weissmuller required special body make-up to diminish unsightly bulges, and that a make-up man had to pencil individual hairs onto Reginald Denny's pate because the actor was allergic to toupees.

A rather unusual make-up publicity story is reported by Bob Schiffer:

> At Metro, we concocted a special makeup for Jeanette MacDonald. Nowadays we have these iridescent makeups that glitter and shine, but in those days makeups were heavier, so, to get an iridescent effect, I mixed gold dust in the powder. The publicity department picked up on it and said, "What a great gimmick!" They hired an armed guard and cooked up a story about how they needed him to bring the gold in. What happened, though, was that when Jeanette would start to sing and dance her body heat would turn all the little gold flecks green. She looked as if she had the measles.

Management.

Although some talent agencies, like Myron Selznick's, maintained departments which took care of the household bills, investments, and income tax returns of those clients who desired such services, it was inevitable that exclusively business management and investment counseling firms would begin to spring up as the nation's tax structure and the stars' financial lives became more complex.

One of the first film celebrity stabilizers was Rex Cole, a tax authority who founded the Equitable Investment Corporation in 1925, handling the business affairs of such stars as Gilbert Roland, Gloria Swanson, John Barrymore, Marlene Dietrich, and Robert Montgomery. A client like Constance Bennett would be allotted $100 a week pocket money, the rest of her salary being carefully budgeted and invested—with at least $20,000 a year allocated for clothes. In 1935 Cole represented Bennett in contract negotiations which brought her the unprecedented sum of $30,000 a week for ten years—the first contract figure to come over the Dow-Jones Industrial Sheet.

Following the pattern set by Rex Cole was the firm of Hollywood Management, Inc., run by Ralph Ring. Ring's organization would, in effect, take responsibility for the efficient running of his client's life. After receiving his pay check, Hollywood Management would absorb all business, domestic, and personal concerns, ranging from finding Mae West a tall, English-speaking Japanese chauffeur, to denying some other star permission to throw a party because it would bring him $500 over his monthly budget, to meeting the train of a bothersome out-of-town relative, to arranging for a dog-feeding service, to choosing the color of a new telephone. Major purchases would be handled by the firm, making a special effort to circumvent the overcharging of movie stars, which was rampant in Hollywood.

Each client was handled as a separate business concern, with a complete set of books, a bank account upon which checks were drawn by the company and countersigned by the client, and another—rigidly restricted —bank account for personal expenses. In 1937 Ring gave out the following typical monthly budget he would plan for a single male star earning $3,000 a week:

Reserve for federal and state tax	$4,335
Agent's commission (10%)	1,300
Management Company (2%)	260
Apartment rental	435
Servants	550
Automobile upkeep, etc.	540
Allowance for relatives	985
Insurance	465
Studio savings (taken out of pay)	650
Household expenses (food, liquor, light)	555
Entertainment	360
Charity	195
Investments and savings	1,900
Publicity	150
Trainer	170
Doctor	85
Voice, dance coaches	65

Many of the immense fortunes amassed by such performers as Fred MacMurray, Jeanette MacDonald, and Marlene Dietrich were formed under the guidance of Bo Roos. By the mid-forties, Roos estimated that his "syndicate" had invested between four and five million dollars, and controlled property valued at ten times that. The widespread Roos interests included oil wells, cattle ranches, orange groves, hotels, country clubs and apartment houses, a roofing company, a knitting mill, and a Mexican film studio. Directors' meetings would be held regularly to study and discuss financial reports and prospects.

MOTHERS AND OTHERS

A. Morgan Maree's firm was founded in 1932 as an investment counseling firm, to which clients like Humphrey Bogart, David Niven, Ginger
Rogers, Barbara Stanwyck, and Cesar Romero would pay 5 percent of
their gross earnings, in return for a meager weekly allowance and the bliss-
ful feeling of financial security.

M OTHERS AND OTHERS.

The mythical Hollywood mother really did exist. She could be seen at any
studio, sitting a few feet off the set, knitting, watching, coaching, reproach-
ing, keeping an eye on her emotional investment. The fact that she rarely
hesitated to speak her mind did nothing to endear her to the producers,
directors, costume designers, and others who had to work with her offspring, but she could not be ignored. Hollywood even held an annual
Mother's Night at the Beverly Hills Hotel, and in 1939 twenty of these
formidable creatures organized themselves as Motion Picture Mothers, Inc.
Soon the group had more than a hundred members, including the likes of
Ethel Gumm (mother of Judy Garland), Nell Panky (mother of Mickey
Rooney), Lela Rogers (mother of Ginger), Mrs. Tyrone Power, Sr., Mimi
Shirley (mother of Anne), Mrs. C. J. Romero, Ruth Brugh (mother of
Robert Taylor), Annette Y. de Lake (mother of Ann Sothern), Anna
LeSueur (mother of Joan Crawford), and Alice Cooper (mother of Gary).
They met regularly for lunch and paid monthly dues which were used to
provide goods and services for old film actors who had fallen on hard
times. The executive body of Motion Picture Mothers, Inc., felt it under-
stood the unfortunate troupers, making sure that their cupboards were
furnished with luxuries as well as staples and also helping to pay for
utilities. "What picture person can exist without a telephone?" asked Marie
Brown (mother of Tom).

The number of movie star biographies which are almost interchangeable
is quite startling: The strong mother with thwarted theatrical ambitions,
left alone with child by death or divorce, heads for Los Angeles with her
beautiful and/or talented offspring. Carole Lombard's parents divorced
when she was seven, and shortly thereafter, Bessie Peters left Fort Wayne,
Indiana, to settle in Hollywood with her three children. When Loretta
Young's father deserted his wife and four children, Gladys Royal Young

MARY PICKFORD AND HER MOTHER, CHARLOTTE.
CULVER PICTURES.

left Salt Lake City with her brood, opened a boardinghouse in Hollywood, and hired her daughters out as extras. This pattern was repeated over and over again, with new arrivals seeking inspiration from the feats of those who had preceded them. They had only to remind themselves of Charlotte Pickford, the patron saint of Hollywood mothers, who had first served as chaperone, then manager of her daughter's business affairs. According to Robert Windeler, a Pickford biographer, when Mary was twenty-eight, Charlotte was still standing over her in her dressing room, to make sure she was drinking the several glasses of warm milk daily her mother deemed necessary. Mrs. Pickford sat right beside her son Jack when he was directing a film, making production suggestions, and was very active in the running of United Artists.

In 1932 *Modern Screen* ran a feature on "Meddlesome Mothers of Hollywood" (hastily followed up a few months later by "Helpful Mothers of Hollywood"). The first category included the parent of Betty Bronson, a sensation after *Peter Pan,* whose mother's interference was concluded to have wrecked Bronson's career, and the mothers of Anita Page, Olive Borden, and Loretta Young (gossips felt that Mrs. Young tried to have Loretta's marriage to Grant Withers annulled because the family needed her pay check). In the second article, the point was made that Charlotte Pickford, Peg Talmadge (an enormously popular figure in early Hollywood), and Charlotte Selby (mother of Mary Miles Minter) formed a powerful triumvirate of shrewd businesswomen whose daughters had become so popular at the box office that they could virtually dictate their own terms to studio executives. Unfortunately, many other mothers, who lacked the abilities of these three, saw themselves as potential managers and succeeded only in cutting short their daughters' careers.

At times it seemed that the mother's aspirations might have focused on any child in the family. Lillian Grable, a frustrated entertainer, first tried unsuccessfully to thrust her older daughter, Marjorie, into the spotlight. When that failed, she urged little Ruth Elizabeth (called Betty) to work at her tap, toe, voice, and saxophone lessons until she was ready for the move to California. Pearl Darnell was determined that one of her three girls would be a star. When daughter Monetta was eleven, her impatient parent told people she was sixteen and got her a modeling job. Later, Pearl's persistent meddling would cause Linda Darnell acute embarrassment and difficulties with the 20th Century-Fox front office.

Jane Withers' mother allegedly determined very early in life that she would have one child, a daughter, who would go into show business. She is said to have rejected several proposals of marriage from men who disagreed with this notion. Some parents saw their children's gifts as a clearcut means of escape from the banality of their lives. Darla Hood remembers her mother telling her, "Darla, you're my ticket out of Liddy." Anne

JEAN HARLOW AND "MAMA JEAN."

MOTHERS AND OTHERS

Shirley's mother was typical of those who played the game of power through martyrdom, protesting in the August 1935 *Photoplay:*

> I had come from New York to put my baby into pictures and I wept because I could find no other way of surviving in a world that has no work to offer a mother who insists upon keeping her child with her.

Elizabeth Taylor's mother, who had a briefly successful stage career as Sara Southern, denies today that she tried to get both her children into show business, but once Elizabeth had become part of the M-G-M family, her mother would come onto the set and position herself behind the camera (and the director) and communicate with her daughter by a complicated set of hand signals (e.g., a finger on the neck meant "You're overdoing the emotion"). She was active in politicking for parts and even in costume decisions, anxious that designers should emphasize her daughter's wasp waist and developing bosom. Shirley Temple's mother was less overbearing than most, but she was shrewd enough to make sure that she was given a contract as her daughter's professional coach and governess, a job that brought her a salary in excess of $1,000 a week, and it was noted in *Modern Screen* in 1935 that in future any writer who profiled Shirley would have to hand over 10 percent of his payment to Mrs. Temple. According to Sidney Skolsky, Mrs. Temple monitored the famous moppet's entire existence, personally supervising each detail, down to rolling up Shirley's fifty-four curls every night.

JEANETTE MACDONALD AND HER MOTHER.

BETTE DAVIS WITH HER MOTHER, RUTHIE.

BETTY GRABLE AND HER MOTHER.

JOAN BLONDELL WITH HER MOTHER, KATHRYN BLONDELL.

DOROTHY LAMOUR AND HER MOTHER.

GINGER ROGERS AND THE FORMIDABLE LELA, AT THE ACADEMY
AWARDS CEREMONIES, 1942.

DEANNA DURBIN WITH HER PARENTS.

SPENCER TRACY AND HIS MOTHER.

It wasn't always a mother. Mary Astor's forbidding father, Otto Ludwig Wilhelm Langhanke, a German immigrant high school teacher, inspired by the success of such young women stars as Mae Marsh and Mary Pickford, pushed his daughter into a movie career when she was twelve and dominated her for years afterward. The fathers of Alfalfa and Spanky of the Our Gang comedies were involved in constant bickering on the set over whose kid got more lines or close-ups. The situation was resolved only when Hal Roach assigned someone to count the lines in the scripts to make sure that each boy had exactly the same number.

Undeniably, though, mothers dominated the scene. There was never a Hollywood father to compare with Lela Owens McMath, a woman who was far from being merely parasitic on her daughter Ginger. She had been a newspaper reporter in Independence, Missouri, and—after her divorce in 1916—consigned Ginger to the care of her grandparents before

NELSON EDDY EMBRACES HIS MOTHER.

heading for Hollywood to write screenplays, one of which she managed to sell to Fox in 1917. In World War I, Lela was a Marine sergeant, making training films and writing for the Corps magazine. Later she was a reporter for the Kansas City *Post* and the Fort Worth *Record,* and she helped found the Fort Worth Symphony, serving as its first general manager. But her true vocation was the promotion of Ginger Rogers. She had the child appearing in Kansas City advertising films before she was five, and when Ginger toured the vaudeville circuit, her mother acted as agent, writer, and wardrobe mistress, taking a 20 percent commission. Later, at RKO, she interfered with casts and crews, attempting to ingratiate herself, but more often alienating everyone. She kept a particularly sharp eye on Ginger's scripts, making sure that their politics never drifted toward the left, and much of Hollywood felt that she played a major part in the failure of Ginger's marriages. (When she and Lew Ayres separated in 1936, he stated that he couldn't compete with her mother.) The studio eventually put Lela in charge of its new talent school, as much to keep her off the Astaire-Rogers sets as to utilize her skills.

At times, these symbiotic relationships soured and ended up in the law courts. In 1934 Mary Astor's parents sued her for nonsupport, claiming they didn't have the money to continue making improvements on the $75,000 house she had bought them. Similar charges were brought by the fathers of both Gene Tierney and Paulette Goddard, while Veronica Lake's ambitious mother sued her for $500 a month support, plus a $17,416 lump sum settlement, claiming that her daughter was neglecting her. There were other mothers who were actively horrified by their offspring's chosen career. After Clara Bow won a fan magazine "Fame and Fortune" contest, it is said that her mother became so distraught that the future star awoke one night to find the woman standing over her with a knife held at her throat.

Not every parent-child relationship was totally neurotic. Jackie Cooper credits his mother with guiding him away from many of the pitfalls that presented themselves to the child star. She made sure that they lived in an "ordinary" neighborhood and did her best to see that he had "ordinary" friends.

Often an ambitious mother inspired fierce devotion on the part of the child she nudged to stardom. Lucille Ball preserved a close relationship with her mother, DeeDee, until the latter's death, as did Bette Davis with her mother, Ruthie, and Fred Astaire's mother—who engineered his early career and for years was his booking agent and promoter—was living with him until her demise in 1975. Ann Miller, at last report, was continuing to depend upon Clara Collier.

Although Jean Harlow was unscrupulously manipulated by her step-father, Marino Bello, she did not allow this to interfere with her loyalty to her mother, Mama Jean (the woman whose religious beliefs may have made her unintentionally responsible for Harlow's death). John Lee Mahin recalls a New Year's Eve party at which Harlow rose and said, "I want to toast the people who were responsible for what little success I have enjoyed—my mother, my father, and God." When Mahin quipped, "Gee, at least give Him top billing," Jean refused to speak to him for a year.

NEW NAMES.

After Phylis Isley Walker, Spangler Arlington Brugh, Judy Turner, Lucille LeSueur, Hedwig Kiesler, et al. were discovered, tested, and signed, one of the earliest decisions to be made concerned renaming—a decision which often led to the first battle of wills between studio and property. Sometimes the disagreement could be settled in moments (Suzanne Burce was informed by telephone that she had become Jane Powell), sometimes it took months of agonizing. In September of 1941 David O. Selznick wrote, in a memo to his director of advertising and publicity, as quoted by Rudy Behlmer in *Memo:*

> I would like to get a new name for Phylis Walker. I had a talk with her and she is not averse to a change. Normally I don't think names very important, but I do think Phylis Walker a particularly undistinguished name, and it has the additional drawback of being awfully similar to Phyllis Thaxter. . . .
>
> I don't want anything too fancy, and I would like to get at least a first name that isn't also carried by a dozen other girls in Hollywood. I would appreciate suggestions.

Four months later, he was getting impatient:

> Where the hell is that new name for Phylis Walker?
>
> Personally, I would like to decide on Jennifer and get a one-syllable last name that has some rhythm to it and that is easy to remember. I think the best synthetic name in pictures that has been recently created is Veronica Lake.

NEW NAMES

According to his wishes, one of the simplest names in the language was chosen and Phylis Walker became Jennifer Jones.

Some people refused from the start to fit into the romantic images certain proposed names represented. Bette Davis (who had changed the spelling of her first name from Betty after a friend of her mother's read Balzac's *La Cousine Bette* and suggested it) rejected Bettina Dawes. Joan Blondell could not see herself as Inez Holmes, and William Lundigan threatened to quit rather than become Larry Parks (a name later passed on to Samuel Klausman).

Joan Crawford was born Lucille LeSueur, and was also known for a time after her mother's remarriage as Billie Cassin. Harry Rapf, her patron at M-G-M, considered LeSueur too difficult to pronounce, too French, and too similar in sound to the word "sewer," so the studio promoted a national fan magazine contest, with a prize of $500 for the best new name. For a few weeks, Crawford was known as Joan Arden, until an extra by that name threatened to sue. M-G-M then settled for the second-place name in the contest, Joan Crawford, which had been suggested by a bedridden woman in Albany, New York.

The story goes that Garbo's name (which means "spirit" in Swedish) existed in the mind of her mentor, Mauritz Stiller, for years before he saw her, and that the moment they met, he knew that she was the star for whom he had been saving it. (If this is true, one can't help wondering why he first wanted to call her Mona Gabor.) Metro initially had doubts about the name Garbo, fearing that it sounded too much like "garbage."

Early in her career, Jane Peters decided to call herself Carol. When she signed with Fox, the studio asserted that Peters lacked glamour, adding that it was also too closely associated with another contract player, House Peters, whose name was the butt of frequent jokes. Like many others, she dug back into her own genealogy to find something familiar, and almost became Carol Knight. This was nixed, however, because Winfield Sheehan was convinced that two-syllable names were more effective for female stars, and Carol's mother came up with the name of close family friends, the Lombards. Although the addition of an "e" to her first name—making Carol into Carole—was later attributed by publicists to her interest in numerology, it was in fact the result of an accidental misspelling on the display posters for *Safety in Numbers* in 1930. It is said that Lombard's characteristic response at the time was, "What the hell, let's keep it that way." Joan Fontaine, on the other hand, *was* advised by an occultist to select a name ending with the letter "e." She had shed her real name, De Havilland, wishing to avoid the impression that she was exploiting the success of her sister, Olivia, and gave up St. John and Burfield to settle on the name of her mother's second husband.

Arlington Brugh accepted the fact that he would have to change his name and tried to adopt Stanhope, his mother's maiden name (Harlean Carpentier had taken on her mother's maiden name to become Jean Harlow), as it was also the name of the character he had been playing when he was discovered. That was rejected in favor of Ida Koverman's suggestion, Taylor. Still hoping to retain some semblance of the individuality he had grown up with as Arly Brugh, the contractee, together with publicity woman Kay Mulvey, came up with Ramsey Taylor. But Louis B. Mayer insisted on Robert, which had worked so well for two of their other leading men, Montgomery and Young.

Several fledgling performers did take on the names of characters they had some success in playing. Byron Barr (also known as Bryant Fleming) played Gig Young in *The Gay Sisters* and thereafter used that name. Dawn Paris, later Dawn O'Day, became Anne Shirley when she made *Anne of Green Gables,* and the name of Tom Brown came from the character he played in *Tom Brown of Culver.* Though Joe Yule, Jr., played Mickey McGuire in nearly fifty short subjects, legalities prevented the boy from using the name professionally, so he settled for Mickey Rooney. Maxine O'Brien became Margaret after her first role in *Journey for Margaret.* Archie Leach almost took on the name of the character he played in the Broadway musical *Nikki,* Cary Lockwood. The studio consented to the first name, but since there already was a Harold Lockwood in films, and the trend was then toward shorter names, an executive suggested Cary Grant instead.

There were instances when newcomers were given names similar to those of stars of a previous era, in the hopes that a certain glitter would continue to attach itself to the name. Hedwig Kiesler became Hedy Lamarr after Barbara LaMarr, whom many people considered the most beautiful of the silent actresses. Luis Alonso rejected B. P. Schulberg's suggestion of John Adams, instead combining the names of two of his screen favorites, John Gilbert and Ruth Roland, to become Gilbert Roland. Other names came from the most prosaic sources, from streets to cereals (Vera Hruba Ralston). Eve Arden, not doing too well as Eunice Quedens, reputedly combined the names of two of the bottles on her dressing table: Evening in Paris and Elizabeth Arden. Frank Cooper— there were already several actors with that name—is said to have been given a new first name by his agent, who hailed from Gary, Indiana. (Another version of this story has the name being suggested by a friend from Indiana who remarked that Gary was a city that had always sounded romantic to her.)

The transformation of Frances Gumm into Judy Garland came in two stages. The Gumm Sisters were appearing at the Oriental Theater in Chicago on a bill headed by George Jessell. Judy's sister, Virginia, has recalled that Jessel told them that they had better change their name if they wished to avoid being referred to as the Dumb Sisters or the Bum Sisters. Without forewarning, he introduced them at the next show as the Garland Sisters. Virginia believed that he explained at the time that his choice had been determined by his receiving, between shows, a phone call from critic Robert Garland. Jessel himself has claimed that he got the idea of the name Judy Garland from a telegram he sent to Judith Anderson in which he expressed the hope that her new play would add another rose to her garland of successes. Unfortunately, this contradicts the fact that the youngest of the Garland Sisters continued to use the name Frances for several months after that appearance at the Oriental. She herself recalled choosing Judy some time later, inspired by the title of a favorite Hoagy Carmichael song.

NICKNAMES

Amigo	Gilbert Roland.
Babe	Oliver Hardy.
Baby	What everyone called Jean Harlow.
Baby Elephant	What Maureen O'Hara's parents called her.
Bart	Herbert Marshall.
Becka	What Gary Cooper called girl friend Lupe Velez.
Black Bull of Gower Street	What George Murphy called Harry Cohn (also called White Fang by Ben Hecht).
Boz	The way Carole Lombard referred to publicist Russell Birdwell, whom most people called Bird.
Butch	Cesar Romero.

Creeping Jesus or Creepy	How Nicholas Schenck and others referred to Adolph Zukor.
Daisy	Marion Davies (pet name given her by Constance Talmadge, after the character she played in *The Floradora Girl*).
Doc	What childhood friends called Robert Taylor because he was so obsessed with becoming one.
Dodo	What Joan Crawford called husband Douglas Fairbanks, Jr.
Dody	Ann Harding (her real name was Dorothy).
Duke	As a boy, John Wayne (then Marion Morrison) had an Airedale terrier named Duke. The firemen at the local station began calling him Duke after his dog, and it stuck.
Dutch	Constance Talmadge (also what Tallulah Bankhead's father called her).
Eethel	John Barrymore's nickname for his sister. She called him Jake.
Fiddle-dee-dee	Victor Fleming's nickname for Vivien Leigh on *Gone With the Wind*.
Frantic Frog	Claudette Colbert, because of her hectic schedule at Paramount; also Fretting Frog, because of her demands on the cameraman.
Gretch the Wretch	Loretta Young (her real name was Gretchen). Ex-husband Grant Withers referred to her as "The Steel Butterfly."
Hetty Green	A reflection of Kay Francis' tightfistedness.
Hipper	What Douglas Fairbanks called Mary Pickford. Also "Tupper."
The Iron Butterfly	Jeanette MacDonald.
Jumbo	Wallace Beery's childhood name. He was also called Sweedie.

NICKNAMES

Junior	What Carole Lombard called husband William Powell when she wasn't calling him Philo (he once played Philo Vance). Also what Barbara Stanwyck called Bob Taylor.
Ma and Pa	Lombard and Gable. (Gable and Kay Williams called each other that, too.)
The Mad Monk	Victor Fleming.
Mayer's sundial	Producer Harry Rapf, because of his protruding nose.
Mims	Miriam Hopkins.
Minnie	What Bill Powell called Myrna Loy (she called him Mr. Pooh).
Missy	Barbara Stanwyck.
Monkeybitch	How Scott Fitzgerald referred to Joe Mankiewicz.
Monkey Face	Cameraman Charles Rosher's name for Mary Pickford; she called him Lord Plushbottom.
One-Take Van Dyke	W. S. Van Dyke was considered the fastest director in town.
Oomkins	David Selznick's pet name for brother Myron.
Pappy	Henry Fonda's nickname for John Ford. (John Wayne called him "Coach," Jimmy Stewart, "Boss.")
Peaches	What the boys in Brooklyn called Mae West as a kid.
Pete	Ramon Novarro. Also what Douglas Fairbanks, Jr., called his father (Senior called Junior "Jayar").
Pip	Arthur Treacher.
Poppy	What Marion Davies called Hearst.
Presh	What Shirley Temple was called by her mother.
The Queen	How Bob Taylor referred to wife Barbara Stanwyck.

Queenie	What schoolmates in Calcutta called Merle Oberon because she was so regal. (In Hollywood she was often called Princess.) Also what Gable called Myrna Loy after they were chosen King and Queen of Hollywood.
Redtop	What Katharine Hepburn was called by her father.
Slacksy O'Brien	Slacksy came from the fact that Sinatra's mother dressed him in fancy pants; O'Brien was his father's boxing name.
Slug	Joan Crawford's pet name for Spencer Tracy.
Sluggy	Bogart's nickname for wife Mayo Methot.
Speedy	Harold Lloyd.
Sporting Blood	What Errol Flynn called Jack Warner (Warner called Flynn "The Baron").
Tiger Lil	Flynn's nickname for wife Lili Damita.
Whitey	The nickname W. C. Fields preferred as a boy to his given name of Claude.
Willie	Nigel Bruce.
The Windmill	How Lauren Bacall was known in New York because of her swinging walk and long arms and legs; also "Pinwheel."
Winkie	John Barrymore's pet name for wife Dolores Costello (also "Small Egg" and "Shrimp").
Wriggle Britches	Gary Cooper's name for Shirley Temple.
Young Fellow	What DeMille always called Gloria Swanson.

NIGHT LIFE.

Whenever Hollywood made a film about itself, audiences could usually count on an opening panoramic shot—photographed from somewhere high in the hills—of the city at night, with shimmering grids of street lights vanishing in perspective and the beams of searchlights sweeping the sky. Next would come stock footage of local landmarks—the Hollywood Bowl, Grauman's Chinese Theater, and the Hollywoodland sign, all of them floodlit. Then this montage would dissolve to street-level shots of distinguished-looking dress extras, in tuxedos and evening gowns, descending from chauffeur-driven Packards and Rolls. Finally, there would be glimpses of neon signs blinking invitingly against the night sky: Ciro's, Earl Carroll's, the Mocambo, Slapsy Maxie's, the Trocadero, the Cocoanut Grove. For the average filmgoer, the names of these famous night spots were enough to evoke an atmosphere of glamour and sophistication.

If you were a regular reader of the fan magazines, especially in the late thirties, you might easily have formed the impression that the typical movie star spent the hours between dusk and dawn flitting from night club to night club. In fact, the work schedules of most of the contract players were so rigorous that such nocturnal antics would have demanded superhuman stamina, and it was only with the eager co-operation of studio publicity departments that the magazines managed to sustain the illusion of a Hollywood café society. For the benefit of the press, a limo might pick up Loretta Young and George Brent on the set where they were working and deposit them at the Trocadero for just long enough to allow Hymie Fink to snap a couple of pictures. Then they would return to the lot to shoot a few more scenes, or be whisked home to grab a few hours' sleep before they were awakened by the 5 A.M. call. The people who were at the clubs every night were the hangers-on and those who were "between jobs." This does not mean that many Hollywood personalities did not enjoy night life. On weekends, the night spots were generally filled with celebrities, and there were always a few people who could get by on black coffee and Benzedrine. All in all, though, the pace of Hollywood night life was relatively sedate in comparison with that of New York at the same time.

Back in the silent era, Prohibition had effectively put a damper on the growth of night life in the Los Angeles area. Around 1920 the favorites of the movie colony, all offering bootleg liquor, were Al Levy's Café, on Spring Street in downtown L.A., Baron Long's Vernon Country Club (a country club in name only), and Mike Lyman's Sunset Inn. Of these, the Sunset Inn, situated near the ocean in what is now Pacific Palisades, was probably the most fashionable. At any of these spots, however, you might chance upon an impromptu cabaret performance by Fatty Arbuckle or Chester Conklin, and the latter two establishments featured Saturday night dance contests at which gold cups were awarded for the most stylish interpretations of the Turkey Trot and the Black Bottom.

In his book *Incredible Land,* published in 1933, Basil Woon reported that there had been fewer than twenty speakeasies in Hollywood proper during the twenties, none of them very classy, augmented by about the same number of cheap "beer flats." There were, however, hundreds of bootleggers, mostly supplied by Tony Cornero. A grappa brandy made in Riverside is said to have been excellent, and decent gin and bourbon were also available, though drinkable scotch and rum were especially difficult to find. The movie colony had its own favorite bootleggers. Frank Orsatti supplied Louis B. Mayer and other executives, while many stars stocked their cellars with the assistance of a Frenchman called Maurice, who was also an excellent cook and catered parties on the side. Booksellers Stanley Rose and Larry Edmunds serviced the writers, arriving at the studios with sample cases loaded with books and booze. Provided you equipped yourself with a suitable flask, there was nothing to prevent you from enjoying a convivial evening at, say, the Cocoanut Grove.

The Cocoanut Grove—probably the most famous of all movie colony night spots—opened at the Ambassador Hotel in May of 1921. The name and its decor derived from the fact that the room's *maître d'*, Jimmy Manos, was acquainted with Valentino and knew that there were several artificial palm trees left over from the filming of *The Sheik*. He acquired them for next to nothing and an institution was born. It was there that Garbo and Stiller dined on Swedish herring and Joan Crawford and Carole Lombard competed for sterling-silver dance trophies. (When she first arrived in Hollywood, Crawford often found herself in trouble with Louis B. Mayer for displaying a little too much flesh during these contests.) Here Chaplin wooed Pola Negri and Bing Crosby first crooned his way into the hearts of the movie colony. A few years later, Virginia Bruce and Cesar Romero could be seen competing in hobbyhorse races, and, on Greenwich Village nights, dozens of stars would show up dressed as artists and models. On one auspicious evening, Robert Taylor presented a letter of introduction to Joel McCrea in the men's room.

Tuesday night was the night to be seen at the Grove. In the twenties and

Overleaf, THE COCOANUT GROVE IN THE AMBASSADOR HOTEL. CULVER PICTURES.

early thirties, stars like Pickford and Fairbanks, Ben Lyon and Bebe Daniels, Theda Bara, Gloria Swanson, Wallace Reid, Nita Naldi, Barbara LaMarr, and Chaplin would occupy the same table week after week, sporting their newest finery and dancing to the music of Gus Arnheim, or serving as guest judges for the Charleston contests. (If you were not one of the privileged few, you could tune in to the regular radio broadcasts from the Ambassador, introduced by Freddy Martin, who was known as "The Voice of the Grove.") Stars-to-be, like Judy Garland—still known as Frances Gumm—were showcased there as well. Tuesday was also the night for special events and elaborate decorations. The evening reached its climax when toy monkeys, attached to long strings, were lowered from the trees. (Once Lionel Barrymore released live ones.) Each male guest was invited to grab a monkey for his date, but since there were never enough to go around, this often led to violent free-for-alls.

The Grove was famous for fights. On opening night, Jimmy Manos established the tradition by flattening two male stars, and by 1937 publicists were claiming that 126 major fights had taken place there. One of the most celebrated occured when M-G-M gave a party for one of L. B. Mayer's top aides, Eddie Mannix. Mannix became drunk quite early in the proceedings and decided to replace Gus Arnheim's drummer. This was tolerated for a while, but eventually began to irritate a Warner Brothers contingent headed by Wilson Mizner, then on the Warner's payroll as a writer. When Mannix refused to leave the bandstand, Mizner decided to take matters into his own hands. Metro and Warner men poured onto the dance floor, throwing punches wildly, like teams coming off the bench in a hockey game. Mannix, an ex-bouncer, was usually able to take care of himself, but on this occasion, Mizner—said to have been the model for the Clark Gable character in *San Francisco*—subdued him. The Warners crowd claimed that Mannix performed a triple somersault before coming to rest. Mizner himself did not go unscathed, repairing to a nearby hospital to have several bones set. (See also FIGHTS.)

Another attraction of the Grove was its floor show, which featured near-naked showgirls perched on elaborate floats. On one occasion, Adrian placed a nude girl in what appeared to be a solid block of ice, causing a sensation among the patrons. The hollow center was in fact heated by an electric coil. On New Year's Eve, it was a tradition that the most beautiful of the Grove's chorus girls, clad in small posies of flowers, be lowered from the ceiling at the stroke of midnight. One year it was decided to supplement this popular spectacle with the concurrent release of a covey of snow-white doves. As the showgirls descended toward the merrymakers, the birds—each sporting a strategically placed strip of adhesive tape to prevent an aerial bombardment—were tossed from a balcony. Unfortunately, they refused to fly and instead settled themselves on tables, congregated on the

HOWARD HUGHES DEMONSTRATES ONE OF THE CONSEQUENCES OF HOLLYWOOD NIGHT LIFE IN THE COMPANY OF STARLET JUNE KNIGHT AND AGENT PAT DI CICCO, AT THE BEVERLY WILSHIRE HOTEL, 1935.

dance floor, and sampled the meringues and napoleons elegantly displayed on the pastry cart.

Of all the other Hollywood night spots, only three—the Trocadero, Ciro's, and the Mocambo, all situated on the Sunset Strip—ever approached the long-term popularity of the Grove. The Strip was an unincorporated zone—not belonging to any city—located halfway between Hollywood and Beverly Hills. During the thirties, the section came to life, largely through the efforts of Billy Wilkerson, publisher of the *Hollywood Reporter*. Wilkerson first struck a couple of miles east of the Strip, near the Sunset Boulevard offices of his paper, by opening the Vendôme, which quickly became the most fashionable lunchtime restaurant in Hollywood (see RESTAURANTS). Later, when Prohibition was repealed, he began to import wines and liquor and, while looking for somewhere to store them, came across an abandoned building on the Strip which had once been a gambling joint and speakeasy. He bought it for its spacious cellar, then hit upon the idea of converting the upstairs into a night club. The name he chose for it was the Trocadero. Wilkerson had very little cash to play with but persuaded the contractor and Harold Grieve, the decorator, to accept deferred payments. Even so, the place was still unfinished when he ran out

219

of money. According to an interview he gave *Close-up* magazine in 1960, Wilkerson saw Myron Selznick driving by in the Rolls-Royce that Jack Warner had given him, invited the agent to inspect the premises, then asked him why, despite the fact that he was a great partygoer, he had never given one of his own. Wilkerson proposed that Selznick throw a party for the Trocadero's opening night, at cost. Selznick agreed, and the money he put up for the evening tided Wilkerson over. (Unkind observers have suggested that Selznick bailed Wilkerson out in return for the favor of his clients being well treated by Wilkerson's paper.) The Trocadero was packed for Selznick's blowout, and there were large private parties on the two succeeding nights—but after that, nobody came. Wilkerson told the *maître d'* to put up the velvet rope and keep the band playing. Anyone who arrived at the club or phoned was told that the place was sold out and that no reservations were available for two weeks. This ruse worked and the Troc was soon jammed every evening.

The Vendôme and the Trocadero complemented each other splendidly because, since one was open only for lunch and the other only for dinner, the same staff could service both. The original Café Trocadero, inaugurated in 1933, was a low, graceful Colonial-style building with a long striped canopy and a folksy little weather vane. In 1936 it was remodeled along somewhat eclectic lines, remaining as popular as ever until the war and subsisting for several years more, eventually closing in 1948. In the Troc's heyday, Sunday was the big night. Maurice, the captain, and Jean, the *maître d'*, were masters of Hollywood protocol, skillfully juggling tables and booths to avoid bruising egos. It was there that Rita Hayworth made the spectacular entrance which fired Harry Cohn's imagination and led directly to her being groomed for stardom. It was at the Troc, too, that young hopefuls like Mary Martin and Martha Raye found an outlet for their talents.

Ciro's was located on the north side of the Strip on a site that had once been occupied by the Clover Club (see GAMBLING). When the Clover was closed, in 1938, because of antigaming pressures, it was bought by Al Freitas, who reopened the place as the Club Seville. In this incarnation, its most notable feature was a glass dance floor laid over a pool filled with carp. This gimmick seems to have had something to do with the Seville's quick demise. Women customers did not enjoy the sensation of fish eyes peering up their skirts, and everyone was terrified that the floor might shatter. Billy Wilkerson took it over, installed a conventional dance floor, and renamed it Ciro's.

The Mocambo, owned by Charlie Morrison, was across the street, not far from the Trocadero. The ASPCA tried to prevent its opening because live exotic birds, displayed behind glass windows, featured prominently in the decor. It was argued that the club's hours and the noise of the orchestra

ELSA MAXWELL INVESTIGATES CAFÉ SOCIETY, HOLLYWOOD STYLE,
WITH DOUGLAS FAIRBANKS, JR., CESAR ROMERO,
BETTY FURNESS, AND MARLENE DIETRICH.

would upset the birds' eating and sleeping habits, but the situation was resolved when a carefully devised schedule was arranged to accommodate them. It was at the Mocambo that Frank Sinatra had his first Hollywood success, and it was a favorite haunt of Bogart and Bacall, for whom Emil Coleman, the orchestra leader, would always strike up "That Old Black Magic."

Other clubs enjoyed passing vogues. The Cotton Club, in Culver City, was another popular Sunday night venue for a while—when Jean Harlow was under contract to Howard Hughes, they could often be seen there together. In the early thirties, the Pom Pom Club, halfway between Hollywood and Beverly Hills, attracted a late-night audience to its "girl show." The Club Marti, the Casanova, and the Century Club all catered to the movie crowd around 1937, as did the Club Bali and the Roosevelt Hotel, which were mainly for dancing. The Hawaiian Paradise—part-owned by Frank Borzage's wife—received a good deal of attention in the columns, and so did the Famous Door. Maxine's was an early arrival on the Strip, and Eddie Brandstatter's Montmartre was, for a while, a successful Tuesday night alternative to the Grove, featuring dance contests in which the most celebrated of stars participated (it was also popular with female stars for lunch on Wednesdays). Brandstatter had previously operated the Embassy Club—said to have had the best food in town in its day—a private club whose members included Richard Barthelmess, Ronald Colman, William Powell, Marion Davies, Marian Nixon, Billie Dove, and Howard Hughes. Later, his Sardi's on Vine Street enjoyed considerable popularity with the luncheon crowd.

In 1928 Fatty Arbuckle—unable to appear in front of the cameras in the wake of the scandal that had befallen him—became a partner in the Plantation Club in Culver City. Cedric Gibbons, head of the M-G-M art department, designed the decor without accepting payment, and opening night saw Hollywood's elite turning out in force. Tom Mix, Buster Keaton, Chaplin, Pickford and Fairbanks, Harry Langdon, Mickey Neilan, Ruth Roland, Bebe Daniels, and the three Talmadge sisters provided entertainment, while Mabel Normand presented Arbuckle with his own likeness—life-size—modeled in flowers. George Olsen led the band, with his wife providing vocals, and for a while the Plantation was a big success, but a series of police raids (this was still during Prohibition) diminished its popularity.

In the early thirties, a place called the New Frolics Gardens was patronized by comedians like Groucho Marx and Jimmy Durante, who occasionally provided extemporaneous entertainment. Ad-lib celebrity shows were also a major attraction at Grace Hayes's Roadhouse, out in the San Fernando Valley, which was extremely popular with movie people. In

1939 Grace Hayes initiated nightly take-offs on *Gone With the Wind,* picking the cast at random from her famous customers.

Very different kinds of night spots were Slapsy Maxie's and Earl Carroll's—Californian outposts of the Folies Bergères tradition. Situated in Hollywood, in a building that rather resembled an early supermarket, Slapsy Maxie's was run by Maxie Rosenbloom, who acted as master of ceremonies, setting the stage for one of the city's best floor shows with his own brand of deadpan humor. Earl Carroll had made his name in New York as a showman in the manner of Flo Ziegfeld. His Hollywood theater-restaurant opened on Christmas Day, 1938—the impresario having announced that a thousand-dollar lifetime cover charge would entitle patrons to a private room padded with patent leather. Opening night attracted Marlene Dietrich, Dolores Del Rio, Jack Warner, Sonja Henie, Edgar Bergen, Richard Barthelmess, Louis B. Mayer, Gable and Lombard, Tyrone Power, Jackie Coogan and Betty Grable, Claudette Colbert, Constance Bennett, Darryl Zanuck, David Selznick, and Franchot Tone, among other luminaries. At one point during the show that night, Bob Hope, Jack Benny, Errol Flynn, Milton Berle, Joe E. Brown, Walter Pigeon, Don Ameche, Robert Taylor, and W. C. Fields were all on stage together. The regular show included a variety of games which invited audience participation. During the war years, servicemen would be brought on stage to fasten the Merry Widow corsets of wriggling chorus girls.

As at the Grove, there were spectacular tableaux featuring flimsily draped models. Carroll's top show girl—also his mistress and later his wife—was Beryl Wallace. When LeRoy Prinz had recommended her to Carroll in New York, the showman had thought she was a little hefty for his taste, but, in California, he installed her at the Sunset Towers—where many of the best-kept women were housed—and they enjoyed a lasting liaison which ended only when they were killed together in an airplane crash after World War II. Carroll was a vain, self-important, faintly pompous man, but—despite his exposure to hundreds of attractive women—he seems to have remained faithful to the statuesque Beryl (though it has been said that he was not averse to "lending" girls to visiting celebrities). Los Angeles architecture buffs remember Earl Carroll's as having a facade which was one of the most extravagant examples ever of the art of strip lighting. Similar to Earl Carroll's, but cruder, was a big honky-tonk barn of a place called the Florentine Gardens. Here, too, seminude girls were the main attraction and audience participation was encouraged.

Farther off the beaten track was the "Little Harlem" section located south of downtown Los Angeles. The black population of the area had grown rapidly since the end of World War I, and there was a thriving night life on and around Central Avenue. The clubs there presented top bands, like Cab Calloway, and the Summerville Hotel, known as "the colored Ritz," housed performers like Stepin Fetchit. Billie Holiday and other black headliners were often booked into Billy Berg's night club in the San Fernando Valley, another spot that was very popular with the Hollywood crowd. Special tastes were catered to at Mary's, a lesbian club on the Strip, and at the Café Gala, a famous gay bar in the hills above Sunset.

OFFICES.

As a group, studio heads were not averse to being thought of as benign dictators, and one of their common symbols of power was the grandiose office, often soundproofed and containing a desk which housed a complicated communications system extending to every corner of the fiefdom. Several of them used the psychological ploy of situating the desk at the far end of a thickly carpeted room, so there would be a long, torturous walk for the visitor before he reached it. Sam Goldwyn, whose own executive throne was located a mere twelve feet from the door, once grumbled to Louis B. Mayer, "You need an automobile to reach your desk!" Mayer's office had walls of white leather, and he sat, on a chair constructed to make him seem taller than he actually was, behind an enormous, horseshoe-shaped desk, his back to a window equipped with drapery and venetian blinds that could be adjusted so that his own face remained in shadow while those of his visitors were fully lit. To one side of the desk was an elaborate switchboard, and hidden on the floor were buzzers that could be used to summon various key aides.

Richard Arlen has testified that when he visited Harry Cohn's office in 1927, there were tops of tin cans nailed to the baseboards to keep the rats out, but as Columbia became more successful, Cohn installed himself in a suite comparable to Mayer's, making use of some of the same devices. There was a substantial door, with no knob on the outside—it opened only when he pressed a buzzer—and a window overlooking Gower Street, which enabled him to check on the comings and goings of his employees. Behind his circular desk was an autographed portrait of Mussolini (upon whose office Cohn's was modeled), which was eventually replaced, when it became less acceptable to admire Il Duce, by a row of Oscars. Like Mussolini and like Mayer, Cohn sat on an elevated chair and could control the lighting so that his own features remained obscure. (Cecil B. DeMille was more obvious when it came to the psychology of lighting. At the kick of a switch under his cluttered desk, a glaring beam would focus on some already intimidated visitor.)

Another apparatus of control was the wait to enter the sanctuary, and again Harry Cohn exploited this to the full. Occasionally he would leave his office on an imaginary mission just to see whom he was keeping waiting, or else he might steal a glimpse of the encamped supplicants from the side door held an inch or two ajar. The most legendary waits, however, were outside Irving Thalberg's office at M-G-M. People were known to return there day after day, seeking an audience. According to a famous anecdote, the Marx Brothers once lit a fire in the outer office to attract Thalberg's attention during just such a wait. It seems likely that Thalberg played the waiting game rather less consciously than Cohn—the work load he took on was extraordinary, and his obsessive attention to detail made it all the more time-consuming. Still, he must have been aware of the effect he was having. (Mayer, interestingly enough, seldom kept people waiting, though his own work load was comparable to Thalberg's.) The atmosphere in Thalberg's quarters was, however, rather civilized by the standards of Hollywood's executive suites. His office was comfortably furnished, and, in the afternoon, a black butler would serve tea and highballs. In 1932 *Fortune* provided the following description of the inner sanctum:

> Thalberg seats himself, in his moderne beaverboard office, at a massive, shiny desk, in front of a dictograph which looks like a small pipe organ and partially hides a row of medicine bottles. Before him are huge boxes of cigarettes, which he never opens, and plates of apples and dates into which he sometimes dips a transparent hand.

David Selznick's office was unusual in that it was downright homey in feeling, complete with chintz curtains and overstuffed chairs and sofas. Bright and sunny, the room featured an antique mahogany desk, upon which rested, in addition to the usual accessories, a jar filled with cookies, which the producer nibbled on in an attempt to check his hyperglycemic condition. Darryl Zanuck's high-ceilinged green and gold working quarters were filled with stuffed and skinned mementos of African safaris—boar heads, jaguar skins, and rhinoceros feet.

Not only studio chiefs and production bosses had impressive work spaces. Billy Grady, during his years as head of casting at M-G-M, had a five-room bungalow as his headquarters. His own office was protected by two secretaries, double sets of doors, a private switchboard, and a window of one-way glass. Relatively severe, the room contained a desk, two chairs, three telephones, a bookcase crammed with actors' records, and an antique umbrella stand filled with Grady's collection of canes.

Of course, not all echelons of studio employees found themselves in particularly spacious or comfortable surroundings. Writer Winston Miller remembers that when they ran out of offices at Republic, he was put to work in a film vault, and John Lee Mahin recalls that the old writers' building at Metro—affectionately dubbed the Triangle Shirtwaist Factory —was alive with mice. S. J. Perelman has recorded his wife's reaction to the office they were assigned in that building in 1936:

> She looked around the gloomy little lazaret we were to occupy, furnished with a worm-eaten desk, two gumwood chairs and a spavined divan. It was a pity, she observed mildly, that the studio's prodigality did not extend to its decor.

PARENTAL PROFESSIONS

STAR	FATHER
Abbott, Bud	Advance man for Ringling Brothers circus; mother a bareback rider
Allyson, June	Bronx building superintendent
Annabella	French publisher
Arlen, Richard	Lawyer
Arliss, George	Printer-publisher
Arthur, Jean	Photographer
Astaire, Fred	Beer salesman
Astor, Mary	German teacher in Illinois public schools

Ball, Lucille	Lineman for Anaconda Copper Company
Bankhead, Tallulah	Congressman; 48th Speaker of the House of Representatives (William Brockman Bankhead)
Bara, Theda	Tailor
Bari, Lynn	Clergyman
Barnes, Binnie	London policeman
Baxter, Anne	Sales manager of Frankfort Distilleries; grandfather was Frank Lloyd Wright
Beery, Wallace	Police sergeant
Bellamy, Ralph	Advertising executive
Bendix, William	Musician in local bands and handyman at Vitagraph Studios in Brooklyn
Bennett, Constance and Joan	Actor (Richard Bennett)
Bergman, Ingrid	Camera shop owner
Bickford, Charles	Coffee importer
Blondell, Joan	Vaudevillian
Bogart, Humphrey	Internist; mother was prominent magazine illustrator, Maude Humphrey (used Humphrey as model for Mellin's baby food ad)
Bow, Clara	Coney Island waiter; part-time handyman
Bruce, Virginia	Insurance broker
Burke, Billie	Barnum & Bailey clown
Byington, Spring	Educator; mother was a doctor
Cagney, James	Bartender
Carradine, John	Newspaperman; mother a doctor; grandfather founded the Holy Rollers
Chaney, Lon	Owned a barbershop
Chatterton, Ruth	Architect
Chevalier, Maurice	House painter
Colbert, Claudette	Banker
Colby, Anita	Pulitzer Prize-winning cartoonist (Bud Counihan)
Colman, Ronald	Silk merchant
Cooper, Gary	Justice of the Montana Supreme Court (Charles Cooper)

227

Parental Professions

Costello, Lou	Owned a small silk mill
Crabbe, Buster	Overseer on pineapple plantation of Libby, McNeill & Libby
Darnell, Linda	Postal clerk
Darwell, Jane	President, Louisville Southern Railroad
Davies, Marion	City magistrate
Davis, Bette	Patent attorney; mother a portrait photographer
Day, Laraine	Grain dealer and government interpreter for Ute Indians; great-grandfather one of the Apostles of the Mormon Church
De Havilland, Olivia, and Joan Fontaine	English instructor at Imperial University, Tokyo; also operated patent law firm
Del Rio, Dolores	Bank manager (left Mexico to flee Pancho Villa)
Devine, Andy	Hotel owner
Dietrich, Marlene	Father and stepfather Prussian officers
Douglas, Melvyn	Concert pianist (Edouard Hesselberg)
Dressler, Marie	Piano teacher
Drew, Ellen	Barber
Dunn, James	Stockbroker
Dunne, Irene	Mississippi riverboat operator; government ship inspector
Durante, Jimmy	Side-show barker
Dvorak, Ann	Biograph director (Sam McKim)
Fairbanks, Douglas	Lawyer (founding President of U.S. Law Association)
Farmer, Frances	Lawyer
Faye, Alice	Policeman
Fetchit, Stepin	Key West cigar maker
Fields, W. C.	Fruit and vegetable peddler (with a horse named White Swan)
Fitzgerald, Geraldine	Lawyer
Flynn, Errol	Marine biologist on staff of University of Tasmania; commissioner of Tasmanian fisheries
Ford, Glenn	Railroad executive
Gable, Clark	Oil driller
Garbo, Greta	Laborer

Garfield, John	Coat presser in factory; cantor
Garland, Judy	Movie theater owner
Gaynor, Janet	Paper hanger
Gilbert, John	Strolling player
Grable, Betty	Bookkeeper
Grant, Cary	Suit presser for local clothing manufacturer
Grayson, Kathryn	Contractor-realtor
Greenstreet, Sydney	Leather merchant
Harding, Ann	Army officer
Harlow, Jean	Dentist
Hart, William S.	Builder of flour mills
Hayward, Susan	Coney Island barker; subway guard
Heflin, Van	Dentist
Henie, Sonja	Fur merchant
Hepburn, Katharine	Urologist; cofounder of Connecticut Social Hygiene Association; mother a Suffragette and early advocate of birth control
Hope, Bob	Stone mason
Hopkins, Miriam	Insurance salesman
Horton, Edward Everett	Printer
Hutton, Betty	Railroad brakeman
Jones, Jennifer	Owner of summer tent stock company; later a film distributor
Karloff, Boris	In the Indian Civil Service
Keaton, Buster	Vaudevillian
Lake, Veronica	Seaman on Sun Oil Company tankers
Lamarr, Hedy	A director of the Bank of Vienna
Laughton, Charles	Hotel owner
Leigh, Vivien	Stockbroker
Lloyd, Harold	Photographer, shoe salesman, sewing machine salesman, proprietor of pool hall
Louise, Anita	Antique dealer
Loy, Myrna	Cattleman; member of Montana Legislature
Lupino, Ida	Headline comedian (Stanley Lupino)
MacDonald, Jeanette	Contractor
McLaglen, Victor	Anglican clergyman (Bishop of Claremont, South Africa)

Parental professions

MacMurray, Fred	Concert violinist
McQueen, Butterfly	Stevedore
Main, Marjorie	Minister
March, Fredric	Manufacturer
Margo	Surgeon
Mature, Victor	Scissors grinder
Menjou, Adolphe	Hotel man and restaurateur
Milland, Ray	Construction engineer
Miller, Ann	Criminal lawyer
Miranda, Carmen	Wholesale produce merchant
Montez, Maria	Spanish Consul and Embassy delegate to Dominican Republic (later Paris, Belfast, Liverpool)
Montgomery, Robert	Vice-president, New York Rubber Company
Moorhead, Agnes	Presbyterian minister
Morgan, Frank and Ralph	Son of cofounder of Angostura bitters
Muni, Paul	Strolling players
Murphy, George	Track coach (trained Jim Thorpe)
Nolan, Lloyd	Shoe manufacturer
Novarro, Ramon	Dentist
Oberon, Merle	Railway official
O'Brien, Virginia	Captain of Detectives, L.A. Police Department
O'Hara, Maureen	Dublin clothing merchant
Olivier, Laurence	Clergyman
Pickford, Mary	Ran the refreshment concession on a Lake Ontario excursion boat
Pigeon, Walter	Haberdasher
Powell, William	CPA
Power, Tyrone	Stage actor
Quinn, Anthony	Cameraman for William Selig
Raft, George	Route supervisor, John Wanamaker warehouse
Ragland, Rags	Building superintendent
Rathbone, Basil	Mining engineer
Robinson, Edward G.	Candy store owner

Rogers, Ginger	Electrical engineer
Roland, Gilbert	Bull-ring owner
Romero, Cesar	Importer-exporter of sugar-refining machinery
Rooney, Mickey	Vaudevillian
Russell, Rosalind	Trial lawyer
Rutherford, Ann	Metropolitan Opera tenor
Ryan, Robert	Building contractor
Sanders, George	Rope manufacturer; mother a horticulturist
Sheridan, Ann	Mechanic
Sinatra, Frank	Prize fighter (under the name of Marty O'Brien); Mother leader of the 3rd Ward, 9th District, Hoboken, N.J.
Sondergaard, Gale	Professor, University of Minnesota
Sothern, Ann	Grandfather a pioneer in submarine design
Stanwyck, Barbara	Bricklayer (worked on Panama Canal)
Sterling, Robert	Baseball player (Walter S. Hart)
Stewart, James	Hardware store owner
Sullavan, Margaret	Stockbroker
Swanson, Gloria	Civilian transport agent for U.S. Army
Taylor, Robert	Doctor
Temple, Shirley	Bank manager
Tierney, Gene	Insurance broker
Tone, Franchot	President, Carborundum Company of America
Tracy, Spencer	Sales manager, Sterling Motor Truck Company
Turner, Lana	Mine foreman
Twelvetrees, Helen	Advertising manager for Brooklyn edition of New York *Evening Journal*
Valentino, Rudolph	Veterinarian
Velez, Lupe	Colonel in Mexican Army
Walker, Robert	Editor, Salt Lake City newspaper
Wayne, John	Druggist
West, Mae	Heavyweight boxer ("Battling Jack" West), later a private detective; mother a corset model
Wong, Anna May	Laundry man

231

PARTIES.

Since early Hollywood had little to offer in the way of public entertainment, aside from weekly dances at the large hotels, the pioneers of the movie colony—many of whom were used to the livelier pace of New York and other large cities—were forced to create a self-contained social life for themselves. Parties of all kinds, ranging from informal get-togethers to bacchic orgies at Mack Sennett's place to extravaganzas staged on the scale of a DeMille epic, have always been an integral part of the Hollywood scene. Prohibition and the watchful eye of the Hays Office reinforced the tradition (it was safer to get drunk behind the wrought-iron gates of a Beverly Hills mansion than in some restaurant open to the public), as did the ever-growing need for privacy. Movie people generally felt more comfortable with their peers, socializing with those who understood the problems attendant upon stardom, weekly grosses, and production schedules.

Hollywood parties were different from parties anywhere else, if only because the private personas of many of the party-goers were often so at variance with their all too well known public images. It must have been delightful, for example, to see Ronald Colman performing square dances dressed in blue jeans, plaid shirt, and red bandanna—a common sight at one time. Then, too, Hollywood parties forced hostesses to confront delicate decisions that were peculiar to that locale. Should Hymie Fink and the other fan magazine photographers be permitted to attend? Should Hedda and/or Louella be invited?

A few people were above such petty considerations. William Randolph Hearst and Marion Davies, for example, had little to fear from Hedda or Louella (Louella, after all, was a Hearst employee and Hedda was a long-time court favorite). W. R. and Marion were the movie colony's most inveterate and extravagant party-givers. Marion, in particular, was never more ebullient than when she was playing the role of hostess. Charlie Chaplin has reported in his autobiography that in the early twenties, whenever Hearst was called East on business, Marion would immediately throw a large-scale party in her Beverly Hills home (this was before W. R. built the famous Santa Monica beach-front house for her). And this would

232

AT ONE OF WILLIAM RANDOLPH HEARST'S MANY COSTUME PARTIES:
CLARK GABLE, CAROLE LOMBARD, HEARST, ANN WARNER, AND
FRANCES MARION.

invariably trigger off a whole round of parties, with Valentino and Chaplin himself reciprocating.

Later, the Santa Monica house and Hearst's San Simeon ranch (see HOMES and SAN SIMEON) were the scenes of dozens of parties, the most famous of which were the costume balls given each year for Hearst's birthday. There was nothing W. R. liked better than to get dressed up. A theme was chosen and suitable outfits ordered (by the gross) from Western Costume. In 1933, for Hearst's seventieth birthday, the theme was pioneer days, and covered wagons were used as props. The hostess was the picture of simplicity in a sunbonnet and a gingham dress, while W. R. chose to appear as a Mississippi riverboat gambler. At a later party, with an all-American theme, Norma Shearer, who disliked being dictated to, chose to disregard the terms of the invitation and arrived as Marie Antoinette. Her

233

period skirts were so voluminous that the seats had to be removed from her car before she could enter it, and she was unable to pass through the main door of the Davies beach house. Marion, according to her own account, told Shearer she would have to take off the dress. A noisy argument ensued, which was joined by Hedda Hopper, who berated Shearer for indelicately appearing as a Frenchwoman when Mr. Hearst had just been thrown out of France. The Queen of the M-G-M lot eventually managed to effect an entrance by way of the ballroom.

The theme of W. R.'s seventy-first birthday party was Tyrolean. Two years later he celebrated with a Spanish fiesta. In 1937 his seventy-fourth birthday was marked by a circus party for which one wall of the Santa Monica house was torn down to accommodate a carousel borrowed from the Warner Brothers back lot. (The hostess rode it half the night, trying to catch the brass ring.) There were side shows and a huge birthday cake, baked in the shape of a circus tent, for the five hundred guests. Marion was costumed as a bareback rider (so was Dolores Del Rio), and Hearst (as well as Henry Fonda) was dressed as a clown. Cary Grant and Paulette Goddard were acrobats, Errol Flynn and David Niven elephant boys, and Bette Davis, after some persuasion—she considered the whole thing silly—appeared as a bearded lady. Marion enjoyed riding the carousel so much that she borrowed it again, a month later, for another party. The wall had been rebuilt in the meantime and had to be torn down once more. For a baby party at Davies' Beverly Hills house, Clark Gable came as a Boy Scout, and Joan Crawford dressed as Shirley Temple. On yet another occasion, Groucho Marx impersonated Rex the Wonder Horse.

It is odd, if perhaps predictable, that these people who spent so much of their working day in heavy costume and make-up would choose to play yet another role in their free time, but barely a month went by without a masquerade of some sort. In the twenties, in fact, there was a group known as the 8080 Club, which held regular costume parties, each member taking a turn in his own home. Dagmar Godowsky has described how she threw a baby party at which Nazimova appeared in diapers pinned with a cluster of cherries, and Wallace Reid arrived as Buster Brown, complete with blond wig. Dagmar greeted her guests in the guise of a Chinese infant, with bound feet and squared-off bangs. There were "come as you are" parties (with invitations often hand-delivered by the hosts at some odd hour when they could hope to find the guest in his or her underwear, preferably with cold cream liberally smeared on the face); "come as you were" parties (with hours spent trying to guess whose baby pictures belonged to whom); and there were "come as your first ambition" parties (a notable one was thrown by the Edgar Bergens). One leap year there was a party for married couples only who were instructed to "come exactly as you were when your romance began." Lee Tracy arrived wearing nothing but a shower curtain. In 1937 there was the inevitable "come with the wind" party, thrown by the Jack Oakies to celebrate their wedding anniversary, at which the likes of the Jimmy Cagneys, the Pat O'Briens, the Dick Powells (Joan Blondell), Robert Young, and Elaine Barrie Barrymore cavorted in southern attire. (The agonizing production progress of *Gone With the Wind* was the butt of countless jokes. At one large dinner party, Sid Grauman installed at the table a life-size wax effigy of an aged David Selznick, bearing the legend "Selznick after the final shot of *Gone With the Wind*.")

To commemorate their eleventh anniversary, indefatigable costume-ball, garden-fete, and white-tie party-givers Ouida and Basil Rathbone invited 250 guests, to come attired as famous brides and grooms, to the Victor Hugo restaurant, which they had had converted for the evening into a papier-mâché cathedral. The host and hostess presented themselves as the Emperor Franz Joseph and the Empress Elizabeth of Austria. Fredric and Florence March, as a caveman and woman, walked off with the "most original costume" prize, while Theda Bara, as a vampire, was chosen "most dramatic" and Dolores Del Rio, a Spanish bride, the "most beautiful." Among the other guests who dined on squab and champagne till 5 A.M. were Jeanette MacDonald and Gene Raymond (Romeo and Juliet), Anna Neagle and Adrian (Camille and Armand), Cole Porter (a Bowery groom), Mervyn LeRoy (a hillbilly), Loretta Young (Mrs. Satan), and the Edward G. Robinsons (Napoleon and Josephine). At another Rathbone party, for the cause of war-torn Poland, Leopold Stokowski and Artur Rubinstein were guests of honor, and the Rathbones' dining hall was extended into the garden by means of a canopy. The dining area was redecorated for the occasion in silver lamé and "Dubonnet" red, and the opening bars of Chopin's "Polonaise Militaire" were inscribed on a cellophane frieze that was stretched around the walls.

The *Hollywood Reporter* of June 4, 1934, called the gala thrown for the Mervyn LeRoys at the Laemmle estate, "probably the most original and colorful party ever staged here." A "Ziegfeld artist" was called upon to turn the house and grounds into a pastiche of the Chicago World's Fair, and the living room into a night club. Sonja Henie converted her tennis court into a New York street for one of her parties, complete with plastic sky and cloud projections. Errol Flynn on one occasion filled his pool with lotus blossoms, while a bubble-making machine produced multicolored bubbles all night long. The West Side Tennis Club had an annual "Bowery" party, and in 1936 the Donald Ogden Stewarts held a "Nervous Breakdown Ball" at Jock Whitney's estate. This started at noon, with guests arriving in white tie and tails. At four in the afternoon, an ambulance arrived and from it emerged Louella Parsons and her husband, Doc Martin, followed by four "interns" carrying Carole Lombard on a stretcher. Lombard seems to have had something of an obsession with ambulances,

Overleaf, A PARTY AT PICKFAIR WITH, AMONG OTHERS, FAY WRAY, GARY COOPER, PICKFORD, AND FAIRBANKS.

DURING A COSTUME PARTY AT THE WEST SIDE TENNIS CLUB,
JEAN ARTHUR RECEIVES A PRIZE FROM IDA KOVERMAN, WHILE
ROBERT MONTGOMERY LOOKS ON.   CULVER PICTURES.

stretchers, hospitals, and all the paraphernalia of medical science. She once staged an elaborate party with an infirmary theme, turning her living room into a ward filled with equipment rented from a medical supply house. Each guest was given a hospital gown to don over his evening clothes, was led to a white iron bed (complete with medical records), and was served dinner on an operating table. On one nonclinical evening, Lombard threw a party for her current boyfriend, writer Robert Riskin. Guests had been requested to appear in evening dress and were taken aback to be greeted by their hostess in rolled-up dungarees and a checkered shirt, a straw bonnet, bare feet, and with a blackened front tooth. Bales of hay were piled outside her house, which had been stripped of its usual furnishings. Chickens ran about inside, and there was livestock in a corral in the back yard, along with a portable outhouse.

Lombard's most memorable party, however (she announced it as her final fling), occurred in 1935 when she took over the entire Ocean Park amusement pier and invited several hundred people to come in their most relaxed clothes. Guests ranged from Marlene Dietrich, Claudette Colbert, Cary Grant, Randolph Scott, Cesar Romero, and newcomer Errol Flynn, to the grips and extras who were also her friends. (Romero injured an ankle spinning in one of the attractions, and Kathryn Menjou bruised the base of her spine, thus earning herself the nickname "Coccyx Katie.") Later, Romero threw a similar bash on Venice Pier. There were parties at roller rinks and parties on trolley cars. Even those held in restaurants or night clubs strained for the novel touch. Kay Francis once had the entrance to a restaurant converted into the prow of a ship, and arriving guests were obliged to slide down a gangplank into a ballroom decorated with nautical devices. Sonja Henie rented Ciro's for a night and made her entrance atop a baby elephant.

The more sedate side of Hollywood entertaining was centered for many years at Pickfair, the residence of the reigning monarchs, Douglas Fairbanks and Mary Pickford. Formal dinners there attracted any visiting dignitaries in town—Fairbanks was drawn to his counterparts in orthodox royalty (it was said that his frequent trips to the capitals of Europe were for the purpose of booking his next season's guests), and his conquests included the Crown Prince of Japan, the King and Queen of Siam, Lord and Lady Mountbatten and the Duke and Duchess of Alba. Notables from other fields also found their way to the Pickfair dining table (which was set every evening for fifteen), and reading from the printed menus, seated before the gold place settings, might be found Babe Ruth, Charles Lindbergh, Guglielmo Marconi, Amelia Earhart, or Henry Ford, along with the cream of motion picture society. Fairbanks often asked his guests to give a five-minute speech on a subject he assigned them—one night Albert

239

PARTIES

Einstein demonstrated the theory of relativity with the dishes and eating utensils on the table.

Mary Pickford was also one of the organizers of the Mayfair Society, the club comprising the aristocracy of the film community, which held ceremoniously elegant white-tie dinner-dances each month, first at the Biltmore, later at other hotels (see HOTELS). In 1936 Carole Lombard was chairman of the ball and her escort that evening, Cesar Romero, recollects an incident that came close to upsetting the decorous traditions of the society:

> Carole was in charge of the ball and she decreed that all of the ladies should wear white. Carole and I got there early, because she was to be in the reception line. The ladies were all coming in, everybody beautifully gowned in white. Except Norma Shearer. She was wearing bright red. And Miss Lombard had a few words to say to her! But nobody was going to tell Norma Shearer.

The subject of who were the best party-givers in Hollywood was much discussed in the fan magazines. In an August 1939 *Photoplay* story, Elsa Maxwell—who certainly qualified as an expert—rated her movieland correspondents. High on her list were the Bennett sisters, Constance and Joan, Kay Francis, the Gary Coopers, Mrs. Samuel Goldwyn, Myrna Loy and Arthur Hornblow ("best chicken sandwiches and cake at their Sunday afternoons"), the Rathbones, Louella Parsons ("greatest barbecue thrower"), Chaplin ("educational evenings" with Albert Einstein and Thomas Mann), Douglas Fairbanks (the "Continental touch"), the Darryl Zanucks ("most elaborate dinners west of the Hudson"), and the Jack Warners ("spectacular").

Joseph Cotten gave an annual Fourth of July blowout, and Cary Grant was famous for his New Year's Eve parties. In the early forties, Atwater Kent, retired millionaire inventor and radio manufacturer (and formerly a leading light in East Coast social circles), took over from W. R. and Marion as Hollywood's most extravagant host. Capo di Monte, his twenty-nine-room mansion on Bel Air Road, was the setting for a dinner, musicale, costume party, or ball on an average of once a week. On one occasion, he spent $40,000 on entertaining fifteen hundred guests. (Seemingly rather shy of the movie crowd, he liked to hang around in the background, watching the proceedings without really participating.) Usual fare at Atwater Kent's parties included vintage champagne and Beluga caviar. Such delicacies were not as commonplace as might be expected. Guests at the Thalbergs' home, for example, were apt to be confronted with such unsavory sounding tidbits as peach halves with mayonnaise and fish and chicken in patty shells.

AT CAROLE LOMBARD'S PARTY AT THE VENICE FUN HOUSE, GIVEN
FOR A. C. BLUMENTHAL AND WILLIAM RHINELANDER STEWART:
MARLENE DIETRICH, LOMBARD, LILI DAMITA, AND ERROL FLYNN.

GINGER ROGERS, ALFRED GWYNNE VANDERBILT, AND
JOAN CRAWFORD AT GINGER'S SKATING PARTY AT THE CULVER
CITY ROLLERDOME.

It was not only major stars, top executives, and eccentric millionaires, of course, who gave parties. Jimmie and Lucille Gleason threw big garden parties, chiefly for character actors. The luncheons at Francis Marion's Adrian-decorated home, or outside in her spacious gardens, were graced by many stars, but were also an occasion to meet the hostess' fellow writers. Paul Lukas and his wife provided a center for the sportier members of the European set, while screenwriter Salka Viertel's salon in Santa Monica Canyon was a haven for literary émigrés. Literary figures also tended to gravitate to the home of Edmund Goulding, and to George Cukor's, where some of the more sophisticated stars—Garbo, Hepburn, Tallulah Bankhead—could often be found on Sundays. The German-speaking colony tended to socialize on Ernst Lubitsch's terrace, and a cosmopolitan group that included Aldous Huxley, Artur Rubinstein, Gladys Cooper, and Constance Collier was apt to be found at the elegant dinner parties Ethel Barrymore hosted in Palos Verdes. Another front-runner in the hostess stakes was Countess Dorothy Taylor Di Frasso, whose friends ranged from Mary Pickford to some of the less respectable members of the Hollywood social set.

Since most people in the industry worked on Saturdays, Sunday was the obvious time for all-day, relaxed gatherings. *The* place to be seen on your day off was at Doug and Mary's tea and swim parties, unless you were going to play tennis at Chaplin's, where tea was served from an elegant silver pot, and crumpets, along with delicately trimmed, very English sandwiches, were piled on gigantic platters. Norma Talmadge also had Sunday luncheon parties for forty or fifty at her beach house. Among the regular guests were Lionel Barrymore and his wife, Irene, Ben Lyon and Bebe Daniels, Billie Dove, Marilyn Miller, Conrad Nagel, Louella Parsons and her husband, Doc Martin, the Buster Keatons, and the Myron Selznicks. Director James Cruze had an open house every weekend at his Flintridge estate, featuring a huge table loaded with turkey, roast beef, and bathtub gin (uncorked, so his guests would not be tempted to carry the bottles away). He also had a jardinière, just inside the door, filled with coins, so that anyone who was hard up could help himself to a few dollars. Louis B. Mayer held court at large Sunday brunches at his Santa Monica home. Phil Silvers has described these occasions as being like an audience at the Vatican, adding, "Of course, it wasn't His Highness's ring you kissed." Mayer's sometime son-in-law David Selznick was another whose Sunday parties were an institution. In the late thirties, people would begin arriving early in the afternoon (perhaps after partaking of L. B.'s hospitality). There would be tennis, swimming, drinks, and lots of shoptalk before dinner, and later the inevitable screening of a new movie. After the war, when Selznick was married to Jennifer Jones, the parties would continue from 11 A.M. Sunday until the early hours of Monday morning.

243

PARTIES

Beautician George Masters has revealed in his book how the hostess managed to remain fresh for so long a period of time. Whenever an opportunity presented itself, she would sneak downstairs for a shower, shampoo, set, and a new make-up job, then slip into a clean outfit identical to the one she had been wearing (three copies of each were always on hand).

Studio parties, intended to reinforce the spirit of the corporate family, were a fixture of Hollywood life. Louis B. Mayer loved to preside over staff picnics, and the M-G-M Christmas party was an occasion on which caste lines were permitted to become blurred, as alcohol allowed grips and executives to meet on equal terms. Thalberg was generally a center of affectionate attention at these celebrations. Amorous photographs were taken in the stills department, and stag films ran in tandem in projection rooms. Much the same kind of thing went on at other studios. At one Columbia Christmas party, Harry Cohn invited a secretary to point out anyone in the room she disliked, promising to fire the person as her Christmas present.

Premieres of major productions provided another suitable excuse for celebration. One of the Warners' most lavish efforts was planned to celebrate the premiere of *A Midsummer Night's Dream* in 1935. An orchestra estimated at 125 pieces played against the background of a ship festooned with orchids. Unfortunately, the premiere did not end until 2 A.M., and everyone was so exhausted that only about half of the expected five to six thousand guests showed up. Before the initial showing of *Wuthering Heights,* Sam and Frances Goldwyn threw a dinner party which was attended by Eleanor Roosevelt, Irving Berlin, Norma Shearer, and Merle Oberon. Following the premiere of *The Good Earth,* Leila Hyams and her husband, the agent Phil Berg, gave a party at which a huge statue of a Mandarin princess, bearing an assortment of leis from which arriving guests could select, was installed in the front hall of their Sunset Boulevard home. Postproduction parties were also popular. Pat O'Brien always gave one at the completion of each of his movies, and Woody Van Dyke was famous for the bashes with which the wrap-ups of his pictures were celebrated.

One feature of Van Dyke's parties was the expectation that everyone would perform; indeed, impromptu entertainment was a feature of many social gatherings. Chaplin liked to dance to Balinese recordings, sing Irish ballads, and perform bullfights in mime. Judy Garland was the first one up at the merest hint of an arpeggio, Marlene Dietrich would sometimes play the musical saw, and Gloria Swanson offered judo exhibitions, while Noah Beery specialized in Indian tribal dances. Norma Shearer performed various gymnastic feats, standing on her head or sinking to the floor and rising again with a glass of water balanced on her forehead (never spilling a drop). Reginald Gardner was for years a popular guest,

ANN RUTHERFORD PLAYS "THE GAME" AT A HARDY FAMILY PARTY,
WATCHED BY LANA TURNER, MICKEY ROONEY, AND OTHERS,
INCLUDING WRITER CAREY WILSON AND DIRECTOR GEORGE SEITZ,
1938.

famous for his imitations of trains, lighthouses, and wallpaper. Cary Grant
would sit down at the piano and he and Ida Lupino sometimes favored the
company with selections of the bawdier British music hall songs. Mischa
Auer was fond of exposing himself, and Lenore Coffee has described an
anonymous host who liked to amuse his guests by balancing three silver
dollars on his erect penis.

Inevitably, there were fads that swept through the Beverly Hills party
circuit for a season or two and then were gone. The Ronald Colmans were
not alone in their temporary addiction to square dancing—the Andy
Devines and the Carl Esmonds, along with Edna Best and others, would
gather regularly in the early forties to doe-si-doe with great enthusiasm
to the rhythms of the fiddler and the chant of the professional caller. For
a while the popular game was "Murder," in which guests were divided into
two teams, one plotting the crime and the other attempting to solve it.
Probably the most enduring craze was for a form of charades variously
known as "The Game," "Indications," and "Quotations." This was already
a popular pastime at San Simeon in the twenties, and in the thirties the
Marx Brothers were noted as leading exponents. Former M-G-M composer
and arranger George Bassman recalls a version which was popular a few
years later:

245

Parties

A lot of people from the Freed unit at Metro would come—Judy Garland, Roger Edens, Chuck Walters, Gene Kelly. Also Keenan Wynn, Nancy Kelly and David Selznick, who she was going with at the time, along with Tallulah Bankhead, Geraldine Fitzgerald and anyone who was in from New York. Laird Cregar used to come with three sweatshirts, because of the strenuous way we played.

Suppose there were 17 people. There would be two team captains, and they would choose sides, so there would be eight in one room and eight in another room some distance away. Then there would be the seventeenth person, who made up all the slogans—a lot of which were theatrical subjects. The two captains would come to the center room to get the slogans, the stopwatch would click and they would dash madly to their teams. As soon as the first person guessed it, the next one would run in to get another slogan. It was a relay, trying to beat the clock.

During the nerve-racking days of *Gone With the Wind,* Vivien Leigh is reported by Roland Flamini to have attempted to introduce a macabre variant of the game called "Ways to Kill Babies."

Card parties, usually rigidly segregated by sex, were as popular as elsewhere, with extremely high-stake poker games a regular form of recreation of the executives. Tim McCoy, Warner Baxter, Ronald Colman, Richard Barthelmess, and William Powell would play poker once a month at Baxter's house. (Later, Colman had the group over for drinks every Friday evening prior to a club hop which would end at Ciro's for dinner.) Kay Francis got together regularly with Jessica Barthelmess, Beatrice Stewart, and Dorothy Di Frasso for backgammon, just as, in the twenties, Colleen Moore, Bebe Daniels, Marion Davies, and Constance Bennett had made up a bridge foursome.

Whether your party was large or small, squadrons of service people were on call to help orchestrate the event. Upon request, florist John Berstal would insert fresh-cut (and sometimes dyed) flowers into your garden just before the guests arrived, and he would fly white orchids in from the East if you were prepared to pay full fare for a passenger seat. (In those early days of flying, blooms were apt to become frostbitten in the unheated freight compartment.) He could also supply you with a movable wall, so that early arrivals would not be wandering around in a vast, empty space while the later crowd would still have ample room. B. F. "Nighty" Nightingale, of Kim Lighters, was the man you were likely to hire to hang Chinese lanterns from your trees, install floodlights, or otherwise enhance the atmosphere. H. B. Mueller manufactured and rented a nonskid portable dance floor to lay over the rug or the swimming pool—"Any Room a Ballroom in Just Thirty Minutes."

246

PETS.

The Hollywood pet was pampered from prenatal days to death and burial. A North Hollywood gentleman named Louis Ray custom-manufactured dog beds, ranging in design from Indian teepee to covered wagon to Queen Anne. J. J. Roberts constructed redwood houses for monkeys, cats, and dogs, including at least one, for Bob Hope's six dogs, large enough to accommodate a human. Edgar and Charlotte Meyer's Beverly Hills beauty shop for animals was regularly patronized by the pets of Claudette Colbert, Sonja Henie, Rise Stevens, Constance Bennett, Ann Sheridan, even Clifford Odets, and the office of Dr. Stanley Meyer, one of the leading Los Angeles veterinarians of the period, featured soothing music piped in for benefit of the animal patients. Carl Spitz's eleven-acre Hollywood Dog Training School, which serviced the canines of Clark Gable, Loretta Young, and Jack Oakie, covered kindergarten, grammar school, high school, and college, with bona fide diplomas issued to graduates. There were, in addition, a Motel for Cats (one section of which was labeled "Cat's Maternity Room") and an even more anthropomorphic Dude Ranch for Dogs at Big Bear Lake. The advertisement for the latter read, "The ranch affords pets a refuge from the strain and confinement of city life." Each dog, bedecked with red bandanna and straw hat, had its private frontier-style bunkhouse, with corral and sun deck, and a choice of such activities as hiking, squirrel hunting, water polo, toboganning, and dog-team racing. In the end, there was the Los Angeles Pet Cemetery, where, after a eulogy was spoken, dogs and cats were usually buried with their favorite toys. Other creatures interred there included a rooster, a lizard, a duck, a marmoset, an alligator, a lion, a horse, and a rat.

The annual Beverly Hills Charity Dog Show was a major social event, where the prize Afghan hounds of Jack Oakie, the fine chihuahuas of Lupe Velez, and Errol Flynn's Rhodesian ridgebacks could be found on promenade. Joan Crawford, who perhaps took the responsibility of being a Movie Star more seriously than anyone else, told a reporter that her poodle, Cliquot, usually eats white meat of chicken, ground sirloin, ice cream and ginger ale. He wears custom made jackets from Hammacher Schlemmer. They are red with black velvet collars with "CC" on them. They have heart-shaped pockets with Kleenex in them in case he has to blow his nose. Cliquot and I wear matching costumes. He wears his red jacket when I wear red slacks and sweater. When I wear green, he wears green. And he has a rhinestone collar for evening.

Another lucky poodle was Topsy, pet of Bing and Dixie Lee Crosby. When Topsy began to show signs of being pregnant, Dixie Lee dashed over to Saks to order a fancy crib and baby quilt. When the pregnancy proved false, there was great disappointment in the house.

Relationships between master or mistress and canine could become intensely symbiotic. When Jack Benny suffered with bronchitis, his poodle (also called Topsy) did, too. When Joseph Schildkraut had severe gas problems, his chihuahuas, Bambi and Boychik, did, too. When Marie Wilson felt the pressure of anxiety, her little Yorkshire terrier, Hobbs, would hysterically begin to chew his own coat, which often led to a condition of intestinal gastritis. Hobbs, who accompanied his mistress everywhere, from the theater to the Brown Derby, became the subject of a bitter divorce battle. It was finally decreed that the small pet would spend equal time with both parents.

Other dogs and their owners were equally inseparable. There is hardly a candid photograph of Marion Davies without Gandhi (or—more formally—Mahatma Coatma Collar Gandhi), the abandoned dachshund Hearst bought for her in Bad Nauheim, which she had for eleven years. Hearst himself had, until his death, a royal succession of dachshunds— at one time, there were over fifty at San Simeon. When his favorite, Helena, died, Hearst wept and had her buried under a stone engraved, "Here lies dearest Helena—my devoted friend." When Gandhi went, the entire staff of San Simeon gathered to hear the funeral service conducted by a local priest. Errol Flynn was more devoted to his comedic schnauzer, Arno, than to many of his female companions. Lupe Velez had a specially constructed basket attached to her bicycle for her chihuahuas, Mr. Kelly and Mrs. Murphy, and it was not unusual to see Lupe pedaling the little group down Hollywood Boulevard, engaging in animated conversation.

Douglas Fairbanks, Sr., was attached to his 150-pound mastiff, Marco Polo, and Laraine Day to hers (Igor); Carole Lombard doted on her dachshund, Commissioner, while Bette Davis lavished affection on her wire-haired terrier, Boojum; Paul Muni was devoted to an Airedale named Simon (after the lawyer in *Counselor-at-Law*), then to a Dalmatian called Toto, while Robert Taylor adored his cocker spaniel, Rumba. When Humphrey Bogart's champion Sealyham died in 1938, Bogart not only hung a small black crepe on his front door but had the dog buried in his back yard in an all-steel vault. Mary Pickford's wire-haired terrier, Zorro, would bite any man or beast in sight, and cost his mistress a pretty penny in lawsuits. Buster Keaton had a succession of eccentric dogs, including Trotsky, an Irish wolfhound, who in warm weather slept completely submerged—except for his floating head—in the Keaton pool, and Elmer, a long-haired St. Bernard who each day ate three lunches at M-G-M: one in his master's bungalow, one with Marion Davies an hour later, and one with the executives an hour after that.

Occasionally stars got a kick out of sneaking their dogs into their films. Ann Sothern's Scottie, Doonie, made an appearance in *Maisie Goes to Reno;* Judy Garland's poodle, Chou Chou, walked on in *The Clock;* and Greer Garson's Gogo got to stroll down a country lane with her in *Valley of Decision*. Lombard's Pekinese, Pushface, was used in *My Man Godfrey,*

ERROL FLYNN WITH HIS PRIZE RHODESIAN RIDGEBACKS.

and Ida Lupino's Scottie, Edward, was engaged to play a scene in *From Pillar to Post,* but the excitement was too much for his tummy and he had to be replaced.

Some of the more eccentric Hollywood personalities favored more outrageous pets. Valentino's menagerie included, in addition to a stable of horses and a number of dogs (notably Kabar, a Doberman, and Sheik, a shepherd), lion cubs, a monkey, and a pet snake. Fanny Brice kept a white rat which she fed on ham and eggs, and during the filming of *The Crusades,* Cecil B. DeMille became intrigued with the falcons used in the picture and with the aid of expert Orin Cannon, trained twenty of them with hood and bell. Along with her dogs, Lupe Velez kept seventy-five canaries, each of which she claimed to know by name.

At his hilltop home, Bella Vista, John Barrymore housed an opossum, a kinkajou, a mouse deer, scores of Siamese cats, and numerous dogs, including Shake, Quake, and Shock, Kerry blue terriers born during an earth tremor. His aviary was stocked with over three hundred specimens of exotic birds, but Barrymore's most notorious pets were Maloney and Clementine. Maloney was a king vulture the actor would take with him on all of his cruises. To the fascination and horror of the boat's crew, Maloney would sit on Barrymore's shoulder and preen his master's eyebrows and mustache, then present his beak for a kiss. A major problem in the bird's upkeep was finding meat sufficiently decayed to appeal to his taste. One day, according to legend, the vulture appeared disconsolate and began to moan. The yacht was moored and Barrymore took Maloney ashore, surrounded him with goodies, and kissed him farewell. The next morning, through binoculars, Barrymore saw the vulture on the beach where he had been left. "There were tears in his eyes. What could I do?" the Great Profile asked. He pulled for shore, leaped out, and brought back the once more ecstatically happy bird.

Clementine, a gift from English actress Gladys Cooper, was a monkey who bit everyone else in the house, but unutterably adored Barrymore. She would sit opposite him for hours, staring with absolute devotion. After his family forced him to give her to a zoo, Barrymore was told by the vet that she had been fascinated not by his divine looks or sterling personality, but by the alcohol fumes he emitted. Thereafter, he would make special visits to the zoo, just to breathe on Clementine.

PHOBIAS.

In November of 1940 Harry Brand, publicity chief of 20th Century-Fox, put out a press release which made his studio sound very like a glamorous insane asylum. Rather conveniently, almost every Fox star displayed the symptoms of some phobic condition fashionable at that time. According to Brand, Alice Faye was acrophobic to the point that during the filming of *In Old Chicago,* she became so jittery at having to descend a flight of stairs that she fell and hurt her back. For *Alexander's Ragtime Band,* the prospect of dancing up a stairway threw her into an absolute faint. Warner Baxter and Gregory Ratoff were both claustrophobic. June Lang was afraid of elevators, Annabella of thunder. Claire Trevor couldn't stand bells, so her door had a knocker and her telephone chimed. Slim Sommerville's fear of crowds made him ochlophobic, and Joan Davis had a morbid fear of disease.

As a matter of fact, a horror of germs and a compulsion toward immaculateness *was* a common condition among the movie colony elite. Joan Crawford would carry a strong disinfectant with her wherever she traveled, and give a hotel room a thorough going over before she could comfortably settle in. Clark Gable refused to have tubs in his home, finding showers more hygienic, and showered several times each day. According to Bill Davidson's *The Real and the Unreal,* Gable, in an effort to protect the pool on his Encino ranch, employed a chemical substance which would turn the water an embarrassingly bright red around any unsanitary swimmer.

One source reports that Peter Lorre had a neurotic quirk about his position in the space around him, and would have to situate himself in special ways in restaurants in order to feel comfortable. W. C. Fields suffered from more conventional but more extreme claustrophobia. Not only could he not bear to be confined in an elevator, he could not even tolerate the pressure of a ring on his finger. Ronald Colman had a mania about punctuality, and Robert Taylor detested talking on the phone, to the point where it would make him stutter. Cecil B. DeMille refused to touch used currency and might send his secretary to the bank several times a day to exchange tired bills for fresh ones. According to an article in the

May 1934 *Modern Screen,* readers newly attuned to psychological termi-
nology shortly before Bedford Drive in Beverly Hills was becoming
known as Freud Street, were informed that Garbo, Sylvia Sidney, and
Constance Bennett were agoraphobic, Maureen O'Sullivan claustrophobic,
and Crawford and Lombard acrophobic. Richard Dix and Claudette
Colbert were said to share a fear of speed (despite the fact Colbert was an
expert skier!), and Edmund Lowe was described as suffering from the
phobic feeling he had swallowed something.

Politics.

Hollywood's political life became a national issue in the late forties and
early fifties when the ugliness of the House Un-American Activities Committee hearings, and the subsequent horrors of blacklisting, brought years
of ideological conflict to a nightmarish climax. Until that time, the general
public had been led to believe that serious thinkers in the movie colony
limited themselves to idolizing Drs. Albert Schweitzer and Einstein, and
other such innocent mental activities. The news that some movie people
felt that society could be changed for the better came as an unpleasant
shock. Show business and politics, it was thought, were incompatible. The
fact is, of course, that from the very beginning politics was an everyday
concern of the motion picture industry. People had been choosing sides
for forty years.

Moviemaking in America had become big business overnight, and the
men who ran it quickly discovered the political pressures that accompany
corporate success. When, in 1909, the Motion Pictures Patents Company
attempted to monopolize the industry, independents had little trouble attracting support from trust-breaking forces in Washington, so that, although not declared illegal until 1917, the Patent Company cartel was
actually rendered ineffective by 1914, largely because of political pressure
from within the Woodrow Wilson administration.

Almost immediately, new giants emerged—Paramount, Loew's, First
National, Fox—which, by controlling both production and exhibition
through theater ownership and the block booking system, provoked new
antitrust moves. This happened to coincide with the highly publicized
Hollywood scandals of the early twenties—all of which produced a climate

in which much unfavorable attention was focused on the movie industry and federal censorship became a real possibility.

In 1922 the studios and their East Coast parent companies responded to this unwelcome scrutiny by forming the Motion Picture Producers and Distributors Association and seeking out "a distinguished and financially uninterested" citizen to front the organization. The man they selected was Will Hays, an important functionary in the postwar Republican revival and, for a short term, Postmaster General in the Harding Cabinet. Hays was an astute choice, since he could be counted upon to still criticism within the then dominant Republican machine. At the beginning of his regime—which was to last almost two and a half decades—he proclaimed in grandiloquent prose that the industry was bent on reform, that henceforth it would regulate itself, both its monopolistic practices and the moral tone of its product. There was little evidence of immediate change, however. The giant corporations still ran the business much as they chose to— in 1928 William Fox almost succeeded in establishing an outright monopoly—and Hays's fervent censorship campaign did not acquire real teeth until well into the Depression, when economic pressures on the industry gave him more leverage. The Production Code, Hays's Bible of censorship—as conceived in the twenties and enforced in the thirties and forties—was absurd even by the standards of the day, but without it federal censorship might well have become a reality, with dire consequences for the industry, and for freedom of expression in general.

The men who ran the movie business, as it settled into its mature configuration, were mostly new to power—rising, as they had, from humble beginnings as furriers, salesmen, and junk dealers—but they were not slow to recognize the importance of political connections. Since they consolidated their own power during a period which saw Republicans victorious and the country enjoying unprecedented prosperity, it was not surprising that most of them would ally themselves with the Grand Old Party, and that a self-made man like Louis B. Mayer would identify himself with the GOP's unstinting support of the free enterprise system.

Mayer became friendly with Herbert Hoover when the latter was Secretary of Commerce, and it can be presumed that Hoover was anxious to recruit support from the burgeoning film industry. Hoover promoted Mayer to the post of treasurer of the California Republican National Committee, and Mayer responded by raising large sums of money for Hoover's presidential campaign. (Among his fund-raising techniques was a "request" that all M-G-M employees contribute a day's salary to the campaign coffers.) His commitment to the cause can be gauged by the fact that Mayer and his wife were Hoover's first overnight guests at the White House.

Hoover bestowed another favor on Mayer when he recommended Ida

POLITICS

Koverman to him. Mrs. Koverman had been a top Republican aide—campaign secretary for Hoover and for Calvin Coolidge before him—and for personal reasons, she was anxious to leave the East Coast. Hoover realized that if she could be absorbed into the M-G-M family, it could benefit all concerned. Once established in Culver City, Koverman became a studio mother figure and an invaluable asset to Mayer in a dozen different ways. Having a background in finance, she was able to reorganize M-G-M's accounting system. And, being accustomed to the corridors of power, she was less than overwhelmed by the ego trips of stars and other creative personnel, and thus could be utilized to keep temperamental employees in line. Since she shared Mayer's taste and sense of values, she could help evolve codes of behavior and dress for contract players and even serve successfully as a talent scout. Primarily, however, she retained her impeccable political credentials and, with her ready access to the innermost GOP circles, was able to serve as a powerful lobbyist. During Republican administrations, no Hollywood figure was a more frequent visitor to the White House than Ida Koverman, doing all she did without ever challenging Mayer's eminence as public spokesman for Republican causes. Mrs. Koverman exercised her power with no apparent interest in its outward trappings—when asked to run for Congress, she refused—and she lived modestly, supplementing her $250 weekly paycheck with the income she gained from small real estate deals.

While few industry leaders acquired quite the political clout enjoyed by Mayer, many shared his aspirations, and most of them—from Mary Pickford to Walt Disney—were ardent Republicans. Cecil B. DeMille was another force to be reckoned with in GOP circles. In 1938 the California State Republican Committee endorsed his nomination for a Senate seat, but he rejected the offer. Later, his foundation for Americanism was responsible for channeling witch-hunt "evidence" to the House Un-American Activities Committee. Jack Warner, on the other hand, was an early supporter of Roosevelt and the New Deal and had the distinction of being placed on Hitler's extinction list because of the film *Confessions of a Nazi Spy*. During the war, Sam Goldwyn and FDR became good friends, and later, Goldwyn fraternized with President Eisenhower, who often stayed with the Goldwyns when visiting California.

By the end of the twenties, the studio establishment—like the leaders of any other industry—had come to identify its interests with those of the political establishment. Increasingly, too, the industry found itself bound to a variety of banking and investment groups, a fact that tended to encourage the adoption of establishment attitudes. The influence of outside business interests worked at many levels. For example, Dr. A. H. Giannini—founder of the Bank of America, which was an early major investor in motion pictures—was instrumental in the formation of the Catholic

League of Decency, a powerful ally of Will Hays in his campaign for "cleaner" movies. The coming of the talkies made the Morgan group and the Rockefeller group—which, between them, through patent ownership and investment, controlled the manufacture, distribution, and licensing of sound equipment—enormously influential in the movie business and this helped cement the bond between the producers and the political establishment, particularly the Republican party.

This inevitably precipitated what can only be called a "class struggle" in Hollywood—though it was one that hardly fitted any classic Bolshevist model. By the late thirties, the spectacle of "millionaire Marxists" provided conservative journalists with an easy target and aroused dreams of glory in the minds of publicity-hungry politicians. The left wing that sprang up in Hollywood in the thirties had a totally unique character. Hard-nosed union organizers and battle-scarred radicals sat in elegant drawing rooms with movie queens and $3,500-a-week writers. It was an environment dripping with irony. Some members of the movie colony may have been drawn to the left by guilt, but others moved in that direction because of a general dissatisfaction with Hollywood values and the paternalistic attitudes of the studio heads. Leftists, with considerable justification, protested that extras were treated like cattle and paid miserably as well, yet thousands of people waited to register with Central Casting, hungry for the meager ration of glamour that working as an extra would afford them.

George Bassman, who joined the M-G-M music department in the mid-thirties, after arranging for bands like Fletcher Henderson's and Duke Ellington's, recalls that you almost had to take sides:

> Life was very cerebral. People got together and really talked of marvelous ideas. If you weren't willing to talk, you were considered a reactionary, and if you did get together and talk, you were called a Communist.

He emphasizes that in the thirties the mildest evidence of leftist sympathies could bring you into conflict with the front office:

> I was in my office one day and I got a call from Eddie Mannix—I'd never even talked with the man before—and he said, "Bassman, meet me in front of the commissary. I want to talk to you about something." I had no idea what he wanted. I met him in front of the commissary and he said, "What is this thing that you're doing?" He talked with a rasp. "What is this organization you're with?"
>
> Now the thing I was involved with at the time was a composers' group, but I knew what he was getting at. I told him that I was not especially active in the American League against War and Fascism, but a group of composers was putting on a benefit concert for the League and they had asked me to write something for it, and I had said yes.

255

POLITICS

He didn't even hear me. He just went into a whole lecture on Americanism, what a wonderful country we have and what a wonderful studio we have, and what did I want to fool around with anything like that for, with all those un-American people? I listened and I said, "I'm not involved with them. I'm merely writing a piece of music."

In the early days of Hollywood, Actors' Equity had tried to establish a beachhead in the movie industry several times—attempting to organize a strike in 1929—but had always been repulsed by management with little difficulty. This was largely due to the indifference of contract players who were making too much money to think they needed protection. The first serious move toward unionization did not come until 1933, at the time of the bank closure crisis which threatened the entire industry.

Studio employees, from stars to stenographers, accepted a 50 percent pay cut in good faith—but it dawned on some of them almost immediately that they might have been duped. The crisis was genuine enough—nobody disputed that—but was it being dealt with at their expense? Noisy meetings erupted all over Hollywood and embryo guilds began to form. For the next several years, strikes and other work actions would disrupt studio life from time to time as the move toward unionization gained momentum.

In *The Kindness of Strangers,* Salka Viertel recalls the atmosphere that surrounded labor unrest in Hollywood in the thirties. One strike began with set dressers demanding higher wages and recognition as a separate union. Carpenters, painters, readers, and cartoonists joined in, the latter two groups "young men and women in blue jeans and pullovers, red scarves around their necks, cigarettes sticking in the corners of their mouths"—conspicuous as the fermenting element in the "revolution."

On Olive Avenue, pickets paraded in front of Warner Brothers while writers and secretaries held separate meetings in the cafeteria opposite the studio, trying to decide whether or not to honor the line. One writer suggested that they wait and see what the secretaries did, because he "could not dream of working without his secretary." The secretaries stood outside for a while, then one said, "What the hell!" and made a dash for the studio gates, where the pickets made no effort to stop her. Most of the others followed immediately. Later they said that the majority of them had been in sympathy with the strikers at the outset, but one girl, who worked for Ayn Rand, swayed them by insisting that the strikers were just a bunch of Commies and that no decent person could support them. The writers, however, decided to stay out until the picket lines were withdrawn. Their boss, Jack Warner, apparently watched the whole drama from the roof of a sound stage.

The studios fought the trend with every weapon they could muster, attempting to turn the Academy of Motion Picture Arts and Sciences into a company union and sometimes using strong-arm methods, but Roosevelt's National Industrial Recovery Act ensured the legitimate unions a future. The NIRA stipulated that industries were to develop guidelines for fair competition, enforceable by law. In return for this, a blind eye would be turned to antitrust issues, but it was understood that collective bargaining rights would be upheld.

The Code of Fair Competition for the Motion Picture Industry became law in November of 1933. Labor was ostensibly allowed to organize freely and company unions were banned, but the studios disputed every issue. One tactical move involved top executives taking large and well-publicized pay cuts in an effort to blame the studios' financial problems on the high-priced talent they employed, the stars, writers, directors, etc. While the code was being drafted, the studios attempted to insert clauses intended to curb such things as star salaries and the negotiating rights of talent agents. It took a flurry of angry protests and a visit to the White House by Eddie Cantor, representing the fledgling Screen Actors Guild, to quash these efforts.

In 1935 the NIRA was declared unconstitutional by the Supreme Court, but by then there was no stopping the momentum of the union movement in Hollywood. Unfortunately, however, many of the motion picture trade and craft unions were organized under the jurisdiction of the International Alliance of Theatrical Stage Employees, which had been penetrated by organized crime figures who exploited both employees and employers—though the bosses were quite willing to pay for protection in return for an acquiescent union leadership. There is every reason to believe that some studios actively collaborated with the IATSE mobsters (see CRIME). The Screen Actors Guild was finally recognized as the bargaining agent for performers in May 1937, then, under the leadership of Robert Montgomery, resisted affiliation with the IATSE and helped expose its ties to the mob. The Screen Writers' Guild, the first to have been organized, was certified by the National Labor Relations Board in August of 1938, and the Screen Directors' Guild achieved the same status a couple of years later. By the time Pearl Harbor was attacked, the industry was almost completely unionized and the unions had been purged of criminal influence.

All of this had of course been played out against the background of the Depression, during the decade of the massacre at Dearborn, the rout of the Bonus Army, Hoovervilles, apple sellers, and the Dust Bowl. Hollywood liberals were cushioned from such realities by the peculiar character of their industry, but many of them kept their eyes open and were pushed toward at least nominal radicalism. Nearer to home, people were appalled by the role played by the Hollywood studios in the sabotaging of Upton Sinclair's campaign for the governorship of California in 1934.

Running on the Democratic ticket, Sinclair was not so much a spokesman for the established party machine as for his own EPIC movement, which took its name from his campaign slogan, "End Poverty in California." Sinclair had visions of a socialist utopia, and in newspaper interviews, as well as in his biography of William Fox, he had been highly critical of the movie industry, expressing his belief that its profits should be rechanneled into the state exchequer for the benefit of the people.

The studio bosses, headed by Joe Schenck, an avowed Democrat, were unanimous in agreeing to use any available means to wreck Sinclair's bid. Large contributions were made to the re-election campaign of the Republican candidate, a bland Iowan named Frank E. Merriam, much of which was raised by imposing a quasivoluntary levy on workers' paychecks. On a more sinister level, employees—Katharine Hepburn for one—were threatened with dismissal if they supported Sinclair. In addition, fake newsreels of stunning crudeness were manufactured, purporting to show all manner of bums, vagrants, anarchists, and agitators, unshaven and speaking in accents that originated far to the east of Ellis Island, gathering at the border, waiting to cross into California the moment Sinclair was elected. In another "newsreel," a white-haired character actress —the picture of vulnerability—was shown on a back lot front porch bemoaning the fate that would overtake her in the wake of a Sinclair victory.

Irving Thalberg is said to have been the architect of this propaganda barrage.

Not everyone in Hollywood allowed himself to be stampeded—James Cagney and Jean Harlow led a rebellion against the "Merriam levy"—but Sinclair was defeated, although it was by a narrow enough margin to suggest that he would have won comfortably had it not been for the slick and well-financed smear campaign devised by the studios. A degree of revenge was gained four years later when Merriam was soundly defeated by Democrat Culbert L. Olson, who was vigorously supported by a number of Hollywood personalities.

Throughout this period, too, the international situation and the rise of fascism helped form many political consciences, although there were some who, for a while at least, admired the "style" of Europe's "strong men." In 1933 Columbia released a documentary feature entitled *Mussolini Speaks,* which was narrated by Lowell Thomas and supported by an advertising campaign that asked such questions as "Is this what America needs?" Because of this film, Harry Cohn was invited to Rome, where he was decorated by Mussolini and presented an autographed photo of Il Duce which hung in Cohn's office for some time (see OFFICES). Walter Wanger had a similar picture in his office. That same year, William Randolph Hearst's Cosmopolitan Pictures produced *Gabriel over the White House,* in which Walter Huston played an American version of the "strong man"

—a President who solved the nation's problems with such tactics as having gangsters executed by a firing squad beneath the Statute of Liberty. Both these pictures arrived in first-run houses at about the time that Hitler became Chancellor of Germany. The man with the toothbrush mustache began to appear on American screens with increasing frequency, though in some neighborhoods theater managers cut him out of newsreels because of the hostility his image provoked.

Unlike Mussolini, Hitler found few admirers in Hollywood, even among the most conservative elements. The studios were, after all, dominated by Jews, and Irving Thalberg, for one, saw for himself the anti-Semitic nature of Nazism while in Europe during the summer of 1933. To aggravate matters, the Hitler regime banned many Hollywood movies as "decadent."

Not many executives, however, went so far as to associate themselves with groups like the controversial Hollywood Anti-Nazi League, which was later denounced as a Communist-front organization. The Anti-Nazi League was, in fact, founded in 1936 by a rather mixed group of individuals including Prince Hubert von und zu Lowenstein, a progressive Catholic; Rupert Hughes, a Republican; Eddie Cantor, essentially a liberal; a German Communist, Otto Katz, then using the assumed name "Breda"; and Hollywood leftists such as writer-producer-director Herbert Biberman. Donald Ogden Stewart, a screenwriter and former regular of the Algonquin Round Table, was elected chairman. The league claimed five thousand members, boycotted Nazi goods, published a weekly paper, produced a weekly radio show, and organized mass rallies. When Mussolini's son, Vittorio, came to Hollywood in 1939 to learn the business of filmmaking at the Hal Roach Studio, the Anti-Nazi League contrived to make his stay as uncomfortable as possible.

In 1939, soon after the Munich Pact, Melvyn Douglas, Edward G. Robinson, and Herbert Biberman drew up a petition, modeled on the Declaration of Independence, asking Americans to pressure FDR into a boycott of goods from Nazi Germany. This was signed by fifty-six Hollywood celebrities, including Joan Bennett, Bette Davis, Myrna Loy, Joan Crawford, Alice Faye, George Brent, Don Ameche, and Henry Fonda.

The Spanish Civil War also sparked a flurry of activity. The Motion Picture Artists' Committee, of which Dashiell Hammett was chairman and Sylvia Sidney vice-chairman, brought Ernest Hemingway to Hollywood and raised enough money to supply the Loyalist forces with eighteen custom-built ambulances. Earlier that same year, 1938, Franchot Tone—another strong supporter of the Loyalist cause—and Joan Crawford sent an ambulance to Spain. Melvyn and Helen Gahagan Douglas were also ardent sympathizers; among their activities on the home front was organizing a committee to aid migrant workers.

Many of the people who had involved themselves with these causes

259

were shocked to find themselves, in 1940, under investigation by the recently formed House Un-American Activities Committee, chaired by Texas Democrat Martin Dies. Dies was notoriously anti-Semitic, anti-British, anti-Hollywood—and there were those who felt he distrusted any-one born west of El Paso or east of Texarkana. From the beginning, the tone of the committee's hearings was spookily surreal and frighteningly anti-intellectual. When one witness quoted Christopher Marlowe, Joe Starnes of Alabama, Dies's top lieutenant, interrupted, "You are quoting from this Marlowe. Is he a Communist?" The red scare of 1919 was being reactivated, and this time the movie industry was a prime target.

Not to be outdone by Dies, Los Angeles District Attorney Buron Fitts, facing re-election, launched a smear campaign against Hollywood celebrities based on the unsupported testimony of a confessed former Communist, John L. Leech. Leech accused Fredric March, James Cagney, Humphrey Bogart, Melvyn Douglas, Franchot Tone, and a dozen others of being either party members, Communist sympathizers, or fellow travelers. Not wanting Fitts to steal his thunder, Dies hurried to California where a delegation of Hollywood personalities—led by Paramount head Y. Frank Freeman—confronted him in his hotel room and demanded that he either substantiate specific charges or withdraw his campaign of innuendo and clear their names. (Dies even suspected Shirley Temple of being a Communist.) Having no real evidence to support his case, Dies backed down. This took the wind out of Buron Fitts's sails, too, and he lost his bid for re-election.

For a few years, the witch hunt abated, but Hollywood's critics in Washington found another cause. A number of politicians were openly critical of the moral support being offered to the besieged British by certain Hollywood movies; such anti-Nazi sentiment was interpreted as a violation of America's neutrality. When Jimmy Fidler began to vociferate this view-point on his Saturday night radio broadcasts, public awareness was raised to the point where isolationists were able to successfully lobby for a Senate subcommittee to investigate "war propaganda" in the movies. According to Wendell Willkie, the film industrys' chief counsel, the aim of this sub-committee was to pressure producers into avoiding "accurate and factual" pictures of Nazism, to block national defense, and to divide the American people into "discordant racial and religious groups."

The charges made were as follows:

1. An industry dominated by "foreign born" producers persisted in making pictures calculated to draw America into the European conflict.

2. Administration officials had asked producers to do this.

3. Filmmakers had a stake in a British victory because of British rental fees.

4. The movie industry—"a tightly controlled monopoly"—was guilty

of turning seventeen thousand theaters into locations for "daily and nightly mass meetings for war."

The films that bothered the subcommittee were productions like *The Mortal Storm* and even *Waterloo Bridge*. This was, after all, the period when Charles Lindbergh—once the honored guest of Louis B. Mayer—could tell an America First rally that Jews were dangerous because of their ownership of motion pictures, radio, the press, and their infiltration into government.

The hearings offered moments of pure farce. Jimmy Fidler was elevated to the status of star witness, whose testimony was countered by an extraordinary cable to the committee from Harry Brand, head of publicity at 20th, who said in effect that Fidler was the kind of person who would do anything for money. As evidence of this, he recalled the time Fidler had fast-talked Alice Faye into buying a $500 dress which fell apart the first time she wore it, causing her great embarrassment and public humiliation. The subcommittee, quite understandably, found this information wholly irrelevant.

In any case, the attack on Pearl Harbor rendered the issue academic, as politics became subordinated to the war. The year 1940 had provided a fitting swan song to the era, with Hollywood throwing itself wholeheartedly into the fury of the Roosevelt-Willkie election. The Hollywood for Roosevelt Committee conducted a vigorous radio campaign, featuring Pat O'Brien, Joan Bennett, Doug Fairbanks, Jr., Alice Faye, Edward G. Robinson, Rosalind Russell, and Henry Fonda. Aligned against them were Bing Crosby, Walt Disney, Mary Pickford, Gloria Swanson, Robert Montgomery, Harold Lloyd, Lionel Barrymore, Adolphe Menjou, Cecil B. DeMille, Louis B. Mayer, and most other studio executives.

For all the passion and occasional violence, this had been a period of relative innocence. At the Communist party's national convention of 1938, *The Daily Worker* conducted a poll which established that the delegates' favorite movie stars were Claudette Colbert and Gary Cooper. Lionel Stander managed to perpetrate the ultimate inside joke by whistling "The Internationale" on screen while waiting for an elevator. Ring Lardner, Jr., and Budd Schulberg visited the U.S.S.R., to see for themselves, and Joseph Freeman, editor of *New Masses,* was once able to charm and cajole guests at a Beverly Hills party into donating $20,000 to the cause. The political adventures of the thirties were ripples on the surface of an ocean where, before long, a whirlpool would swallow hundreds of gifted people. Neither the postwar activities of the House Un-American Activities Committee nor the abominations of black-listing need be recapitulated here, but it is important to remember that the paranoia of the forties and fifties fed on the idealism of the thirties.

The first real black list had been published as far back as 1934. Compiled and published by a fanatical rightist, Elizabeth Dilling, this booklet titled *The Red Network* saw revolutionaries around every corner, implicating organizations such as the YMCA along with individuals like Clarence Darrow and Eleanor Roosevelt—the latter presented as a "dangerous pacifist." This publication, although endorsed by the likes of William Randolph Hearst, had little immediate effect, but it did offer a model for later self-appointed witch-hunters with a penchant for list-making.

When the witch hunt began in earnest, in the late forties, the industry at first presented a united front against HUAC—even the studio bosses briefly supported the civil rights of employees with liberal or leftist leanings —but this front soon crumbled, partly because the bosses had problems of their own. In 1944 antitrust proceedings were once more instituted against the major companies, and, though they dragged on for several years and eventually reached the Supreme Court, this time they were to prove successful. None of the companies' establishment connections could help them. The consent decrees sought and obtained by Paramount and RKO in 1949, effectively divorcing production from exhibition and destroying the block booking system, marked the beginning of the end of the studio system as it had functioned in the Golden Age.

PRANKS.

Actors have often been called children who've never grown up, and Hollywood's penchant for practical jokes and other pranks is certainly evidence in point. According to David Niven, for example, Douglas Fairbanks, Sr., was one of the most active of the early practitioners, delighting in such naïve pleasures as exploding cigars and, at elegant Pickfair gatherings, crawling under the table to delicately unbutton the fly of some sedate gentleman guest.

Even more notorious as a joker at that time was Sid Grauman, who relished arriving at meetings in hearses and having himself delivered in coffins. (For some reason, many members of the movie colony found disease and death, ambulances, stretchers, and coffins hysterically funny.) Grauman liked to stage his gags as carefully as he staged his premieres. In *Whatever Happened to Hollywood?* Jesse Lasky, Jr., describes a typical Grauman stunt, of which Lasky's father was the victim. Lasky, Sr., then head of Famous Players, received a phone call from Grauman, who begged him to hurry to the Million Dollar Theater in downtown L.A., to address a group of important exhibitors. Grauman was counting on Lasky's predilection for extemporaneous—if pompous—speech-making, and, as expected, the mogul immediately called for his limo and headed for the theater. After a few brief words of introduction from Grauman, Lasky stepped on stage, barely able to make out, through the glare of the footlights, rows of soberly suited men gazing attentively at the stage. He told a couple of jokes, to break the ice, but when this did not produce the desired response, he moved onto the more serious part of his discourse, belaboring his audience with facts and figures. In the words of his son, "He held them quite spellbound. . . ."

When the house lights were raised, Lasky discovered that he had been lecturing to a collection of wax dummies.

Marion Davies relished stirring up a little mischief on the set. When Hearst was away on business, she sometimes consumed thousands of dollars' worth of film with such antics as blacking out a tooth in order to break up her leading man during a tender love scene, or pretending, with the aid of a pillow, to be pregnant.

The queen of the pranksters was Carole Lombard, who seemed to spend almost as much time dreaming up whacky stunts and gifts as she did learning her lines. On location, one time, she replaced all the light bulbs in the crew's quarters with flash bulbs, so that darkness was broken with a series of brilliant explosions. She and cohort Gene Fowler convinced Russell Birdwell to let them take over the Selznick publicity department for one day, which they spent devising manic press releases and improbable stunts. On the first day of shooting *Mr. and Mrs. Smith,* Alfred Hitchcock —who not long before had made his infamous remark about all actors being cattle—arrived to find three cows in a corral, each tagged with the name of one of the picture's principals. On the set of the same picture, she provided cast and crew with ice-cream cones filled with cold cream, then photographed the results. After Gable's picture *Parnell* received devastating reviews everywhere but in China, Lombard hired a plane to drop thousands of leaflets over M-G-M, each reading, "Fifty million Chinamen can't be wrong." One of her most famous hoaxes involved her agent, Myron Selznick. When presented with the standard contract renewal form, she took the three copies he left with her and reversed the usual split, so that she would get 10 percent of *his* earnings. Selznick cosigned them as a matter of routine and was horrified a few weeks later when she wrote asking why she wasn't receiving her commission.

David Niven also played the percentages when he was annoyed at Sam Goldwyn for taking half of his radio paychecks. After he had done a

PRANKS

Kraft Music Hall show, the sponsor sent Niven a large basket of cheeses and other tidbits. He scrupulously halved each Velveeta, each box of crackers, each can of sardines—even the basket itself—and had it hand-delivered to Goldwyn.

Although he couldn't hope to compete with his spouse, Clark Gable had been known to pull off a few good capers in his early days. When a young woman he was spending the evening with blacked out after overimbibing, Gable stopped at a flower stand and bought several dozen lilies, took the woman home, laid her out with her hands folded in the appropriate position, and surrounded her with the flowers and lighted candles.

Vince Barnett, a character actor who appeared in such films as *Scarface* and *I Cover the Waterfront,* moonlighted as a professional joker, enlivening parties by appearing as a soup-spilling waiter and the like. Raoul Walsh brought him to one party where he went around accusing everyone of stealing the silver. At another, he bawled Chaplin out for trying to attract attention to himself, and once, observing that Winston Churchill—on a visit to Hollywood—had placed an arm on a girl's chair, Barnett batted the offending limb away, remarking, "We have rooms upstairs for that kind of thing." At one of Norma Shearer's parties, Barnett impersonated an East Coast executive and when the hostess ventured a business opinion, he berated her mercilessly, saying that housewives shouldn't poke their noses into matters they knew nothing about, and telling her that if she paid more attention to her house, it wouldn't be such a mess.

Introduced to Helen Hayes, he told her he could only feel sorry for somebody who was married to a no-good bum like Charlie MacArthur. Not everyone took his barbs sitting down. When he interrupted a tête-à-tête between Tom Mix and Lupe Velez, Mix tried to choke him, and when, at a Joan Crawford gathering, Barnett accused Clark Gable of playing the big star and walking away from him, Gable did not hesitate to take a swing at him.

A more subtle response to Barnett was devised by the unlikely duo of Howard Hawks and Paul Muni. Deciding to turn the tables on him, they arranged for a pinch of snuff to be placed between the clapper boards right before one of Barnett's big close-ups, making him sneeze uncontrollably, while Muni pretended to be furious. Barnett continued to sneeze and apologize, as Muni raged on—so convincingly that he even deceived his omnipresent wife.

According to biographer Charles Higham, young Katharine Hepburn, with fellow conspirators Leland Hayward and Laura Harding, once sneaked through the back entrance of Walter Wanger's home during a dinner party. Bribing the catering staff and borrowing their uniforms, they proceeded to serve the meal. After dinner, Mrs. Wanger asked, "Has anyone told you that you look like that new girl in town, Katharine Hepburn?" At a larger party, Errol Flynn once planted a microphone in the powder room of his house and wired it to speakers in other rooms, so that his few hundred guests were privy to the ladies' room gossip.

It was a temptation for jesters to utilize the facilities and personnel accessible around the studios. Casting director Billy Grady once arranged for two Chinese extras to impersonate visiting foreign dignitaries who were supposedly personal friends of Nicholas Schenck. All day long, they were showered with the most magnanimous hospitality by the top executives until, late in the afternoon, an official asked if there was anything further that could be done for them by the studio. "Yes," was the reply, as one of the Oriental gentlemen extended his Central Casting voucher, "can you tell me where we cash these?" Darryl Zanuck once passed off an actor as the British ambassador to Mexico, and disguised himself as the ambassador's secretary. Zanuck, who was big on rubber chocolates and the like, was, along with Fairbanks, Chaplin, Hearst, Harold Lloyd, Warner Baxter, Victor Fleming, Edmund Goulding, Oliver Hardy, John Barrymore, Wilson Mizner, and Wallace Beery, a regular customer of Charles Hoffman and Max Asher's Hollywood magic shop.

Writer Charles MacArthur scorned Hollywood and delighted in putting one over on the studio brass. While having his car refueled at a Beverly Hills gas station, he struck up a conversation with the young, handsome Englishman who was performing the task. He invited the grease monkey, who was making forty dollars a week at most, to get cleaned up and come along with him to the studio. When they got there, MacArthur introduced him to Metro production executive Bernie Hyman as "Kenneth Woolcott, the well-known British novelist, who is against doing any movie writing because he insists there's no room for creative talent in them." Before long, the gas station attendant, who had never written a word in his life, had signed a year's contract as a Metro writer for one thousand dollars a week. He lasted the year without ever being found out.

At the heart of many of these shenanigans was a genuine core of sadism. Humphrey Bogart and Peter Lorre would sit in their favorite booth at Romanoff's, and if they found someone objectionable or dull, they would blow smoke in his face until he began to choke. When Ernst Lubitsch, then head of production at Paramount, who was terrified of planes, was forced to fly to San Francisco in a chartered aircraft for the sneak preview of a new Mae West film, he became petrified when they hit some turbulence over Santa Barbara. Suddenly, two "pilots" burst out of the cockpit, shouting, "We don't know what you're going to do, but we're getting the hell out of here," opened the hatch, and jumped. Lubitsch, not knowing that they were stunt men hired for the gag, bit through his cigar and had a heart attack.

PREMIERES.

Although Sid Grauman had introduced the concept of modest first-night festivities in San Francisco in 1916, the Hollywood-style gala premiere as an art form is generally acknowledged to have evolved from the opening of Grauman's Egyptian Theater in 1922 (with Douglas Fairbanks as *Robin Hood*) and the even more fabulous opening of Grauman's Chinese Theater on May 19, 1927. On the latter occasion, an estimated 100,000 people (guarded by 500 policemen and 1,000 members of the 160th Infantry) packed Hollywood Boulevard for the initial showing of Cecil B. DeMille's *King of Kings*. Much of Hollywood had been draped with bunting and decorated with flags and flowers. Two dozen searchlights raked the heavens, and Mary Pickford became the first star to plant her feet in cement in the forecourt of the theater, where an enormous fountain spurted water a hundred feet into the air to the accompaniment of an orchestra. In place of an ordinary curtain, Grauman installed a waterfall illuminated by a rainbow of lights. He had invited President Calvin Coolidge to push a button in Washington to signal the waterfall's initial rush, but when the invitation was declined, Pickford's finger was chosen to press the button that would "change stone and celluloid into screen history." The usherettes were a troupe of Oriental girls imported from San Francisco's Chinatown. Twenty-two hundred invitations were sent out to the cream of screenland society, and the mayor, chief of police, and fire chief were on hand (in Chinese costume) to greet DeMille. Unfortunately, after listening restlessly to long speeches by D. W. Griffith, Mary Pickford, and Will Hays, and sitting through half the epic film, only 2 percent of the audience was still seated when an intermission was announced at 1 A.M.

At early premieres, stars would greet their fans from open cars. On a few occasions, a wooden ramp was built down the center of Hollywood Boulevard for the luminaries to walk on. For the opening of Chaplin's *The Gold Rush* at the Egyptian, Grauman convinced Mary Pickford, Douglas Fairbanks, and Rudolph Valentino to make introductory shorts. Doug and Mary were shown in their pool at Pickfair. A title flashed on the screen reading, "Good Heavens! It's 7 o'clock!" They then emerged from

266

A CROWD GATHERS OUTSIDE GRAUMAN'S CHINESE THEATER FOR
THE PREMIERE OF *Strange Interlude*. WHEN THE STARS APPEARED,
A RIOT ENSUED AND THE YOUNG WOMAN IN GLASSES AND BLACK
AND WHITE HAT, SEATED LEFT CENTER IN THE FRONT ROW,
WAS CRUSHED BY THE MOB, SUSTAINING A BROKEN LEG AND
LOSING HER GLASSES.   CULVER PICTURES.

the pool, dressed in evening clothes, and set off for the premiere. Valentino
went a step further. He was shown swimming at the beach, when some
thieves came along and stole his clothes. He hitchhiked to the premiere
in his bathing suit. As he was shown on screen arriving in his bathing suit,
he made his real-life entrance—still in the bathing costume. At another
Grauman opening, Valentino came on stage in pajamas, apologizing that
he had overslept. He then slipped out of his night clothes to reveal white
tie and tails underneath.

An ordinary premiere in the thirties would cost from $5,500 to $10,000,
while the real extravaganzas could often run to $50,000. The biggest

267

cost was always the outdoor lighting, with a large amount budgeted for fresh flowers. For the long-awaited premiere of *Hell's Angels*—which Howard Hughes did not attend—Grauman planted searchlights all through the Hollywood hills, and the theater itself was ablaze with lights from the roof and forecourt. As an added touch, the souvenir programs were made of hand-tooled leather, embossed with gold.

A premiere was often a greater spectacle than the movie it celebrated. Wilson Mizner referred to the institution as "a bloody Indian raid in top hat and tails." Preparations for these events were a familiar sight along Hollywood Boulevard. Bleachers were erected in advance and fans would begin arriving before dawn on the big day, settling in near the theater with blankets, cushions, and picnic baskets. Before the stars began to arrive, to be greeted by a master of ceremonies (often the premieres were broadcast over the radio), a red carpet would be unfurled and a canopy of flowers erected above it. Appropriate tableaux—for *The Great Ziegfeld,* models dressed in costumes from the picture, standing in shadow-frame boxes, lined the sidewalk leading to the theater—were installed, then the ritual could begin. Generally, the crowds were well behaved, though scenes like those portrayed by Nathanael West at the climax of *Day of the Locust* were not unheard-of. Sid Grauman was the undisputed dean of gala premiere concepts, but he did have some rivals. Spectacular premieres were also staged at the Carthay Circle, the Pantages, and other large theaters around town. For the opening of *The Garden of Allah,* publicist Russell Birdwell had imitation oriental carpeting painted over six boulevard blocks in Culver City.

In the late thirties it became fashionable to hold the world premieres of major films in a location associated with the subject matter of the picture. (New York, of course, had always had its own premieres, parallel with those staged in Hollywood.) The gala opening of *Gone With the Wind* took place in Atlanta, with usherettes in Civil War period costume and ushers in Confederate uniforms. A special portico was built for the theater so that it would resemble Twelve Oaks, and the entire building was draped in Confederate flags. The celebrations lasted three days and the day of the premiere itself was declared a state holiday. Such welcomes were not uncommon when Hollywood decided to visit itself upon the provinces. The Omaha opening of *Union Pacific* in 1939 was a three-day civic celebration, with all expenses (and profits) shared by Paramount, the city, and the railroad. Businessmen, ministers, teachers, and salesmen allowed their beards to grow, women went shopping for calico dresses and sunbonnets, Indians pitched tents in front of the railroad station, and shopkeepers built false fronts on their stores. All these preparations culminated in a pioneer costume ball and banquet for five thousand people. The railroad also sent two special trains on a national tour: one a brand-new streamliner, the other pulled by a facsimile of the first Union Pacific locomotive. Actors in costume rode the specials, making thousands of platform appearances and being feted in fifty-three cities.

The premiere of *Northwest Mounted Police* in Chicago (which, after all, is nearer than Hollywood to the Canadian border) was preceded by two days of festivities, including a contest in which twelve thousand women competed for the thrill of sitting next to Gary Cooper and five thousand men vied for the privilege of sitting beside Madeleine Carroll or Paulette Goddard. *Virginia City*'s opening attracted the governors of six states, and when Dorothy Lamour appeared at the Detroit opening of *Disputed Passage,* in 1939, officials estimated that the crowd that came out to greet her was the third largest in the city's history. A trainload of celebrities from motion pictures, politics, and sports joined 100,000 others in South Bend, Indiana, for the premiere of *Knute Rockne*. At a banquet on the Notre Dame campus, Kate Smith sang "God Bless America" and Franklin Delano Roosevelt, Jr., read a letter from his father. After a competition between Tacoma and Seattle for the premiere of *Tugboat Annie Sails Again* (in the film, Annie's home town on Puget Sound is called Secoma), the victorious city of Tacoma proclaimed an official "Tugboat Annie Day." All the local schools were closed, forty thousand troops posted nearby were granted furloughs, and the cast of the movie chugged up the bay, escorted by several hundred flag-draped local tugs, yachts, freighters, and dredges. One of the most unlikely sights ever to grace a premiere occurred in Port Huron, Michigan, when Henry Ford, his son Edsel, Louis B. Mayer, and Mickey Rooney arrived at the opening of *Young Tom Edison* riding a bicycle made for four.

World War II brought an abrupt end to the gala premiere, since kleig lights were out of the question and formal dress came to be considered frivolous. But the coming demise of the practice had been signaled previously by the Albany, Georgia, opening of *Biscuit Eater,* a grade B opus about a hunting dog. Paramount's publicity chief, Cliff Lewis, decided to make it a "doggy premiere" and announced that Bing Crosby's dog, Dorothy Lamour's dog, and other celebrity canines would be on hand. Lewis decreed that the animals, who occupied the first two rows of the theater, had to wear formal attire—the gentlemen in white tie and tails, the ladies in satin and net—with corsages presented by Paramount Pictures.

PUBLICITY.

Publicity was the lifeblood of Hollywood, and its top operatives were men who, although unknown to the general public, wielded considerable power. Close to the executives who made the key decisions, they were the guardians of the industry's secrets, and they effectively controlled the channels of communication between the stars and their fans.

In the beginning, publicity was little more than a synonym for stunts. The most famous press agent of that era, Harry Reichenbach, displayed a highly developed sense of the outrageous, and although he was based in New York, he worked with many movie people and was a major influence on early Hollywood publicity. It was he who smuggled a lion into the room of a man who had registered at a Times Square hotel under the pseudonym "T. R. Zann," just as a jungle picture was about to be released. It was Reichenbach who caused Francis X. Bushman to be followed by a mob through the simple device of having Bushman's pockets stuffed with nickels, which were then allowed to trickle through small holes and fall to the sidewalk. It was Reichenbach again who, in 1919, took eight swarthy men off the streets of Manhattan, dressed them as Turks, and registered them at the Hotel Majestic, where they spread the word that they were in New York to search for a missing virgin. The story soon caught the attention of reporters, and the mysterious Turks were written up in several papers, to the chagrin of their editors when they began to see advertisements for a new Priscilla Dean film, *The Virgin of Stamboul,* appearing in their own publications.

Hollywood's most successful Reichenbach disciple was Pete Smith, who had worked for the master before moving to Hollywood, where he set up its first independent publicity organization, representing such clients as Colleen Moore, Marshall Neilan, and Conway Tearle. Early in 1925, soon after Louis B. Mayer took control of Metro, there was a shake-up in the studio's publicity department. Joe Jackson, who had been its head, had become involved with Carmel Myers—one of the stars of *Ben Hur*—apparently to the detriment of his work with other Metro players. When Mayer decided to replace him, he was advised that Pete Smith was the best publicity man in town. The problem was that Smith already had his own thriving business and would not give it up for less than one thousand a week—an astronomical salary at that time. Mayer balked at this, but asked Irving Thalberg and Harry Rapf to try to talk to him. Smith repeated his demands, and Mayer finally gave in. (He never had any reason to regret his decision. For one thing, it was Smith who masterminded the plan that forced Loew's, the parent company, to add Mayer's name to Metro-Goldwyn—a move that some officers of Loew's deeply resented.)

Like Reichenbach, Pete Smith specialized in opportunism and the fabricated event. When President Wilson was delayed on his way to San Francisco, Smith had an actor who was playing Wilson in a Marshall Neilan film driven to the St. Francis Hotel. The look-alike's arrival caused great consternation and garnered a creditable amount of news coverage. A few years later, Smith had the idea of flying Leo, the M-G-M lion, from California to New York. Since anything to do with flying attracted attention in the twenties, this was a sure-fire stunt. A plane was specially modified to carry a lion—no small feat in those days—and a famous aviator, Martin Jensen, was hired to pilot it. The flight attracted more attention than Smith had bargained for when Jensen was forced to crash-land in a remote Arizona canyon and could not be found for several days.

In 1931 Smith left the publicity department (though he continued to handle advertising for a while) to write and narrate the popular Pete Smith short features which were a staple for many years in theaters showing M-G-M pictures. Smith's successor, and the epitome of the studio publicist, was Howard Strickling, who began his publicity career with the old Metro company in 1919, after a brief spell as a reporter. In 1924 when Louis B. Mayer was installed at the studio, Strickling left to join Rex Ingram in Europe, but he returned a couple of years later, at Smith's invitation, to become the number-two man in the M-G-M publicity department. After Smith left for his shorts unit, Strickling became head of publicity and eventually held the title of vice-president in charge of publicity and advertising.

In theory, Strickling was subordinate to Howard Dietz, his opposite number in the New York office of Loew's, Inc., but in practice—while he and Dietz had an amicable relationship—he was answerable to no one but Louis B. Mayer. More than just a publicist, he was one of Mayer's most trusted aides; and his department was more than just a publicity machine, concerning itself with the over-all welfare of the studio's contract players. If a new star was arriving from New York or Europe, Strickling's assistants would locate a suitable house and hire servants to staff it. It was understood, at Metro, that the publicist's job included making the lives of their performers as comfortable as possible and protecting them from unpleasant situations.

JOAN CRAWFORD AND DOROTHY SEBASTIAN, BEING "COACHED" BY
FRANK HOLBORROW, SWIMMING INSTRUCTOR AT THE CLUB CASA
DEL MAR IN SANTA MONICA.

All this reflected Mayer's policy of developing stars systematically,
rather than attempting to exploit them with a single burst of publicity. According to Strickling, Mayer felt that everyone would be best served if
contract players thought of themselves as part of an organization that had
their long-term welfare at heart; Mayer was nothing if not paternalistic, and
liked to consider the studio his extended family. Since Mayer believed in
the careful grooming of stars, Strickling's department could take its time
about building images. There was never any question of engineering
spectacular stunts—which would have been alien to Strickling's character
—or gambling everything on a single roll of the dice. When a performer
signed with the studio, one of the first things he or she did was to fill out
an elaborate form which solicited biographical information. This began
with conventional inquiries—professional name, real name (if different),
date of birth, family relationships, education—then proceeded to other
subjects that might be of particular use to the publicist:

Athletic or other achievements.

Radio, vaudeville, etc., experience if any.

Previous occupations aside from pictures or stage—where and when.

Ever do any writing (specify short story, novel, drama, with titles)?

Business activities aside from pictures, if any.

How often attend picture shows?

What would do if out of pictures.

Convictions regarding stage and screen—do they conflict?

Any forebears in the theatrical profession? Other arts?

Any kin at present so engaged?

Give any personal convictions about acting, also any rules observed.

Any ambition outside present career? Greatest ambition is . . .

Childhood ambition was . . .

Favorite actor is (screen) . . . (stage) . . .

Favorite actress is (screen) . . . (stage) . . .

Opinion of Hollywood.

Outstanding impression of Hollywood.

Favorite motion picture is . . . stage play . . .

Favorite role you have portrayed.

Detail any unusual adventure.

Do you govern your life by any rule or rules?

What are they?

Most treasured possession (like an heirloom, keepsake, etc.) is . . .
State why.

Any superstitions?

Believe in hunches? Details if ever successfully followed a hunch.

Active in what sports (golf, etc.).

Hobbies.

Favorite recreation (dancing, bridge, etc.).

Musical instrument played, if any.

Pets (dogs, etc.) and their names.

Any particular phobia?

According to Strickling, the principle applied at M-G-M was that if a star was to sustain an image over a long period of time, then that image had better be based on the star's actual character and preferences—at least to a reasonable extent. Every effort was made to involve the new contract player in the determination of the image to be projected. Strickling credits Pete Smith with developing this system, although it seems to have evolved quite slowly and did not reach its refined form until after Strickling took charge. It most certainly was not in operation when Garbo arrived at M-G-M in the summer of 1925. Herbert Voight, the Metro publicist assigned to meet Garbo and Mauritz Stiller at the boat in New York, couldn't induce a photographer to shoot a picture of Garbo until he finally had to pay one ten dollars to expose a couple of plates. Once she reached California, Smith's department set about rectifying the situation in a most unfortunate way, perpetrating a series of publicity stills in which she was shown holding a tiger cub and posing with a lion, surrounded by the USC track team, and crouched—as if to start a race—while the track coach pointed a pistol at her head. (Smith quickly recognized his error and switched to exploiting Garbo's desire for privacy.)

Typical of the campaigns launched during Strickling's tenure at M-G-M (which lasted over five decades) was that which presented Clark Gable to the public as the all-American outdoorsman, addicted to hunting, shooting, and fishing. In fact, Gable had had little experience of the outdoor life when this campaign was launched, but he did agree that it was a style of life which might appeal to him, and before long, guns and rods and bivouacs and campfires became his passion, providing an escape from the pressures of Hollywood that he took advantage of whenever possible.

In some instances, however, Strickling's strategy had to be modified. Wallace Beery, for example, was a very difficult man in real life, yet it was necessary to present him as the lovable old scoundrel he generally portrayed on screen. This was a harmless enough evasion of reality—it was certainly not the publicist's job to shatter millions of illusions—but more complex problems were presented by some of Metro's younger players. An example given by Strickling is Van Johnson. Here was the case of a former chorus boy becoming, overnight, the darling of American mothers, who saw him as the freckle-faced son they wished was their own. Suddenly, reporters were asking him what he thought about the international situation and if he believed FDR should run for another term in the White House. Since Johnson was not equipped to handle such questions, the publicity department was obliged to provide him with answers and to create for him a persona which fitted the image that the public had thrust on him. Similarly, youngsters like Mickey Rooney, Lana Turner, and Elizabeth Taylor had to be presented with simplified philosophies of life which they could spout to interviewers. And, since adolescents could not be counted upon to contribute much mature thought to the building of their images, it was necessary to take more liberties, which could prove dangerous. The accounts of Judy Garland's childhood that began to appear in the press within weeks of her signing with M-G-M were grossly distorted. To what extent Judy and her family contributed to these distortions is a matter for speculation, but the false picture of her comically tragic childhood in

AN EARLY PUBLICITY SHOT OF GARBO.   CULVER PICTURES.

vaudeville became a fixed item in her legend, which she came to eventually
believe herself. This confusion about her childhood seems to have contributed much to the unhappiness of her later life.

You didn't have to be as young as Judy to be overwhelmed by the pressures of stardom. Some celebrities, Gable for instance, had a knack for
dealing with fans and the press, but others, like Spencer Tracy, found such
confrontations rather painful. Robert Taylor received his baptism of fire
during a trip to Europe. On the *Super Chief,* en route to Chicago, a young
woman reporter sat on his knee and promptly wired her paper a story
announcing that she had found the experience less thrilling than sitting on
her own husband's lap. She added that she doubted if the star even had
any hair on his chest. It was an echo of the "pink powder puff" slur against

275

EVERY YEAR, FROM 1922 TO 1934, HOLLYWOOD PUBLICISTS ELECTED WAMPAS (WESTERN ASSOCIATION OF MOTION PICTURE ADVERTISERS) BABY STARS. PICTURED HERE, LILLIAN ROTH AND JEAN ARTHUR, 1929.

Valentino a dozen years earlier, and by the time Taylor arrived in Chicago, a mob was waiting for him—apparently eager to tear his clothes from his body to check out the woman's theory. Another crowd was waiting in New York, but a terrified Taylor managed to avoid them and board the Cunarder on which he was to cross the Atlantic without being observed.

When it became evident that an even larger horde would be waiting when the boat docked at Southampton, a wire was sent to Strickling, already in Europe with Louis B. Mayer, asking him to intercept the vessel before it berthed. Strickling took a tender out to the liner while it was still in the Solent and found Taylor in a state of panic, asking to be smuggled ashore. But Strickling, with the assistance of a young British woman journalist, persuaded him that hiding would only make matters worse. The best way to deal with the situation, they argued, was to confront the newspapermen with his side of the story. An on-deck press conference was arranged, at which Taylor succeeded in restoring his romantic image and his confidence in himself.

In its day-to-day operations, Strickling's department was a model of efficiency. Forty or more people—including unit publicists, planters, etc.—would attend his Monday morning staff meetings, and the ideas discussed would then provide the basis for the hundreds of memos—always typed on pink paper—which flowed from Strickling's office to each of his publicists. All of Strickling's top employees, many of whom were women, had at least two jobs. They might gather information on the sets, prepare copy for distribution, or be engaged in channeling material to Louella or to the trades or to *Collier's,* but, apart from this specialized activity, they would be assigned two or more contract players who were their personal responsibilities. Strickling's chief aide, Eddie Lawrence, specialized in working with ladies of temperament like Norma Shearer, while Strickling himself, with Otto Winkler, handled Gable's publicity. (Gable had a clause in his contract providing that if Strickling should ever leave the studio, he would remain his press agent. Winkler was recruited after writing newspaper articles sympathetic to Gable at a time when the actor was embroiled in a paternity suit.) Kay Mulvey worked with Jean Harlow and Spencer Tracy, and Emily Torchia was assigned to younger actresses like Lana Turner. It was the publicist's responsibility to look after his charges in every possible way, working out stories with them, accompanying them to interviews, and shielding them from unwanted attention. Often this led to close friendships, as in the cases of Strickling and Gable and of Kay Mulvey and Jean Harlow.

The publicist most often compared with Strickling is Harry Brand, who was once secretary to Mayor "Pinkie" Snyder and, coincidentally, worked with Strickling at the Los Angeles *Express* and the Los Angeles *Tribune*

PUBLICITY

(both wrote for the sports pages) before graduating to publicity. His first job in the field was at the old Warner Brothers Zoo, at Washington and Main in downtown L.A. Later, he became Joe Schenck's right-hand man at 20th Century, and when 20th merged with Fox, he took over the publicity department, building it into one of the strongest in Hollywood. Like Strickling, Brand emphasized systematic, low-key promotion. His contacts both inside and outside the industry—from judges and politicians to bartenders and bus boys—were legendary, making him one of the most formidable behind-the-scenes figures in the movie colony.

The Los Angeles press corps provided more than its share of top Hollywood publicists. Arch Reeve, who went on to run the Paramount publicity department for many years, worked on the sports pages of the *Tribune* with both Strickling and Brand. Jock Lawrence, Sam Goldwyn's able publicity head, started as a reporter on Hearst's *Examiner*.

Another top publicist was Perry Lieber, who started with RKO in 1928 and ran the department from 1937 to 1962. He was very close to stars like Cary Grant, Ginger Rogers, and Irene Dunne, and during Howard Hughes's tenure at the studio he became one of Hughes's most trusted aides. When RKO folded, Lieber worked briefly under Harry Brand at 20th, then moved to Las Vegas to handle press relations for Hughes's Summa Corporation.

ADOLPH ZUKOR POSES WITH SOME OF HIS PARAMOUNT STARLETS, INCLUDING CLARA LOU (ANN) SHERIDAN, STANDING SECOND FROM RIGHT. SEATED WITH ZUKOR ARE TOBY WING, CHARLOTTE HENRY, GAIL PATRICK, AND IDA LUPINO.

OLIVIA DE HAVILLAND "PERSONALLY" ANSWERS HER FAN MAIL.

It was not unusual for publicity men to move into other branches of the movie industry, and at least one, Hal Wallis, did so with great success. His sister, Minna, was casting director at Warner Brothers when he joined her, in the late twenties. He started in the publicity department, but within a few years he had graduated to producing and, when Darryl Zanuck left the company, he became its top producer.

Charles Einfeld, who worked out of the New York office of Warners, was the acknowledged master of the press junket, establishing his reputation in 1933 when he organized a cross-country expedition to promote the Busby Berkeley musical, *Forty-second Street*. His "Forty-second Street Train" consisted of several Pullman coaches, furnished by General Electric and other sponsors, which carried half a dozen Warner stars and scores of pretty girls to a number of cities where the local fans were given the opportunity to catch a glimpse of their favorites and gape at a forest of well-turned calves. At each stop, members of the press were invited aboard and plied with refreshments, given access to the movie luminaries, and en-

couraged to enjoy such facilities as "the Malibu lounge," which was equipped with potted palms and sun lamps. The expedition was a huge success, attracting vast throngs wherever it went. The final destination on the schedule was Washington, D.C., on the eve of Franklin D. Roosevelt's inauguration. Historians tend to ignore the gaily decorated Warners float, a touch incongruous on that drab Depression morning, just as there is little mention of a similar M-G-M float, from which Amos 'n' Andy broadcast a description of the inaugural parade. At the time, however, newspapers rewarded the efforts of both studios with extensive coverage.

Apart from perfecting the junket technique, Einfeld was also noted for his ability to turn bad publicity around. When Harvard students voted Ann Sheridan the unenviable title of actress least likely to succeed, Einfeld countered by having her photographed with a mule and sending prints to thousands of newspapers with a caption commenting on the relative salaries of Hollywood actresses and Harvard graduates. It was Einfeld's

SUSAN HAYWARD: A TYPICAL PUBLICITY BUILD-UP.

publicity department, too, that released one of the most grotesque stories of all. The press was informed that Pat O'Brien had been forced to have a tattoo removed from his chest because of his screen work. So attached was O'Brien to this tattoo, the release continued, that he had had all the skin peeled off his chest and made into a lampshade! (Some sources say this story was concocted by James Cagney.)

The splashy Reichenbach style did not vanish entirely from Hollywood in the thirties, finding a champion in the person of Russell Birdwell. A slight, dapper Texan with a neatly trimmed mustache, Birdwell had a natural leaning toward the flamboyant. (Some of his contemporaries felt that his main concern was promoting himself.) After more than fifteen years as a journalist—most of them spent with the Hearst papers—he accepted David Selznick's invitation to try his hand at publicity work. This was in 1935, just after Selznick left Metro to embark on a career as an independent producer. Birdwell promoted Selznick International's first picture, *Little Lord Fauntleroy,* by hiring hundreds of painters to execute a sign over two miles long on a Culver City street. Next he employed an armed ex-FBI man to guard the "ideas" at the Selznick Studio. David Selznick was appalled by this gimmick, and Birdwell, according to a profile of the publicity man which appeared in *The New Yorker* in 1944, was rather shocked to learn that good taste was supposed to be an element of his work. Pointing to a portrait of Selznick's father, a freewheeling producer in his day, Birdwell said, "I seem to be working for the wrong Selznick." The younger man agreed that his father would have approved of the G-man idea.

Birdwell's success was in large part attributable to his knowledge of the newspaper world, his shrewd understanding of editorial instincts. When David Selznick informed him that the shooting of *Gone With the Wind* would begin with the nighttime burning of Atlanta, Birdwell decided against sending out a press release, knowing that the sight of flames soaring into the sky above Culver City would act as a magnet for newsmen from all over Southern California, and that the element of surprise would give added impact to the story.

It was Birdwell's theory that government officials and agencies lent respectability to a P.R. campaign. When Carole Lombard remarked casually, to a foreign director who was complaining about his taxes, that she felt her own tax bill was reasonable, considering the salary she was fortunate enough to earn, Birdwell forwarded her statement to the Internal Revenue Service, who quickly made good use of it. Soon Lombard was being publicly praised for her patriotism by politicians of every persuasion. When Dick Powell's career was slipping, Birdwell arranged for the actor to have lunch with a senator from Arkansas, Powell's home state. Seventeen other senators attended and, inevitably, made speeches. The publicity resulting from this event performed miracles for Powell's popularity. And when Franklin D. Roosevelt innocently observed that Janet Gaynor was "cute as a button," Birdwell lost no time in broadcasting the news to the world.

In 1939 Birdwell left the Selznick organization to set up business as an independent press agent. Immediately he landed half a dozen clients who were willing to pay his asking fee of $25,000 a year (for corporate accounts he demanded double). Representing illustrous clients like ex-King Carol of Romania and Howard Hughes did nothing to temper his disdainful attitude toward good taste. In 1940, to promote *So Ends Our Night* for United Artists, Birdwell had Gerta Rozen—a bit player—call a press conference in front of the studio, at which she removed her coat and announced that she would take off another item of clothing every day until the producers relented and gave her a better part. The papers billed this as the world's slowest striptease, but, needless to say, the producers gave in before the assembled photographers got so much as a glimpse of lingerie.

For one client, Birdwell invented the cellophane bathing suit, and for the opening of *The Prisoner of Zenda* he flew the entire population of Zenda, Ontario—twelve people—to New York. Hoping to make Norma Shearer more accessible and less the *grande dame,* he had her photographed riding a roller coaster. Martha Scott recalls another of his techniques:

> Russell Birdwell was very helpful to me for a couple of years. He got me in national publications along with a lot of other gals. He used to do it by getting about six of his clients together, like Marlene Dietrich and Carole Lombard and a couple of others and say that some fraternity had elected them such and such. I'll never forget that one of them was I had "carefree legs." He always made these up—Bird was a brilliant con man.

There was considerable antipathy between company men like Howard Strickling and independents like Russell Birdwell. (Even in his Selznick days, Birdwell never had the responsibility of running the long-term promotion of a large stable of stars.) When Clark Gable and Carole Lombard were married, Gable called Strickling and asked him to share arrangements for the event with Birdwell, who was Lombard's press agent. Strickling refused to set a precedent by working with someone he considered an upstart rival.

The Atlanta premiere of *Gone With the Wind* provided the occasion for another confrontation between the two publicists. The M-G-M party—angered because it was felt that insufficient credit was being given to director Victor Fleming—refused to co-operate with the Selznick forces which were marshaled by Birdwell. Gable, who counted Fleming as one of his closest friends, was so incensed that he almost refused to attend the

STARS RELAXING ON THE SET BETWEEN SHOTS WAS A FAVORITE
SUBJECT OF THE PUBLICITY DEPARTMENT'S STILL CAMERAMEN:

KATHARINE HEPBURN (RIGHT), KNITTING ON THE SET OF
Quality Street, WITH ESTELLE WINWOOD AND FAY BAINTER.

BETTY GRABLE PASSES THE TIME WITH HER NEEDLEWORK.

BETTE DAVIS AND PAUL HENREID BETWEEN TAKES OF
Now, Voyager.

premiere, but was finally persuaded that such a gesture would only make things worse. Strickling borrowed an American Airlines DC-3—promising the carrier valuable exposure in return—and flew to Atlanta with Gable, Lombard, and the M-G-M entourage. When they arrived, Birdwell cornered Strickling in a hotel bar and attempted to badger him into collaborating. Gable, seeing what was going on, came over and threatened to flatten Birdwell unless he left Strickling alone.

It would be misleading to suggest that publicity departments were simply well-oiled machines programmed to keep the names of a given studio's stars before the public with the aid of a constant stream of clever stories and glossy photographs. The business of publicity had its less savory aspects, and some of its more unscrupulous practitioners worked on the assumption that any publicity was good publicity. An anonymous article in *The American Mercury,* dated January 1942, details various instances of this at an unnamed Hollywood studio where the publicity department was run by a lugubrious individual the author refers to as "Mr. Tolliver." One of Tolliver's exploitation men, according to this piece, was the lawsuit specialist whose job it was to make sure that somebody sued the studio for something at least once every thirty days. All pictures were considered to have an "actionable quotient . . . a loophole whereby someone can bring a libel or plagiarism suit." Naturally, a *real* libel or plagiarism suit was the last thing in the world the studio would want—the only kind that was desired was one that could be totally controlled by the publicity department. The author cites the example of a litigation which arose from a movie based on a famous sea story. The suit specialist found "a thirsty barfly" and persuaded him to pose as the grandson of the villain of the book, and to begin action to halt the showing of the picture on the grounds that "it libeled the name of his ancestor." This particular suit went to court and attracted considerable attention from the press. An injunction was, in fact, granted, but never enforced. The bogus plaintiff was then paid off in liquor and drinking money.

More often, however, it was the publicist's job to keep people out of the courtroom. Covering up scandals was an integral part of the work, and there were plenty of people ready to assist in this task—at a price. If a drunk was subdued after a fracas at a bar, for example, and there was any reason to think he might be associated with the movie industry, in however humble a capacity, the barman would check his wallet for a studio pass. If he found one, he would call the studio and the chances were that someone from the publicity department would be sent over with a few dollars to square the barman and make sure the police were not called. If the drunk happened to be a contract player, or a director, the sum involved might be quite substantial.

DURING WORLD WAR II, RITA HAYWORTH DEMONSTRATES
HER PATRIOTISM.

PUBLICITY

Hedda Hopper, in her book *The Whole Truth and Nothing But,* describes the situation:

> The police departments, often reported to be openly cozy with mobsters, have a long record of blinking at other kinds of lawbreakers, providing a nimble press agent can get on the case in time. Clark Gable, returning home from a party at Paulette Goddard's after downing too much of the bubbly, banged up his car in a traffic circle, but it was happily announced that a passing motorist was really to blame.
>
> Eddie Mannix has related how it cost a total of $90,000 to keep the reputation of a celebrated MGM star intact when he was caught in the same desperate situation that sent Big Bill Tilden, the tennis ace, to prison as a homosexual.
>
> Studio cops worked hand in glove with custodians of the law outside the studio gates. Some days the telephones of top public-relations men like Howard Strickling at Metro and Harry Brand at Fox rang like a four-alarm call in the firehouse, as police dutifully reported that they had this or that star safely locked up for speeding, drinking, or mixing it up in a public brawl.

On the other hand, some judges in the Los Angeles area could be extremely harsh toward Hollywood personalities who strayed into their courts—Bebe Daniels once served a ten-day jail sentence in Orange County for speeding! To make sure that valuable employees were not subjected to such perils, it was the job of the troubleshooters in the publicity departments to establish friendly relations with the DA's office and the various local police departments, so that—when stars got into trouble—things could be squared in such a way that charges were not brought. The studios could offer a variety of favors in return, ranging from tickets to premieres to substantial donations to police benevolent associations. Newspapermen presented a trickier problem, since they had a vested interest in not concealing stories, but often enough they too could be squared. (In Prohibition days, a supply of quality liquor was sometimes sufficient to ensure against press leaks.)

The movie business was the biggest game in town and could afford to pay through the nose in order to buy itself protection.

R ACING.

During the twenties and early thirties, fans of horse racing had nowhere to go in Southern California—the nearest track was across the border in Agua Caliente. When thoroughbred racing was legalized in 1934, it was the movie colony that provided the reservoir of enthusiasm and financial support which was needed for it to succeed. The new Santa Anita track was the brain child of Hal Roach, and its elegant clubhouse soon became an important gathering place for the movie elite. Directors Woody Van Dyke and Henry King both had holdings in the Santa Anita Turf Club, as did Bing Crosby, who was later president of the Del Mar track, near San Diego. The Hollywood Park Turf Club was organized by Jack Warner, who was chairman of a board that included Raoul Walsh. Mervyn LeRoy became the track president. The track soon became a passion with all echelons of studio society, to the point where both trade papers, *Daily Variety* and the *Hollywood Reporter,* would print racing news and charts, and it became difficult to get work accomplished on the set during periods of track activity.

Horse owners whose colors were seen at the track included Crosby, Walsh, Jack and Harry Warner, Robert Taylor, George Raft, Spencer Tracy, Howard Hawks, Errol Flynn, William LeBaron, Don Ameche, Myron Selznick, William Goetz, and Joe E. Brown. Fred Astaire owned a string of thoroughbreds including Triplicate, which—having been bought for $6,000 as a three-year-old—went on to win over $250,000 for victories that included the Hollywood Gold Cup and the San Juan Capistrano Stakes. Barbara Stanwyck and Zeppo Marx were partners in a stable called Marwyck.

By far the most ambitious and successful horseman in the movie colony, however, was Louis B. Mayer. Mayer performed the unprecedented feat of building one of the finest racing stables in the country in less than a decade and almost singlehandedly raising the standards of California racing to a level where it had to be taken seriously, even within the traditional eastern bastions of thoroughbred racing. He built his stable in much the same way he had built his studio, by sparing no expense and concentrating on the goal of developing a string of star performers. When he gave up

289

racing in 1949, he had over forty stakes victories to his credit, and the bloodlines that were established at his stable are still an important factor in thoroughbred breeding today.

According to Jack Baker, chief veterinarian at Mayer's Perris farm, Mayer had a comprehensive grasp of the day-to-day running of the stable, interesting himself in every detail from track records to the grain mix in the horse's feed. He obtained animals from the East Coast and from Australia and, at the outset of World War II, managed to purchase some choice thoroughbreds from top European breeders, including the Aga Khan, who were anxious to see their bloodlines—which had often been in one family for generations—survive the international hostilities. The terms generally demanded were that the owners be allowed to select a mare at the war's end, in order to pick up the bloodlines once more. Mayer was, in fact, offered many horses on this basis, but could only import a few because of transportation difficulties—they often had to come by way of Africa and South America.

It has been said that Mayer was forced to give up his horses because of IRS pressures and because his bosses at Loew's thought he was devoting too much time to his stable. Myron Fox, Mayer's personal business manager and the man who was directly in charge of the stable, says this is not true. Fox asserts that Mayer—once he had been shown the financial advantages that would accrue—sold out when he did chiefly because his new wife, Lorena, had no interest whatsoever in racing. Jack Baker adds that Mayer may have become somewhat disillusioned by the public's response to his success, citing an occasion when Mayer's horses finished first, second, and third in a stakes race at Hollywood Park. For this triumph Mayer was roundly booed by the crowd.

Hollywood's obsession with the race track inspired Errol Flynn to organize white mice races, for which he had printed an elaborate race card and a tip sheet. The mice were named for various movie world personalities, and the tip sheet—"Selections by Smokey 'Never Loses' Flynn"— was full of in-jokes and sexual innuendo:

AVA GEE: Has had Plenty of Chances—Should Repete and Repete
CRAWFORD: One of the Country's Tops—Winning Form
HOPPER: Long Time Out—Sharp—Waiting for her Connection
CROSBYTYM: Sounds like a Winner
DOCKEY BOY: No Gamble. From a Solid Stable.
IRIS B. Classy. Not Scared by a Big Field. If Hand Ridden, Will Go.
ORREBOY: Erratic. Might be Backing up at the Pole.
SINATRA: In Light, and Should Last.

GREER GIRL: Tab Now for Best Effort.

CLARK G.: Breaks and Cuts—Especially with Fillies

HIS HIGHNESS: By Czar Out of Ellis Isle

GEORGIE GEE: From the Hurdles to the Flat. Might Have Made a Great Stud If He'd Cleared the Last Fence.

PIDGEON II: Still Trying. Needs Slightly Softer Spot.

LOOEYBEE: Recently Came to Life.

JACK BENNY: No Hope.

BIG PETER: Been Beaten Many Times.

LANA GIRL: Bit Hard to Handle but Not with Good Boy Up.

BUDDY BOY: Wearing Greer Garson's Silks—Buddy Boy Looks Like Sheer Breeze.

TIGER LIL: Ran Out When Backed with Smart Money—Mine!

EDDIE G: Likes Any Track. Get Down on This One.

Q-COR: Frequently Nosed Out by Younger.

FREDDY MAC: Runs Best for a Big Purse—Nose Always in There.

Some of these names scarcely need elucidation. Among the slightly more obscure examples, Dockey Boy refers to Louella Parsons' husband, Dr. Martin; Orreboy is presumably named for Warner Brothers designer Orry-Kelly; His Highness for Mike Romanoff; Buddy Boy for Elijah E. ("Buddy") Fogelson, the Texas oil magnate Greer Garson later married; and Tiger Lil for Flynn's former wife, Lili Damita.

Another mouse was named Flynn's Folly. Of this entry, the tipster remarked, "Might Act Better If Gelded."

RECREATION.

The Hollywood crowd was as addicted to sport as was any other sector of American society. Experienced celebrity hounds knew that among the best places to see stars were the race tracks (see RACING) and the American Legion Stadium in Hollywood on Friday nights. Friday night was fight night, and the ringside seats were generally packed with stars. Lupe Velez frequently climbed into the ring to give encouragement to Latin fighters, artfully flashing parts of her anatomy the Hays Office kept under

291

wraps on screen. Los Angeles was a great boxing town, with local heroes like Fidel La Barba, Henry Armstrong, Newsboy Brown, and Bob Walker, the fighting grip, who battled Joe Louis at Wrigley Field in the mid-thirties. Since there was no major-league baseball on the West Coast, movie people turned out to watch the hapless Hollywood Stars, who hosted visiting Triple-A teams at Gilmore Field, and also watched from the fifty-yard line at the Coliseum as Jackie Robinson carried the ball out of the UCLA backfield. Occasionally, you might even catch a Hollywood personality watching the girls' softball games at Fiedler Field. The motion picture colony was, however, full of highly competitive people who were not satisfied with the role of spectator, and were eager to demonstrate their own athletic prowess.

RANDOLPH SCOTT, PHYLLIS BROOKS, AND CARY GRANT AT THE FRIDAY NIGHT FIGHTS.

A number of Hollywood stars were, in fact, ex-athletes. Johnny Weissmuller and Esther Williams both held world records for swimming, and Sonja Henie, like Weissmuller, was the winner of several Olympic gold medals. Johnny Mack Brown had been an All-American football star on the powerful Texas teams of the mid-twenties (he was eventually elected to the College Football Hall of Fame), and John Wayne was on the University of Southern California gridiron squad a couple of years later. Errol Flynn, an accomplished horseman, swimmer, and fencer, had boxed his way into the quarter-finals of the Amsterdam Olympics. John Payne had professional experience in both boxing and wrestling rings, as did Victor McLaglen, who was at one time heavyweight boxing champion of eastern Canada. Robert Ryan was heavyweight champion of Dartmouth College four years in a row, and Jimmy Cagney and Bob Hope both had early experience as amateur fighters, as did Robert Preston, who was a Golden Gloves medalist. Claudette Colbert was a winner of ski trophies, and Hollywood boasted many low handicap golfers, including Ruby Keeler and Fred Astaire (who has said that if he had his life to live over, he would probably forget about movies and devote himself to the PGA tour). The best known golfer in town was, of course, Bing Crosby—a stylish player who practiced constantly (often on a strip of lawn on the Paramount lot) and brought his handicap down to 2, winning the championship of the Lakeside Golf Club on five occasions. He launched the famous Pro-Am competition that bears his name in 1937, at the Rancho Santa Fe course, near San Diego. In 1947 he moved this contest to the Monterey Peninsula, where it still thrives, pitting the skills of professionals and celebrities alike against three of the most challenging golf courses in the world: Spyglass Hill, Cyprus Point, and Pebble Beach.

In addition, a number of top-flight professionals—Babe Ruth, Bobby Jones, Jack Dempsey, and Red Grange, to name just a few—made movies in Hollywood, and in some instances took up residence there for a while, so the amateurs did not lack for models.

For several years, there was an interstudio baseball league, the most fanatical devotee of which was Buster Keaton, who could always find a job for someone with the potential of helping his team. The British colony was given to the more sedate pace of cricket, filling its Sunday afternoons with the crack of willow on leather and the click of bails, evoking nostalgia for distant village greens. It was C. Aubrey Smith who founded the Hollywood Cricket Club in 1932, and its membership included Ronald Colman, Clive Brook, Basil Rathbone, Nigel Bruce, Harry Warner, Errol Flynn, Cary Grant, Herbert Marshall, David Niven, and Boris Karloff. Some members of the British colony preferred soccer, however, and were fervid supporters of a local team called the Sons of St. George, which included several English ex-pros and played against visiting Mexican clubs.

RECREATION

Karloff, as well as being a charter member of the cricket club, played for the local field hockey team and was an avid tennis buff. Tennis was headquartered at the West Side Club, famous for its beautiful girls, and at the Beverly Hills Tennis Club, which at one time had Fred Perry for its head coach and tended to be patronized by the more serious players. Milton Holmes, the owner of the club, was a top pro himself. Members included Groucho Marx (whose son, Arthur, became an outstanding player), Charlie Chaplin, Flynn, Norman Krasna, Billy Wilder, Frank Capra, Robert Riskin, and William Wyler. Donald Woods, another member, recalls fiercely fought games between Peter Lorre and Paul Lukas, with Lukas disputing every call. Gilbert Roland was one of the best tennis players in Hollywood—strong on his ground strokes, but reluctant, according to Woods, to come into the net. Among the women, Ginger Rogers was a regular at the Beverly Hills Tennis Club who could hold her own with most. Carole Lombard was another enthusiast, once remarking that she'd gladly quit movies if she ever became good enough to beat Alice Marble. Frank Morgan and Charles Butterworth were strong players, and W. C. Fields could sometimes be seen chopping balls across the net, racket in one hand, martini in the other. According to one biographer, his game was accurate, powerful, and ruthless, though he was disinclined to chase balls that were out of reach.

Another player who preferred to remain immobile was William Randolph Hearst. He came to the game late in life and often invited players of the caliber of Fred Perry, Bill Tilden, Ellsworth Vines, Frank Shields, Helen Wills, and Alice Marble to be his guests at San Simeon. Hearst himself, apart from his lack of mobility, was quite proficient. Ben Lyon, who often played with him, recalls that Hearst preferred to play doubles, so that he could let his partner chase the ball. The tournaments at San Simeon were famous, and so were the tennis weekends at Ronald Colman's home on Mound Street. The latter were, in fact, all too famous, attracting dozens of fans who climbed trees and scrambled for vantage points until Colman surrounded his tennis court with a high tarpaulin stretched on fencing.

Apart from Perry and Tilden, top tennis pros in town included Harvey Snodgrass and Frank Feltrop. Feltrop, attached to the Beverly Wilshire Hotel, coached Rita Hayworth, Lana Turner, Mickey Rooney and many others.

Since most people had their own pools, swimming was a back-yard activity, unless you preferred the beach. Amid the mansions on the Santa Monica shore were the Santa Monica Swimming Club and the Santa Monica Beach Club. The former was perhaps more show business populated than the latter, but, since members tended to wander from the bar of one to the bar of the other, it made little difference. Screenwriter

LOUIS B. MAYER WARMS UP FOR A STUDIO PICNIC SOFTBALL
GAME, IN WHICH HIS TEAM IS OPPOSED BY ONE CAPTAINED BY
IRVING THALBERG.   CULVER PICTURES.

JOAN CRAWFORD AND DOUGLAS FAIRBANKS, JR., HER FIRST
HUSBAND, PLAYING BASEBALL.

Winston Miller began going there in the twenties, when he was still in his
teens:

> I spent most of my weekends there and I remember that the big fun
> was the volleyball games between the Swimming Club and the Beach
> Club. We'd alternate playing at one club or the other, and the whole member-
> ship would come across to support its team. There was a lot of excitement.
>
> We played seven men on a team. Joel McCrea played for the Beach
> Club, and so did George O'Brien. Buster Crabbe was one of the stars for
> the Swimming Club. Cary Grant was down there a lot, getting a wonderful
> tan, but we used to see so many people—celebrities—that we didn't pay
> much attention to them.

Other sports, from roller skating to croquet, enjoyed vogues of varying
duration. Croquet was, in fact, extremely popular for a while. Champion-

BING CROSBY ON THE LINKS, 1934. CULVER PICTURES.

ship courts were built all over Beverly Hills, and moguls like Darryl Zanuck and Sam Goldwyn clashed for stakes of up to one thousand dollars a game. Goldwyn was a health fanatic, but he had been forced to give up his first love, handball, after a broken ankle, and his second love, golf, because he became so frustrated at his own errors on the fairway. He was introduced to croquet by Harpo Marx and George S. Kaufman, and enjoyed it from the outset, but it was his wife, Frances, who had the court built for him. Alongside it was a "score-keeper's hut," where contestants could find soft drinks and read the house rules which Goldwyn had chalked onto a blackboard:

1. Don't get excited.
2. Correctly remember balls you are dead on.
3. Have patience with fellow members who are not as good as you are.

Ronald Colman, William Powell, and Richard Barthelmess took up water skiing, and, in the mid-thirties, Central Casting had an all-black basketball squad. A few years later, an overage motorcycle gang—the Morango Spit and Polish Club—met every Sunday at Howard Hawks's home. Victor Fleming, Keenan Wynn, Bill Wellman, Andy Devine, and Clark Gable were among the regulars. In a show of drunken bravado and true Hell's Angel spirit, Wellman once rode his Harley-Davidson off the diving board into the deep end of the Beverly Hills Tennis Club swimming pool.

The need to escape from public scrutiny could be an important factor in selecting leisure activities. Clark Gable was not an unsociable man—he liked to dress up and attend parties and premieres and play the movie star —but there was another side to his personality which demanded freedom from that responsibility. The hunting and fishing trips originally undertaken for the sake of his professional image quickly became an essential part of his private life. When he was married to Carole Lombard, the two spent a great deal of time at a duck club run by Harry and Nan Fleischmann, south of Bakersfield. Another hideaway for the couple was La Grulla Gun Club in the Baja California mountains, near Ensenada, and the Gables and Fleischmanns often went fishing on the Rouge River in Oregon, staying at the Ask U Inn, which was run by old friends of Gable's.

Sailing was another way to find privacy, and Hollywood yachtsmen were an assorted bunch, ranging from the expert to the rank amateur. Harry Cohn boasted—or joked—that sailing was his favorite pastime. He owned an extravagantly appointed cruiser, the Jobella (named for his parents), which was moored in the San Pedro yacht harbor, with ship-to-shore telephone lines permanently in place, but was never seen to make any attempt to reach open water. Chaplin's *Panacea* was another boat that was rarely away from its berth, though Chaplin used it extensively for parties and is

GINGER ROGERS PLAYING TENNIS

FRED ASTAIRE PLAYING TENNIS.

known to have favored it as a romantic setting. On the other hand, a number of Hollywood yacht owners—Humphrey Bogart, Errol Flynn, John Ford, and Frank Morgan among them—were skilled helmsmen.

Perhaps the first Hollywood figure to take sailing seriously was Cecil B. DeMille. In 1917 he purchased a 57-foot cruiser, the *Sea Bee,* then four years later replaced it with a sleek, ocean-going schooner, *Seaward,* 106 feet from stem to stern, which remained one of his great passions until it was requisitioned by the Navy during World War II. (Another DeMille hobby—one that afforded the ultimate in recreational escape—was deep-sea diving.)

An equally enthusiastic early sailor was John Barrymore, who, in 1926, bought a 93-foot gaff-rigged schooner, the *Mariner,* built four years earlier and the holder of a transpacific record. He installed a diesel auxiliary motor and had the boat's living quarters converted to accommodate three state-rooms and an enlarged galley. With its skipper, Otto Mathias, at the helm, the *Mariner* took part in the annual San Pedro to Hawaii race, becoming becalmed in midocean and arriving three days after all other competitors. Chastened by this experience, Barrymore returned to California by steam-ship, but it did not lessen his interest in sailing. In 1929 he commissioned a 120-foot, diesel-powered, steel-hulled boat which he named the *Infanta* in honor of his new baby daughter. The *Infanta* cost $225,000, and its launching at Long Beach was a highlight of the 1930 social season. Capable of fourteen knots, the boat was equipped with every conceivable comfort that could be customized to fit its racy lines. One cabin was decorated as a nursery for the baby, there was a library with wood-burning fireplace, and a glassed-in sun deck. Boxes of soil were provided so that mint could be grown for Barrymore's juleps, and he undertook a number of extended cruises in this vessel, sailing to the South Seas to fish and to Alaska to hunt bear.

Another Hollywood yachtsman who cruised to the South Seas, on more than one occasion, and for two and three months at a time, was Lewis Stone, Commodore of the California Yacht Club and owner of the schooner *Serena.* Most movie world sailing enthusiasts belonged to the California Yacht Club, though the snootier Los Angeles Yacht Club did admit Bogart to membership, perhaps because of his prep school background. Bogart's *Santana,* which he bought from Dick Powell for $55,000, was a serious racing craft, typical of the kind of boat owned by the better Hollywood helmsmen. *Santana* was, in fact, a well-known boat in competitive circles, its record including a second-place finish in the 1934 Santa Monica to Honolulu race. Bogart also owned a 34-foot cruiser, *Sluggy,* which he kept at Newport Beach. Other fast boats were Flynn's *Zacca* and *Sirocco,* Preston Foster's *Zoa II,* and Frank Morgan's *Dolphin.* Morgan won a number of important races and kept detailed scrapbooks as a record of his yachting achievements.

John Ford owned an ocean-going boat called the *Araner,* in which he regularly plied the seas between San Pedro and Hawaii. Ronald Colman, who had few serious pretensions as a helmsman but knew how to look the part, sailed the *Dragoon,* while Jimmy Cagney skippered the *Martha,* and Spencer Tracy's ketch was called the *Carrie B.* in honor of his mother.

Although several boats were named—perhaps out of guilt—for mothers, wives, and daughters, the Hollywood yachting scene was essentially male-oriented (though Errol Flynn, as is well known, had few superstitions about inviting women aboard). It was a weekend diversion from the demands of domesticity and gossip column romance—a chance to escape the scrutiny of landlubbers like Louella Parsons and Hedda Hopper. The stars who sailed were able to enjoy, for a couple of days, the companionship of their crews, which tended to be a mixture of full-time sailors and enthusiasts drawn from the rank and file of studio employees. Bob Schiffer often crewed for Bogart and recalls the experience with affection:

> Bogie was a great helmsman, but he let us apes—he called us his deck apes—do all the hard work. The best times I've had in my life, I think, have been with Bogart. Wonderful guy. He had a deal with his wife Betty [Lauren Bacall] that he would take off every Thursday and be back

MERLE OBERON AND DAVID NIVEN PLAYING PING-PONG.

DON AMECHE IN HIS POOL.

on Sunday night at six. There were no women, except occasionally Betty would come along, and she would bring the social side of the yachting circle in.

But the most fun we had was just the fellows. We'd sit down in the boat, around a table—Bogie had a great faculty for getting people angry with one another, and when he got them to the point where they would beat one another up, he was happy. Someone would swing at someone else and it was all his fault—but you would never realize that as it was going on, till you thought it over, that Bogart was the guy who started it. He had a cook and a captain and every Saturday he'd get them into a fight. He loved it! He just loved to see them get into fights.

RECREATION

Schiffer also sailed with Errol Flynn:

> I was in Acapulco, with Flynn, on the *Zacca*. He drank a lot then, but he was still in great shape. Every day we'd sail out of there, and for the cocktail hour he'd drink beer—or anything he could get his hands on—and by the time we sailed into that harbor, he was smashed. But he could sail that boat! He would sail right up between rocks—just a beautiful sailor. Then we'd anchor and the two of us would go up to a little bar and drink tequila—he was always bare chested, with a knife stuck in his belt. Then he'd walk out and sleep with a prostitute. He'd go up to the whorehouses and come back in the morning.
>
> He met a girl in Acapulco—her father was the owner of the Las Americas Hotel, which was a big hotel in those days—and he was really on the make for her. She was a beautiful girl, but her father was chaperoning her. Flynn kept asking her out to the boat, but she would never come.
>
> Well, I was sitting on the fantail of the boat one day and Flynn had brought back one of these Mexican prostitutes with him. She had hair all over her legs, and a moustache. You just wanted to shave her! It was eight or nine in the morning and I was looking at this apparition. They hadn't been to sleep and I was looking at this horrible girl, in the bright light of day, and I was thinking, "How can this good-looking famous guy end up with this real baggage?"
>
> Suddenly, out from the beach comes a motor launch, and in this motor launch is the owner of the Las Americas and his daughter—they had finally decided to come out and visit. Flynn, as the boat came alongside, walked over and asked them to come aboard. They stepped onto the boat. Flynn brought them back to the cockpit and said, "I'd like you to meet Mr. and Mrs. Schiffer."

Almost as many people devoted themselves to flying. Bill Wellman had been in the Lafayette Flying Corps, and LeRoy Prinz was also a World War I pilot. Cecil B. DeMille, although over age, had attempted to gain a commission in the Army Air Corps, learning to fly in 1917. After the war, he built his own airfield and began a flying service, the Mercury Aviation Company. In 1919 Sidney Chaplin launched a company which pioneered float plane service between Catalina and the mainland, and later Richard Arlen was part owner of a charter company.

Ben Lyon learned to fly for Howard Hughes's *Hell's Angels,* then bought a Stinson for his personal use:

> Flying was a lot of fun in those days before smog and air traffic control. You didn't have to register your route, or anything like that. Suppose you wanted to go to Palm Springs. No fuss, and the air was so clear you could see forever.

CLARK GABLE AND JOHN BARRYMORE AT BARRYMORE'S SKEET-
SHOOTING RANGE.

DICK POWELL ABOARD HIS YACHT, THE *Galatea,* 1938.

I used to fly Bebe up to San Simeon—down near the sea there was a long, flat field and you'd have to buzz the pasture land to get the cows out of the way—and Hearst would say, "Bebe, you're crazy to fly up here in that thing!" He was against flying then, but later he used to fly his guests up there in a Stinson trimotor.

Wallace Beery was an excellent flier, Clarence Brown, too, and so were Henry King and Reginald Denny. Hoot Gibson, though, was not so good. He had quite a few accidents, turning the plane over—that sort of thing —damaging the aircraft more than himself. It was a lot of fun, in those days. You could just take off and go anywhere you wanted to—any route, any altitude, any weather.

Bebe Daniels eventually learned to fly from her husband, and among the many other Hollywood pilots were Ruth Chatterton, Ray Milland, Leland Hayward (a big enthusiast), Margaret Sullavan, Jimmy Stewart, and George Brent.

306

During the years prior to the reopening of the Santa Anita race course, the tradition of thoroughbred horse breeding in Southern California was kept alive chiefly by the polo crowd. The young bloods who grew up in Pasadena or wintered in Santa Barbara provided some of the best competition in the country, and there was a large contingent of people in the movie colony anxious to prove themselves on the polo field. Walt Disney was so eager to gain acceptance in this world that he recruited teams from among his staff and had them practice with him, before work, under the watchful eye of an ex-army player, on a vacant lot in the San Fernando Valley, until he had gained sufficient experience to join his peers at the Riviera and the Uplifter's Club. Later he was forced to quit polo when he sought financing for his new Burbank studio and was told that he would have to abandon the sport because of the danger involved before the bankers would agree to a loan. Other Hollywood devotees of polo included Spencer Tracy, Darryl Zanuck, Walter Wanger, Robert Montgomery, Frank Borzage, Gary Cooper, Hal Roach, Clarence Brown, Jack Holt, Leo Carillo, Michael Curtiz, Wallace Beery, Charles Farrell, Johnny Mack Brown, Jimmy

ERROL FLYNN ABOARD THE *Sirocco*.

Gleason, and Will Rogers—the latter generally conceded to be the pre-eminent player among the movie crowd.

Clark Gable wanted to take up polo—and even bought a pony and all the necessary equipment—but was forbidden to play by the M-G-M front office. Spencer Tracy ran into similar problems. In June of 1933, while playing in the Brandeis Cup matches at the Riviera Country Club's polo green, Tracy—a good, but sometimes reckless player—was involved in a bad spill in which he suffered a sprained arm, a wrenched back, and facial cuts. Fox, his studio at the time, refused to renew his contract unless he agreed to give up polo, but he continued to play under such assumed names as Ivan Catchanozoff. This got him into hot water when he took another bad fall in 1934, during the filming of *Marie Galante.*

No sport in Hollywood was pursued with more passion, and skill on a polo pony was a useful accomplishment for anyone who wanted to get ahead in the movie industry. Nobody was too surprised, then, when Aiden Roark was appointed to Darryl Zanuck's executive board at 20th. Roark was a crack polo player.

Hollywood even invented its own sport, officially called Dougledyas, but commonly referred to as "Doug," after Mr. Fairbanks, its originator and champion. It was actually a variant of badminton, played with tennis rackets, heavily taped shuttlecocks, and a high net. The strenuous game was played regularly at Pickfair by such stalwart competitors as Victor Fleming, Howard Hawks, and Raoul Walsh, the last of whom had his nose broken in the course of a particularly vigorous match.

RELATIVES.

There is a famous Hollywood story, possibly apocryphal, that has the head of a major studio naming his brother to a senior executive position, installing him in a lavishly appointed office, and providing him with an endless supply of yellow memo pads. "Always use these yellow pads," the brother was told. "They're for your exclusive use and when people see them, they'll give them the appropriate priority." The studio head then returned to his own office and circulated to all departments a notice which read, "Ignore all memos written on yellow paper."

Most motion picture executives came from a background in which it was traditional to look after your relatives and in which the family business was the norm. It was natural for them, when they found themselves in a position to do so, to hire brothers, cousins, and in-laws—but we should pause before labeling this blatant nepotism, which would imply placing relatives in positions of real power. This did go on to some extent, but family members were more often put into sinecure positions where they drew a salary for performing some innocuous task that had little bearing on studio policy or the *Realpolitik* of the movie business. There were several Schencks at Loew's, Zukors and Balabans at Paramount, and enough Mayer kin at Metro for one wit to explain the initials of the studio as standing for Mayer's-Ganze-Mespuchah (Yiddish for Mayer's entire family). Few of these relatives had any clout, however, though Louis B. Mayer's quarrels with his brother Jerry did occasionally upset M-G-M's smooth routine. L. B. had made Jerry general manager of the studio, so he was, nominally at least, responsible for much of the day-to-day efficiency of the operation. When the two brothers fought, which happened frequently, they often reached the point of refusing to speak to each other, breaking the chain of command and creating problems on the floor. As for Mayer's two sons-in-law, Bill Goetz and David Selznick, Goetz was never a factor at Metro (although it was Mayer who got him his executive positions at 20th and at Universal), and Selznick can hardly be accused of needing his father-in-law's assistance to make it to the top. (This did not save him from the inevitable "the son-in-law also rises" jokes.) Mayer's nephew, Jack Cummings, a producer, may actually have been held back because of his family ties, finding himself assigned to B properties through most of his career. When he was finally given his head, he turned out successful films like *Seven Brides for Seven Brothers*.

The studios at which nepotism was most rampant were Universal and Columbia. Carl Laemmle, head of Universal Pictures, was not known as "Uncle Carl" for nothing. Jokes about his legion of relations constituted a cottage industry in Hollywood, and even Ogden Nash was moved to compose the couplet:

> Uncle Carl Laemmle
> Has a very large faemmle.

At times it seemed that half his *lanzmen* from Laupheim, Germany, had followed the scent of his success, to beg employment of him. Few were refused and fewer still met with any degree of success in the movie industry. One notable exception was William Wyler, whose mother was a cousin of Uncle Carl's, and who started out as a messenger boy at the studio. The Columbia payroll was heavily weighted with kinsmen of Harry Cohn, along with those of General Manager Sam Briskin and of Briskin's brother-in-law Abe Schneider. In this instance, they so choked up the higher echelons of the studio that many able men found it impossible to achieve advancement there. Because of the many Cohns on the lot, Robert Benchley nicknamed Columbia "the Pine Tree Studio."

Given the fact that Hollywood was a highly self-contained community, founded by a relatively few individuals, it was almost inevitable that relationships by blood and marriage would become significant. This all began back in the days when film pioneer Jesse Lasky's sister married the young glove salesman Samuel Goldfish (who later changed his name to Goldwyn). A generation later, Lasky's cousin Mervyn LeRoy married Harry Warner's daughter Doris. As in other societies all over the world, and throughout history, dynasties were shored up by intermarriage with competing but interdependent dynasties.

This applied chiefly to the executive levels of the film industries. In the creative sphere, there was a comparable number of intermarriages, but these carried little real significance, except insofar as such unions gave the box office an occasional jolt. More interesting, perhaps, is the number of performers related by birth who achieved success in the movie industry.

Several sets of siblings made it to the top—either separately or together —the most prominent being Lillian and Dorothy Gish, the Marx Brothers, the Barrymores, Norma and Constance Talmadge, Charlie and Sidney Chaplin, and Constance and Joan Bennett. Wallace and Noah Beery and Olivia de Havilland and Joan Fontaine were among those who were rarely on speaking terms. The rivalry between the De Havilland girls dated back to their childhoods, when Livvy was robust and beautiful and her younger sister was skinny and sickly. According to Sidney Skolsky, when Joan was nine, she actually tried to kill Olivia. Later—and on a less equal footing— were brothers George Sanders and Tom Conway, Barry Fitzgerald and Arthur Shields, and Dana Andrews and Steve Forrest. In *The Story of Alexander Graham Bell,* Loretta Young insisted that her sisters Sally Blane, Polly Ann, and Georgiana Young be cast as her screen sisters, and Marie Blake, best known as Sally the switchboard operator in the Dr. Kildare series, was the older sister of Jeanette MacDonald. Somewhat more distantly connected were cousins Dolores Del Rio and Ramon Novarro, Rita Hayworth and Ginger Rogers, as well as Howard Hawks and Carole Lombard. M-G-M director Norman Taurog was Jackie Cooper's uncle.

Trusted family members were often the logical choices to be the business managers of stars. Spencer Tracy relied heavily on his brother Carroll to take care of financial and other, more personal matters, as did James Cagney on his brother Bill. Alice Faye's brother William handled her business affairs, and Carmen Miranda depended upon her father to perform these functions.

In the early days, several girls found themselves in pictures as a result of payoff deals made by members of their families, especially with D. W.

Griffith. Colleen Moore's uncle, Walter Howey, was an editor on the Chicago *Examiner* who was able to get both *Birth of a Nation* and *Intolerance* past the censors in return for which Griffith rewarded his niece with a contract. Winifred Westover's father was also a newspaperman who had done favors for Griffith and Carmel Myers' father was a rabbi who advised the director on ancient history. Later, all sorts of jobs were found at the studios for relatives of stars. Some mothers and fathers were employed as coaches of diction and dance; some were given stipends for less specific jobs. Brothers and sisters could be found in bit parts, for example Rita Hayworth's brother Vernon Cansino in *The Lady from Shanghai* and *The Loves of Carmen*. Tyrone Power's sister Anne found a position in the writing department at Fox, and Gene Tierney's mother was hired as a press agent by the same studio.

Marriages forged some surprising relationships. Howard Hawks became Irving Thalberg's brother-in-law when he married Norma Shearer's sister. Buster Keaton's marriage to Natalie Talmadge made him brother-in-law to Joe Schenck, his backer. Gary Cooper's wife was the niece of Dolores Del Rio's husband, M-G-M art director Cedric Gibbons (whose brother married costume designer Irene). Loretta Young is the sister-in-law of Ricardo Montalban. Marion Davies' nephew, screenwriter Charles Lederer, married Anne Shirley, and her niece Patricia's husband was Arthur (Dagwood) Lake. Rod Cameron took things one step further when he married the mother of his third wife and became his own son-in-law, a procedure which Gloria Grahame reversed when she married her ex-stepson, Tony Ray.

RESORTS.

Movie people who wanted to get away between pictures or just for a quiet weekend had many seductive destinations from which to choose, for within easy driving distance of Hollywood is a variety of natural splendor—beautiful beaches, wild mountain areas, spectacular desert scenery. Inevitably, of course, certain places became favored as resort areas. Aside from the long-established Santa Monica ocean front (see HOMES), there were film colony beach heads at Laguna, Balboa, and, much more important, Malibu.

RESORTS

When the Rindge family, who had purchased the 13,000-acre Rancho Malibu property in 1891 (for ten dollars an acre), was forced to give up its strangle hold on it in 1927, actors and actresses led by Anna Q. Nilsson, began to settle on the sandy spit, near Malibu Creek, that came to be known as the Malibu Colony. Eventually this would become a year-round community, but most of the early lease holders treated it very much as a summer resort. Around 1930, a lot with thirty feet of ocean frontage could be leased for ten years at thirty dollars a month, and those who took advantage of these terms included John Gilbert, Clara Bow, Barbara Stanwyck, Ronald Colman, Dolores Del Rio, Ruth Chatterton, Bill Powell, Richard Barthelmess, Constance Bennett, Chico Marx, Warner Baxter, George O'Brien, and Louise Fazenda. Their names were to be found on the old-fashioned mailboxes which stood in the post office—a small white hut at the entrance to the Colony. The property was protected from the outside world by a high stone wall, and the gate was always manned by an armed guard, while a staff of seven security men was employed to patrol the grounds. During the thirties, more homes began to appear along the beaches to the south of the Colony, and in the mountains that rise alongside the Coast Highway. The chic Malibu watering hole in those days was the Glass Slipper.

On clear days, you can see Catalina Island from Malibu, and even from the Hollywood Hills. Catalina was popular with film world yachtsmen and aviators who tended to congregate either at the Hotel St. Catherine or La Conga Club, which was situated at the water's edge and provided a private dock for members' boats.

South of Los Angeles, Del Mar—where the race track was governed by a Board of Directors headed by Bing Crosby—became a popular venue, and the Coronado Hotel, across the bay from San Diego, was another favorite destination. Over the border, in Baja California, Tijuana, Agua Caliente, and Ensenada were much frequented by the faster-living elements of the movie crowd. Joe Schenck had almost half a million dollars invested in the opulent casino and resort—which included a dog track and golf course—at Caliente (see GAMBLING), and Jack Dempsey built a Monacoesque casino-hotel in Ensenada, where a favorite hangout was The Hut.

Inland, Big Bear Lake and Lake Arrowhead were popular summer resorts—with the High Hat and North Shore Tavern known as the smart rendezvous at the latter. The Arrowhead Springs Hotel was financed by Schenck, Zanuck, Jolson, and others (see INVESTMENTS). As the thirties progressed, Palm Springs began to feature more and more as the winter retreat for the movie colony. The Desert Inn had been established there, in 1909, by Nellie Coffman, and for two decades it was patronized chiefly by tuberculosis victims who would take bubbling mud baths under the supervision of the local Indians, who charged twenty-five cents a dip. When

Hollywood discovered Palm Springs, the Desert Inn was joined by El Mirador (for a while the "Amos 'n' Andy" radio show was broadcast from its roof). The Stables and the Dunes were other well-patronized establishments of the thirties, as was La Quinta, a smart bungalow resort in the desert twenty miles beyond Palm Springs proper.

In those days, Palm Springs was like a gigantic dude ranch. Hotels employed hosts who dressed like the Riders of the Purple Sage in tooled cowboy boots and embroidered shirts. It was their job to organize "Western" picnics, horseback rides, and moonlight barbecues. For those with a taste for dice or roulette, there were several little all-night spots featuring gaming tables in the back room. An important institution was the Racquet Club, founded by two Hollywood notables—Charles Farrell and Ralph Bellamy—who in 1934 bought fifty-two acres of desert for $3,500 (see INVESTMENTS). (Some protaganists claim that the "folding farrell," served at the Clubhouse bar, was the original bloody mary.) The Palm Springs Tennis Club was set up in competition in 1937 by Pearl McManus, and although it served as headquarters for the wealthy British colony that wintered there, it never quite matched the prestige of the Racquet Club with the movie crowd.

RESTAURANTS.

Although Hollywood has never challenged New York or San Francisco, let alone Paris or Marseille, as a mecca for the gourmet, restaurants have played a significant role in its social history. From the early days when night after night, Charlie Chaplin and Mabel Normand and their cronies made their way out to the Ship Café in Venice, there has always been an "in" place, since, for the movie crowd, eating out has essentially meant being seen at the right place by the right people.

Writing in *Scribner's* in 1937, Lucius Beebe observed that Hollywood's habits at table were something to make Brillat-Savarin fairly whisk about in his grave. Telephones at the table, he remarked, were considered the height of chic, and no personality of consequence dared sit through an entire meal without having a phone ostentatiously installed in his booth in order to conduct a conversation of suitably impressive length. Another peculiarity of the Hollywood restaurant scene was the custom of serving

313

dinner, not course by course for all the company together, but, rather, individually to suit the convenience of late arrivals, "so that while Mr. Flynn and Miss Damita may be in their salad, Mrs. Sam Hoffenstein directly across the table from them will be only at the caviar stage." In defense of guests' tardiness, it should be noted that this was often caused by shooting schedules conflicting with social arrangements. There can be little excuse offered, however, for the kind of service which Beebe observed to be the norm in fashionable Hollywood eating places. Unless you were a friend of the house or a recognized celebrity, you were likely to find yourself treated with a minimum of courtesy. As an example of this, Beebe cited an occasion at the Vêndome when he had seen noncelebrity customers forced to vacate their table in the midst of a meal to accommodate the tardy appearance of Douglas Fairbanks.

Paul Henried, arriving in 1940 with an open mind and a European palate, loved Hollywood, but was appalled by the culinary standards he found there:

> There was terrible food, with one or two exceptions. One was Romanoff's—the Romanoff's that used to be on Rodeo Drive, north of Wilshire. . . . It had one room that was the bar and a few tables, and whoever was anybody was seated there by Mike, so that when you walked in there would sit Gable and Carole Lombard, and David Niven—the lineup was there. This was an eating place that was, as the British would say, plausible —good food, nothing extraordinary. They would give you a good sole, that was flown in, they would give you an excellent charcoal broiled steak for two, which they sliced, with a very good mustard sauce, so that it became like an *entrecôte*. They did quails very well, particularly if you talked to the head waiter and told him you wanted it well done and crisp.
>
> Then there was Perino's, which was very good, in some ways better than Romanoff's because it had more variety. They would have something that was then unheard of, like a crêpe filled with lobster or with crab. And there was Chasen's. That was about it. Those were the three places you could go and get a decent meal. There were some private homes, of course, where you could expect a good dinner. At Jules Stein's, for instance. Jules Stein was well traveled and had excellent taste, and he imported cooks. At that time he had one cook who did nothing but bake his bread and rolls and cake.

The first real restaurant in Hollywood was John's, a stone's throw from Hollywood and Vine, which had its heyday during and immediately following World War I. John was a Greek who ran an unpretentious establishment, but everybody ate there, and it was one of the key meeting places of early Hollywood. In 1919 John's was joined by Musso and Frank's—still a landmark along Hollywood Boulevard—which was destined to become the favorite of the literary set, attracting the likes of F. Scott Fitzgerald and William Faulkner during their stints on studio payrolls. In the early twenties, Armstrong and Carlton opened at the corner of Hollywood Boulevard and Cherokee and quickly established itself as *the* new spot.

One evening in 1925, Herbert Somborn (one of Gloria Swanson's husbands), Sid Grauman, and Abe Frank, manager of the Ambassador Hotel, were lamenting the dearth of decent eating places in Los Angeles. Somborn remarked that in his opinion you could open a restaurant in a back alley and call it anything, and—as long as you provided good food and service—the patrons would come flocking. To prove his point, he hired a friend, Robert Cobb, who came from a family of caterers, and set about acquiring suitable premises. The outcome was the first Brown Derby, which opened—not in a back alley, but across the street from the Ambassador—in 1926. Cobb eventually bought out Somborn's interest in the business and opened the Vine Street Derby in 1929 and the Beverly Hills branch in 1931. In the thirties, they were almost like private clubs for the show business community, open twenty-four hours a day to accommodate actors wanting breakfast before starting out for location and others dropping in after late-night sessions at the studio. At the Vine Street branch, the booths near the entrance and along the north wall were reserved for the movie and broadcasting elite. Wallace Beery had a regular table, eating there three nights a week, and Friday evenings saw the place packed with celebrities, since Friday was fight night and the Vine Street Derby was just a short walk from the American Legion Stadium, where the matches were staged. Wilson Mizner, one of Cobb's partners, had a regular Friday night table, as did Hollywood's "Irish Mafia," which included Spencer Tracy, Pat O'Brien, Frank McHugh, Ralph Bellamy, and Frank Morgan. At precisey 8 P.M. everybody made a dash for the stadium, and the restaurant remained very quiet until the feature fight was over, at which point it quickly filled up again.

Many of the waitresses were pretty, aspiring actresses. (In George Cukor's *What Price Hollywood?* the character played by Constance Bennett is discovered while working in the Vine Street Derby.) Wearing highly starched derby-shaped skirts, they spent much of their time dropping and provocatively retrieving silverware near tables occupied by directors and producers.

One of the major reasons behind the success of the first Brown Derby had been a man called Pete Schroeder, who had been the *maître d'hôtel* on the *Chief,* the Santa Fe train that ran between Los Angeles and Chicago.

RESTAURANTS

Everyone going east traveled on the *Chief,* and Schroeder—who was something of a ham himself—knew how to cater to celebrities (see COAST TO COAST). Somborn decided he would be the ideal *maître d'* for his new restaurant, and soon Schroeder, handsome in high hat and livery, was welcoming guests at the Derby. Schroeder was so good at his job that before long he was offered a partnership by the Armstrong half of Armstrong and Carlton, the Derby's rival on Hollywood Boulevard. Armstrong and Carlton promptly became Armstrong-Schroeder and moved to Beverly Hills.

Another early restaurant, one that retained its popularity for many years, was Victor Hugo's, which was originally situated in downtown Los Angeles, on Hill Street between Seventh and Eighth. Edmund Wilson's impressions of this restaurant, jotted down in 1928, have been published in his posthumous book, *The Twenties:*

> You pay a certain amount for lunch and then get all you want to eat of enchilada, goulash, spaghetti, *pâté de foie gras,* glazed tongue, glazed beef, salads (hot red Spanish sauces and purple ripe olives), rolls and cornbread fingers, eggs with chopped-up chicken à la king, like all entrées, in a chafing dish—ravioli—pickle sauce, eggs stuffed with anchovies, coffee in glasses, French pastry, strawberry cake with glazed, deadly-looking strawberries rather like the decorations of the restaurant itself, where a long carpeted staircase led to a luxuriously curtained interior—mirrors, Empire ornaments, birds of paradise behind white looped window curtains. . . .

The *prix fixe* Wilson mentions was at that time $1.50 a head. In the thirties, when Victor Hugo's moved to Beverly Drive, near the Beverly Wilshire Hotel, it was increased to $2.00, considered rather stiff at the time. Dinner could cost you as much as $5.00, quite sufficient to keep the riffraff away.

Perino's, on Wilshire, was opened by people who had been associated with Victor Hugo's, and it quickly established a reputation for providing the best food in Los Angeles. It was probably the one restaurant patronized by the movie colony that could have been set down in New York or London without seeming out of place: the ambiance was conservative and the service excellent by any standard.

Not long after he founded the *Hollywood Reporter,* in 1930, Billy Wilkerson opened a small sandwich shop on Sunset Boulevard, near the offices of his paper. As sandwich shops go, this was an ambitious operation (Wilkerson imported many delicacies from Europe, especially from Fortnum & Mason in London), and soon he expanded the operation into

316

ESTHER RALSTON STANDING BEFORE THE ORIGINAL BROWN DERBY
ON WILSHIRE BOULEVARD.   CULVER PICTURES.

a proper restaurant, the Vendôme, which remained the chic luncheon spot for a number of years. The celebrities who ate there provided Wilkerson with tidbits of gossip which he promptly published in the *Reporter*—an admirable arrangement for all concerned. The Vendôme was open for lunch only; at night, the staff moved a couple of miles west to Wilkerson's Trocadero (see NIGHT LIFE). Later, Wilkerson opened another fashionable restaurant, La Rue, with characteristic Hollywood aspirations to the grand manner—spaghetti, for example, was served in huge, silver tureens. La Rue was a favorite of Humphrey Bogart's, the first booth being known as the Bogart booth.

Chasen's, still popular today, was opened in December of 1936 by Dave Chasen, a well-known ex-vaudevillian, who was backed in this enterprise by Harold Ross, publisher of *The New Yorker*. Originally known as the Southern Pit, the restaurant started in a shack on Beverly Boulevard, with a barbecue pit dug in the back yard, and soon became one of the most popular spots in town. Its success owed much to Chasen's famous chili and a good deal to impromptu performances by the patrons. Since Chasen kept autograph hounds, photographers, and gossip columnists at bay, the stars felt free to relax and enjoy themselves. On any night, Durante might get up and sing, Ray Bolger might perform one of his eccentric dances, Cagney sing Yiddish dialect songs, or Frank Morgan oblige with a strip-tease. Members of the convivial Irish contingent might harmonize in a corner booth, while W. C. Fields and Gregory La Cava would often be found playing Ping-Pong in the back yard.

Later, Chasen expanded the place and installed a steam bath on the second floor. His men's room was supplied with reading lamps so that its occupants could browse through the newspapers and magazines which were provided there. When this facility was inaugurated, Chasen premiered it Hollywood style with kleig lights and bouquets of flowers. Often, privileged customers stayed on at the restaurant until the small hours, playing cards or celebrating. On one such occasion, at 4 A.M., Chasen told writers Nunnally Johnson, Charles MacArthur, and Joel Sayre that he was about to close. The revelers unceremoniously threw Chasen out into the rain and locked the door.

Ronald Colman, Leslie Howard, Cary Grant, and James Stewart were all regulars, but Chasen's best customer was Billy Grady, an old Broadway buddy who had become head of casting at M-G-M. At Grady's expense, Chasen had a special booth built for him, and the casting director held court there every night.

"Prince" Mike Romanoff came to Hollywood in 1937 with a checkered past and a rosy future. He began his career as a New York garment worker named Harry Gerguson, but then, assuming the mantle of royalty, gained fame as a rubber-check artist in the era of the speakeasy. A con man un-rivaled in his blatancy, he was hounded by the law on both sides of the Atlantic and actually served time in France. In Hollywood he found his spiritual home; when he finally arrived there, he was welcomed with open arms. Studios paid him handsome fees to act as a technical adviser on films with exotic locales, and when he launched his first restaurant in 1938, movie greats were happy to pay for the privilege of giving Mike an op-portunity to insult them.

Cesar Romero explains how the original Romanoff's, on Rodeo Drive, was financed:

> Harry Crocker, who was a great friend of Mike's, came to all of us and said, "Come on now, Mike's going to open a restaurant and we've all got to pitch in." So we all bought stock. I bought a share for $50 and every time I went to Romanoff's, I would say, "I own a bar stool." Of course, the place was a tremendous success and at the end of the first year, Mike bought back all of the stock. But I did get one dividend check from him during that first year—for three cents!

On opening night there were no cooking facilities and food was sent in from a nearby hash joint, but enough money was raised that evening to install a kitchen. Later, the restaurant moved a few blocks to larger premises. Access to the hexagonal main room was by way of the cocktail bar and a short flight of stairs so situated that everyone in the restaurant was able to see new arrivals. Booths were arranged to eliminate any se-cluded corners, making every detail of every patron's attire, conduct, and gastronomical preference visible to everyone else. Kurt Nicklas, the *maître d'hôtel,* kept a watchful eye on the proceedings.

When he was not working, Bogart ate lunch there almost every day, always occupying the second booth from the left of the entrance. This was reserved for the Bogarts, Robert Benchley, Herbert Marshall, Sir Cedric Hardwick, and a handful of others whose names were recorded on a plaque over the booth. Bogart would arrive at 12:30 precisely and gen-erally ordered bacon and eggs with toast and beer or milk, followed by coffee and Drambuie. Other lunchtime regulars included Jack Benny, Frank Sinatra, Gary Cooper, and Groucho Marx.

Don the Beachcomber's was more famous for its drinks than for its food. With bamboo fences, exotic vegetation, and open porches and bal-conies, this establishment aimed for the atmosphere of a South Seas watering spot. One "shack" was reserved for movie personalities—Tom Brown and Mischa Auer were regulars—and there they could sample Don's celebrated alcoholic concoctions, such as the Zombie and the Dr.

RESTAURANTS

Funk, secure in the knowledge that they would be protected from cameras and fans. It was, incidentally, in Hollywood restaurants, clubs, and bars, especially those along the Sunset Strip, that vodka was first popularized in the United States.

One of the earliest spots on the Strip was the Cock 'n' Bull, which featured (and still does) a comfortable atmosphere reminiscent of an English pub. Opened in the early thirties, it soon became a favorite hangout of the Hollywood press corps. The Cock 'n' Bull was within easy striking distance of the Troc and several other gossip factories, and since it was also popular with cameramen, make-up artists, and the like, it was a good place to pick up snippets of studio scandal. Some of the harder drinking celebrities, like Errol Flynn, put in an appearance from time to time. Also on the Strip was the Café Lamaze, where the menus were written on large slates, carried from table to table by the waiters. This was popular with the younger set.

Lucey's, a bar and restaurant across the street from Paramount, was a writers' hangout which drew a regular clientele from both Paramount and RKO. A number of other well-populated eating spots grew up near studios. Frances Edwards, long-time hostess of the M-G-M commissary, eventually opened her own establishment in an alley near the main gate to the Metro lot. Since Columbia had no commissary for many years, studio employees tended to congregate at Billingsley's, on Sunset near Gower. Close by was Brewer's Tavern, an extras' hangout where the Gower Street cowboys annually elected a "mayor." The Toad-in-the-Hole, a couple of blocks north, was celebrated for its thick steaks and baked potatoes.

Elsewhere, there was Henry's—originally opened by a rotund Chaplin stock company actor named Henry Bergman (Chaplin is reputed to have bankrolled him)—then taken over by Eugene Stark, who also operated the Bohemian Café. Von Klein's The Berries was famous for its sandwiches, and the Gotham was a Jewish delicatessen on Hollywood Boulevard that attracted the New York crowd. Garbo, even in her most enigmatic period, sometimes stopped there for a quiet, early dinner. Nearby, adjacent to Grauman's Chinese, was Brown's Hot Fudge Sundae, patronized by stars like Cagney and George Raft. Ted Snyder's and the Cinebar and Cinegrill were low-keyed establishments in favor with the movie colony, and Omar's Dome was a late-night meeting place in downtown L.A. where one might repair for a snack after a dance at the Biltmore or a visit to a burlesque show. Thelma Todd's famous Roadhouse was situated out on the Pacific Coast Highway. The Marx Brothers, Gene Markey, and Fanny Brice were fond of a place called Bublichki, on whose premises Stan Laurel was once married. The Crillon was a satellite of the Mocambo, and the Hollywood Café was a popular dinner spot, as were the

It Café, run by Clara Bow and Rex Bell, and Sugie's in Beverly Hills.

The Players Club, owned by Preston Sturges and Ted Snyder, was at the eastern end of the Strip and heavily patronized by the residents of the nearby Château Marmont and Garden of Allah. Nominally open to the public, Sturges really looked on it as his private club, and, if he wanted to be alone with his friends, he would sometimes just hang a "closed" sign on the door. There was a table of puzzles, a card room, and a billiard room, and at one point a serious chess club met there regularly. Music was provided by an old player piano, and a small theater was installed at the top of the building. Representative of the famous feats performed there was Donald Ogden Stewart eating twelve dozen oysters on a dare.

A two-minute walk from the Players was one of the greatest of all Hollywood institutions, Schwab's Drug Store. Schwab's was the natural successor to the drugstore that Sam Kress had opened in 1918 at the intersection of Hollywood and Cahuenga boulevards. This had been a popular hangout for extras and small-time actors in the silent era. Because Kress was willing to cash checks and extend credit, so many would-be Western stars congregated on the premises that his establishment gave birth to the term "drugstore cowboy."

Schwab's was operated by the four Schwab brothers—Jack, Leon, Bernard, and Marvin—and their formidable mother, who had owned a drugstore downtown. When they opened in Hollywood—taking over a failing enterprise next to a Ruben's market on Sunset, and brightening it up with a new soda fountain and a pinball room in the back—Leon made the rounds of the nearby studios to drum up business. He can hardly have imagined how successful he would be. Among the earliest patrons were Charlie Chaplin and Harold Lloyd, both pinball addicts, and with customers of this stature, the crowds soon followed. What made Schwab's so special, however, was the fact that it was the opposite of exclusive, attracting people from all ranks of the film industry. Credit was virtually automatic, and starving bit players could always be sure of a free meal. (Down-on-their-luck actors also congregated at Joe Halff's Laurel Drugstore, just across the street.) Agents and managers conducted business there, packing the phone booths, and Schwab's also served as an informal real estate office, providing an exchange for information on everything from cheap apartments to Beverly Hills mansions. When Charles Laughton arrived in town, Jack Schwab took him all over the city shopping for a suitable car.

Although it is not true that Lana Turner was discovered there, she did frequent the place, as did Ida Lupino, Olivia de Havilland, Orson Welles, Rita Hayworth, Frank Morgan, Mickey Rooney, and any number of refugees from the Garden of Allah seeking cures for their latest hangovers. The lineup of celebrities led Sidney Skolsky—who virtually used it as an office—to nickname the drugstore "the Schwabedero." Sometimes, when the fountain was busy, stars would mix shakes or man the cash register. And until pinball machines were banned, they often took part in noisy contests, with enthusiastic cheering sections packing the back room.

SALARIES.

In the days of the Nickelodeon, movies cost next to nothing to make, and the salaries paid to players, directors, and writers were far from princely. The incredible escalation of salaries that occurred in the period 1914 to 1920 was due (in combination, of course, with the growing success of the movies themselves) very largely to two stars, Mary Pickford and Charlie Chaplin, who had a strongly developed sense of their own value and made their demands at crucial moments in the development of the industry.

When Pickford went to work for D. W. Griffith at Biograph in 1909, she earned $5 a day. Her wages there eventually amounted to $40 a week, the following year she jumped to Imp at $175 a week, and in 1911 she worked briefly for Majestic at $275 a week. She returned to Biograph for a while, then, in 1913, accepted Adolph Zukor's offer to shift her allegiance to his Famous Players Company at a salary of $500 a week, which quickly rose to $1,000. (It was Zukor who was to complain, later, that "Little Mary" had a mind like a cash register.) When Mary's mother, Charlotte, who pursued her daughter's interests with single-minded determination and a shrewd business sense, overheard a salesman saying, "As long as we have Mary on the program, we can wrap everything around her neck," Charlotte confronted Zukor, and, on January 15, 1915, a new contract was signed in which it was agreed that Mary would appear in ten pictures a year for a guaranteed $2,000 a week plus half of the profits. Within a matter of months, Charlotte was informing Zukor that her daughter was worth $7,000.

Chaplin, meanwhile, had started his screen career in 1914 with Mack Sennett at a salary of $150 a week. Having established the tramp character, he moved to Essanay the following year at $1,250 a week. So popular had he become that, in the spring of 1916, Mutual offered the twenty-six-year-old comedian the unprecedented salary of $10,000 a

322

week plus an annual bonus of $150,000, for a total of $670,000 a year—a figure which made international headlines.

News of this contract prompted Charlotte and Mary Pickford to make fresh demands, leading Zukor to set up two new companies, the Mary Pickford Studio and Artcraft, to produce and distribute Mary's pictures. Like Chaplin, she was now guaranteed $10,000 a week. In 1919 she made three pictures for First National, on even more favorable terms, then joined forces with Chaplin, Griffith, and Douglas Fairbanks in the formation of United Artists.

Prior to the final stage of this escalation, around 1916, few stars had earned more than $1,000 a week, and many of the best known names in the business pulled in less than half that. Character actors and comedians seldom earned more than $250 a week, and top directors could hope for maybe $500. The negotiating successes of Pickford and Chaplin, along with the post–World War I movie boom, changed all this. By the end of the decade, major stars were earning between $3,000 and $7,000 a week, and top character actors were breaking into the $1,000-a-week bracket. By the early twenties, some directors could ask for $50,000 a film, and even some scenario writers—till then the lowest of the low—were receiving $2,500 a week.

The salary situation remained fairly stable until the coming of sound, when many established and well-paid stars were dethroned. This factor, plus the great influx of newcomers from the stage and other sources, combined to bring salaries down for a while, but the success of the talkies, along with the high-powered methods of a new breed of artists' representatives—men like Myron Selznick—soon pushed them up again. By this point, however, taxes, although much lower than today, were beginning to take a sizable bite out of the weekly pay check. Five thousand a week in the thirties no longer had the real value that $5,000 had had in the twenties.

The figures that follow were issued by the IRS in 1935, 1936, 1937, 1940, and 1941. (Occasionally conflicting—and usually higher—figures have appeared in other sources: e.g. $588,423 for Abbott and Costello in 1941, $350,000 for Charles Boyer in 1941, $351,562 for Cary Grant in 1941, and $307,014 for Shirley Temple in 1936.) The fact that they were made public is generally attributed to anti-Hollywood elements in Washington, men who felt that movie people were reaping the wages of sin and deserved to be exposed to the masses. The masses responded with appropriate awe. The publication of the figures also had the effect of reinforcing the motion picture colony class structure. As pointed out by Robert Sklar, it took a brave man in Hollywood to fraternize with those earning substantially less than himself. Such egalitarianism might give others the impression that he was on the way down.

SALARIES

	1935	1936	1937	1940	1941
Abbott and Costello					291,905
Adrian, Gilbert (costumes)	38,666				
Ameche, Don		34,499	51,833	147,824	
Arthur, Jean		119,000	79,999	110,833	
Astaire, Fred	127,875	211,000	271,711	133,332	
Ayres, Lew	71,500		52,500		
Bacon, Lloyd (director)	122,625				192,000
Barry, Philip (writer)	54,000				
Barrymore, Lionel		129,174	132,739	79,875	
Baxter, Warner	203,000	284,000	225,961		
Beery, Wallace	75,000	203,750	190,000	278,750	251,250
Bennett, Joan	72,833		72,000		
Berkeley, Busby (director)	69,750	73,750	83,416		101,958
Berlin, Irving (composer)	150,000				
Berman, Pandro (producer)	138,000	202,000	251,347		156,000
Blondell, Joan		84,799	74,833		
Blore, Eric		20,888			
Boyer, Charles	129,448	249,000	265,191		220,833
Brown, Clarence (director)		156,000	159,000	201,666	220,000
Brown, Joe E.	173,438		267,500		
Cagney, James	147,167				362,500
Cantor, Eddie	150,000		150,000	119,600	78,000
Capra, Frank		208,000			
Carrillo, Leo	30,333	57,832			
Carroll, Madeleine	360,000	287,000	114,795	98,599	
Chaplin, Charlie	216,000	125,000	106,000		
Cohn, Harry (executive)		182,000		149,766	145,600

	1935	1936	1937	1940	1941
Colbert, Claudette	100,000	350,000	375,055	275,000	390,000
Colman, Ronald	108,916	362,000			
Cooper, Gary	311,000	370,000	238,416		287,671
Cortez, Ricardo	67,917		38,208		
Crawford, Joan		302,307	351,538	318,365	266,538
Cromwell, John (director)	135,729	137,000	110,500		
Crosby, Bing	318,000	156,000	190,000	452,314	302,314
Cukor, George (director)		194,166		182,000	189,975
Curtiz, Michael (director)	102,325	107,200	123,400		187,200
Del Ruth, Roy (director)	206,333	238,000			
Dieterle, William (director)	76,875	90,833	88,667		
Dietrich, Marlene	368,000	269,000	370,000	100,312	100,000
Dietz, Howard (publicity)	39,000		52,500		
Durban, Deanna				209,833	203,166
Dwan, Allan (director)		52,660	69,666		
Erwin, Stuart	36,541		30,000		
Evans, Madge	43,733	48,386	48,196		
Faye, Alice	45,500	45,500	145,499	157,958	119,166
Fields, W. C.	76,875		121,333	255,000	140,000
Fleming, Victor (director)	65,416		160,000	185,666	142,000
Flynn, Errol			94,761		240,000
Folsey, George (cameraman)	18,215				
Fonda, Henry	56,208		47,503		172,208
Francis, Kay	115,167	227,100	209,100		
Gable, Clark		253,333	289,000	298,544	357,500
Garbo, Greta		190,000	472,499		203,333
Garland, Judy					100,902

SALARIES

	1935	1936	1937	1940	1941
Gaynor, Janet	169,750	220,000	100,000		
Gibbons, Cedric (art director)	52,000		68,250	91,000	91,000
Goldwyn, Samuel (executive)	127,500		189,000		
Grant, Cary			175,625	206,250	256,250
Grey, Zane (writer)	90,000	36,000			
Hammerstein, Oscar (lyricist)	72,541				
Hammett, Dashiell (writer)	29,500				
Harding, Ann	93,750	60,000			
Hardy, Oliver	85,316	88,600	101,200		
Harlow, Jean		146,130	104,967		
Hathaway, Henry (director)			101,666	144,250	
Hawks, Howard (director)	61,055		130,416		
Hellman, Lillian (writer)			50,000		
Henie, Sonja		72,500	210,729		
Hepburn, Katharine	121,572	206,000	203,751		188,916
Hitchcock, Alfred					157,375
Hopkins, Miriam	86,250		130,000		
Hornblow, Arthur (producer)	71,375		130,833	159,000	
Howard, Leslie		185,000	140,000		
Howe, James Wong (cameraman)	21,257				
Huston, Walter			25,333		
Johnson, Nunnally (writer)		123,000	106,260	89,000	
Jones, Buck		143,000			
Kalmus, Natalie (technicolor adviser)		65,525	56,775		

	1935	1936	1937	1940	1941
Karloff, Boris			40,000		
Kelly, Patsy		45,216	43,199		
King, Henry (director)	143,000	143,000	157,444	157,500	
Lang, Fritz (director)	33,166		67,763		
Lasky, Jesse (executive)	124,500	71,330	109,166		
Laughton, Charles				170,496	
Laurel, Stan	156,366	135,000	75,000		
Leisen, Mitchell (director)				143,750	
Le Maire, Rufus (casting director)	27,500				
LeRoy, Mervyn (producer/ director)	198,583	146,000	153,517	182,000	182,000
Lombard, Carole	156,083	450,000			
Loy, Myrna		123,916	152,583	160,666	138,166
Lubitsch, Ernst	260,000		260,833		
MacDonald, Jeanette		319,400	238,299	300,000	173,333
McLaglen, Victor	50,000	143,000	164,325	76,666	
MacMurray, Fred			92,000	248,333	
Mahin, John Lee (writer)	36,500		72,791	116,791	96,250
Mamoulian, Rouben (director)	86,666		68,000	118,750	
Mankiewicz, Joseph (producer/ director)	50,041	79,066	86,774	156,000	156,000
Mannix, E. J. (executive)	129,057	130,000	157,500	201,912	208,579
Mayer, Louis B. (executive)	151,500		1,161,753 *	697,048	704,452

* Highest salary paid in the United States.

SALARIES

	1935	1936	1937	1940	1941
Mayo, Archie (director)	75,750		100,750	116,708	
Montgomery, Robert		142,000	243,250	191,250	211,416
Morgan, Frank	70,955	74,367	84,983	99,720	99,691
Newman, Alfred (composer)		52,000			
Niven, David	5,200				
Oakie, Jack	101,625	47,500	164,416	78,416	82,812
O'Brien, Pat		108,750	119,500		
Oliver, Edna Mae	58,166	71,791	94,458		
Pigeon, Walter		40,000			
Pitts, ZaSu	18,333				
Plunkett, Walter (costumes)		17,216			
Porter, Cole (composer)		75,000	76,500		
Powell, Dick	69,500	96,000	176,249		
Powell, William	66,666			267,500	256,250
Power, Tyrone			68,691		169,009
Raft, George	90,000	51,041	219,399		
Roach, Hal (executive)	104,000	129,000	104,000		
Rogers, Ginger	74,483	124,000	184,583	254,416	215,000
Rogers, Will	258,000				
Rooney, Mickey					172,416
Ruggles, Charlie	106,278		133,236		
Ruggles, Wesley (director)	163,717		203,151	199,999	120,384
Schenck, Nicholas (executive)	193,434	260,785	489,602	318,881	334,204
Selznick, David (producer)		115,000	203,500		
Selznick, Myron (agent)			110,825		

	1935	1936	1937	1940	1941
Shearer, Douglas (sound technician)	25,000				
Shearer, Norma	80,000			150,000	150,000
Sheehan, Winfield (executive)	344,230				
Sidney, Sylvia	63,000	226,000	114,100		
Skouras, Spyros (executive)	189,500	341,000	320,054		
Sothern, Ann		33,666			
Stanwyck, Barbara	80,833	151,000	142,499	75,937	190,000
Sten, Anna	96,833				
Sternberg, Josef von (director)		95,000			
Stone, Lewis	58,084	51,914	48,500		
Stromberg, Hunt (producer)		197,583	265,500	332,267	297,409
Sturges, Preston (director)			134,250	147,583	113,933
Sullavan, Margaret	102,431	63,333			
Summerville, Slim	70,833	69,062			
Swarthout, Gladys	101,883			16,333	
Taurog, Norman (director)	88,750	68,000	122,000	156,000	156,000
Taylor, Robert			173,352	199,999	197,490
Temple, Gertrude (mother)		68,666	52,166		
Temple, Shirley	69,999	121,000	110,256		
Thalberg, Irving (executive)	151,762				
Thau, Ben (executive)	31,200		81,750	139,178	151,989
Tone, Franchot		76,250	107,291		125,694
Tracy, Spencer	36,250		91,750	208,000	247,383
Treacher, Arthur	28,900				

SALARIES

	1935	1936	1937	1940	1941
Trevor, Claire	27,655				
Tucker, Sophie			48,888		
Vallee, Rudy	166,348	238,000			
Van Dyke, W. S. (director)		164,500	178,916	229,750	201,583
Vidor, King (director)	140,000			195,078	180,089
Wallis, Hal (producer)	136,750	184,833	208,083		260,000
Walsh, Raoul (director)	25,500	67,500	145,000		97,750
Warner, Jack (executive)	88,333	86,666	137,333		182,000
Weissmuller, Johnny	24,600				
West, Mae	480,000 *	323,000			
William, Warren	95,458				
Wurtzel, Sol (executive)	149,500	163,000	182,503	146,500	
Wyatt, Jane	20,000				
Young, Loretta	21,000	118,000	150,019	170,000	
Young, Robert	32,293		58,625	87,208	113,208
Zanuck, Darryl (executive)	134,833	260,000	260,000		

* Highest paid woman in the United States.

SAN SIMEON.

Although it was two hundred miles from Hollywood, San Simeon was a focal point of the movie colony's social life. Built high in the Santa Lucia mountains, William Randolph Hearst's "ranch" was a spectacular complex of palazzos and pavilions, an architectural fantasy worthy of the mad King Ludwig of Bavaria. Here the publisher and his mistress, Marion Davies, hosted the legendary house parties that were attended by *le tout Hollywood*.

Dorothy Jordan remembers seeing the ranch for the first time in 1929:

> Since everyone called it a ranch, I expected a Monterey-type California lodge. As we drove up from the train, someone said, "Do you see that Spanish castle over there?" It was a bright moonlit night, but all I could see was a pile of crates. That was the castle! Hearst hadn't assembled it yet.
>
> We passed through a gate—it was late and I was trying to keep my eyes open—and I saw deer and other animals cavorting about. We came to another gate and there was a camel! I said, "Good gracious! Is that a camel?" I was told it was always at that gate because the foreman of the ranch had a car with a canvas top, and the camel was crazy about canvas, so it just waited nearby hoping to get a nibble. They told me that Hearst had a whole zoo there—with lions and everything.
>
> We drove in through the last gate and I'll never forget that first sight. All of a sudden, in the moonlight, this beautiful marble house with a dome. I believe it had eight marble terraces off it, then steps down, flower beds, and then another marble terrace—all leading down to the guest houses.

Ben Lyon, who was a frequent guest at San Simeon, recalls the ritual that was attached to these weekends:

> When you got your invitation, it would come from Marion or W. R.'s secretary. They would merely call up and say are you available to go up to the Hearst ranch on a certain date? Then an envelope would arrive with instructions to be at Glendale on the Friday night and your tickets

331

DINING AT SAN SIMEON: CHARLIE CHAPLIN, GEORGE BERNARD
SHAW, MARION DAVIES, LOUIS B. MAYER, CLARK GABLE, AND
GEORGE HEARST.

would be waiting. There would be a private train sidetracked, consisting
of an engine, a baggage car, a couple of diners, and three or four sleepers.
There might be thirty to fifty people going at the same time. Drinks would
be served, and a specially planned dinner, and then you'd get off at San
Luis Obispo at about two in the morning. Cars would be there to drive
you the five miles to the castle. You would be assigned to what they called
bungalows, but they were like Italian villas, with marble and seventeenth
century velvet covering entire walls.

Whole buildings had been imported from Europe, and every room was
furnished with priceless works of art, almost as if Hearst looked on the
treasures of the Od World as his personal Erector set. French tapestries,
Italian bronzes, English fireplaces, and Greek columns were combined
according to no known canon of style, masterpiece battling with masterpiece and symbol canceling symbol. Everything was on the grand scale—
the gardens alone are said to have cost a million dollars—and construction was always in progress, since Hearst entertained the superstitious be-

lief that if he stopped building, he would die. Tons of furniture, statuary, and disassembled masonry remained crated at the bottom of the hill and in a San Francisco warehouse. But according to Ben Lyon, Hearst knew where everything was:

> Joe Willicombe was his right-hand man and Hearst used to say to him, in that little high voice of his, "Joe, call up San Francisco and tell them on the third floor, in bin 267, there's an ormolu clock. Have them send it down."

Visitors to San Simeon were confronted with exotic meals and a rigorously enforced one-cocktail-only code, but, as Lyon recalls:

> Of course, you always had a bottle of something in your suitcase. If you were found out, and reported by a maid or someone, a secretary would inform you that you were leaving.
>
> It was a fabulous place—forty people seated at a long, narrow table for

MARION DAVIES AND CHARLIE CHAPLIN IN THE PROJECTION ROOM AT SAN SIMEON; MARION'S EVER-PRESENT DACHSHUND AND TELEPHONE BOTH ON HER LAP.

dinner, and at each meal, a different person would be placed on either side of Marion or W. R., who sat opposite each other. The most fabulous food was served there, usually out of season—strawberries from China, asparagus from Siberia—but, strangely enough, you had your paper napkins, your bottle of catsup, your bottle of A-1 sauce. I guess they were trying to save money.

The long narrow table Lyon speaks of was a fifty-four-foot refectory table, dating from the seventeenth century, which had originally been built for a European monastery. The food on the written menus was prepared by a team of three chefs. As for the banishments for secret drinking, these did happen, although Marion's friends and Hearst's favorites were sometimes let off more lightly. On one occasion, Lyon's future wife, Bebe Daniels, along with Constance Talmadge and Eileen Percy—regulars at at the ranch—had a little too much to drink and amused themselves by decorating the classical statuary on the grounds with some of their lacy undergarments. When they came in to dine, they found that their place cards had been isolated at one end of the table, and their place settings littered with empty liquor bottles. Marion herself was more than fond of a tipple, and her habit of concealing a bottle of gin in the water tank of her toilet was hardly a secret.

Colleen Moore has described how sometimes the guests would play hide-and-seek after dinner—a wonderful game, she remarked, when you had an entire castle at your disposal. Gilt chests from Venice, she said, made wonderful hiding places, "especially with a beau." A less successful hiding place, she found, was a suit of armor made for Charles of Burgundy. After almost suffocating, she toppled over in the armor and received a stern scolding from her host.

Bridge became another pastime at the ranch, and there were also two large puzzle tables in the salon where guests pored over jigsaws so elaborate they might take months to finish. Dorothy Jordan remembers San Simeon as a place at which it was not difficult to stay amused:

There was everything in the world you wanted to do. Swim—indoors and outdoors—ride horseback, go look at the zoo, which was the largest wild animal collection in the nation. Or you could just sit and read, play tennis or backgammon—it was all there. But you never had the feeling of being in a crowd. That was Marion Davies' gift, of being able to entertain 40 or 50 people, and they never had the feeling of being in a crowd. It was just a lovely, relaxing, country weekend. But there were two things Mr. Hearst particularly enjoyed, and it was sort of the unwritten law that you participated in them if you were requested to—those were the picnics and the costume parties.

For one typical overnight picnic, the guests rode on horseback over miles of rugged trails, while Hearst's cousin and major-domo, Randolph Apperson, loaded sixteen pack mules with provisions (such necessities as caviar, freshly caught lobster, duck stuffed with tangerines, and a fifty-pound baked salmon), sleeping bags, etc., as well as the musical instruments for a hillbilly band W. R. had hired for the occasion. (For those who didn't care to ride, limousines and drivers were provided. Ray Milland recalls another picnic where only five guests actually rode horses.) A quaint aspect of such overnight expeditions was the provision of chaperones—generally Hedda Hopper and Frances Marion!—to ensure that no improprieties occurred between unmarried guests.

As for the costume parties (see PARTIES), these were spectacular affairs for which dozens of outfits would be rented and shipped from Western Costume.

While the movie colony provided the nucleus for these house parties, the guest lists often included politicians, foreign dignitaries, celebrities from all branches of the arts, and executives of Hearst's publishing empire. Most came for the weekend, but some stayed longer—at times too long. Marion Davies has described how these guests would find, as their stays lengthened, that their place cards were gradually moved farther and farther from the center of the table. "It was a gentle reminder that time was passing and they could go home."

SCREEN TESTS.

The screen test has been a prominent feature in the folklore of Hollywood. There is, for example, the legendary story of an executive's reaction to Fred Astaire's 1928 test: "Can't act. Can't sing. Balding. Can dance a little." Whether or not this tale is in fact apocryphal is anybody's guess, just as there is probably no way we can ever ascertain the truth about Clark Gable's tryout at M-G-M. The most usual version of this has Lionel Barrymore spotting Gable in a Los Angeles stage performance of *The Last Mile* and arranging for a test to be made at Metro. Gable was then outfitted as a loin-clothed Polynesian, with a gardenia behind his ear, and asked to do a scene from *Bird of Paradise*. (Hollis Alpert, in his family biography of the Barrymores, claims that he was costumed as an Indian warrior.) It has further been reported that when the resulting footage was screened for Irving Thalberg, he protested, "It's awful—take it away." Lionel Barrymore, however, has insisted that Thalberg viewed the test in silence and simply shook his head to indicate a negative reaction. But whether Barrymore's recollections regarding Gable's beginnings at the studio are to be trusted is a matter of conjecture, since, in his auto-biography, he claims that he reported for work a month later and found Gable locked in a torrid embrace with Norma Shearer—when in fact Gable made eight pictures for Metro before he first worked with Shearer in *A Free Soul*. Who countermanded Thalberg's judgment is another question. One candidate for this honor is Ida Koverman, Louis B. Mayer's personal assistant. It is said that she saw the screen test and decided that Gable had sex appeal. To prove her point, she ran the footage for a roomful of female employees. Their reaction to it was so enthusiastic that the Metro brass admitted they had made a mistake.

Nor is this the end of the assemblage of contradictory information. Minna Wallis, Gable's first agent in Hollywood, insists that her client never took a screen test. On the other hand, Jean Garceau, Gable's secretary for twenty-one years, states in her biography of him that both Minna Wallis and her colleague, Ruth Collier, saw the *Bird of Paradise* test and promptly signed him up. After obtaining parts for him in *Painted Desert* at Pathé (see AGENTS) and *Night Nurse* at Warners, Wallis got him tested by Darryl Zanuck for a part in *Little Caesar*. Jack Warner's supposed reaction to this test was, "What can you do with a guy with ears like that?" Gable, according to Jean Garceau, was then retested at Metro, this time in a well-fitting suit, carefully directed by Barrymore, and by December 4, 1930, he was under contract to M-G-M for $350 a week.

When Cary Grant tested in the twenties, nothing came of it until Paramount finally hired him as a "test horse," feeding lines to actresses on trial. Often an actor was passed over by one studio before being picked up by another. James Stewart, for example, was rejected by Fox before being successfully tested at M-G-M. After seeing Robert Montgomery featured in the Broadway play *Possessed,* a Goldwyn scout had him screen-tested for the lead in *This Is Heaven,* opposite Vilma Banky. A debate ensued as to whether the actor's neck was too long or his shirt collars too short, but the final judgment was that he was too skinny and looked more like Banky's son than her sweetheart. All was not lost, however, since Edgar Selwyn, author-director of *Possessed,* persuaded Joe Schenck (who happened to be his brother-in-law) to give Montgomery a part in *Three Live Ghosts* at United Artists. Schenck's brother, Nicholas, president of Loew's, screened the original Goldwyn test and was sufficiently impressed to bring pressure on Louis B. Mayer to sign Montgomery to an M-G-M contract.

Occasionally a performer passed over one studio in favor of another. In 1934 Rosalind Russell was brought to California by Universal, who submitted her to two weeks of rather degrading testing. Executives there were happy enough with what they saw to offer her a seven-year contract. But she had also tested for Metro, who presented a more appealing proposal, so Russell confronted Carl Laemmle, Jr., at Universal—wearing smeared make-up, an unflattering, cast-off dress of her sister's, and tacky accessories, and asked to be released from her contract. Laemmle readily agreed, and, after changing her clothes, she rushed off to sign with M-G-M. Three years later, Metro tested Orson Welles, and everyone there was extremely enthusiastic about the results. They offered him a contract which apparently promised excellent terms and a great deal of freedom, but for some reason he turned it down and returned to his theater and radio work before eventually signing with RKO.

In 1928 Walter Wanger had Joan Bennett tested at Paramount's Long Island studios. Afterward he told her mother, "Your daughter is very sweet, but she'll never photograph." Goldwyn tested her the following year and put her into *Bulldog Drummond,* thus launching her on a decade of mediocre roles. She worked at United Artists and Fox before being picked up by, of all people, Walter Wanger, whom she finally married in 1941.

While appearing in a Broadway comedy, *Broken Dishes,* Bette Davis was tested by Sam Goldwyn. On viewing the results, he is said to have grumbled, "Who did this to me?" She tested for Universal and was placed under contract, though Carl Laemmle, when he met her face to face, had a reaction similar to Goldwyn's. "She has as much sex appeal," he observed, "as Slim Summerville." If an article in *The Saturday Evening Post,* dated August 15, 1942, is to be believed, the Davis screen test caused quite an uproar in Hollywood. It seems that executives and casting directors were concerned as to whether or not her ankles were good enough for the silver screen. Phil Friedman, her agent at the time, argued that this was irrelevant since she was an intellectual actress. Disturbed by this notion—and despite Davis' subsequent success—studio heads began to order that legs should be emphasized in all future tests. For a while, the article continued, candidates for all kinds of roles—"Calamity Janes, Carrie Nations, Aunt Jemimas and Ma Pettigills"—were screen-tested in bathing suits or ballet costumes.

One of the most elaborate tests ever made was the one prepared by Paul Muni, who took on the roles of all seven characters in Chekhov's *The Stage Doorman,* each in a different make-up and with a different voice. William Fox and Winfield Sheehan were both enthusiastic. They labeled

Muni "the new Lon Chaney" and gave him a seven-year contract, beginning at $500 a week. When Edmund Goulding had David Niven try out at Metro in 1935, Niven was a trifle more flippant in his choice of dramatic material. He simply faced the camera and recited a spicy limerick. Goulding was delighted, but his boss, the moralistic Mr. Mayer, was not amused.

Spencer Tracy was another who had unsuccessful screen tests. In 1930 he was dressed up as a sailor and given scars on his face, along with a beard, for a test at Fox Movietone Studios in New York. He never heard from them again. For Universal, he did a dramatic scene, playing an older character, and again got no response. Finally, John Ford saw him play "Killer" Mears in *The Last Mile* on Broadway and convinced Winfield Sheehan to hire Tracy for Fox's *Up the River*.

A number of Hollywood directors, George Sidney, for example, got their starts directing screen tests. Top cameramen were often used (one reason why actors were advised to refuse to test in New York, where you were apt to be shot by a newsreel cameraman), and the candidate for stardom would receive all the benefits of the expertise available in the studio's make-up and hairdressing departments. The cinematographer would experiment with lighting for perhaps thirty minutes before a silent test was shot. After any necessary corrections were made, a sound test would be taken to reveal voice quality, acting ability, and general personality. The cost was considerable, often running as high as $25,000 a test.

Screen tests could, quite understandably, be traumatic experiences. To this day, Martha Scott winces at the memory of her *Gone With the Wind* trial. She and Paulette Goddard played Melanie and Scarlett in a joint test directed by George Cukor, who, Scott believes, was anxious for the leading role to go to his friend Katharine Hepburn:

> They did everything they could to make it awful. There were no close-ups. We were just two tiny figures coming in the door. And our voices were very high. To me, it was just an obvious throwing of the staging, the lighting and the sound of the thing.

As everyone knows (and assuming that Martha Scott is correct in her assessment of Cukor's motives), this was a case where neither faction triumphed.

SHOPPING.

If you were Franchot Tone or Jeanette MacDonald or Hunt Stromberg and it was late 1935, where would you have done your Christmas shopping and what might you have gotten for your friends? The December 14 issue of Rob Wagner's *Script* had a few snappy suggestions. How about the Marconiphone, that unique combination phonograph and radio that was being featured at Cryson's? Or, for the man who had everything $12,000 a week could buy, Desmond's in Westwood was offering the "Cravat Jolie," a hand-loomed batik-effect tie in Jacquard moiré, which came in a genuine leather box with the lucky gent's name embossed on the cover, for $10. Zeppelin brassware was the latest thing at Bullock's-Wilshire: "Light and durable, because it's the same material used in making airplanes and zeppelins. Stunning for buffet suppers and you can easily think of three people who'd bless your blondined hairs if you'd send them the salad bowl ($15)." Robinson's was highlighting a modern electric clock built in the form of a bar, with "an inebriated figure with a red nose lying as natural as W. C. Fields right across the top" for $27.50. A. Schmidt & Son on Wilshire was offering a dazzling array of Georgian silver; Foster's in Westwood had the "cunning iridescent crystal bubble links for flowers that have panicked the town" as well as triple-size coffe cups. H. L. Geary had some of the most attractive chrome-finished fruit sets you've ever seen, and at Orviatt's you might have picked up a lady's combination hatbox and suitcase for $60 or the popular Chuck-a-Luck game for $13.50, "without which no self-respecting playroom is complete." For more fun, the Broadway-Hollywood was presenting the new Paddleball game. "Set one up in *your* backyard, and when Una Merkel or Carole Lombard come drifting over on Christmas morning, grab a paddle and get busy." At the same store, you could find a set of transparent rubber boots, made especially for California dogs. Cannell and Chaffin, the poshest purveyors of furniture in town, had recently added a new gift room to their Wilshire Boulevard establishment, in which you could find a splendid assortment of crystal decanters from Czechoslovakia. Monogrammed satin nightgowns, chiffon velvet hostess gowns, and Shetland bed jackets might be purchased either at Dennison Lewis or Denwitt's in Beverly Hills. Park Lane on

SHOPPING

Wilshire would be happy to supply you with mirrored dressing tables in a delicate peach hue, while the St. Denis Asia Bazaar on Sunset had a menagerie of tiny rose quartz animals which "would feel at home on any Bel Air bookcase." And if one was too tired after a long day on the set to shop, the Elsey-Fraser Children's Shop would bring a selection of its exclusive line of handmade imported frocks to your home.

The gift list taken care of, one would have to think of one's own needs. Men were most apt to have their clothes made either by a tailor named Watson, by John Roche—who had been an actor in silent films—or by Eddie Schmidt, who was Gable's Beverly Hills tailor for years. Pesterre's on North Beverly Drive was *the* place to buy riding and polo outfits, suede came from Voris on the strip, and the Asia Bazaar was where gentlemen bought their silk shirts.

In women's fashion, Bess Schlank was a leader in *haute couture* for quite some time, but the key factor in film society fashion was the fact that over the years—beginning with Howard Greer in 1927—several of the top motion picture costumers opened retail shops catering to the stars they had dressed on screen. Royer and Wakeling left Fox in 1939 to go into a retail partnership, and Adrian followed in 1942, quitting M-G-M to offer two important collections a year. Irene worked out of Bullocks-Wilshire, quickly establishing a clientele which included Marlene Dietrich, Loretta Young, and Joan Bennett. Personal wardrobes by Adrian and Irene, whose clothes were instantly recognizable by style and material, were a major status symbol during this period.

In the days of co-ordinated outfits, the buying of accessories was equally important and equally socially stratified. Jewels were most likely to come from Flato's on Sunset or one of the smart shops on Hollywood Boulevard, and furs from Willard George, Colburn's, or Al Teitelbaum in Beverly Hills. It was not uncommon for a star to have a wardrobe of twenty or more fur coats, most of which were ermine, sable, and mink. Teitelbaum would occasionally fashion his pelts into more esoteric items, like a $400 ermine toilet seat for the Bing Crosbys.

In the early days, Sam Kress, who opened his first drugstore at the corner of Hollywood Boulevard and Cahuenga Pass in 1918, supplied the film colony with its imported perfumes. Stars like Gloria Swanson, Pola Negri, and Wallace Reid bought hundreds of bottles a year. Kress's establishment, which expanded into five stores, also stocked expensive *cloisonné,* fine leather goods and tobaccos, and imported theatrical make-up (regularly tested behind the counter by Lon Chaney). Kress himself later became a wardrobe executive at M-G-M.

The other luxuries which became necessities in screenland society were in ample supply. Pre–World War I bourbons were stocked at Akins & Co.

in Beverly Hills; rare books could be bought from Maxwell Hunley, who was heard to remark that at Christmas, the red bindings always went first; and at Darrin from Paris, designer of luxury automobile bodies, you might find Gable, Dick Powell, or Chester Morris in the back room, watching their old cars take on new life.

SNEAK PREVIEWS.

In the thirties and forties, few major Hollywood films were released without at least one sneak preview. From Oakland to San Diego, signs would appear outside movie theaters announcing MAJOR STUDIO FEATURE PREVIEW TONIGHT—if the event was not being conducted in total secrecy—and cards would be distributed to the audience, soliciting comments and opinions on the picture being shown. Theaters used for previews were equipped with "double projection" equipment, which meant that they could run the separate sound and visual strips in sync, just as they were run on the Movieola editing machines at the studio. If audience reaction was satisfactory, the negative would be cut and the two strips "married" to create an answer print. If the sneak went badly, the picture would be recut, and, quite often, new scenes would be added or old ones reshot. *Bringing Up Baby,* for example, seemed to be too slowly paced for the preview audience, so it was cut from 11,800 feet to 9,200. When *Lost Horizon* was tested, the viewers found that the initial action dragged, so Frank Capra threw out the first two reels.

Sometimes changes would be brought about as a result of an audience's discomfort or dissatisfaction, often with the ending of a film. As originally shot, Wallace Beery lost his final fight in *The Champ* and died, obviously not the happy ending the audience wanted. At the next preview, Beery won the match and the audience cheered. In the case of *The Big House,* Robert Montgomery's wife was changed into his sister, because of the unfavorable reaction to the hero's spouse having a romance with Chester Morris. When *For Me and My Gal* was given a sneak preview in Westwood, 85 percent of the people said that George Murphy, not Gene Kelly, ought to have won Judy Garland in the end. Louis B. Mayer ordered that the entire cast be recalled and new scenes—incorporating footage from King Vidor's *The*

Big Parade—be added, so that Kelly could redeem himself by becoming a war hero. Three weeks of additional production was involved, but the new version satisfied everyone—except, perhaps, George Murphy.

One of the most famous instances of a film being radically changed after a preview occurred in 1930, when *All Quiet on the Western Front* was first shown to the public. Lewis Milestone had cast ZaSu Pitts in the poignant role of Lew Ayres's mother. Unfortunately, Miss Pitts was thought of as a comedienne, and, to make matters worse, one of her comedies, *Honey,* was the regularly scheduled attraction at the theater where the sneak was being held. The audience laughed the moment she appeared on screen, and continued to titter through even her most tragic scenes. Panicked, the producers had all her scenes reshot with Beryl Mercer in the role. Similarly, the film previewed as *Complete Surrender,* starring Joan Crawford and Johnny Mack Brown, was released as *Laughing Sinners,* with Joan Crawford and Clark Gable, when Brown's personality failed to register in the part. Gable was an example of a newcomer spotted by a preview audience. When *The Easiest Way* was sneaked at the Alexander Theater in Glendale, Irving Thalberg asked people after the show how they had liked "the new fellow who played the brother-in-law" and got an excited response. Thalberg then met with other executives in the parking lot and told them that the studio had a new star.

During Thalberg's reign, M-G-M previews—sometimes as many as five for a single picture—were an important social ritual. Since they were often held at some distance from Los Angeles, the journey would be made in one of the two dozen or so plush, sixty-foot private trolley cars which could be rented from the Pacific Electric Railway. The trip from the M-G-M siding, at Lot One in Culver City, could take as long as two hours, and studio executives would gather to play cards in the front lounge. A cold buffet was provided by the commissary.

At the screening, Thalberg would shift seats several times to gauge the reaction of different sections of the audience. Frank Whitbeck, of the advertising department, would check with ushers and ladies' room attendants for overheard remarks. While Thalberg was alive, Louis B. Mayer generally stayed away from previews, except for very important productions. After Thalberg's death, Mayer often rode the Big Red Car to the sneaks, usually amusing himself en route by playing pinochle with cronies such as music director Georgie Stoll. Howard Strickling recalls that Mayer did not make any effort to conceal his reactions at a preview. If he strode silently from the theater, that signaled trouble. If he lingered in the lobby and chatted, everyone relaxed.

While other studios tended to employ limousines rather than trolley cars, their systems were basically the same as Metro's. The producer would be accompanied by his associate producer, the director, the cutter, and often the writer. One of them would have a sound modulator, or "fader," in hand to control the sound level. Sometimes they would cluster in an anxious group, sometimes they would scatter through the audience, taking notes on outbreaks of whispering or restlessness, and timing laughs with a stop watch. If it was felt that jokes were coming so frequently that some were being lost in the laughter of previous ones, a few feet of film—called a leader—usually consisting of close-ups, would be inserted to enable the audience to catch up. In the case of *Stage Door,* the wisecracks came so rapidly that a score of leaders had to be inserted after the first showing.

An average of four hundred cards would be brought to a sneak, although a B picture might rate only half that amount. They ranged from very simple postcard questionnaires, asking such stock demands as "Did you like the picture or not? Why?" to the far more elaborate system devised by Selznick, who found that he received twice the response when he asked more provocative questions. Sam Goldwyn, who often got a 70 percent return, would methodically tabulate the responses of the audience himself. For *The Adventures of Marco Polo,* he handed out a fold-over letter, stating:

Dear Friends:

This picture is in rough form and I have brought it to you to get your aid in completing it before its release to the world. I tender you my grateful thanks for your answers to the following questions:

How did you like *The Adventures of Marco Polo?*

Did you enjoy the performances of Gary Cooper, Sigrid Gurie, Basil Rathbone, Ernest Truex, Binnie Barnes, Alan Hale and George Barbier?

Was the action of the picture entirely clear?

If not, where was it confusing?

Have you any other constructive criticism to make?

The sneak preview dated back to the early silent days. Some people have credited Cecil B. DeMille with being the originator of the idea; others point to the silent comedians. Irving Thalberg believed that Harold Lloyd was the first to initiate previews, but Lloyd himself, in an interview with Kevin Brownlow, would only say that he was "one of the early ones." Certainly, Lloyd, Mack Sennett, Roscoe Arbuckle, and others did take their one-reelers to local theaters, in rough-cut form, and ask the managers to run them to make sure they were getting the laughs in the right places. It's very logical that comedians should have been in on this idea from the very beginning, since gags are notoriously difficult to judge and there's really no way of knowing if they will have the desired effect until you get the reaction of an audience. Walt Disney understood this very well—his Mickey Mouse cartoons were often tightened up as the result of exposure to a preview audience.

Sneak previews

By the late thirties, the preview had become quasi-scientific. It was worked out that various towns and suburbs in California could be taken to accurately represent analogous groups in the nation at large. If, for example, you wanted to know how a picture would do in college towns, you previewed it in Pomona. Huntington Park was a surrogate for manufacturing cities like Cleveland and Pittsburgh, while the Riverside audience corresponded with the smaller city audiences of Albany or Des Moines. If you wanted to predict a picture's reception in Jersey City or Brooklyn, you previewed it in Oakland; Long Beach was taken to parallel the Corn Belt, and San Diego provided a testing ground for small western cities. As for the critical New York audience, its equivalent in sophistication was sought in Santa Barbara.

The similarity between Pasadena and the censorious population of Back Bay Boston was established early, when, at a 1925 showing of *The Merry Widow,* in the midst of a fiery love scene between John Gilbert and Mae Murray, the film suddenly stopped, the house lights came on, and Mayer and Thalberg were requested by the Pasadena police chief to step into the manager's office. Thinking on his feet, Mayer explained that they had brought the film to Pasadena precisely because it was known to have the strictest censorship, and they were grateful for having been shown just how far they could or could not go. The screening continued and the love scenes were subsequently tempered.

In the case of a major picture, the film would often be literally sneaked in, to discourage the presence of the press, rival producers, and artificially packed audiences. Hal C. Kern, David Selznick's supervising editor, recalls the strategy he evolved for the *Gone With the Wind* previews:

> Selznick told me, "Hal, I've got to preview the picture. It's too big not to know that we're right. And we cannot get caught. Russell Birdwell tells me that the newspapers and magazines are just dying to see the picture, but I don't want them to until I have seen it in a preview.
>
> I said, "David, the people find out about previews through you. The only way I can assure you of a preview is not to tell you where it's going to be. I'll send a car to your house at 6 o'clock. I'll take the film to a theater, but you won't know where it's going to be till you get there."
>
> I went to Santa Barbara, to the Fox theater, and I was never so disappointed in my life. There were probably 200 people in the house. I looked up the manager and he said, "Oh, have we got a lemon!" I told him what I had and he said well, the theater down the street's just packing them in. We walked down to the other theater and it was full.
>
> I took six officers with me and I told them to go around to the different fire exits and stand there, so that nobody came in. I had had a tape made

for the end of the other picture that said, "Ladies and gentlemen, you are about to see one of the great pictures of the year. But nobody not in the house now will be allowed to enter. If you have an appointment with anybody, leave now, but you won't be allowed back in the theater and there will be no telephone calls." Well, when the film started and they got to the name of Margaret Mitchell, people just stood up on their seats and yelled. Mrs. Selznick was crying like a baby. Nobody got to make one phone call and we were not caught.

Russell Birdwell just about died. He was so hurt that he was the publicity man and he wasn't even told about it. He said, "Well, you'd never get away with another one because the magazines have advertised that anyone in the theater when *Gone With the Wind* is previewed who lets us know will get $500." Then I got a call from David saying he wanted another preview. So I called Hunt, who was the manager of the big theater in Riverside and I said, "What kind of a house are you getting these nights?" He said, "I'm getting about 1800 people." I said, "Well, I have a picture called *Intermezzo* that I want to preview. People think we're going to show *Gone With the Wind,* but all I want is a regular crowd—no sign, no nothing."

So I went there with my cops and I took a look around and everything was quiet. I went in and saw the manager and then the boys started bringing in the film and when he saw how much film there was, he just looked at me and said, "You bastard!" And that's how we got by with the second preview.

Spy Systems.

In interviews with Hollywood veterans, the image of the studio "family" is one that crops up again and again and, in the sense that the studios were paternalistic institutions, it is surely appropriate. Filial piety was often put to the test, however. At M-G-M, for example, the cinematographers deeply resented what they considered to be a spy system employed by middle management, which suspected the cameramen of delaying shooting schedules. Under the scrutiny of the unit manager, the assistant director and the script clerk—both of whom owed their jobs to the unit manager—would keep careful notes on the time which the cameraman took to light each setup. The cinematographers considered themselves conscientious and responsible craftsmen and found this practice extremely humiliating.

Paranoia was the motion picture mogul's occupational malady. Most of them had grown up in tough, competitive businesses back East, and their suspicious natures developed early in life. Spying was a natural recourse for many of them. At Columbia Harry Cohn had an elaborate intercom system with open mikes on every sound stage hooked up to a speaker in his office, so that he could listen in at the flick of a switch. If he heard something he didn't like, he could push the "broadcast" button and yell out to the startled company, "I heard that!" (Notoriously lecherous, Cohn on occasion used this intercom to address a surprised starlet, asking her if she was keeping herself in a state of sexual readiness.) As time went on, however, directors like Howard Hawks, Leo McCarey, and George Stevens hit back at Cohn, deliberately broadcasting unflattering remarks, and the system fell into disuse.

In addition, there were always volunteers who traded information for power. Cohn's most trusted communicant was a black woman who worked in the front office. At Metro, executive Eddie Mannix made use of a girl friend, Betty Asher—who worked in the publicity department—to report to him on studio activity. (Mannix himself had originally been sent out from New York as a spy for Nick Schenck.) William Randolph Hearst apparently got detailed reports on Marion Davies' movements from her dear friend Louella Parsons.

People were also followed from time to time, as John Lee Mahin recalls:

> On *Treasure Island,* Wally Beery had his leg bound up all the time as Long John Silver. They were shooting on Catalina and he said that he had cramps in the leg and would have to go over to the mainland to see the doctor. So they stopped shooting, or tried to shoot around him, and he got on the boat and headed for the mainland. Well, Eddie Mannix was suspicious of Wally so he got hold of a guy with a 16 mm. camera and had him follow him. Wally went to his house, he got his station wagon out, he put his fishing rods in it and he drove all the way up to Bishop, with this guy following him the whole way. He followed Wally up the stream, catching trout, drinking in the tavern.
>
> When Wally got back on Tuesday, as he said he would, they asked him, "How's your leg?" He said, "It feels a lot better. The doctor put me on something over the weekend." Mannix said, "Come down here—I want to show you a test we made." So they showed him this whole thing and Mannix said, "That will cost you about $5,000."

S UPERSTITION AND THE OCCULT.

In Hollywood in the twenties and thirties, traditional show business superstition, endemic to all branches of the theater, was heightened by the craze for the occult that was sweeping the entire country at that time. Charlie Chaplin, in his autobiography, wrote of this tendency, observing that ectoplasm loomed over the city "like smog." And while Chaplin himself did not frequent the séances which were common in movie star homes, he did report that Fanny Brice had assured him that she had been present when the table rose from the floor and floated about an elegant drawing room. In the early days, the group around Nazimova, June Mathis, Valentino and his wife, Natacha Rambova, was deeply involved with séances, astrology, and the notion of reincarnation. Valentino claimed to receive spiritual messages and to have a "familiar" named Black Feather—an American Indian —whom he consulted before making any important decision.

Many stars depended completely on their astrologers and numerologists when it came to making both career and personal decisions; others relied on fetishistic objects and practices. Advisers like Carroll Righter, Myra Kingsley, Blanca Holmes, and Norvell began to wield a certain amount of power over their clients. In the thirties, Earl Carroll's and Ciro's featured the omniscient Madame Juno, and a woman prophet named Louise Lockridge would come into the House of Westmore, by appointment, to tell customers their fortunes as their nails were drying. A somewhat less orthodox mystic, revered by elements of the movie crowd, took a drop of blood from each of his clients with instructions that the client should call if he felt the onset of a headache or depression, or if he was experiencing a run of bad luck. According to Leo Rosten, when a call for help arrived, the psychic healer would bombard the client's blood sample with what he claimed were "health rays," produced by a "power-giving" machine in his possession. By some miraculous process, these "health rays" were then transmitted into the body of the troubled customer.

John Barrymore met theosophist Harry Hotchener and his wife, Helios —a student of East Indian philosophy and an astrologer—through Mary Astor's father. They became close friends, Henry serving as Barrymore's business manager for a decade and Helios drawing up a chart in relation to any important step the actor was contemplating. Douglas Fairbanks and Mary Pickford had their horoscopes presented to them each morning, and Pickford, in particular, planned her day accordingly. Miriam Hopkins, who read palms and cards at parties, relied equally heavily on psychic advisers. She abided by their decisions on scripts, and would avoid certain film locations, as well as addresses and hotel rooms, if they were unfavorable numerologically. Marie Dressler was in constant communication with her New York astrologer, Nella Webb. Sessue Hayakawa is said to have been able to read unopened letters, and Basil Rathbone claimed to possess extrasensory perception and reported a number of occult experiences. According to Donald Ogden Stewart, Countess Dorothy Di Frasso—once hired a voodoo priest to stick pins into the wax image of the wife of a star she fancied for herself.

Ernst Lubitsch was involved with a numerologist named Mrs. Thomas Platt, and William Dieterle had complete faith in the occult powers of his wife, Charlotte, particularly in regard to starting dates on his films. Production of *Dr. Socrates* had to begin at precisely 9:02 on the morning of June 6, 1935, and finish shooting at 5:20 P.M. on July 15, times deemed fortuitous by Charlotte for both her husband and star Paul Muni. In order to meet Mrs. Dieterle's starting date for *Juarez,* one insert was shot several weeks ahead of schedule. She was delighted that the title of that film contained six letters, but would not allow another six-letter word to be uttered on set during production, lest the magic be diminished. Thus, instead of shouting "Camera" or "Action," Dieterle introduced every shot with "Here we go!" Other directors were known to insist on certain conditions in order to be able to proceed with a film. Anatole Litvak liked to have a staircase with thirteen steps on at least one set in each picture, Mervyn LeRoy attempted to get the number 62 onto the screen somewhere in a movie, and Lloyd Bacon felt more secure if his name appeared on some visible prop.

Performers often attached magical attributes to some special talisman: Edward G. Robinson to an old silver dollar, Barbara Stanwyck to a gold medallion she wore around her neck, Fred Astaire to an ancient plaid suit, and Claude Rains to an intaglio ring (he claimed that when he lost it for two years, everything he appeared in flopped). Neither Mary Pickford nor Norma Shearer would remove her wedding ring for a role, preferring to cover it with flesh-colored tape. John Garfield owned a worn pair of shoes which had to appear somewhere in each of his pictures, and John Barrymore insisted on having a red apple on his dressing room table—a Barrymore family tradition.

According to legend, Margaret Sullavan was six days late reporting for *Three Comrades,* claiming she never started a picture until it rained—not the most reasonable practice in terms of the California climate. It is also said that Ida Lupino stayed away from the filming of *They Drive by Night* on the advice of her astrologer, Richard Gulley, costing the studio a small fortune. Mary Astor considered it a bad omen if the first scene shot on a new picture went well, Bessie Love wouldn't start a picture, take a trip, or make an important decision on a Friday, and Bruce Cabot wouldn't work on the thirteenth—and had a clause to that effect in his contract. Eric Stacey, the first assistant on *Gone With the Wind,* had a superstition about not tying his shoelaces until the first shot of the day was in the can. Sometimes he would flop around the set for hours in unlaced shoes.

One superstition shared by a great many actors was the belief that to die on screen at the start of a film career was a good omen. It seems to have worked for Bogart, Cagney, Gable, Raft, Edward G. Robinson, Alan Ladd, and William Bendix, to name a few.

TEMPERAMENT.

According to Hollywood tradition, it was essential for a performer to win the respect of the men in coveralls who kept things running smoothly on the set. Rising stars went to extreme lengths to court them, and Tom Drake recalls he perils of alienating them:

> If you got the crew drunk—and this didn't happen too often, maybe on an airplane trip when you were going on location and they were serving free drinks—all the hostility would come out. Those guys would tell you, "Don't talk to me about those people. Wallace Beery—any of them—we can drop a sandbag on them anytime we want to. Look at what happened to Lionel Barrymore."

Barrymore was injured during the filming of *Saratoga.* The official version of the incident had him tripping over a power cable, but gossip on the M-G-M lot hinted that the injury might not have been quite that accidental.

Wallace Beery, despite his lovable image, succeeded in antagonizing crews on many occasions. A particularly vexatious habit of his was to invest his film punches and slaps with all the power at his command. In *Slave Ship,* for example, instead of faking the blows he was directing at cabin boy Mickey Rooney, he was hitting so hard that the blood was trickling down Rooney's face. In this instance he had to be cautioned by director Tay Garnett, who took him aside and pointed out that every guy on the set and up in the catwalks loved Rooney, and it would be most unfortunate if someone decided to part Beery's hair with a sun arc.

George Raft had a similar experience with Beery while making *The Bowery*. They were doing a big fight scene on a barge and Beery asked to get things rolling with the first punch. According to Raft, Beery hit him with all his might, knocking him out cold. When Raft came to, they squared off and several punches were thrown in earnest before the crew pulled them apart. Raft himself had a knack of making enemies on the set, but this was due less to rambunctiousness than to a sense of insecurity. Since he never thought of himself as a competent actor, he was quick to imagine slights and inequities. Charles Laughton, although surer of his talents, had trouble learning lines and accepting suggestions of interpretation. His agonies and frustrations would lead to contentiousness, lateness, and blaming other members of the company for his own shortcomings. Margaret Sullavan's uncertainties about herself earned her the reputation of being one of the most hypersensitive of actresses, and Fred Astaire and Cary Grant were both chronic worriers who were apt to be peevish and fractious.

Such temperamental tendencies hardly qualified these performers as full-fledged bitches and bastards, however, whereas there were plenty of people around who did enjoy such reputations. Grace Moore, Hedy Lamarr, Sonja Henie, Betty Hutton (given to hysterical crying jags), and Luise Rainer (who had a habit of throwing fainting fits when she disagreed with her director) were among those who were known as prima donnas. One of the worst was Constance Bennett. Indeed, all costume designer Walter Plunkett had to say to restrain any headstrong tendencies in the young Katharine Hepburn was, "From the way you're starting out, you'll be worse than Connie Bennett." Because of Bennett's frequent displays of temper and her unreasonable demands, many performers refused to work with her. While making *Three Faces East,* after a scene in which she was kissed by Erich von Stroheim, she shouted to her maid to bring her a mouthwash at once, and later demanded retakes of scenes in which Stroheim made gestures which might have attracted attention away from her.

Ruth Chatterton was also given to tantrums. On *Dodsworth* she slapped director William Wyler across the face and locked herself in her dressing room. Norma Shearer's methods were different—haughtiness was her chief weapon—but she too had great success in alienating her co-workers. After playing with Shearer in *The Women,* Joan Crawford is reported to have said, "I love to play bitches and she helped me in the part," a remark that was prompted by a long series of incidents. The two actresses fought over priority to the services of hairdresser Sidney Guilaroff, and Shearer was constantly keeping everyone waiting while she fought over lines, costumes, and other production details. Crawford deeply resented the fact that—despite her strong box office appeal—she never got the glossy, million-dollar movies that were habitually assigned to Shearer, and seems to have felt that Shearer's furies were directed at her personally. On the final day of the shoot, Crawford retired sobbing to her dressing room, then refused to attend the cast party which was hosted by Shearer, who regaled her captive audience with her low opinions of other female stars.

It was not only women who were capable of arousing antagonism. In an interview with Richard Schickel, William Wellman reminisced about the making of *Beau Geste,* observing that everybody hated Brian Donlevy because he lorded it over everyone else. "They wouldn't even sleep with the guy—I've never seen a guy that could completely get everybody to dislike him as he could." Ray Milland was one of the performers on that picture who was exasperated by Donlevy's attitude. During a fencing sequence, he found an unpadded spot on Donlevy's body and managed to nick it with his sword. To the crew's delight, Donlevy fainted at the sight of his own blood.

Paul Muni irritated many people by remaining aloof from his colleagues. On the set of *Juarez,* his wife positioned herself outside the dressing room door and informed would-be visitors that "Mr. Muni does not communicate with anyone." Spencer Tracy's stubbornness, smugness, and alcoholic binges often got on the nerves of both cast and crew. In 1933, after a big argument with Winfield Sheehan at Fox, Tracy got drunk and passed out on a sofa on one of the sets. To keep him there safely till morning, Sheehan had him locked inside the huge sound stage. The next day, the entire set was in a shambles. Tracy had completely smashed everything in sight, including thousands of dollars' worth of lights.

The cardinal sin on the set was upstaging, and Tracy—with all his reputation for professionalism—was a master of the art. In *Test Pilot,* according to Clark Gable, Tracy died "the slowest, most lingering death in history." Just as he was about to expire in Gable's arms—again and again and again—Tracy would force a weak smile and live on for another couple of seconds, until Gable finally dropped his costar's head and burst out, "Die, goddammit, Spence! I wish to Christ you would!" Fireworks exploded between Gable and Charles Laughton during the filming of *Mutiny on the Bounty.* Gable complained to director Frank Lloyd, "Laughton's treating me like an extra. He didn't even look at me when he addressed me. The audience won't see me in the sequence. Laughton hogged it!" Gable refused to continue working that day and Irving Thalberg had to fly to Catalina to smooth his ruffled feathers.

Edward Arnold was a virtuoso of a technique that was popular among scene stealers. He would deliberately blow his lines, take after take, until the rest of the cast was ready to drop (and/or kill). Exhausted directors would then have to accept any take that he completed, no matter how bad the other actors looked in it.

In her autobiography, Bette Davis describes the methods of two more scene-stealing experts, Robert Montgomery and Miriam Hopkins. Montgomery, she wrote, "added elements to his close-up performance" that had not existed in the shooting script. By reacting to things that Davis had not done on camera, he made her close-ups worthless. Hopkins—who knew every trick in the book and added a few of her own—caused Davis all kinds of problems:

> When she was supposed to be listening to me, her eyes would wander off into some world where she was the sweetest of them all. Her restless little spirit was impatiently waiting for her next line, her golden curls quivering with expectancy.

Davis also gives the example of a two-shot (a shot in which both characters appear) which was supposed to favor them both equally. Hopkins kept easing farther and farther back onto a couch so that, in order to look at her, Davis would have to turn away from the camera.

Edward G. Robinson's autobiography is another treasure trove of Miriam Hopkins prima-donna stories. On *Barbary Coast,* Robinson complained, she was always late, would never speak a line as written (thus not giving him his proper cue), would make everybody stand around while she fussed about her costume, and would indulge in every trick she could to cause confusion and delay—and to prove that she was, after all, the real star. Eventually, Robinson could tolerate this no longer. Breaking an unwritten rule of studio etiquette, he berated her in front of the entire company, telling her that temperament had gone out of fashion and that she was defeating her own ends by attempting to hog the camera. The scene they were about to play was one in which he was supposed to slap her. Speaking loudly enough for everyone to hear, she said, "Eddie, let's do this right. You smack me now so we won't have to do it over and over again. Do you hear me, Eddie? Smack me hard!"

When Robinson did as she asked, there was a resounding burst of applause from the entire cast and crew.

THE TRADES.

Trade papers have existed since the beginning of the movie industry. *Variety,* which published its first issue in 1905, always gave Hollywood its due, but was not a Hollywood paper. It was published in New York, as were most of the early trade papers—such as *Film Daily*—which, while they gave a certain amount of space to studio news, were primarily geared to the exhibitors. Weekly trade papers made their appearance in Hollywood proper in the mid-twenties, but the production end of the industry did not have its own daily trade paper until 1930, when Billy Wilkerson launched the *Hollywood Reporter.*

Wilkerson was a dapper, mustachioed little man who had once sold cemetery lots in Buffalo, New York. He graduated from that to operating a fashionable speakeasy in Manhattan—apparently Mayor Jimmy Walker was a silent partner—then came out to Hollywood to try his hand at the motion picture business. After an abortive attempt at becoming a producer, he turned his attention to the idea of starting a paper, a notion which, according to a 1960 interview in *Closeup,* he had been toying with for some time. By his own account, Wilkerson borrowed $5,000 from a New York friend, with an option to double the loan, then went to see Frank Whitbeck and Eddie Eckles, who were in charge of advertising for the Fox West Coast theaters, and asked them to design the paper. No sooner did the *Reporter* hit the stands—the first issue appeared on September 3, 1930— than the studios barred its staff from their lots. But because informants at the studios phoned in news items, the paper survived.

In its early years the *Reporter* was essentially pro-worker and pro-creative personnel. Wilkerson regularly attacked, in print, high-paid "yes-men," a fact that won him few friends in the administrations of the major studios. Actors, writers, and directors were the heroes of the new paper, even receiving free subscriptions for a while, so that when the moguls turned their fury on the *Reporter,* the talent they employed rushed to its defense and the paper soon built up a sizable following, though its free subscription policy was crippling Wilkerson financially. He was on the verge of being forced to abandon the whole venture when a South African theater owner, Albert E. Schlesinger—who had his own vendetta against the moguls—loaned him enough money to get the paper over the hump.

The *Reporter*'s short-lived "democratic" phase reached its peak in 1933 when it campaigned with the workers against the imposition of an across-the-board 50 percent pay reduction for all studio personnel. This was supposed to be a temporary measure, made necessary by the Depression, and most workers accepted it in good faith, until it became evident that some executives were hoping to parlay it into a permanent pay cut. For the first time, trade guilds and labor unions began to organize—a movement that was bitterly fought by the Hays Office and the executives (see POLITICS). Wilkerson and the *Reporter* gave the workers much needed support.

Although Wilkerson's own Tradeviews column was highly influential, it was the Rambling Reporter column—originally written by Edith Gwynne, the fourth of Wilkerson's six wives—which probably did more to boost circulation. In its early years this was the hardest-hitting gossip column in Hollywood. Wilkerson, as owner of first the Vendôme, then the Trocadero, Ciro's, and La Rue, could provide Gwynne with a fountainhead of gossip, so there was no need for her to rely on studio flaks for handouts. And, while managing to avoid libel suits, her copy was never so oblique as to prevent insiders from guessing just who was doing what to whom, and under what sordid circumstances.

During the mid-thirties, however, there were changes in the *Reporter*. As the moguls began to take a less bilious view of Wilkerson, since he was clearly around to stay, his paper became accordingly more friendly toward them. We can assume that the Vendôme and the Troc were important factors here. It must have become increasingly difficult for Wilkerson to attack executives who were regularly paying through the nose for the privilege of eating his broiled pompano and Maryland terrapin. Success had brought Wilkerson and the establishment together. Soon he was playing cards with old enemies like Louis B. Mayer and Joe Schenck (though he continued a bitter feud with Harry Cohn, who had once campaigned for Wilkerson to be run out of town, by finding or inventing some dirt with which to sully his reputation).

Uncharitable observers began to murmur that the moguls had Wilkerson in their pockets—after all, he had come to rely increasingly on the studios for advertising revenue—and some critics went so far as to suggest that he had never really been his own man. Considerable speculation centered on the source of the original $5,000 that had been used to launch the *Reporter*. The check had been signed by one H. H. Sonn, an executive of a New York real estate company, but there were people who believed that Mr. Sonn had laundered it on behalf of someone closer to the motion picture business. Some fingers were pointed at Myron Selznick, whose clients were handled by the *Reporter* with kid gloves. If Selznick did rate preferential treatment, however, it was probably due to the helping hand he had offered when Wilkerson was preparing to launch the Trocadero (see NIGHT LIFE). In any case, the rumors persisted and people remembered that when Wilkerson first arrived in Hollywood, he had been heard to say, "This town is a racket. I'm going to play it like a racket—get mine as fast as I can, then duck."

Billy Wilkerson was far from the most popular man in town—he was a prickly antagonist and there were many who questioned his claims to probity, but nobody could deny that he was colorful or that he had a penchant for rocking the boat. One that he rocked especially violently was *Variety,* a weekly published three thousand miles from Hollywood. In the early thirties the *Reporter* scooped its august competitor so often that paranoid *Variety* staffers decided that the *Reporter* was somehow intercepting their best stories and a $46,500 lawsuit was brought against the upstart daily. The *Reporter* showed no signs of backing down, however, and *Variety* dropped its suit in favor of setting up a rival trade paper in California. Thus, *Daily Variety* was born. The new paper's first editor was Arthur Ungar, a virtuoso of the personal feud, who opened his attack on the *Reporter* in his first editorial, on September 6, 1933, by remarking, "We don't know about that vanity thing. There will be none of that sickening stuff in *Daily Variety.*"

Vanity advertising was a phenomenon that thrived in the Hollywood trades as naturally as mosquitoes do in the Everglades. Billy Wilkerson is usually given credit for its invention, but one does not have to look far for precedents, and the idea hardly needed inventing in the first place. Actors, agents, directors, and producers simply took it for granted that by placing full-time advertisements in the *Reporter,* on a fairly regular basis, they could expect favorable attention in the paper's editorial pages. The fact that vanity advertising was indigenous does not mean, however, that Wilkerson did not milk it for all it was worth. If a star was remiss in placing his annual Christmas message to a few hundred of his closest friends, the *Reporter*'s advertising salesmen were prompt to remind him, through his agent, that such neglect could lead to diminished coverage on the editorial pages. So eager were most Hollywood personalities to contribute to the *Reporter*'s revenues (it was always nice to see your name in print, in conjunction with a flattering studio portrait and a message thanking some hack for making your last picture such a success) that Wilkerson hit on the idea of bringing out special editions and anniversary issues to provide them with further opportunities.

And despite Arthur Ungar's protestations, this kind of thing was not entirely alien to the *Variety* tradition either. In the 1932 edition of *Variety* celebrating the opening of Radio City Music Hall, everybody from the president of RKO to obscure vaudeville comedians took out ads—close to one hundred pages of them. Certainly no one in Hollywood took Arthur Ungar's bluster seriously, and *Daily Variety* was soon swamped with vanity advertising, none of which seems to have been refused.

Sime Silverman, founder of *Variety,* had always had a strict policy of protecting the independence of his reviewers, but out West, this independence was gradually eroded. It was not so much that Ungar dictated how reviews should be written, but that those reviewers with a tendency toward the vitriolic were apt to find themselves assigned to movies made by Poverty Row studios and independents, while the more positive reviewers got to cover the films produced by the major studios, which, after all, accounted for a good deal of the advertising space sold by *Daily Variety*.

As the *Reporter* had its moment supporting the workers in 1933, so *Daily Variety* had an authentic journalistic triumph a few years later, leading the print crusade against the mobster-controlled union bosses, Willie Bioff and George Browne. Arthur Ungar justifiably took much credit for this—the men he was exposing were not afraid to break heads—but this does not mean that he was especially pro-labor. He was, in fact, an ardent anti-leftist—although in this regard he was eclipsed by Wilkerson, who, in his fervor to rid Hollywood of Marxist influence, printed in the *Reporter* the first comprehensive list of movie personalities with leftist affiliations, thus greatly facilitating the task of the House Un-American Activities Committee.

Although the *Reporter* and *Daily Variety* are open to much criticism, it must be said that throughout the thirties and into the forties they were lively publications, and their back issues remain among the most reliable sources for information on old Hollywood—even if a working knowledge of the way in which friendships and alliances affected editorial policy is sometimes needed to read between the lines.

A minor, but interesting, competitor was *The Hollywood Filmograph,* one of the weekly trade papers which began publication in the mid-twenties. (Others were the short-lived *Hollywood Vagabond* and *The Film Spectator*—later *The Hollywood Spectator*—which survived until 1939.) *The Hollywood Filmograph* was run by a man called Harry Burns, who seems to have been a popular figure around town, perhaps because he possessed far less ego and ambition than either Wilkerson or Ungar. He catered more to the lower echelons of the movie colony, giving as much space to character actors, comedians, specialty dancers, newcomers, and independents as he did to the major studios and established stars. Not a trade paper, but also oriented toward Hollywood insiders, was Bob Wagner's *Script*—a weekly that aspired, with some degree of success, to be L.A.'s equivalent of *The New Yorker*.

Although *Motion Picture Daily* and *Motion Picture Herald* were New York based, they should be mentioned here because their publisher, Martin Quigley, played a considerable role in Hollywood politics for several years. In 1929 he did the studios a favor by ridding them of several minor New York trade papers, merging them into *Motion Picture Herald*. The producers rewarded him with five-year advertising contracts. At the same time, he was successful in courting the friendship and trust of censorship czar Will Hays and became very adept at playing the Hays Office against the studios while appearing to serve as mediator. He was instrumental in the foundation of the Legion of Decency and seems to have been influential in winning Joseph Breen the job of administering the production code, a position that gave Breen day-to-day control over the content of Hollywood movies. This won Quigley the undying animosity of Louis B. Mayer, who had wanted the job for his nominee, Colonel Jason Joy.

In the thirties Quigley tried to launch his own Hollywood-based trade daily, but—though he poured $175,000 into the project—it was doomed because the rank and file recognized immediately that it would be, to all intents and purposes, a mouthpiece for studio executives. Quigley was regarded with increasing suspicion after it was made public that he had accepted a $50,000 loan from a subsidiary of AT&T, which led many people to believe that his support of such rightist organizations as the American Liberty League was not motivated entirely by high-minded idealism.

The circulation of the trades was small, but their influence was great. Their subscribers included men of enormous wealth and power—Franklin Delano Roosevelt had an airmail copy of the *Reporter* on his desk every morning—and the stories they printed found their way into newspapers all over the world. Billy Wilkerson once boasted to Louis B. Mayer that his paper was far more effective in propagating information about the motion picture business than any wire service. To prove his point, Wilkerson had Mayer supply a dummy story about Clark Gable which was printed in the *Reporter* the following day. Before long, that one story had generated more than five thousand clippings around the globe.

TREND SETTING.

Hollywood, particularly from the late twenties through the early forties, had a tremendous influence on style trends, not only in such obvious areas as fashion, make-up, and hair style, but in interior decoration, eating habits, speech, and even facial expression. One line or one image in a film could precipitate a rush for some item not yet even in the shops. Women waited for the next Gloria Swanson, Kay Francis, Norma Shearer, or Garbo vehicle before planning their season's wardrobe, while men kept their eyes on sharp dressers like George Raft.

Entire industries could be affected by a few frames of film. In 1922 Wallace Reid appeared in a scene wearing an unstarched shirt. Manufacturers besieged the Motion Picture Producers Association to have Reid stick to the classic starched, detachable collars. When they were asked, "Why don't you start making soft white shirts instead?" a trend was immediately reversed and millions of men made more comfortable. When Clark Gable was revealed without an undershirt in *It Happened One Night,* hundreds of thousands of he-men discarded theirs, causing a panic in the men's underwear industry. Because of Jean Harlow (and M-G-M promoting over three hundred Platinum Blonde Clubs), the sale of cosmetic peroxide almost doubled. A 1941 test showed that 80 percent of an audience was aware of what brand of cigarette Bing Crosby was smoking in a picture, and the entire tobacco industry suffered from the movie identification of cigar smoking with gangsters. Asta, of the Thin Man series, created a demand for wire-haired terrier puppies. Sonja Henie wore white ice skates in a film and such was the public demand that a week after the picture's release, it was impossible to find a pair of white skates in any store from coast to coast. Charles Boyer ordered pink champagne for Irene Dunne, and restaurants were suddenly bombarded with requests.

At times, innovations created primarily to accommodate the cameraman would be adopted by the public. Rosalind Russell made a film in which she emerged from a shadowy hallway in a mink coat. Since dark fur wouldn't show up, a light mink was used, beginning a rage for such garments all over the country. In 1930 Joan Crawford, tired of waiting for lighting adjustments because of the shadows thrown by the brim of her hat, flipped the brim back against the crown, and another style was born.

JOAN CRAWFORD IN THE FAMOUS *Letty Lynton* DRESS, 1932.

TREND SETTING

Article after article in the print media of the thirties pointed out Hollywood's pervasive influence. In the August 1931 *Motion Picture,* Adrian declared that movies were responsible for the world-wide vogue for daytime pajamas. His competitor, Travis Banton, considered them out of place in public restaurants and ballrooms. Sides were chosen. Members of the "pants brigade" included Sylvia Sidney ("a boon for women if there ever was one"), Lupe Velez ("She would think nothing of attending the coronation of a King in a pair of blazing red and yellow pajamas with three feathers stuck up on top of her head"), Marlene Dietrich, Katharine Hepburn, Frances Dee, and Joan Crawford ("They lend the necessary harmony with penthouses, airplanes and the modern way of living"), while Dolores Del Rio, Ann Harding, Hedda Hopper, Connie Bennett, Norma Shearer, Fay Wray, and Mary Pickford definitely would not wear them to formal dinners or dances. The *Literary Digest* of May 27, 1933, suggested that the vogue for slender figures was due to the fact that lightweight actresses appeared on the screen to have lost five or six pounds because of the distortion caused by the motion picture projector and that there was, therefore, "a grave responsibility upon the motion picture engineer in the interests of public health to prevent the screen from setting up an ideal of dangerous emaciation." The April 1937 issue of *Nation's Business* accused the tight-fitting "sex dress," introduced in films around 1930, of causing many auto accidents. The November 1939 *Current History* concluded:

> No fashion magazine, however skillfully edited, can compete with them [the movies] when it comes to making it imperative to own a particular hat or necklace. Neither adjectives nor photographs nor drawings can make a woman feel about an evening wrap as she feels when she sees it on the shoulders of Irene Dunne or in the arms of William Powell.

Gilbert Adrian's influence was enormous. He was responsible for Garbo's chic, exemplified by the simple, high-necked, long-sleeved evening gowns he created for her. His 1932 *Letty Lynton* dress made a brief screen appearance on Joan Crawford, but it was enough to create a great demand in the retail market, and thousands of copies were made. This led indirectly to the square-shouldered "coat hanger" look which became the mode of the forties, when women, many of them alone during the war, needed to project a strong, almost masculine image. As David Chierichetti points out, Schiaparelli had already launched the padded shoulder look in Paris, and it had even been seen in the work of other Hollywood designers a year or two earlier, but it took a big star in a big commercial movie to put the idea across.

Adrian was also responsible for the evening polo coat—Crawford had worn this casual daytime style so well that he designed one of gold cloth for her. He began an oriental trend with his costumes for *The Painted Veil;* he tilted Garbo's Eugenie hat in *Romance* at a steep angle, which dominated ladies' millinery throughout the thirties; and, for *As You Desire Me,* he created the pillbox hat, which tied under the chin, and soon became another indispensable item of every chic woman's wardrobe. When he was in New York in 1931, Adrian predicted a rage for puffed sleeves. The editor of one of the top fashion magazines remarked on "the impudent pretensions of studio gown designers." On a return trip the following year, Adrian invited the journalist to his Plaza Hotel room and asked her to look out the window and count the women in puffed sleeves. She stopped at fifty. Like major Paris and New York couturiers, Adrian guarded his latest ideas with the utmost secrecy. Until a film's premiere, the costumes and sketches were kept locked away, so no manufacturer's spies could copy the design in advance. The opening of a new Garbo or Shearer opus would have the impact of a Paris opening on the fashion world of that day.

Travis Banton, master of shimmer and slink, designed a full-length beaded shirtmaker dress for Carole Lombard to wear in *Ladies' Man* and caused a sensation in the fashion industry. During the war, he often dressed Rita Hayworth in strapless gowns which were boned or wired, an innovation that became one of the foundations of Dior's New Look four years later. Orry-Kelly contributed the basic jumper which Ingrid Bergman wore in *Casablanca,* and when Edith Head designed Dorothy Lamour's sarong for *Jungle Princess* in 1936, she set off a trend for tropical patterns and sarong draping that endured for almost ten years. Head exerted considerable influence again in *The Lady Eve,* in which she emphasized Latin motifs. This, coupled with the impact of the exotic women stars of the forties, had a marked effect on style. Maria Montez' and Carmen Miranda's wardrobes of turbans and Miranda's high platform shoes, bare midriffs, and gaily colored, ruffled long shirts were seen on women from Montana to Massachusetts, as they learned how to rumba and do the other Latin dances they saw at the picture show.

Around 1930 the Dietrich persona was marketed wholesale. Women in all strata of society suddenly became sunken-cheeked and bored sophisticates, with tweezed and penciled brows and staring, faintly taunting eyes. Her affinity for male attire (along with Garbo's and Hepburn's) was a major factor in the ultimate acceptance of slacks as an item of female dress. Women's pants were a Southern California invention, yet no merchant outside the Los Angeles area would take them seriously until the manufacturers started to distribute photographs to the press of stars wearing them. The Associated Apparel Manufacturers of Los Angeles would supply hundreds of pictures to the news services of leading actors and actresses at the Santa Anita race track, wearing the latest sportswear styles.

ALWAYS A SHARP DRESSER, GEORGE RAFT HAD A SIGNIFICANT
INFLUENCE ON MEN'S FASHION.

Many individual performers exerted a wide influence. In hair styles, thousands of girls imitated Colleen Moore's Dutch bob (created when her mother whacked off her long curls, although Perc Westmore has been credited with it), Claudette Colbert's short, curly coiffure (which she has worn for over forty years), and Bette Davis' bangs in *Elizabeth and Essex*. When Garbo returned to America in 1935 wearing her hair perfectly straight just above the shoulders, she very nearly precipitated a national hairdressing crisis—until a well-organized publicity campaign persuaded the female population that only Garbo could carry off this daring style and that others would have to have their ends curled under in a pageboy. After Norma Shearer's appearance in *Romeo and Juliet* in 1936, every other girl in the country wore her hair smooth on the crown and curled up into a soft fluff below her ears. (The same film started a trend toward high-waisted, Renaissance-line coats and dresses of beaded fabrics, which swung from the shoulder to the floor.) Before too long, women were encasing their long bobs in the snoods seen in *Gone With the Wind*. Hedy Lamarr's striking appearance inspired many women to dye their hair black. Others emulated Mary Astor's skull-sculptured hairdo and during the war, of course, Veronica Lake's peek-a-boo look, which the government urged her to change because so many female defense workers were getting their tresses caught in the machinery.

The ubiquitous Westmore brothers (see MAKE-OVERS) were behind many cosmetic, hairstyle, and even fashion looks. It was Mont Westmore who, in 1927, inadvertently initiated the flat-chested flapper look by strapping Clara Bow's breast• with adhesive tape for the film *It*—a look that was further popularized to no small extent through the fashions of Irene. Perc Westmore created the center-part hairstyle for Ann Sheridan, and launched another fad when he hit on the idea of using orange lipstick to set off her red hair. It was Perc, too, who pulled Katharine Hepburn's unmanageable hair into the topknot she still wears. According to Frank Westmore's book *The Westmores of Hollywood,* it was his brother, Ern, who "with a few swipes of his lipstick brush over the mouth of Bette Davis" did much to change the shape of lips for millions of women. (Joan Crawford, who had been severely criticized when she enlarged the corners of her mouth to play Sadie Thompson in 1932, was another key influence on lip fashions.)

When Garbo was seen wearing berets in her private life, thousands of young women bought berets. Deanna Durbin popularized the hair bow with long streamers, and Shirley Temple had a tremendous impact on children's fashion. Her Royer-designed dress styles were immediately snatched up by manufacturers—with a healthy cut of the profits going to the Temple family. At the National Hairdressers and Cosmetologists Annual Convention in 1939, it was reported that Shirley was responsible for the large number of juvenile beauty salons springing up everywhere, in which little girls of three and four were subjected to permanent waves and manicures. In 1939 Ann Rutherford confided to David Selznick that all the girls she knew were letting their eyebrows grow in as a result of Ingrid Bergman's unplucked brows. And Paulette Goddard was thirty years ahead of the hot-pants fad when she introduced sequinned evening shorts in 1941.

Men were also influential. Douglas Fairbanks was responsible for the resurgence of the mustache, and his naturally bronze complexion was a major factor in the sun-tanning fad following World War I. In male attire, Hollywood popularized the slack suit, the polo shirt, the Tyrolean hat, and the roll-collar shirt. The vogue for colored shirts is reputed to have been introduced into society by John Gilbert, who left the studio so late for a party one afternoon that he didn't have a chance to change from the blue shirt he was wearing for the benefit of the camera. In 1932 Clark Gable inspired a craze for turtle-neck sweaters worn to match jackets, and was one of the first to display the padded shoulder look for men. When George Raft abandoned the high-waisted trousers he had long been identified with, in 1936, it was a fashion news event of some consequence. Raft also popularized the black pin-striped suit and highly polished black shoes with pointed toes. Gary Cooper was reported to have been slightly dismayed when the twelfth-century Chinese robes he wore in *Marco Polo* in 1940 set a new trend for women's clothes, and William Powell's sapphire cuff links also started a feminine fashion. When Carole Lombard told Travis Banton that she wanted to wear a similar set, he produced the first tailored dinner clothes for women, complete with shirts with cuffs.

Cedric Gibbons' use of white *intérieures modernes* in such Metro-Goldwyn Mayer productions as *When Ladies Meet, Dinner at Eight, The Thin Man,* and *Private Lives* did a great deal to advance the "Hollywood" or "White Telephone" look, a trend in decor that lasted at least ten years. For *Dinner at Eight,* he and Hobart Erwin designed a bedroom for Jean Harlow which employed eleven different shades of white (and gave Bill Daniels, the director of photography, nightmares—white being so highly reflective). Wealthy clients often asked Gibbons to design interiors for their homes, sometimes requesting exact copies of sets that had appeared on screen. In addition, affianced couples and newlyweds by the score wrote to the various studios for blueprints and specifications of homes they saw in movies. Venetian blinds (first shown on screen in *Our Dancing Daughters* in 1928), the elaborate tiled and mirrored bathroom, the one-handed phone, western American style furniture, as well as porch and lawn furnishings, all caught the public imagination in motion pictures.

Expressions commonly used on screen—such as "big shot," "take him for a ride," "sez you," and "it ain't a fit night out for man nor beast"—

became current in everyday language (as did at least one off-screen Hollywood expression, "in like Flynn"). Popeye helped increase the popularity of spinach, men learned the seductive trick of lighting two cigarettes at once from Paul Henreid, and it was reported that girls were so impressed with the way Myrna Loy crinkled her nose that they would practice the mannerism in front of their mirrors. On a more serious level, *I Was a Fugitive from a Chain Gang* was instrumental in bringing about the reformation of the Georgia penal system.

It is often difficult to tell to what extent an idea actually originated in Hollywood—the movie industry was itself subject to many influences—but there can be no doubt that as a popularizer of ideas, especially those concerning style trends, Hollywood in its heyday had no equal anywhere in the world.

A WEEK IN THE LIFE OF A HOLLYWOOD BACHELOR.

In 1936 the following newspaper piece appeared under the title "Life of a Hollywood Bachelor," purporting to be a diary kept by Milo, Cesar Romero's Filipino "Man Friday." Although it is impossible to know the extent to which a publicist's hand was involved, the journal seems quite credible in its balance of glamour, work, and social obligation.

MONDAY: Romero rises at 9:30. Breakfast. For two hours plays tennis with Lili Damita, Errol Flynn and Gloria Stuart. 1 PM: at the Vendome —lunch with Pat Di Cicco, his agent. 3 PM: conference with business manager, Charles Walton, about annuities. 4 PM: back to apartment; reads book. Roger Pryor calls . . . 7 PM: buffet dinner at the George Murphys. Then a treasure hunt on roller skates with the Monday Night Gang: Mr. Pryor, Ann Sothern, the John Alden Blanchards, the Robert Stallmans, Betty Furness and the Murphys. Mr. Romero and Mrs. Blanchard win the prizes: two bottles of champagne. Midnight: bed.

TUESDAY: Up at 6:30 and off to downtown railroad station for first scene of *Public Enemy's Wife*. En route, stops at 15-cent barber shop and loses six-year-old moustache. 1 PM: lunch at studio commissary.

365

CESAR ROMERO WITH CLOSE FRIEND JOAN CRAWFORD AT THE
VICTOR HUGO CAFÉ.

Waits in dressing room all afternoon for call. Sends regrets for invitations
to two cocktail parties and one dinner. Light supper in dressing room.
7 PM: call finally comes for scenes to be shot in baggage car. Works
till 11. In bed by midnight.

WEDNESDAY: Up at 9:30. Breakfast. Two hours fitting with tailor.
12:30: to Assistance League (society charity organization) for lunch.
4:30: cocktail party . . . 7 PM: dinner at apartment of sister Maria.
8 PM: back at studio. 11 PM: home again. Reads and to bed at 1 AM.

366

A week in the life of a Hollywood bachelor

THURSDAY: Rises at 9 AM. To studio for publicity pictures with Pat O'Brien and Margaret Lindsay. 11 AM: makes radio transcript of prepared material on styles for men. No like. 1:30: lunch with Robert Taylor at Vine Street Brown Derby. 3 to 7 PM: works in studio on process shots, also scenes of gangster shooting. 8:30: at the Trocadero after hurried change to white tie and tails. Mr. Romero is host of party for President-elect Gomez of Cuba . . . He escorts Virginia Bruce. They dance until 2 o'clock curfew.

FRIDAY: Sleeps until noon. Drives to Edward Everett Horton's ranch for lunch. ZaSu Pitts, Louise Fazenda and a London theater owner also there. 7 PM: takes Virginia Bruce to dinner at Perino's. Then to *The Children's Hour* at the Biltmore. No like. After theater, to the Cafe La Maze for dancing until closing.

SATURDAY: Sleeps until 11. 12:30: lunch at Levy's with fan magazine writer. 2 PM: a turn along the boulevard. Buys six shirts. Back to apartment to read mail. 7 PM: dinner at his apartment with Maria, Betty Furness, Robert Taylor and Carole Lombard. Then into Los Angeles and two burlesque shows. Bed at 1:30.

SUNDAY: Up at noon. To Riviera Country Club for horse back ride . . . Lunch. 3 PM: to Santa Monica Swimming Club. Cocktails, but not much swimming. 8 PM: dinner with radio producer. Conference on program broadcast at 10 PM. Midnight: to bed.

BIBLIOGRAPHY

Allvine, Gordon. *The Greatest Fox of Them All*. Lyle Stuart, 1969.

Alpert, Hollis. *The Barrymores*. Dial Press, 1964.

Anger, Kenneth. *Hollywood Babylon*. Straight Arrow Books, 1975.

Astor, Mary. *A Life on Film*. Delacorte Press, 1967.

Balio, Tino, ed. *The American Film Industry*. University of Wisconsin Press, 1976.

Banham, Reyner. *Los Angeles*. Allen Lane, The Penguin Press, 1971.

Barrymore, Lionel, as told to Cameron Shipp. *We Barrymores*. Appleton-Century-Crofts, 1951.

Basten, Fred. *Beverly Hills, Portrait of a Fabled City*. Douglas-West Publishers, 1975.

Baxter, John. *Stunt*. Doubleday & Co., 1974.

———. *The Hollywood Exiles*. Taplinger Publishing Co., 1976.

Behlmer, Rudy, selected and edited by. *Memo from David O. Selznick*. Viking Press, 1972.

Benchley, Nathaniel. *Humphrey Bogart*. Little, Brown & Co., 1975.

Blesh, Rudi. *Keaton*. Macmillan Publishing Co., 1966.

Brough, James. *The Fabulous Fondas*. David McKay Co., 1973.

Brownlow, Kevin. *The Parade's Gone By*. Alfred A. Knopf, 1968.

Cagney, James. *Cagney by Cagney*. Doubleday & Co., 1976.

Cawkwell, Tim, and Smith, John M., eds. *The World Encyclopedia of Film*. Galahad Books, 1972.

Cannom, Robert C. *Van Dyke and the Mythical City, Hollywood*. Murray & Gee, 1948.

Capra, Frank. *The Name Above the Title*. Macmillan Co., 1971.

Carey, Gary. *Doug & Mary: A Biography of Douglas Fairbanks and Mary Pickford*. E. P. Dutton, 1977.

Chaplin, Charles. *My Autobiography*. Simon & Schuster, 1964.

Chaplin, Charles, Jr., with N. and M. Rau. *My Father, Charlie Chaplin*. Random House, 1960.

Chierichetti, David. *Hollywood Costume Design*. Harmony Books, 1976.

Clarke, Charles G. *Early Filmmaking in Los Angeles*. Dawson's Book Shop, 1976.

Clymer, Floyd. *Cars of the Stars*. Floyd Clymer Publishers, 1954.

BIBLIOGRAPHY

Coffee, Lenore. *Storyline*. Cassell & Co. (London), 1973.

Colman, Juliet Benita. *Ronald Colman*. William Morrow & Co., 1975.

Crawford, Christina. *Mommie Dearest*. William Morrow & Co., 1978.

Croce, Arlene. *The Fred Astaire and Ginger Rogers Book*. Galahad Books, 1972.

Crowther, Bosley. *Hollywood Rajah*. Henry Holt & Co., 1960.

Curtiss, Thomas Quinn. *Von Stroheim*. Farrar, Straus & Giroux, 1971.

Dardis, Tom. *Some Time in the Sun*. Charles Scribner's Sons, 1976.

Davidson, Bill. *The Real and the Unreal*. Harper & Brothers, 1957.

Davies, Marion. *The Times We Had*. Bobbs-Merrill Co., 1975.

Davis, Bette. *The Lonely Life*. G. P. Putnam's Sons, 1962.

Day, Beth. *This Was Hollywood*. Doubleday & Co., 1960.

Dempsey, Jack, with Barbara Piatelli Dempsey. *Dempsey*. Harper & Row, 1977.

Eames, John Douglas. *The MGM Story*. Crown Publishers, 1975.

Eells, George. *Hedda and Louella*. G. P. Putnam's Sons, 1972.

————. *Ginger, Loretta and Irene Who?* G. P. Putnam's Sons, 1976.

Ellis, Vivian. *Ellis in Wonderland*. Hutchinson & Co. (London), 1940.

Field, Alice Evans. *Hollywood, USA*. Vantage Press, 1952.

Feinman, Jeffrey. *Hollywood Confidential*. Playboy Press, 1976.

Flamini, Roland. *Scarlett, Rhett and a Cast of Thousands*. Macmillan Publishing Co., 1975.

Fordin, Hugh. *The World of Entertainment*. Doubleday & Co., 1975.

French, Philip. *The Movie Moguls*. Weidenfeld and Nicholson (London), 1969.

Furnass, J. C., and the staff of the *Ladies' Home Journal*. *How America Lives*. Henry Holt & Co., 1941.

Garceau, Jean, with Inez Cocke. *Gable, a Pictorial Biography*. Grosset & Dunlap, 1961.

Garnett, Tay. *Light Your Torches and Pull Up Your Tights*. Arlington House, 1973.

Gebhard, David, and Von Breton, Harriette. *LA in the 30s*. Peregrine Smith, 1975.

Geduld, Harry M. *The Birth of the Talkies*. Indiana University Press, 1975.

Giesler, Jerry, as told to Pete Smith. *The Jerry Giesler Story*. Simon & Schuster, 1960.

Godowsky, Dagmar. *First Person Plural*. Viking Press, 1958.

Goodman, Ezra. *The Fifty-Year Decline and Fall of Hollywood*. Simon & Schuster, 1961.

Graham, Sheilah. *The Garden of Allah*. Crown Publishers, 1970.

Griffth, Mrs. D. W. (Linda Arvidson). *When the Movies Were Young*. Dover Publications, 1969.

Griffith, Richard. *The Talkies.* Dover Publications, 1971.

Guiles, Fred Laurence. *Marion Davies.* McGraw-Hill, 1972.

Hagen, John Milton. *Holly-Would!* Arlington House, 1974.

Halliwell, Leslie. *The Filmgoer's Companion* 4th ed. Hill & Wang, 1974.

Hampton, Benjamin B. *History of the American Film Industry.* Dover Publications, 1970. (Originally published as *A History of the Movies,* Covici, Friede, 1931.)

Hart, William S. *My Life, East and West.* Houghton Mifflin Co., 1929.

Hayward, Brooke. *Haywire.* Alfred A. Knopf, 1977.

Hecht, Ben. *Charlie: The Improbable Life and Times of Charles Mac-Arthur.* Harper & Brothers, 1957.

Hendon, Booton. *Mary Pickford and Douglas Fairbanks.* W. W. Norton & Co., 1977.

Higham, Charles. *Hollywood Cameramen.* Indiana University Press, 1970.

———. *Cecil B. DeMille.* Charles Scribner's Sons, 1973.

———. *Kate: The Life of Katharine Hepburn,* W. W. Norton, 1975.

———. *Charles Laughton.* Doubleday & Co., 1976.

Higham, Charles, and Greenberg, Joel. *Hollywood in the Forties.* Paperback Library, 1968.

Holstius, E. Nils. *Hollywood Through the Back Door.* Geoffrey Bles (London), 1937.

Hopper, Hedda, and Brough, James. *The Whole Truth and Nothing But.* Doubleday & Co., 1963.

Hurrell, George (photos), and Stine, Whitney (text). *The Hurrell Style.* John Day Co., 1976.

Hyams, Joe. *Bogart and Bacall.* Warner Books, 1975.

Israel, Lee. *Miss Tallulah Bankhead.* G. P. Putnam's Sons, 1972.

Jacobs, Lewis. *The Rise of the American Film.* Harcourt, Brace & Co., 1939.

Jobes, Gertrude. *Motion Picture Empire.* Archon Books, n.d.

Kanfer, Stephen. *A Journal of the Plague Years.* Atheneum, 1973.

Kanin, Garson. *Hollywood.* Viking Press, 1974.

Keylin, Arleen, and Fleischer, Suri, eds. *Hollywood Album.* Arno Press, 1977.

Kiesling, Barrett C. *Talking Pictures.* Johnson Publishing Co., 1937.

Knight, Arthur (text), and Elisofon, Eliot (photos). *The Hollywood Style.* Macmillan Co., 1969.

Kobler, John. *Damned in Paradise: The Life of John Barrymore.* Atheneum, 1977.

Kohner, Frederick. *The Magician of Sunset Boulevard.* Morgan Press, 1977.

Koury, Phil A. *Yes, Mr. De Mille.* G. P. Putnam's Sons, 1959.

Lambert, Gavin. *On Cukor.* G. P. Putnam's Sons, 1972.

BIBLIOGRAPHY

————. *GWTW: The Making of Gone With the Wind.* Little, Brown & Co., 1973.

Lamparski, Richard. *Whatever Became of . . . ?* Vol. 2. Ace Books, 1968.

————. *Whatever Became of . . . ?* Vol. 3. Ace Books, 1970.

————. *Whatever Became of . . . ?* The New Fifth Series. Crown, 1974.

————. *Lamparski's Whatever Became of?* Bantam Books, 1976.

Lasky, Jesse L., Jr. *Whatever Happened to Hollywood?* Funk & Wagnalls, 1975.

Lawrence, Jerome. *Actor: The Life and Times of Paul Muni.* G. P. Putnam's Sons, 1974.

LeRoy, Mervyn, as told to Dick Kleiner. *Take One.* Hawthorn Books, 1974.

Levin, Martin, ed. *Hollywood and the Great Fan Magazines.* Arbor House. 1971.

Lindsay, Cynthia. *Dear Boris.* Alfred A. Knopf, 1975.

MacCann, Richard Dyer and Perry, Edward S. *The New Film Index.* E. P. Dutton & Co., 1975.

Macgowan, Kenneth. *Behind the Screen.* Delacorte Press, 1965.

McWilliams, Carey. *Southern California: An Island on the Land.* Peregrine Smith, 1973.

Madsen, Alex. *William Wyler.* Thomas Y. Crowell Co., 1973.

Marion, Frances. *Off with Their Heads.* Macmillan Co., 1972.

Marx, Arthur. *Goldwyn.* W. W. Norton & Co., 1976.

Marx, Samuel. *Mayer and Thalberg, the Make-Believe Saints.* Random House, 1975.

Messick, Hank. *The Beauties and the Beasts.* David McKay Co., 1973.

Meyersberg, Paul. *Hollywood, the Haunted House.* Stein & Day, 1968.

Milland, Ray. *Wide-eyed in Babylon.* William Morrow & Co., 1974.

Moore, Colleen. *Silent Star.* Doubleday & Co., 1968.

Morella, Joe, and Epstein, Edward Z. *Lana. Citadel Press,* 1971.

Murray, Ken. *The Body Merchant.* Ward Ritchie Press, 1976.

Niven, David. *Bring On the Empty Horses.* G. P. Putnam's Sons, 1975.

O'Brien, Pat. *The Wind at my Back.* Doubleday & Co., 1964.

Parish, James Robert. *The Fox Girls.* Castle Books, 1971.

————. *The Paramount Pretties.* Arlington House, 1972.

————. *The RKO Gals.* Arlington House, 1974.

————. *The Tough Guys.* Arlington House, 1976.

Parish, James Robert, and Bowers, Ronald L. *The MGM Stock Company.* Arlington House, 1973.

————, and Leonard, William T. *Hollywood Players: The Thirties.* Arlington House, 1976.

————, and Stanke, Don E. *The Debonairs.* Arlington House, 1975.

————. *The Glamour Girls*. Arlington House, 1975.

Parrish, Robert. *Growing Up in Hollywood*. Harcourt Brace Jovanovich, 1976.

Payne, Robert. *The Great Garbo*. Praeger, 1976.

Powdermaker, Hortense. *Hollywood, the Dream Factory*. Little, Brown & Co., 1950.

Preminger, Otto. *Preminger*. Doubleday & Co., 1977.

Rivkin, Allen, and Kerr, Laura. *Hello, Hollywood*. Doubleday & Co., 1962.

Robinson, Edward G. *All My Yesterdays*. Hawthorn Books, 1973.

Robinson, Edward G., Jr., with William Duffy. *My Father, My Son*. Frederick Fell, 1958.

Rose, Helen. *Just Make Them Beautiful*. Deanes-Landman Publishers, 1976.

Rosenberg, Bernard, and Silverstein, Harry. *The Real Tinsel*. Macmillan Co., 1970.

Rosten, Leo C. *Hollywood: The Movie Colony*. Harcourt, Brace & Co., 1941.

Rothenstein, Jaik. *Hollywood Leg Man*. Madison Press, 1950.

Russell, Rosalind, and Chase, Chris. *Life Is a Banquet*. Random House, 1977.

Schickel, Richard. *The Men Who Made the Movies*. Atheneum, 1975.

Silvers, Phil, with Robert Saffron. *The Laugh Is on Me: The Phil Silvers Story*. Prentice-Hall, 1973.

Sklar, Robert. *Movie-Made America*. Random House, 1975.

Skolsky, Sidney. *Don't Get Me Wrong—I Love Hollywood*. G. P. Putnam's Sons, 1975.

Springer, John, and Hamilton, Jack. *They Had Faces Then*. Citadel Press, 1974.

Shipman, David. *The Great Movie Stars: The Golden Years*. Bonanza Books, 1970.

————. *The Great Movie Stars: The International Years*. St. Martin's Press, 1972.

Stewart, Donald Ogden. *By a Stroke of Luck*. Paddington Press, 1975.

Swanberg, W. A. *Citizen Hearst*. Charles Scribner's Sons, 1961.

Swindell, Larry. *Spencer Tracy*. New American Library, 1969.

————. *Screwball*. William Morrow & Co., 1975.

Sylvia, Observations of, as noted by her secretary. Brentano's, 1931.

Taylor, Robert Lewis. *W. C. Fields: His Follies and Fortunes*. Doubleday & Co., 1949.

Teichman, Howard. *George S. Kaufman: An Intimate Portrait*. Atheneum, 1972.

Thomas, Bob. *King Cohn*. G. P. Putnam's Sons, 1967.

BIBLIOGRAPHY

————. *Thalberg*. Doubleday & Co., 1969.

Thomas, Tony. *Cads and Cavaliers*. A. S. Barnes & Co., 1973.

Tornabene, Lyn. *Long Live the King*. G. P. Putnam's Sons, 1976.

Tuska, John. *The Filming of the West*. Doubleday & Co., 1976.

Vaughn, Robert. *Only Victims*. G. P. Putnam's Sons, 1972.

Viertel, Salka. *The Kindness of Strangers*. Holt, Rinehart & Winston, 1969.

Von Sternberg, Josef. *Fun in a Chinese Laundry*. Macmillan Co., 1965.

Wagner, Walter. *You Must Remember This*. G. P. Putnam's Sons, 1975.

Walker, Alexander. *The Celluloid Sacrifice*. Hawthorn Books, 1967.

————. *Stardom*. Stein & Day, 1970.

————. *Rudolph Valentino*. Stein & Day, 1976.

Warner, Jack L., with Dean Jennings. *My First Hundred Years in Holly-wood*. Random House, 1964.

Wayne, Jane Ellen. *Robert Taylor*. Manor Books, 1973.

Weinstock, Matt. *My L.A.* Current Books, 1947.

Wellman, William A. *A Short Time for Insanity*. Hawthorn Books, 1974.

West, Mae. *Goodness Had Nothing to Do with It*. Prentice-Hall, 1959.

Westmore, Frank, and Davidson, Muriel. *The Westmores of Hollywood*. J. B. Lippincott Co., 1976.

Whittemore, Don, and Cecchettini, Philip Alan. *Passport to Hollywood*. McGraw-Hill Book Company, 1976.

Windeler, Robert. *Sweetheart: The Story of Mary Pickford*. Praeger Publishers, 1974.

————. *Shirley Temple*. W. H. Allen (London), 1976.

Wood, Michael. *America in the Movies*. Basic Books, 1975.

Woon, Basil. *Incredible Land*. Liveright, 1933.

WPA Guide to Los Angeles. 1941.

Yablonsky, Lewis. *George Raft*. McGraw-Hill, 1974.

Yallop, David. *The Day the Laughter Stopped*. St. Martin's Press, 1976.

Zeltner, Irwin F. *What the Stars Told Me*. Exposition Press, 1971.

Zierold, Norman. *The Moguls*. Coward-McCann, Inc., 1969.

Zimmer, Jill Schary. *With a Cast of Thousands*. Stein & Day, 1963.

Zolotow, Maurice. *Billy Wilder in Hollywood*. G. P. Putnam's Sons, 1977.

Among the periodicals consulted on this project were:

American Magazine
American Mercury, The
American Speech
American Weekly, The
Atlantic Monthly
Business Week

Christian Science Monitor Magazine
Close-up
Coast
Collier's
Commonweal
Coronet
Current History
Daily Variety
Editor & Publisher
Family Weekly
Film Pictorial
Films and Filming
Films in Review
Fortune
Good Housekeeping
Harper's
Holiday
Hollywood Citizen News, The
Hollywood Filmograph, The
Hollywood Quarterly
Hollywood Reporter, The
Ladies' Home Journal
Liberty
Life
Lion's Roar, The
Literary Digest
Look
Los Angeles Daily News, The
Los Angeles Examiner, The
Los Angeles Herald-Express, The
Los Angeles Magazine
Los Angeles Times, The
McCall's
Modern Screen
Motion Picture
Motion Picture Herald
Movie Life
National Board of Review Magazine
Nation's Business
Newsweek
New West
New Yorker, The

BIBLIOGRAPHY

New York Times, The
Pageant
Paramount News
Photoplay
Picturegoer
Reader's Digest, The
Saturday Evening Post, The
Screen Book
Screenland
Scribner's
Script, Bob Wagner's
Sight and Sound
Stage
Time
Variety
Wall Street Journal, The
Washington Post, The
Westways
Woman's Home Companion

ACKNOWLEDGMENTS

A large number of people gave freely of their time and knowledge in assisting us to compile this book, but we would like to offer our special gratitude to Howard Strickling, who spent many days helping us understand what it was like to live and work in Hollywood forty and fifty years ago. In conversations and detailed memos, he conjured up a world that he knew as few others can claim to have known it. He patiently corrected misunderstandings and offered glimpses of little-known aspects of the movie colony. Mr. Strickling's standing is such that, through his good offices, we were able to meet with and talk to key figures who might otherwise have been disinclined to see us. Gail Strickling, as well as being a gracious hostess on numerous occasions, added her memories and knowledge to her husband's. Kay Mulvey, a former associate of Mr. Strickling's at M-G-M, joined us for several of our talks and added many valuable recollections of her own.

Among others who granted us interviews, we would like to thank Leon Ames, Art and Barbara Babbitt, George Bagnall, Jack Baker, George Bassman, Albert Cavens, Charles G. Clarke, Joseph Cotten, Samson De Brier, Tom Drake, Carl and Ruth Esmond, Paul Fix, George Folsey, Myron Fox, Paul Henreid, Tom Jones, Dorothy Jordan (Mrs. Merian C. Cooper), Hal C. Kern, Henry King, Maurice Kusell, Charles Lane, Ernest Laszlo, Anna Lee, Queenie Leonard, Ben Lyon, John Lee Mahin, Winston Miller, Virginia Kellogg Mortensen, Robert Nathan, Lloyd Nolan, Walter Plunkett, LeRoy Prinz, Frances Richardson, Cesar Romero, Bob Schiffer, Martha Scott, Walter Scott, George Seaton, Jack Staggs, Emily Sundby, Minna Wallis, Lyle and Donna Wheeler, and Donald Woods.

Ron Haver and Joan Cohen, of the film department at the Los Angeles County Museum, were of assistance in a dozen different ways, and extensive research was done at the library of the Academy of Motion Picture Arts and Sciences where the entire staff—in particular Sam Gill, in charge of the archives—was unfailingly helpful. Further library research was done at the University of California's Doheny Library; at the American Film Institute in Beverly Hills; at the Lincoln Center Library for the Performing Arts, and other branches of the New York Public Library system; and at various branches of the Los Angeles Public Library and the Santa Monica Public Library.

ACKNOWLEDGMENTS

Many people were helpful in finding photographs, but we wish to single out Ron Alter, of Ron's "Now and Then," in New York City, and Gene Andrewski, both of whom were especially responsive to our needs and diligent in searching out rare and unusual pictures.

Joan Cohen, Mark Obenhaus, and Toby Spiselman all read parts of the manuscript and made useful suggestions. Clive T. Miller performed an invaluable service by giving us a detailed commentary on an early draft of the text. His knowledge of the movie industry is matched by his feeling for words, and there is hardly a chapter in the book that has not been improved as a result of his scrutiny. It would be difficult to overestimate the importance of his contribution, and we wish to thank him for taking so much time from his own work in order to help us.

Susan Brockman, Jeanie Courtney, Julie Dolan, Kathy Dolan, Jeff and Judy Harris, Joan Hartley, Judith Stonehill, and Tim Street-Porter all provided assistance that made our task easier. Finally, thanks are due to Betty Anne Clarke, of International Creative Management, and to Lisa Drew, of Doubleday & Company, for helping make the whole project possible.

INDEX

Index

380

INDEX

INDEX

INDEX

INDEX

INDEX

INDEX